1989

1100–1600 Music		Art and literature		History and philosophy
Beginning of period of troubadours and trouvères	**1100**	St Mark's, Venice, completed		Bologna University founded
		Notre-Dame, Paris, begun		Beginnings of Paris University Oxford University founded
Léonin, Pérotin: early polyphony (organum) at Notre Dame, Paris	**1200**	Chartres Cathedral in progress		Third Crusade begins
Guiot de Dijon: *Chanterai por mon corage*				Cambridge University founded
Franco of Cologne establishes notation of rhythm		Westminster Abbey begun Sainte-Chapelle, Paris, begun Cologne Cathedral begun		Mongols invade Russia St Thomas Aquinas: *Summa contra Gentiles* Marco Polo goes to China
Adam de la Halle: *Jeu de Robin et de Marion*	**1300**	Doge's Palace, Venice Duccio: *Maestà*; Giotto: Padua frescoes		Avignon Papacy (to 1377)
Philippe de Vitry: *Ars nova*		Dante: *Divine Comedy* Petrarch: *Poems* Boccaccio: *The Decameron*		Beginning of 100 Years' War (England/France: to 1453)
Machaut: *Messe de Nostre Dame*		Chaucer: *Canterbury Tales*		Black Death plague ravages Europe
Landini: *Ecco la primavera*	**1400**	Brussels Town Hall, Seville Cathedral begun Donatello: *David*		
		Florence Cathedral Van Eyck: *Arnolfini Wedding*		
Dunstable: *O rosa bella*; Dufay: *Ce moys de may*		Piero della Francesca: *Baptism of Christ* King's College Chapel, Cambridge		Burgundian court flourishes (1364–1477)
Dufay: *Mass 'Se la face ay pale'*	**1450**	Mantegna: *Adoration*		Gutenberg Bible printed
Earliest music printing (chant books, by woodblock)		Botticelli: *Primavera*		
Josquin: *Ave Maria . . . virgo serena*		Leonardo: *Last Supper*		Columbus discovers New World
Ockeghem dies (*c* 87); Josquin: *Nymphes des bois*	**1500**	Michelangelo: *David*		
First music printing from movable type (Venice)		Leonardo: *Mona Lisa*; Ariosto: *Orlando furioso* Dürer: *Hands of an Apostle*		Erasmus: *The Praise of Folly*
Isaac: *Choralis constantinus*		Raphael: *Alba Madonna*; Michelangelo: Sistine Chapel ceiling		Machiavelli: *The Prince* The Reformation begins Magellan circumnavigates the world
Josquin dies (*c*81)				Luther translates New Testament into German
Rise of the Italian madrigal	**1525**	Rabelais: *Gargantua*		Henry VIII head of English church Calvin: *Christianae religionis institutio*
		Titian: *Venus of Urbino*		
Lassus: *Prophetiae sibyllarum*		Palladio: Villa Rotonda, Vicenza		Copernicus: *De revolutionibus orbium coelestium*
	1550	Bruegel: *January* (The Months)		Elizabeth I becomes queen of England Council of Trent
Palestrina at height of career in Rome		Tasso: *Gerusalemme liberata*		Mercator produces first map of the world
	1575			
Victoria: *Music for Holy Week* Andrea and Giovanni Gabrieli: *Concerti* Italian madrigals published in England *(Musica transalpina)* Palestrina (*c*69) and Lassus (62) die Dowland: *First Booke of Songes or Ayres*; G. Gabrieli, *Sacrae symphoniae*	**1600**	Guarini: *Il pastor fido*		Spanish Armada defeated Janssen invents the microscope

1600–1750 Music	Art and literature	History and philosophy
Earliest opera, *Euridice* (Peri and Caccini) *The Triumphs of Oriana*, English madrigals (incl. Weelkes: *As Vesta was*) Byrd: *Ave verum corpus (Gradualia)* Monteverdi: *Orfeo* Monteverdi: *Vespers* Gesualdo: *Responsories for Holy Week*	**1600** Caravaggio: *Christ and the Apostles* Shakespeare: *Hamlet* Cervantes: *Don Quixote* Rubens: *Self-portrait with Isabella*	Galileo discovers the laws of dynamics
Schütz: *Veni, Sancte Spiritus* Byrd dies (80)		Harvey demonstrates the circulation of blood 30 Years' War begins (Germany) Mayflower sails to Plymouth (Mass.)
	1625 Bernini: Colonnade of St Peter's, Rome	
First public opera house opens, Venice Monteverdi: *The Coronation of Poppaea* Monteverdi dies (76); Frescobaldi dies (59); Cavalli: *Egisto* Carissimi: *Jephte*	Rembrandt: *Nightwatch*	Harvard University founded Descartes: *Discourse on Method*
	1650 Velázquez: *Maids of Honor* Milton: *Paradise Lost*	
Lully becomes chief composer at French court Schütz: Passion settings; Cavalli: *Ercole amante* Buxtehude becomes organist at St Mary's, Lübeck; Cesti: *Il pomo d'oro* Lully: *Le bourgeois gentilhomme* Schütz dies (87)	Molière: *Le bourgeois gentilhomme*; Levau and Mansard: Versailles	Louis XIV comes to French throne Pascal: *Pensées* Newton discovers the laws of gravity
First German opera house opens (Hamburg) Purcell organist of Westminster Abbey	**1675** Racine: *Phèdre*	Spinoza: *Ethics*
Lully: *Armide* Purcell: *Dido and Aeneas* Purcell dies (36) Earliest pianoforte made Beginning of greatest period of Stradivari's violin-making	Wren: St Paul's Cathedral, London	
	1700	Leibnitz: *New Essays on Human Understanding*
Handel in Italy; Bach in Weimar Handel in London – *Rinaldo* Vivaldi: Concertos op. 3 Corelli dies (60); Couperin: First harpsichord book Bach in Cöthen; Couperin: *L'art de toucher le clavecin* Handel: *Acis and Galatea* Bach: *Brandenburg Concertos* Rameau settles in Paris, *Treatise on Harmony* Bach in Leipzig – intensive cantata composition Bach: *St John Passion*; Handel: *Giulio Cesare* Vivaldi: *The Four Seasons*; A. Scarlatti dies (65) Bach: *St Matthew Passion* Pergolesi: *La serva padrona*; Rameau: *Hippolyte et Aricie*; Telemann: *Musique de Table*	Watteau: *Embarkation for Cythera* **1725** Canaletto: *The Bucintoro*	
Handel: *Messiah* J. Stamitz appointed concertmaster at Mannheim Bach: Mass in b Bach dies (65)	Gainsborough: *Mr and Mrs Andrews* **1750**	Frederick the Great becomes king of Prussia ; Maria Theresa becomes head of Holy Roman Empire

Stanley Sadie's Brief Guide to Music

Stanley Sadie's
Brief Guide to Music

edited by STANLEY SADIE
with ALISON LATHAM

Prentice-Hall, Inc.

Englewood Cliffs, N.J.

North and South American Editions published by
Prentice-Hall, Inc.
Englewood Cliffs, N.J. 07632

A shorter edition of
Stanley Sadie's Music Guide (1986)

ISBN 013–082173–X

This book was designed and produced by
John Calmann and King Ltd, London

Printed in Great Britain by Butler & Tanner Ltd,
Frome and London

Cover: *The Orchestra of the Opéra* (detail),
by Edgar Degas. 1868–9, 21 × 13$\frac{3}{4}$ ins. Paris, Louvre.

Abbreviations in music examples:
bn., bassoon; cl., clarinet; cont., basso continuo; db.,
double bass; fl., flute; hn., horn; m. (mm.) measure(s);
ob., oboe; orch., orchestra; pf., pianoforte; str.,
strings; tpt., trumpet; trbn., trombone; va., viola; vc.,
cello; vn., violin; ww., woodwind.

In the Listening Notes and lists of works, capital letters
denote major keys, lower-case ones minor keys. The
publishers wish to acknowledge the help of Vance
Jennings in preparing the Listening Notes.

Contents

XI   The Traditions of Popular Music Wilfrid Mellers 326

Preface

The principal aim of this book, a shortened version of the original *Music Guide*, remains to enhance people's pleasure and understanding in listening to music. Although it is designed in the first place for those with little experience or musical knowledge, I hope that its mixture of musical description and background information may also prove attractive and helpful to the general music lover.

The approach here to the repertory of music is perhaps slightly different from those commonly found in introductory books. Description and elucidation remain the first considerations; but some emphasis is also placed on history and context. I do not find myself especially sympathetic to a philosophy in which every work of art is regarded as an independent entity that can profitably be discussed simply for what it is: "what it is" – and thus the understanding of it – depends on when it was created, how men and women were thinking at the time, and the purpose for which it was created, as well as the techniques used in its creation. The mystical complexities of a Bach or the heroic strivings of a Beethoven assume a greater significance if we can begin to realize why these men were drawn to the mystical or the heroic.

The book begins with three chapters on the materials of music. The first treats "elements" (pitch, rhythm, harmony, key, etc), chiefly for the benefit of those not familiar or not fully familiar with them. It is not exhaustive but is designed to equip the reader for what is to come, introducing concepts one at a time and assuming no prior knowledge. The second and third chapters discuss respectively musical instruments and the structures of music, again to a level that should enable the student to understand what ensues.

The main part of the book, Chapters IV to X, discusses the music of seven different eras, in chronological order from the Middle Ages to the present day. The principal author of the first two is Judith Nagley and the last two Paul Griffiths, both of whose contributions I acknowledge with warm thanks. I myself supplied the introductory sections to all seven of these chapters. In them I have made some attempt to draw attention to features of contemporary social and cultural history (political, intellectual and religious history too) that relate in significant or suggestive ways to the music that is to be discussed, and to outline the new stylistic weapons that composers forged to enable them to rise to the challenges of a changing world. The aim is to give the reader a sense of music as a part of the fabric of life, as something that changes as the world does, and so to heighten his or her understanding of it through this broader human context.

With these objectives in mind, we have laid more stress than usual on biography in the main text of the central chapters. Without biographical discussion it is rarely possible to

1 *Previous page* Map of Europe showing the principal centres of musical importance

explain the purpose for which a piece of music was composed, on which its style and structure may acutely depend. Except in the earliest chapters, where the material scarcely exists, and the latest, where the familiarity of the modern world renders it progressively less necessary, biographical information is included for important composers; we also give, in tabular form, summary lists of works. A tabular biographical outline is supplied for the most important composers. I believe that biography can be inherently interesting, can cast light on the society to which a composer belongs, and that, taken with the music itself, it may serve to stimulate the reader's interest and increase his or her involvement. I hope that the enthusiasm and the love of music that I and my co-authors feel, and have made no special effort to hide, may also infect the reader.

Many people come to music first of all through popular music. Our final chapter – written by Wilfrid Mellers, to whom I am indebted – discusses the traditions of popular music in a way that in its different context may be seen as analogous to that pursued in the main historical chapters. I hope this chapter may provide a valuable way in for students more familiar with popular music than with other kinds.

The absence of any substantial discussion of non-Western music ought not to be regarded as a symptom of ethnocentricity. The Western musical tradition (with its relatively recent Afro-American infusion, as treated in Chapter XI) is quite big enough, rich enough and complex enough to be the subject of an entire book. There are in the world other traditions of high complexity and richness, too, and to treat them cursorily or perfunctorily would be unwarrantedly patronizing. This book is in any case primarily for Westerners, who may be expected to be closer to their own traditions than to others'.

I would not claim that this book is a history of music as well as one about its understanding and enjoyment; a history has to be comprehensive in a sense that this book does not aim to be. But my co-authors and I have tried, by the careful selection of material in the composer discussions, and by the provision of some "connecting tissue" outside them, to give some indication of the lines of historical development and continuity.

A set of six records or cassettes is available as a companion to this book (for students, a single-cassette selection is available). The first of the six contains music relating to Chapters II, IV and V, the others respectively to Chapters VI to X. Details of the music included will be found on the Contents pages. All the recorded items are described in the Listening Notes, printed at appropriate points in the chapter concerned. The notes (which follow no uniform scheme, since different music needs to be listened to in different ways) are designed to be read, with help and guidance from an instructor where that is suitable, while the music is actually being heard. Many of them are supplemented by more general discussion of the works in the main text. Suggestions for further listening, based on representative works referred to in the text, are offered on pp. 345–6.

It is never possible in the discussion of music to avoid technical vocabulary. Much of this is explained as it is introduced; but all of it is covered in the Glossary (pp. 350–6), which through its cross-references to the main text embodies something of an index of musical topics. There is also a general index, chiefly of names.

Lastly, I should like to acknowledge the collaboration, at every stage in the preparation of this book, of my close colleague and constant helper Alison Latham, who (among other tasks) prepared the tabular material and the Glossary; also the work as picture editor of Elisabeth Agate, whose imaginative contribution speaks for itself.

STANLEY SADIE

Chapter 1

The Elements of Music

In every society, in every period, men and women have made music. They have sung and danced to it; they have used it in solemn rituals and in light-hearted entertainments; they have listened to it in fields and forests, in temples, in bars, in concert halls and opera houses; they have made it not only with their voices but by adapting natural objects and banging them, scraping them and blowing through them; they have used it to generate collective emotion – to excite, to calm, to inspire action, to draw tears. Music is not a fringe activity or a luxury one: it is a central and necessary part of human existence.

Every culture has found a musical style, and a means of expressing it, that arise from its needs, history and environment. In Black Africa, for example, where the population has in general a strong and subtle command of rhythm, and where there has been a need for quick communication over distances, the musical culture is particularly concerned with

2 Dame Gladness leading a round dance: miniature from *Le Roman de la Rose*, *c*1420, by Guillaume de Lorris and Jean de Meun. Österreichische Nationalbibliothek, Vienna.

drums and drumming. The ancient courtly cultures of the East developed musical traditions of high elaboration and refinement while the rural populations used much simpler music. In the West (Europe and America), the chief concern of this book, musical traditions arose chiefly from chant used in the early church, from the art forms developed at the courts of kings and nobles, from the needs of the wider audiences that industrialization created, and from the technologies of the electronic age – while the rural population, and in more recent times the urban industrial one, has developed a more popular one of its own.

What, then, *is* music? It has been defined as "organized sound". A musical tone is the product of regular vibration, and is perceived when an inner part of the listener's ear is made to vibrate in sympathy. A noise, by contrast, is the product of *irregular* vibration. Of the banging, scraping and blowing we mentioned above, the first may produce music or noise, according to the object banged and the ways it vibrates. Normally, scraping or striking a taut string, or causing a column of air to vibrate, will produce a musical tone. Any piece of music will be made up of a large number of musical tones, intended to be heard in a carefully ordered pattern.

The basic systems of ordering are three: *rhythm*, which governs the movement of music in time; *melody*, which means the linear arrangement of tones; and *harmony*, which deals with the simultaneous sounding of different tones. There are other important elements too, such as color and texture.

Notation

In non-literate societies, there is no need for musical notation; music is passed on by ear, one generation learning a store of tunes by listening to an older generation. The same applied for a time with ecclesiastical chant, in our literate Western society; but eventually, so that repertories could be stored, reproduced or distributed, a system had to be devised to indicate how music should be performed. This was at first done with signs written above or below the words, showing small groupings of notes. Many other notation methods have been devised, some telling the performer not what tone is to be sounded but where to put his fingers on the instrument he is playing. This kind of system is still widely used, especially for the guitar.

Pitch

There are two basic facts that any musical notation has to convey: first, the *pitch* of a tone; second, its *duration*. As regards pitch, we define tones as *high* or *low*. Musical notation, in the standard Western system, shows pitch by the positioning of the symbol (or note), representing each tone, on a five-line *staff* (or stave) of fixed pitch. The staff shown in ex. I.1 carries an indication, in the sign at the left (the *clef* sign, providing the key – *clef* is

ex.I.1

G A   B   C   D   E   F   G   A   B   C

French for key), of where the pitch is fixed. This is a traditional script sign for the letter G, and it means that the second line from the bottom represents the note called by that letter (which is created by a vibration of about 390 cycles per second – or 390 Hertz or Hz). This, the G clef, is also called the *treble clef*. The first note shown on the staff signifies the note G; the notes that follow move up in sequence to form a *scale*. They are placed alternately on the lines and in the spaces. Where the music needs to run off the top or the bottom of the staff, small extra lines (called leger or ledger lines) are added, as we see for the last three notes of ex.I. Music that is lower pitched is written in the F clef or *bass clef*, where the symbol on the fourth line up signifies an F, the note nine below the treble-clef G. The C clef, fixing the note halfway between these, is used for instruments of intermediate

ex.I.2

Octaves

pitch. Ex.I.2 shows the notes on and close to the treble and bass clefs. Notes are labeled alphabetically, in upward sequence, with the letters from A to G, which are then repeated.

The simplest interval – the pitch-distance between two tones – is the *octave*, the interval at which pitches seem to be duplicated. If you sing or play a simple scale, the eighth note seems in some way "the same" as the first, only higher. When women and men sing together, the men automatically sing an octave lower than the women.

There is a natural 2:1 ratio between tones an octave apart. A string two feet long, set in vibration, will produce a particular tone; halve the length to one foot (and keep the tension the same), and the resulting tone will be an octave higher – or double the tension (and keep the length the same), and the sound will also be an octave higher. This applies equally to a column of air; a tube two feet long will produce a tone an octave lower than a tube a foot long. We now understand this phenomenon in terms of vibration: the longer string or tube creates vibrations at half the speed of the shorter. The note to which most orchestras tune their instruments is A, 440Hz (the second note in ex.I.1); the note an octave lower is 220Hz, an octave higher is 880. On a piano, the lowest note is an A, 27.5Hz, and the highest A – seven octaves higher – is 3520Hz; the human ear can cope with musical sounds almost an octave below the lowest A before they degenerate into rumble, and more than two octaves above the highest.

Scales

The notes shown in ex.I are, on a piano keyboard, the white notes; these form a *diatonic scale*. The intervals between its eight notes are made up of five full steps (a whole tone or two semitones) and two half steps (one semitone); the half steps fall at E–F and B–C. This kind of scale was used well into the Middle Ages. Then intermediate steps began to be used, and, as the diagram of the piano keyboard (ex.I.3) shows, the five larger steps of the diatonic scale were filled in, with black notes. The note midway between C and D is called C sharp (notated C♯) or D flat (D♭). This shows how the octave is divided into 12 equal steps (or semitones), forming the *chromatic scale* (ex.I.4). The sharp and flat signs are called *accidentals*; they can be contradicted by the natural sign (♮).

ex.I.3

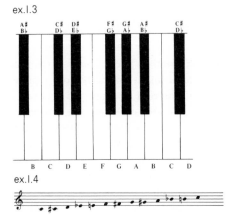

ex.I.4

Intervals

No relationship among the notes is as close as that between two an octave apart, but some of the *intervals* (as they are called) are closer in feeling than others. We have seen the 2:1 octave relationship; there is also a 3:2 relationship for notes a 5th apart, and 4:3 for a 4th (see ex.I.5). There are simple number ratios for all the basic intervals between notes of the scale. Intervals are defined by the number of notes they include, counting both the bottom one and the top one: the octave is eight notes, from one A to the next, the 5th five notes (A–E), the 2nd two (A–B). Some intervals – 2nds, 3rds, 6ths and 7ths – need to be identified as "major" or "minor" as they may include different numbers of semitones: C–E, for example, is a major 3rd, made up of four semitones, while D–F, of three, is a minor 3rd. Intervals of 4ths and 5ths are described as "perfect" when made up of five and seven semitones respectively; in the white-note diatonic scale there is one 4th (F–B) and one 5th (B–F) of six semitones and these are called, respectively, "augmented" and "diminished". Ex.5a shows the intervals in semitones up from C; ex.5b shows them with their inversions (that is, the intervals that complement them in the octave).

ex.I.5

The Western division of the octave into seven and 12, though it has some basis in natural, scientific fact, is not universal. Many folk cultures use a five-note division (called *pentatonic*); a familiar example of a pentatonic melody is *Auld lang syne*. Pentatonic scales are widely used, for example in China, parts of Africa and South-east Asia, and in much European folksong. More complex divisions of the octave are also found, for example in India, where there are 22-note scales. Intervals smaller than a semitone have also been used in Western music, especially by eastern Europeans (who find "microtones" in some of their folk music) and such modern experimental composers as the American John Cage.

Rhythm

The most basic element in music is *rhythm*; some musical systems, in fact, use rhythm alone. While painting and architecture depend on space, music depends on time. Our perception of time in music is related, first, to the establishment of a regular pulse (for which there are models in nature and everyday life, like a person's heartbeat, breathing or walking, or the ticking of a clock), and second, to the use of accent and duration, by means of which groupings can be constructed.

Pulse, tempo

The most usual way for a composer to show the rhythmic structure of his music – that is, the timing of the notes – is for him to indicate the *pulse*: this is done with a conventional word, probably an Italian one (like *allegro* for quick music, *adagio* for slow), to suggest the speed or tempo, though he may be more precise and state exactly how many beats are required per minute. Then he will indicate how the beats are to be grouped, normally in twos, threes or fours:

ONE two ONE two ONE two ONE two ...
ONE two three ONE two three ONE two three ...
ONE two THREE four ONE two THREE four ONE two THREE ...
(Capital letters denote accented beats; in groups of four, a secondary, lighter accent falls on the third beat.)

ex.I.6

ties are used to join notes together
dots increase a note by half its value

The note names work on a mathematical basis of proportional lengths. Eighth-notes and shorter ones may be written with "beams" (as shown on the left of ex.6), to improve legibility and to indicate metrical groupings; the grouping with beams may be shorter (as shown just right of centre) as long as it conforms to the metrical divisions, or the notes may be shown separated (as on the right)). Note the "flags": none on a quarter-note, one on an eighth, two on a sixteenth, and so on.

Meter

Counting in this manner shows the *meter* of a piece of music – that is, the beats and their groupings. The rhythms are heard with the meter as an understood background; in some kinds of music, like music for dancing, for communal singing, or above all in popular music, the meter or beat is strongly emphasized. Marches provide a good example of a meter in twos, or duple – obviously, as we have two legs. Familiar instances of duple meter are *She'll be comin' round the mountain* and *Greensleeves*. Waltzes are always in triple meter; so is *The Star-Spangled Banner*. In quadruple meter are *O Come, all ye faithful* and *Way down upon the Swanee river*. Some music is without meter: early church chant is often performed without meter, taking its rhythm from the words, and there are types of non-Western and advanced Western music that do without it.

Notation of rhythm

If the pitch of a note is the "vertical" element when we look at musical notation, then the horizontal element is rhythm. We have seen how the height of a note on the staff shows its pitch; its placing in horizontal distance along the staff – reading from left to right, as one reads words in Western languages – shows when it is to be sounded.

The modern system of rhythmic notation uses different shapes to express different durations. Nowadays the basic longest note is the whole-note. Ex.I.6 shows the standard note values. Musical notation has to provide not only for notes but also for silences of exact length: so there exists a system of *rests*, equivalent in length to each of the note values.

Time or meter signatures

Regular meter is conveyed in notation by means of a *time signature* or *meter signature*. This, consisting of one number above another, is placed at the beginning of each piece to tell the performer how the beats in the piece are grouped and what the duration of each of them is. The lower number indicates the unit: 4 (the most common) represents a quarter-note, 2 a half-note, 8 an eighth-note. The upper number shows how many of this unit are in each *measure* or *bar*; the measures are ruled off by vertical bar-lines. The first note of each measure has a natural metrical accent.

ex.I.7

The commonest time signature is 4/4 (often notated by its equivalent C): some typical groupings of note values in measures in 4/4 are shown in ex.I.7. Also much used among duple and quadruple signatures are 2/4 and 2/2 (or its equivalent ¢). Easily the most common triple time signature is 3/4. All these are what are known as "simple" time signatures, in that their unit beats are divisible by 2. Sometimes, however, the unit beats need to be divisible by 3, and have to be dotted notes (a dot following a note adds half again to its length); these are called "compound" time signatures, and of them the one most often used is 6/8. This means that there are six eighth-notes in each measure, divided into two groups of three; 6/8 is a duple meter (it is the meter of *Greensleeves*), but a compound duple one. All the most common time signatures are charted in ex.I.8.

ex.I.8

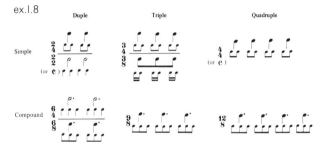

Melody

Melody has been defined as a "succession of tones in a musically expressive order". Certainly, to most people's minds, melody is the heart of music; no aspect of musical skill is as much prized as the ability to compose melodies that are shapely, expressive and memorable.

Anything that involves a perceptible sequence of tones may be regarded as a melody – from a nursery song to a phrase of church chant, from a folk dance to the angular line of a Stravinsky work, from a Bach fugue subject to last week's hit song. Generally we think of melody in terms of tunefulness, in the capacity of a line of music to impress itself quickly and clearly on the memory.

Ex.I.9 shows two melodies: *The Star-Spangled Banner*, of which the tune was composed by J. S. Smith in the late eighteenth century, and the traditional *Auld lang syne*. Each is built out of a series of short phrases, planned sometimes to answer one another, sometimes to repeat or echo. Both are vocal melodies, so that there is a relationship between music and words; mostly, a phrase in the music corresponds with a line in the poem. *The Star-Spangled Banner* consists of two-measure and four-measure phrases, in a 2 + 2 + 4 pattern, so that each pair of short phrases is answered by a longer one; the first group of this kind is immediately repeated, then comes a *sequence* (a phrase repeated at higher or – as here – lower pitch) of two measures, followed by a phrase which echoes at its close one heard earlier. Finally, the concluding phrase takes the music to a clear climax with the ascent to the high note just before the end. The use of upward-leaping phrases and dotted rhythms

ex.1.9

is typical of music intended to be stirring (compare for example the French national anthem, the *Marseillaise*).

The phrase structure of *Auld lang syne* is much simpler: $4+4+4+4$. Further, the last four measures match almost exactly the second four, while the third four follow the first quite closely. The rhythms are also very consistent, but they are largely determined by the meter of the verse. Here again there is a high note near the end to provide a sense of climax.

A number of general points can be made about melodies. First, they are made up of individual phrases, usually of two or four measures; often the composer aims at some variety in phrase length. Second, the music heard at the beginning may recur later, as an immediate repeat or as a recall after other music. Third, there are likely to be resting points in the melody; these are called *cadences* (after a Latin word meaning "fall"), and there is virtually always a decisive one at the end. Fourth, there may be patterns, of line or of rhythms or both, that recur and give the melody a sense of unity. Fifth, there is often some kind of climax point, with a rising phrase and a high note, close to the end.

Cadence

Key, tonality

One matter of particular importance in musical form – that is, the way elements are arranged in a musical work to make it coherent – is *tonality*. If you hear or play the melodies we have just been considering, and break off shortly before the end, you will find that you instinctively know what the final tone should be. The music is drawn to a particular tone as if with a gravitational pull. If, as with these two melodies, that tone is C, the music is said to be "in C". Had we written *The Star-Spangled Banner* beginning one note higher, on A rather than G, and kept all the same relationships between notes, it would have ended on D and been "in D"; we would have *transposed* it from C into D.

It is not, however, simply a matter of the last tone. The fact that the melody is in C affects the role each tone plays in it. C is the central tone, the *tonic*, but G is almost as

Tonic, dominant

important: note how the music comes to rest on G at "light" and "fight", and later (more decisively) at "there" – and it is a G that provides the climax (on "free") at the end. When music is in C, G is called the *dominant* and is the obvious alternative tonic – for in all but very short pieces the composer will generally change the tonal center, or *key*, from time to time. Of course, all this applies equally at different pitches: for music in A, the dominant is E, and for music in E♭ it is B♭. Any piece of music may be transposed from one pitch to another without changing its internal tone relationships; it will merely sound higher or lower.

We saw earlier (p. 14) that the diatonic scale consists of a sequence of notes equivalent to the white notes on the piano keyboard. This group of seven different pitches (the octave duplication does not count), which provided the basic material of music well into the Middle Ages, still can provide all that is necessary for music that does not change key at all (*Auld lang syne*, for example, has no notes with accidentals, and *The Star-Spangled Banner* adds only sharps to the note F when it leans towards the key of G). The white notes on the piano make up the scale of C major. Make all the F's into F sharps, and the notes make up G major; sharpen the C's as well, and it is D major. Or flatten the B's, and a scale of F major results. The process of adding sharps and flats may be continued up to six of each – six sharps is F♯ major, six flats G♭ major (which are different ways of saying the same thing, because on the piano F♯ and G♭ are the same note). Each of the keys has its own *key signature*. When a composer wants to write in (say) D major, all the F's and C's will need to be sharpened, so instead of writing them in every time, they are shown at the beginning, with the understanding that those sharps or flats will be observed throughout.

So far we have dealt only with major keys – those in which, when the tones used are equivalent to the white ones on the piano, the music gravitates towards C. Some work differently: when the same selection of tones is used, the music gravitates not towards C but towards A. These are the *minor* keys. The tonal center in a minor-key piece is a minor 3rd (three semitones) below that of its major equivalent; A minor is called the *relative minor* of C major, and C major the *relative major* of A minor. In reality, the scales are not identical, even though the key signatures are; in A minor, for example, the tone G (and to a lesser extent the tone F) often needs to be sharpened if the melodic line is to run smoothly. It is generally thought that music in minor keys is more sad, more serious, perhaps more threatening in character than that in major keys (though of course there is plenty of sad major-key and cheerful minor-key music).

It will be clear from the special relationship we have noted between a key and its dominant that some keys are more closely related than others. When C is the tonic, G, we saw, is the chief complementary key. But F is also close, one step in the flat direction, while G is one step in the sharp direction (and C, of course, is the dominant of F – which is why we call F the *subdominant* of C). A piece of music in C major is likely to change key first of all to G, but it may well change to A minor, the relative minor, or other nearby keys; composers use such key changes for contrast and to help establish the form of a piece – for the changes are perceptible to the listener and create natural divisions between its sections. In a longer piece, or where the composer is aiming for dramatic effects, changes to more distant keys are usual. The process of changing key is called *modulation*.

Tonality came to be an important element in musical composition around the year 1600. But well before then the pull of a tonic, or a home tone, was a factor. The home tone was not always C or A when the diatonic scale A–B–C–D–E–F–G was used. Medieval theorists, borrowing an idea from the ancient Greeks, devised a series of six *modes* (to which they gave Greek names), with the whole steps and half steps differently related to

Key signatures

Major, minor

Modulation

Modes

the final note. The Dorian mode, for example, had D as the final tone when the white notes were used. Medieval and Renaissance composers were keenly aware of the different expressive character of each mode.

Harmony

So far, we have been discussing music as if it were a single line of sound. In fact, for about the last thousand years almost all Western art music has involved two or more simultaneous sounds. The term used for the combination of sounds is *harmony*.

The earliest forms of harmony in Western music arose when traditional church chant was sung not by all the monks together but by only some of them while others sang something different – usually either a fixed tone or in tones moving parallel with the chant melody (see ex.I.10). This was regarded as adding a clothing to the melody, and an element of depth to the music. Harmony still has that function, as we hear when, for example, a hymn is sung with organ accompaniment, or a guitar plays in support of a voice, or a pianist adds a left-hand part below a right-hand melody. The organ, the guitar or the pianist's left hand will normally play combinations of tones, or *chords*.

Chords

ex.I.10

(chant in white notes, added part in black notes)

te   hu - mi - les   fa - mu - li   mo - du - lis   ve - ne - ran - do   pi - is

Ideas have varied a great deal as to what combinations of notes make good harmony. Some types of early harmony move mainly in 5ths; movement in parallel 5ths is also used in some folk singing. By the Renaissance the *triad* had become the the main unit of harmony. This is a three-note chord built up in 3rds, or by filling in the central gap in the interval of a 5th. The triad has remained the basic element in Western harmony until well into the present century; it is used not only with the notes in their basic order, 1–3–5, as in ex.I.11*a*, but also in *inversions* – that is, with the same notes but in a different vertical order, as in ex.11*b*.

Triads

ex.I.11

(a)   major triad   minor triad   (b)   inversions 1st   2nd   inversions 1st   2nd

Anyone who has tried picking out a melody on the piano and adding chords to it knows that an acceptable harmony can be made for many melodies just by using two or three triads. Ex.I.12 shows the opening of *Auld lang syne* harmonized with three triads, those on the tonic, the dominant and the subdominant. *The Star-Spangled Banner* is a more developed melody, and though it too could be very simply harmonized it sounds much better with a wider range of harmonies, as ex.I.13, with its opening measures, shows; two chords there (marked ★) are inversions. The full stirring effect of the melody can be made only with its proper, rich harmony. The way a note is harmonized often changes its sense; ex.I.14*a* shows the same note with several different harmonies, and if you listen to these you will realize that your expectation of what (if anything) is likely to follow differs from one to another.

ex.I.12

ex.I.13

ex.I.14

Consonance, dissonance

Ex.14*b* shows two of these chords with others that naturally succeed them. The first of each of those pairs is a *dissonance*: it embodies a feeling of clashing or of tension which needs to be resolved. The chord that resolves a dissonance is normally a *consonance* or a smoother-sounding chord. The tension generated by dissonances can provide a sense of movement and energy to a piece of music.

Ideas have differed a great deal from time to time about which intervals are consonant and which are dissonant. In traditional Western triadic harmony, two tones a semitone (or minor 2nd) apart, or the inversion of that (a major 7th), form the strongest dissonance; also quite dissonant is the 4th. These are shown, with their usual resolutions, in ex.I.15*a*. In the fifteenth century, even a full major triad was felt inappropriate for the final chord of a piece and an "open 5th" was preferred (ex.15*b*); full triads were usual for concluding chords in the period 1600–1900.

ex.I.15

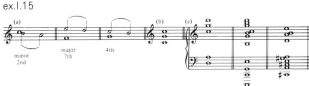

If harmony can give a sense of forward movement in music, it can also do the opposite and provide a musical equivalent of punctuation. We saw, in the melodies of ex.9, that there are natural stopping places or cadences. When they have a clear air of finality they are called "perfect cadences" or "full cadences", and generally lead from the dominant to the tonic; the most important secondary kind, called "imperfect cadences" or "half cadences", lead to the dominant. There are examples of both in ex.I.16, a partial harmonization of a line of *Auld lang syne*. Cadences of these kinds are the most basic material of harmony, for harmony is not simply single chords but progressions of chords, and it derives its character from the way they relate.

ex.I.16

Counterpoint, polyphony

Much music, as we have seen, consists of melody with accompanying harmony. But much, too, consists of melodic lines heard against one another, woven together so that their individual notes harmonize. The word derives from the idea of note-against-note, or point-against-point – for which the medieval Latin is *punctus contra punctum*. Music that uses counterpoint is called *contrapuntal*. An important and more general term for music made up of several strands is *polyphony* (Greek for "many sounds"). A related term is *homophony* ("like sounds", when the voices move in the same rhythm).

Techniques of counterpoint, of composing one line against another, were particularly important in the late Middle Ages and the Renaissance, when it was usual for church music to incorporate traditional chants. Ways were devised of composing melodies to be sung against these chants, or of weaving the chants into the musical texture of a piece (*texture* is a useful term for distinguishing between music that is mainly harmonic, or homophonic, and music that is mainly polyphonic or contrapuntal). The late Renaissance period was a "golden age" of polyphony, when these techniques were brought to the

Imitation

highest refinement. Central to such polyphony was the idea of *imitation* – that is, of one voice (or instrument) imitating what has been sung (or played) by another. Ex.I.17a shows a passage in simple counterpoint where the two lines each have some melodic character but "go" together (the lower is not simply a harmonization of the upper); ex.17b shows

ex.I.17

3 The importance of music in royal ceremonial is shown by this engraving of trumpets and kettledrums in procession: from the *History of the Coronation of James II and Queen Mary* (1687) by Francis Sandford.

a brief passage in imitative counterpoint, where two phrases (*x* and *y*) are heard first in one voice which is then imitated. Imitative counterpoint is familiar to anyone who has tried to sing *Three Blind Mice* or *Frère Jacques*; these are rounds, and the music is in *canon*, a special kind of imitation that is continuous and very exact. In most imitative counterpoint the imitation continues for only a few notes and it is usually at a different pitch.

There was another golden age of counterpoint in the early eighteenth century, with J. S. Bach as its greatest figure. This is a more elaborate, faster-moving type of counterpoint than that of the sixteenth century, more instrumental than vocal. Composers have continued to use counterpoint to enrich and add variety to the texture of their music, and to give it greater depth and intellectual weight – for music in which all the interest lies on the surface is apt to seem thinner than music where the interest, sometimes at least, irradiates the entire texture.

Color, dynamics

Composers can create variety in their music by several different means: by its texture, its rhythmic character, its speed, its key structure. Two other weapons in the composer's arsenal are tone color and dynamic level. A tone may sound quite different on different instruments or sung by the human voice. A composer can also, with most instruments, ask the player to vary the volume. This he indicates, as with speeds, by Italian terms, especially *forte* (or *f*, loud) and *piano* (*p*, soft).

Chapter II

The Instruments of Music

At the beginning of Chapter I, we saw that musical sounds are produced by regular vibration in the air. Human beings have devised numerous ways of creating this vibration: first of all by singing, later by playing instruments.

The simplest, most primitive kinds of instrument are lumps of wood or stone, fashioned so that the player can strike them. Lumps of different sizes were found to produce sounds of different pitches, and hollow objects to produce a fuller sound than solid ones (because the air in the cavity takes up the vibration in resonance). A skin stretched across a hollowed-out object gives a still better sound; this in fact creates a drum. The simplest *wind instruments* came into being when someone thought of blowing across a leaf or a straw, through a hollow bone or horn, or into a reedpipe. Anthropologists have found animal bones with holes made in them which would enable a player to produce sounds of different pitch. The earliest *string instruments* probably grew out of the discovery that a taut string, when plucked, could produce a musical sound, and that the sound could be magnified by the attachment of a box of some sort to the object bearing the string.

Virtually all instruments belong to one of four categories. The simplest are the *idiophones* ("own-sounding"), where the body of the instrument is set in vibration by the player and is itself the sound-producing object. Examples are bells, cymbals, xylophones and rattles. When a skin or membrane – rather than the instrument's actual vibrating body – is struck, the instruments are *membranophones*; this group includes little other than drums, though kazoos also belong to it and so does the comb-and-paper. Wind instruments are called *aerophones*; this category includes trumpets, flutes, clarinets and organs. String instruments, or *chordophones*, range from the piano and the harp to the violin and the guitar. To these four classes a fifth has lately been added, *electrophones*, instruments that produce their sound by electric or electronic means, like the electric organ or the synthesizer.

Voice

The human voice may not exactly be an instrument, but it is certainly the oldest means of music-making. It remains the most natural and the most expressive. Unlike the other sources of sound to be discussed in this chapter, the voice is actually a part of the performer's body. He or she is thus dependent on natural gifts (if a singer's voice fails, he cannot buy a new one). The "vocal cords", which we cause to vibrate when we sing, are folds of skin

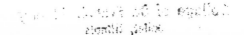

in the throat. We make their vibrations resonate in the cavities of the chest or head, and can adjust the shape and size of those cavities by muscular control according to the note we want to sing and the syllable we sing to it.

Female

We saw in Chapter I that the pitch of a woman's voice is normally in the treble clef and a man's in the bass. But there is a good deal of variation. A high-pitched woman's voice is called *soprano*, a low one *contralto* or simply *alto*, and an intermediate one *mezzo-soprano* (meaning half-soprano and sometimes called just *mezzo*). The normal pitch ranges of these voices are shown in ex.II.1, but voices vary greatly and many singers can range

ex.II.1

wider without loss of quality. The soprano voice is probably the most prized of all. The vast majority of the great women's roles in opera are for sopranos; a significant exception is Carmen, Bizet's sultry gipsy, which is a mezzo part. Sopranos may be gentle and lyrical, or bright and bell-like with a capacity for rapid, high singing, or grand and brilliant. In a large modern choir the sopranos are usually the largest group, not only because it is the commonest voice among women but because the soprano voice is generally the lightest and more are needed if the sopranos are to hold their own.

Male

The highest normal voice is the *tenor*, the lowest the *bass*; between them lies the *baritone*. The pitch ranges are shown in ex.II.2. For the last two hundred years the tenor has been

ex.II.2

regarded as the main voice for heroic singing and for expressing ardent love. Opera composers tend to have tenor heroes and bass villains, though the richness and masculinity of the bass voice have often led to its use for kings or warriors or sympathetic fathers. There is also a tradition of comic bass parts. The strong, warm sound of the baritone voice is often used for dramatic and heroic roles.

All these different voice types are used in large choirs; most of the repertory of choral music is composed for "SATB" (soprano, alto, tenor and bass). Often, boys (known as trebles) are used in preference to sopranos, especially in European church music, much of which was composed at a time when women were prohibited from singing in church. Boys tend to produce a strong and firm, sometimes even raucous sound, less soft and sweet than that of girls or women. In earlier times, too, the alto part was regularly sung by men, as it still is in many church choirs. Good male altos produce a light, sharply defined sound, well suited to contrapuntal music. Some men singing these parts use what is called "falsetto" (meaning an unnatural, "put on" high voice), but with others this type of singing is a natural extension of the top of the tenor voice; it is generally called *countertenor*.

There is another type of high voice. In the sixteenth century, the custom developed in southern Europe of castrating boys who had particularly fine voices, to prevent their voices from breaking. Italian church choirs began to use these *castratos*, and in the seventeenth and eighteenth centuries *castrato* singers dominated serious opera. The combination of a boy's vocal quality and a man's lungs evidently produced a sound of extraordinary beauty, power and flexibility. *Castrato* singers took the roles of heroes, warriors and lovers for two

Castrato

130, 320

centuries (for example Handel's Julius Caesar and Gluck's Orpheus). Most of them had roughly the same range as a mezzo-soprano; the roles they took are nowadays best sung by women. The practice of castration began to be regarded as abhorrent in the eighteenth century and was abandoned during the nineteenth.

Strings

The term "string instrument" (or "stringed") refers not only to those played with a bow – that is, the violin type – but also to many plucked instruments, like the guitar or the harp, as well as keyboard instruments like the piano (where the strings are struck) and the harpsichord.

Bowed instruments

Chief among the bowed instruments are the violin and the other instruments like it – the viola, a large violin of lower pitch, and the cello (its full name is violoncello), a much larger instrument pitched an octave below the viola. To these we may add the double bass, which is larger still but structurally rather different.

Violin

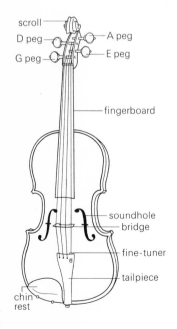

scroll
D peg
G peg
A peg
E peg
fingerboard
soundhole
bridge
fine-tuner
tailpiece
chin rest

4 Diagram of a modern violin showing principal features.

The violin is basically a resonating box with a neck attached, across which, with pegs and bridges, four strings are attached. The strings are made of gut, often with silver wire wound round them, or of steel; they are held taut and stretched across a piece of wood (the fingerboard) in such a way that the player can press them down with the fingers of his left hand and so shorten their vibrating length. With his right hand he draws his bow across the strings, bringing its horsehair (made sticky with rosin) into contact with one of them and causing it to vibrate. The vibration passes into the hollow body of the instrument (the soundbox), which amplifies it and transmits the vibration to the air and to the listener as a musical tone.

Violins have existed since the sixteenth century. The great age of violin-making was in the seventeenth century and the early eighteenth, the time of such men as Stradivari and Amati, who built instruments of incomparable sweetness, richness and power of tone. At this time the violin became the basic instrument in the orchestra and in chamber music, a position in which it is still unchallenged because of the beauty and the expressiveness of its sound and its unrivaled agility. Its capacity to draw a silvery line of tone and to play with great brilliance and rapidity make it specially prized as a solo instrument. Many composers (Bach, Beethoven, Mendelssohn, Brahms) have written concertos for it.

The four strings of the violin are tuned to the tones shown in ex.II.3a. Since the player can modify the length of the string only by shortening it, by pressing it against the fingerboard, all he can do is raise the pitch from these four "open notes", so the first note shown (G) is the lowest of which the instrument is capable. The highest is more than three octaves higher, produced by pressing the E string at the end of the fingerboard. The violin offers an almost infinite range of possibilities for varying the sound: among the most

ex.II.3

(a) Violin   (b) Viola   (c) Cello   (d) Double-bass

8ᵛᵉ lower

important are *vibrato* (when the player's left hand has a controlled wobble, greatly enriching the tone), double stopping (playing on two strings at once) and plucking or *pizzicato*.

Viola

The viola is tuned a 5th lower than the violin (ex.3*b*); the instrument is itself some six inches longer. Its tone is rather darker and less sweet, less brilliant than the violin's. The viola is only quite rarely used as a solo instrument, its main role being to play a middle, accompanying voice in the string texture. In England it was once called the "tenor", and in France it is still called the "alto" – which makes clear the kind of part it is usually asked to play.

Cello

By the rules of acoustics the viola, since its pitch is a 5th below the violin's, ought to be half as big again as the violin. But then it would be impossible, when the player tucked it under his chin to play it, to reach the other end or to support its weight. So the viola has to be made smaller than its acoustical ideal. The cello, however, is built rather closer to its proper acoustical size, since it is played not under the chin but held between the player's knees. Its tuning is shown in ex.3*c*. Otherwise its technique is exactly like that of the violin or viola. The cello is an instrument of outstanding eloquence and warmth, with a rich middle register and an intensely expressive top register; many composers have written for it music of a specially personal quality, like Dvořák and Elgar in their concertos.

Double bass

In the modern orchestra, a deeper foundation is needed than the cellos can provide; this is supplied by the double bass. The most usual tuning is shown in ex.3*d*; note that the strings are set not a 5th apart, as with the upper instruments, but a 4th, for the distances that the player's hands have to travel between notes would otherwise be too great. The instrument's tone is somewhat gruff when it is heard alone, but coupled with the cello an octave higher it sounds firm and clear.

Viols

The way that the shoulders of the double bass slope gently up to the neck mark it out as closely related to the viol family. The viols developed about the same time as the violins and were much used for chamber music in the sixteenth and seventeenth centuries. Their gentle, slightly reedy tone makes them ideal for the contrapuntal music popular at that time. Viols are made in several sizes, of which the main three are the treble, the tenor and the bass. They have six (occasionally seven) strings. All of them, even the smallest, are played with the instrument held vertically, between the knees like a cello.

Plucked instruments

Most of the plucked string instruments work on the same principle as the bowed ones – they have a resonating body, and a neck along which the strings are stretched with a system of pegs and bridges; the player stops the strings against a fingerboard attached to the neck.

Guitar

The best known of these is the guitar. The modern guitar has six strings (earlier ones had four or five), tuned as shown in ex.II.4*a*. Its body has a flat back with incurved sidewalls; the strings are nowadays of nylon, with the lower ones wound in metal. The instrument is specially associated with Spanish and Latin American music, but its appeal has always been wide and it is used in folk music in many countries. The guitar can be plucked or

ex.II.4

guitar   lute

5 *Above* The lute and the guitar.

6 *Girl with a lute:* painting by Bartolommeo Veneto, early 16th century. Isabella Stewart Gardner Museum, Boston.

strummed, either with the fingers or, if a sharper sound is wanted, with a device (a plectrum) made of some hard material.

Lute

Historically, the most important plucked instrument is the lute. In the sixteenth century it was the most popular domestic instrument, like the piano later or the guitar today, and was used for solo music and for accompanying songs or ensembles. The classical lute generally has a flat soundboard and a bowl-shaped or pear-shaped body; there are different sizes with necks of various lengths and shapes but typically lutes have six strings tuned as shown in ex.4*b*. There are numerous other instruments of the lute type, among them the mandolin, a small instrument with four or five double wire strings, whose thrumming adds a special color to Italian (and particularly Neapolitan) folk music; the banjo, a favorite instrument among black American minstrel groups and also much used in parlor music, with a round body and usually five wire strings; and the ukelele, a Hawaiian instrument like a small, four-string guitar.

Harp

Of an altogether different type is the harp, which unlike the other plucked instruments has a place in the modern orchestra. The harp is an ancient instrument known in biblical times and in many cultures, notably in Africa and South America. The orchestral harp is a highly developed instrument with about 45 strings, tuned to a diatonic scale. At its base is a set of seven pedals with which the player can shorten the strings and raise their pitch by one or two semitones; one pedal controls all the C strings, one the D strings, and so on. The harp has always had an important place in folk music, especially in Ireland and Wales; in art music, it can add color and atmosphere to orchestral music with its delicacy and its gentle washes of sound.

Keyboard instruments

Piano, harpsichord

Another, rather better-known example of a struck string instrument is the piano. Here the striking is done at one remove, through a complex mechanism operated by a keyboard. The piano was invented just before 1700 by an Italian, Bartolomeo Cristofori, who wanted to build an instrument that – unlike the harpsichord, the most important keyboard instrument of the day – could be played soft and loud, or *piano* and *forte*: hence its full name, pianoforte (or fortepiano).

Both the piano and the harpsichord consist of a set of tuned strings held taut in a wooden case, with a sounding-board underneath; both possess keyboards in which the keys for the diatonic notes are at the front (they are usually of white ivory) and the keys for the other five notes, the sharps and flats (usually of black ebony), are set a little further back from the player. The harpsichord, however, is a plucked instrument. When the key is depressed by the player, a piece of wood (the jack) is thrown up and the piece of quill (in modern instruments plastic) attached to it plucks the string. The player has no control over the speed at which the jack is projected, so cannot affect the force with which the string is plucked. So each tone on the harpsichord sounds at the same volume. The action of the piano, by contrast, allows the pianist to control, by the force he applies, the speed at which the hammer strikes the strings and, accordingly, the volume of each tone.

The harpsichord went out of fashion in the late eighteenth century, when composers increasingly felt that variation in volume was important for the kind of expressiveness they wanted in their music. It was revived in the present century, when performers began to realize that, if we wanted to hear music in the sense intended by its composers, it was necessary to use the kinds of instrument they had in mind when writing it.

The piano became the principal domestic instrument during the nineteenth century.

7 *Above* Pedal harp by Salvi, 1974.

8 *Man playing the harpsichord:* painting by Gonzales Coques (1614–84). Private collection.

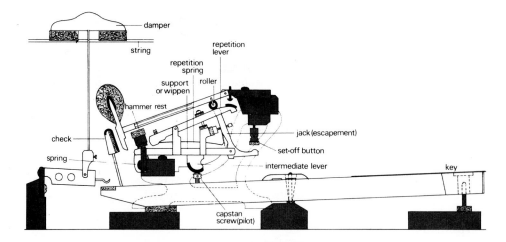

9 Action of a modern grand piano: on pressing the key the movement is transmitted via the pilot to the intermediate lever; the jack then acts on the roller of the hammer which rises towards the string. The moment the backward projection of the jack contacts the set-off button the jack moves back permitting the hammer to escape and to continue in free flight to strike the string and then begin its descent; it is then caught and retained by the check and repetition lever as long as the key remains depressed. If the key is partly released the hammer is freed from the check, and the roller is acted on directly by the repetition lever; it is thus possible to strike the string again by depressing the key a second time (the jack will re-engage with the roller only when the key has been fully released so that a full hammer stroke may be made).

Virtually every cultured home in Europe and the USA had one. It also became the instrument that many composers of the time played and used for much of their most original and most personal music (Beethoven and Chopin, for example). It has a huge repertory, most of it solo music, some of it music with strings, some of it accompanying the voice. The piano has no real place within the orchestra, but there are many piano concertos, in which the piano plays with the orchestra and sometimes contests with it.

The instrument has changed considerably. In the late eighteenth century, its tone was crisper and lighter. Its sustaining power and volume have greatly increased. These changes were made necessary not only by the changes in musical style but also by the rise of public concerts in large halls, where the music has to be loud enough to carry to a substantial audience. To support the extra string tension needed for this extra volume, wooden frames gave way to iron ones in the early nineteenth century. The traditional "wing" shape, derived from the harpsichord and convenient for accommodating strings long in the bass and short in the treble, has remained in use for concert grands and large domestic pianos. The upright piano, in which the frame and strings are mounted vertically, has long been normal for use in the home, occupying much less space and loud enough for an ordinary parlor.

The harpsichord too has smaller, domestic equivalents, the virginal and the spinet. Another domestic keyboard instrument is the clavichord, whose delicate tone is produced by the impact of a tongue of brass on the string.

10 Beethoven's last piano, by Conrad Graf, a gift from the maker. Beethovenhaus, Bonn.

Wind instruments

The basic principle of any wind instrument is that an air column in a tube is made to vibrate to produce a musical tone. There are three main ways in which this can be done: first, by blowing across a sharp edge on the tube; second, by attaching to it a reed that will vibrate; and third, by the player's using his lips in the role of a reed. The choice of method affects the kind of sound. Other factors influence the sound – the nature of the reed, the materials of which the instrument is made, and the bore of the tube (whether it is wide or narrow, and is uniform or widens towards the far end). Wind instruments are usually divided between so-called woodwind and brass. This usage helps clarify the role of each in the orchestra, though it is inexact – some "woodwind" instruments are made of metal, and the category "brass" includes some of wood.

Woodwind

The simplest of all wind instruments are the flute type, in which the player directs his breath at an edge, creating eddies of air that set the column in vibration. (The principle is the one that enables someone blowing across the top of a glass bottle to produce a faint sound; pour water into the bottle, reducing the effective size of the tube, and the tone will rise in pitch.) Every culture uses flutes, like the Arab *nay* and the Indonesian *suling*. Other varieties include the ocarina and the nose-blown flutes of Polynesia. Flutes divide into two main types, the end-blown (like the recorder) and the side-blown (like the true flute).

Recorder

The recorder has a long history in Western music, probably dating back to the fourteenth century. It is built in various sizes, to play at different pitch levels: the four main ones are the soprano (or descant), the alto (or treble), the tenor and the bass (the lowest tone possible in each is shown in ex.II.5). Recorders have traditionally been made of wood, or occasionally of ivory, until recent times when their massive use in schools has led to the manufacture of smaller types in plastic. The instrument has a beak-shaped mouthpiece at the top, with a whistle-like aperture a little below it to provide the edge that sets up the vibration. Its main body, which is cylindrical, has holes which are covered or uncovered by seven fingers and one thumb to produce different tones. With all the holes covered, the tube sounds at its full length and gives its lowest tone, but by blowing in a more tightly focused way the player forces the tube to vibrate in two halves and produce a tone an octave higher.

ex.II.5

The recorder has no place in the normal modern orchestra, but is an important member of the Baroque orchestra. Its chief repertory comes fom the Renaissance and the Baroque periods; around 1700, particularly, many composers wrote sonatas for it. Bach and Handel included it in many of their works. Its clear, piping sound was less well suited to later music and it fell out of use. But it has been revived, partly to answer the need of music educators for an instrument suitable for children's use.

Flute

The flute came into prominence during the late seventeenth century, when a group of French makers devised improvements to what had been a simple tube with finger-holes. It was still difficult to play in tune. More attempts were made to improve it by adding keys, but the first fully successful one was only in the 1840s when Theobald Boehm devised an ingenious system (soon adapted for other instruments) using rings as well as keys.

Early flutes were normally made of wood, or occasionally ivory. Nowadays metal ones – of silver or alloy, occasionally gold or platinum – are much more common. The tone of the instrument, when gently played, is cool and limpid. Its lowest register can achieve a soft, almost sensuous expressiveness, but its extreme top can add sharpness and brilliance to an ensemble. Besides the normal flute, there is a half-size instrument, the piccolo, and a large alto flute. The compasses of these are shown in ex. II.6.

11 *Above* Part of a consort of recorders: woodcut from *Syntagma musicum* (1619) by Michael Praetorius.

ex.II.6

The flute has a large repertory of sonatas from the beginning of the eighteenth century. When the recorder fell into disuse, the flute remained, being particularly well suited to

the character of mid- and late eighteenth-century music and popular among amateurs. Two flutes became the standard in the orchestra by 1800. In the present century its flexibility and its delicate, unassuming sound have won it much favor, especially among French composers.

Oboes, bassoons

All the other orchestral woodwind instruments are reed-operated. There are two types of reed: the single reed, a blade of cane tied to the mouthpiece and made to vibrate against it when the player blows, and the double reed, consisting of a pair of blades which vibrate against each other. The oboe is the principal double-reed instrument of soprano pitch.

The word "oboe" comes from the French *hautbois* ("high wood", a loud wooden instrument). Double-reed instruments of this type are used in many cultures, for example the North African *zurna* and the Indian *shahnai*.

Like the flute, the oboe was improved in the seventeenth century, with the addition of keys to make tuning easier. By the middle of the eighteenth century, it was the first woodwind instrument firmly established in the orchestra. Two oboes have been a basic part of the orchestra ever since. Oboes have been built in various sizes. The most important is the english horn (or *cor anglais*), curiously named since it is neither English nor a horn – it is a tenor oboe, pitched a 5th lower than the ordinary instrument and having a richer, more throaty tone. It is called for in many scores of the nineteenth and twentieth centuries. There is also an oboe d'amore (a gentle-toned "love oboe"), popular in Bach's time. The compasses of these instruments are shown in ex.II.7.

ex.II.7

12 *Top* Modern flutes: alto (*top*), concert, piccolo, by Rudall Carte & Co.

13 *Above* Playing a one-key flute: engraving from *Principes de la flûte traversière* (1707) by Jacques Hotteterre.

Various attempts have been made to build a satisfactory bass oboe; but the existence of the bassoon, a double-reed instrument and the true bass of the woodwind group, makes it unnecessary. It has a smoother, less reedy sound than the oboe. The size of a bass instrument poses special problems: its long tube (nine feet) needs to be doubled back on itself and the finger-holes have to be bored obliquely through the wood if the player is to be able to reach them.

The bassoon came into the orchestra during the eighteenth century as the bass to the oboes. It has had something of a reputation as "clown of the orchestra" because of its capacity for comic effects, but bassoonists resent this since it can also be eloquent or somber. An octave lower than the bassoon is the double bassoon, whose 18-foot tube is twice doubled back on itself; this instrument provides a deep and resonant bass. The compasses are shown in ex.7.

Clarinet

The clarinet has a shorter history than the other orchestral woodwinds, beginning in the early eighteenth century. It has a single reed, fastened to the mouthpiece, against which it vibrates. The tube, normally of African blackwood, is cylindrical. Because of the acoustical properties of a cylindrical tube with a single reed, the player, when he blows more acutely, does not make the sound rise an octave (as with the other instruments we have been considering) but an octave and a 5th. Since players have only sufficient fingers to uncover enough holes for an octave, the clarinetist has to use special keys to fill the gap between the basic tones produced by the full tube length and the next series an octave and a 5th higher. This makes the clarinet's timbre rather different from one register to another – rich and oily in the lowest, a little pale in the middle, clear and singing in the medium-high, quite shrill at the top.

The strength of its upper registers quickly secured the clarinet a place in military bands. It was slower to find its way into the orchestra and was not regularly used until close on 1800. Mozart contributed notably to its repertory. Nineteenth-century composers found its romantic tone appealing and made much use of it for poetic effects. In the twentieth century it held an important place in jazz bands in the hands of men like Artie Shaw and Benny Goodman.

14 *Above left and centre* Modern oboe and english horn, by Howarth of London; *Above right* Modern German bassoon by Wilhelm Heckel.

15 *Opposite Young man holding a clarinet:* painting, 1813, by Johannes Reekers. Frans Halsmuseum, Haarlem.

16 *Right* Modern clarinets: sopranino, soprano in B♭ (Schmidt-Kolbe system, by Fritz Wurlitzer), soprano in A, basset horn in F, bass in B♭, by Leblanc.

ex.II.8

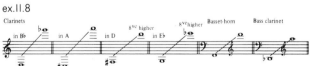

Clarinets are made in a variety of sizes. All are transposing instruments; this means that the tone that is heard differs from the one the player sees in his music and plays. This curious system enables a player to change from one size of instrument to another without altering his fingering. The standard clarinet is said to be "in B♭", which means that when the player plays C the tone that sounds is B♭. There is also a clarinet in A, more convenient for music in certain keys. Smaller, shriller instruments in D and E♭ are used for special effects and in bands. A larger, tenor clarinet usually pitched in F and called the basset horn was used by Mozart and others. The most important of the various sizes is the bass clarinet, pitched an octave below the standard one. The compasses of all these are shown in ex. II.8.

Saxophone

Another single-reed instrument is the saxophone, invented by Adolphe Sax in the mid-nineteenth century. The saxophone is made of metal, with a conical tube. Sax built it in seven sizes. The saxophones never found a regular place in the orchestra, but are used in military bands and above all in jazz, where their smoothness and flexibility find a natural home.

Brass

The so-called brass instruments – they may be of other metals, or even wood or horn – work on a principle similar to that of reed instruments. But here the player's lips act as the reed. The player presses them to a cup-shaped (or funnel-shaped) mouthpiece against which they vibrate, setting the air in the tube in vibration. Anyone who has tried blowing in this way into a simple piece of tubing, like a hosepipe, knows that a musical (or fairly musical) sound can be made but that only a limited number of tones can be sounded, as the length of the air column cannot be varied. But it can be made to vibrate in sections – halves, thirds, quarters and so on. These tones form what is called the *harmonic series*; ex.II.9 shows the tones that may be obtained from a tube about eight feet in length. The lowest tones are produced with the lips very relaxed, the highest with them very tight.

ex.II.9

(the notes shown in black are imperfectly tuned)

Instruments of this type were used in ancient civilizations, commonly for ceremonial or ritual purposes, because the sound produced is generally loud and noble. Animal horns were often used, for example the original Roman *buccina* and the Jewish *shofar*; the alphorn, used in mountainous countries for long-distance signaling, is of wood. An early metal example is the Scandinavian *lur*, a long, conical instrument in the shape of a bent S.

Horn

The first true brass instrument to establish itself in the orchestra was the horn (usually called French horn, but many are German). In the early eighteenth century it was mainly used in outdoor music or pieces referring in some way to the hunt. By the middle of the century there were normally two horns in an orchestra. The style of music then being written could accommodate the instrument's limited range of tones, and horns added warmth and fulness to the sound. At the end of the century it was occasionally used as a solo instrument (notably in Mozart's concertos). In the nineteenth century the horn's

17 Triple horn in F/B♭/F alto, with five rotary valves, by Paxman (first manufactured in 1965).

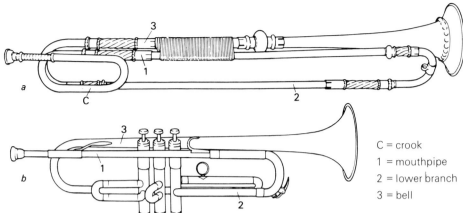

C = crook
1 = mouthpipe
2 = lower branch
3 = bell

romantic qualities brought it into special favor; it was also useful for supplying unobtrusive inner harmony. Four horns were often used, sometimes six or even eight.

By that time the horn could play more than just the tones of the harmonic series. Structurally, it had originally been simply a coiled, slightly conical brass tube, with a flared opening (or bell). But in the eighteenth century, so that it could play its limited number of tones in the prevailing key, the player would use an extra coil of tubing (a "crook") to supplement its basic length. Early in the nineteenth century a system of valves was devised which made crooks unnecessary. The valves enabled the player to switch extra lengths of tubing into action by pressing pistons and so alter the tones available to him. The horn could now manage a full range of tones. Since then, the bore of the tube has been widened to give a smoother tone and make it easier to play. The horn, the least "brassy" of the brass instruments, blends readily with the woodwinds and even the strings.

Trumpet

The highest-pitched of the brass instruments (their compasses are shown in ex. II.10) is the trumpet. A simple cylindrical tube, either straight or twice doubled back on itself, it began to be used in orchestral music during the Baroque period, when the fanfare-like phrases it could play – like the horn, it could manage only the tones of the harmonic series – fitted well with the cut of the melodies. During the late eighteenth century a pair of trumpets came to be used regularly in larger orchestras, especially in music of a formal or ceremonial kind. As with the horn, crooks were used to adapt it to the key of the music.

ex. II.10

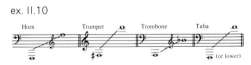

Valves were applied to the trumpet, too, early in the nineteenth century, enabling it to play a full range of tones. Since then composers have taken advantage of its brilliant and forthright sound and its ability to penetrate, or ride over, the full orchestral ensemble. Also sometimes found is a cornet, a gentler-toned instrument looking like a short, stubby trumpet, less noble in sound but much easier to play (it is more commonly used in bands). The trumpet itself, of course, is much used in jazz; indeed its most famous exponent ever is Louis Armstrong. In jazz, and occasionally in orchestral music, the trumpet's tone is modified by the insertion of a mute – a kind of large plug – in its bell. Mutes of various

18 *Above* Hand-horn player, lithograph, *c*1835, by C. Tellier.

19 *Above right* Diagram comparing a Baroque and a modern trumpet.

20 Modern American bass trombone in B♭/F/E♭, with two thumb valves (Vincent Bach model), by Selmer.

shapes and materials affect its tone, enabling the instrument to do anything from moaning to snarling.

Trombone

The "heavy brass" instruments are the trombones and the tuba. A trombone has no need for valves as it has a movable slide; by altering the length of the tube and (as with the horn or trumpet) varying his lip pressure, the trombonist can play any tone in his compass. Trombones are made in two sizes, though nowadays a single instrument fitted with a valve so that it can play the music of both the tenor and the bass is widely used. In earlier periods trombones were much used in church music, and their noble, solemn tones are now often called upon when an effect of grandeur is wanted. They are heard too in noisy, brilliant climaxes.

Tuba

At the bass of the brass ensemble comes the tuba, a large instrument of the horn type with a wide bore and three or four valves. Tubas are made in numerous sizes; the most usual orchestral one has about 16 feet of tubing (not including the lengths controlled by valves). They are made in a variety of shapes, some (like the sousaphone – named after the composer – and the helicon) winding round the player so that he can support it when marching. Its tone is deep, sonorous and well rounded, lacking the bite and edge of the trombones.

Organ

The organ is a wind instrument, although the player fortunately does not have to blow it. The air is supplied by pumps and bellows. An organ may have hundreds, even thousands, of pipes: one (sometimes more) for every tone in every stop. "Stop" is the term used for a group of pipes that produce a particular quality of sound. The player has at his command a series of buttons that he can pull out to engage each of them (hence the expression "pulling out all the stops"). The pipes may be of wood, tin or other metals; they may be flue pipes (on the edge principle) or reed ones; they may be narrow or wide, open or closed, round or rectangular in shape. Each produces a different sound.

A large instrument may have three keyboards, or even more, operated by the hands, and a further one (a pedalboard, laid out like a keyboard but larger) for the feet. Traditionally, the action of an organ – the series of links between the keyboard and the air supply – was purely mechanical, but nowadays electrical systems are widely used. And electronic organs, without pipes at all, have reached a point of development where almost any sound can be accurately and cheaply reproduced – a threat to the traditional pipe organ despite the latter's beauty, variety and grandeur of tone.

The organ's repertory reached a peak in the early eighteenth century, with the incom-

Organs, old and new:
21 Organ by Christian
Müller, 1735–8, Groote
Kerk, Haarlem (*left*).

22 Organ by the Holtkamp
Organ Co. (inaugurated
1967), University of New
Mexico, Albuquerque
(*right*).

parable music of Bach, and includes several masterpieces from the nineteenth and twentieth centuries. A few composers have written organ concertos, notably Handel, but the organ has never had a regular place within the orchestra; its natural home is of course the church and its natural repertory sacred music.

Percussion

Percussion instruments are those sounded by being struck, or in a few cases shaken. Most are made of wood or metal. Some, *untuned percussion*, produce on impact a noise rather than a definite musical tone; others, *tuned percussion*, sound a recognizable pitch. Percussion instruments are used more for rhythmic purposes than melodic.

Drums

The most important percussion instrument in Western music is the drum, in particular the kettledrums, or timpani. Pairs of kettledrums have been used in orchestral music since the early eighteenth century, often with trumpets to add pomp and brilliance. The kettledrum is a large bowl-shaped vessel, usually of copper, with a skin held taut across the top. It sounds a tone of definite pitch, determined by the instrument's size and the tension of the skin, which is adjustable either with hand-screws or with a foot-operated mechanism.

23 Modern percussion instruments.

cymbals

bass drum

timpani

tam tam

side drum

xylophone

glockenspiel

tubular bells

Untuned percussion

Other types of drum include the bass drum, much used in bands, which provides a deep, unpitched thump, and the side drum, a small instrument with strings that rattle against the head when it is struck, producing a sizzling sound. These are basic to the rhythm sections of jazz and dance bands. So is the cymbal, a resonant brass plate that can be played either with a drumstick or – common at dramatic climaxes – clashed one against another. Another instrument often heard at climactic moments is the large gong or tam-tam: struck with a soft, heavy beater, it can produce a solemn, awesome noise that menacingly grows in volume for a few moments after the impact. Gongs play a large role in the music of Indonesia, where the gong-based orchestra is known as the *gamelan*; the type of gong used there, unlike the tam-tam, sounds a definite pitch.

Tuned percussion

Tuned percussion instruments include the bells, or chimes, a series of metal tubes suspended in a frame; they are often called upon to imitate church bells. Smaller bells are represented on the glockenspiel, a series of metal bars struck with small hammers. A similar instrument operated from a keyboard is called the celesta because of its sweet, "celestial" sound. Wooden instruments of this type produce a harder, drier tone. Chief among them is the xylophone, a series of wooden (or synthetic resin) bars laid out like a piano keyboard with metal resonators underneath. It is struck with small mallets. A larger version is the marimba – the name comes from Africa, where (as in parts of Latin America) such instrument types are common. A metal instrument of this kind, with disc resonators made to revolve by a motor and so producing an effect of vibration, is known as the vibraphone or vibraharp (or simply "vibes"); it is much used in jazz.

Electronic instruments

Almost any sound can be analyzed by electronic means and then re-created. The people who have experimented during the present century with electric methods of creating sound have added enormously to the range of sound and the means of organizing it.

There are instruments like the *ondes martenot*, operated from a keyboard and a control panel, and sounding like a de-personalized human voice. More recent are the electric piano, which can sustain in a way that the real piano cannot, the electric guitar – well known from rock music – where the string vibration is resonated by the electric apparatus, and the electronic organ (mentioned above). There is also the tape recorder, with which an ingenious and imaginative musician may devise new ways of making and shaping musical sounds, and ultimately the synthesizer, which has an almost unlimited capacity for the generation of sounds or the modification of existing ones. We stand on the brink of a new world of sound creation – a prospect that must be exciting to the composer, eager to create sounds never heard before.

Orchestras, bands and ensembles

The orchestra

The orchestra as we know it dates back to the late seventeenth and early eighteenth centuries, when groups of musicians began to be employed to play in opera houses and at courts. As early as 1626 a royal band of 24 string players had been assembled by King Louis XIII of France. Later, wind players were added. Orchestras varied in size, depending on the wealth of their patron or employing organization, the kind of music to be played and the size of the building in which they played. Generally, an orchestra of the mid-eighteenth century might be expected to have a dozen violins, eight other string players, a flute, two each of oboes, bassoons and horns, an accompanying (or "continuo") harpsichord, and for important occasions a pair of trumpets and kettledrums.

By the beginning of the next century, when larger halls were in use and music of a grander kind was being composed, an orchestra could well have 24 violins, ten violas, six each of cellos and double basses, and pairs of flutes, oboes, clarinets, bassoons, horns,

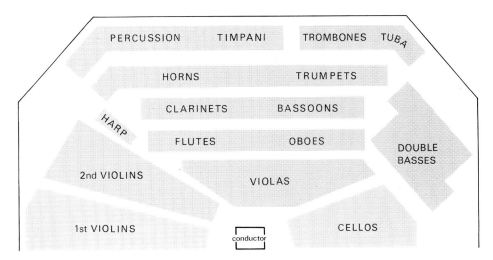

24 Typical layout of a modern orchestra.

trumpets and kettledrums, with a few extra instruments – a piccolo, an extra horn or two, two or three trombones – as required. A modern symphony orchestra at full size might typically have 32 violins (divided into 16 firsts and 16 seconds), 14 violas, 12 cellos and 10 double basses, with a piccolo and three flutes, three oboes and an english horn, three clarinets and a bass clarinet, three bassoons and a double bassoon, six horns, three trumpets, three trombones and a tuba, two harps and four to six percussion players. A typical arrangement of a modern orchestra on a concert platform is shown in fig. 24.

Bands

In early times, many towns had their own wind bands; there were also military bands. In the modern wind or military band the clarinets play a central role, akin to that of the violins in the orchestra. A large band may include 10 or 12 clarinets, along with other woodwinds and a substantial body of brass as well as percussion and sometimes bass strings. Brass bands, popular in industrial societies in the nineteenth and twentieth centuries, are largely based on cornets and various sizes of tuba.

Another important large ensemble is the jazz band. Jazz is commonly played by small groups, for example, a clarinet, a trumpet, a trombone, a saxophone, and a rhythm section with piano, string bass (double bass) and percussion including drums. In the big-band days, however, there might be as many as four or five each of saxophones (with the same players doubling clarinets if needed), trumpets and trombones, with piano, guitar, string bass and drums.

Chamber ensembles

Composers have written music for numerous different combinations of instruments. But there are some standard groups for which large and attractive repertories have been created. These are itemized in the table. Chamber music was originally intended for performance

---

Listening Note II.A   *Side 1, band 1*

Britten: *Young Person's Guide to the Orchestra* op. 34 (1946)

Benjamin Britten (1913–76) composed his *Young Person's Guide to the Orchestra* as music for a film about the instruments of the orchestra. It is in the form of a theme and variations, the theme being a dance by Henry Purcell written in 1695 for use in a play called *Abdelazer*.

Time

Time		Time	
0:00	full orchestra states theme	11:09	tuba
0:21	woodwinds play the theme	11:56	percussion, starting with timpani
0:44	brass play the theme	12:10	bass drum followed by cymbals
1:03	string section enters	12:20	tambourine – triangle
1:18	percussion section plays	12:31	side drum
1:36	full orchestra repeats the theme	12:35	Chinese woodblock
1:55	flutes play their variation	12:40	xylophone
2:28	oboes	12:51	castanets
3:30	clarinets	12:56	gong or tam-tam
4:07	bassoons	13:04	whip
5:00	violins		fugue starts:
5:33	violas (entry on long note)	13:40	piccolo, then other woodwinds
6:35	cellos	14:21	violins, then other strings
7:52	double basses	14:52	harp
8:51	harp	15:04	horns, then other brass
9:38	horns	15:24	percussion
10:24	trumpets	15:35	original theme returns
10:55	trombones	16:21	(end)

ex.i

ex.ii

(fugue subject: given here
in its main key, D major)

not in concert halls but in rooms in a house; works of this kind are written in such a way that they are to be played with just one player to each part.

group	instruments
Trio sonata	2 violins (or recorders, flutes, oboes, or 1 violin and 1 flute etc) and continuo
String trio	violin, viola, cello
String quartet	2 violins, viola, cello
String quintet	string quartet+an extra viola or cello
Piano trio	piano, violin, cello
Piano quartet	piano, violin, viola, cello
Piano quintet	piano, 2 violins, viola, cello
Violin sonata	violin, piano
Cello sonata	cello, piano
Wind quintet	flute, oboe, clarinet, bassoon, horn

25 Nuremberg town musicians playing three shawms and a sackbut; drawing, *c*1660, artist unknown. Stadtbibliothek, Nuremberg.

Chapter III

The Structures of Music

Every piece of music needs to have some kind of organization, or form, if it is to be coherent to the listener. In music, as in the other arts, form has to do with the arrangement of the various elements. For the listener, it has chiefly to do with recognizing. By hearing something you have heard before, and recognizing it, you can perceive a piece as something more than a series of unrelated sounds.

In the first part of this chapter we shall consider some of the ways in which composers have organized their music, which elements they have used, and how they have used them. In the second we shall look at the genres, or types, of music – the symphony, the quartet, the oratorio and so on – in terms of their structure and their history, noting which composers have particularly contributed to each genre.

Musical form

Phrase, motif, theme

The basic elements in the organization of Western music are melody and key. The easiest thing to recognize is a melody that one has recently heard, so composers repeat melodies to give shape and unity to a composition. A structural unit in music, however, may be smaller than a melody. It may be a *phrase*, of perhaps six or seven notes, or even a *motif* (or a *figure*), of two or three, which the composer uses persistently so that it imprints itself

1000	The Middle Ages
1300	
	The Renaissance
1500	
1600	The Baroque
1700	
	The Classical Period
1800	
	The Romantic Period
1900	Modern Times

firmly on the hearer's mind. The term *theme* is often used for a musical idea on which a work is based: longer than a motif but able to give rise to some kind of musical "argument" or working-out. Sometimes its rhythm may be at least as important as its melodic line: Beethoven, for example, takes the "short–short–short–long" figure that opens his famous Fifth Symphony and uses it in different melody patterns, but it remains instantly recognizable.

Key

Second in importance to melody is key. As we saw in Chapter I, most Western music has a strong gravitational pull towards a tonal center. We talk of a Symphony in D, or a Concerto in B♭ minor, when the music feels as though it needs to end on a chord of D major or of B♭ minor. We have seen, too, that composers cause their music to change key during a movement. A piece in C major normally modulates first of all to G major, which as we saw on p. 19 uses the same tones as C major except one (F♯ instead of F). An example of this can be seen in *The Star-Spangled Banner* (see pp. 17–18), which goes from C to G. A listener soon recognizes that change of key and what it signifies in the design of a piece. He also soon recognizes when a piece returns to its home key.

Composers developed subtle ways of handling key to convey structural meaning – for example, by moving to remote keys to create a sense of distance from the home key. They could, further, couple key and melody. In "sonata form" (see p. 47), composers generally – at a point about two-thirds or three-quarters through a movement – moved to the home key and at the same time reintroduced the opening theme. This "double return" creates a moment of particular force in the structure.

Harmony and cadence

There are other ways in which harmony can be used in the structure of a movement. Composers of the Baroque period, for example, often based an entire movement on a recurring pattern of harmonies (much as in jazz). Movements were often constructed over a repeating bass-line; this, called a "ground bass" (because the bass serves as the ground on which the piece is built), is more fully discussed below, p. 48. Numerous other kinds of compositional device exist by which a composer can manipulate the structure of a movement. The use of cadences – punctuation points, or resting points – can mark out its outlines for the listener.

Cantus firmus

Most of these formal devices belong to the Baroque, Classical and Romantic periods. In the Middle Ages and the Renaissance (that is, up to about 1600), the chief organizational device was the *cantus firmus* (Latin for "fixed song" or "fixed melody"). Here the composer chooses a particular melody, which might be sung or played in long notes by one voice or instrument while the others sang faster-moving parts around it; or the melody might be worked into the music in some other way, or might be sung in elaborated form. The fixed melody might be repeated several times over, in a recurring rhythmic pattern: this gave the piece a certain unity. That melody would normally be taken from the traditional repertory of chant, or *plainsong*, drawn up by the church (see p. 63), in which each melody is associated with a particular part of the liturgy (the prescribed form of church service). It would be familiar to the congregation. Later, after the Reformation, the Lutheran church in Germany built up a similar repertory of familiar hymn-tunes, called *chorales*, which composers used as a basis for cantatas and organ pieces. Some were adapted from popular songs, just as were some of the melodies that Catholic composers of the Renaissance had used in their church works. Sacred or secular, from liturgical chant or popular song, the purpose was the same: to provide something familiar to the listener and to give the composer a foundation for his piece.

Plainsong

Chorales

There is an analogy to this in twentieth-century music. In the early years of the century, many composers felt a need for a new method of formal control. Schoenberg (see p. 279)

12-tone music

devised a 12-tone system in which a "series", the 12 tones of the chromatic scale arranged in a specific order, is used as the basis of an entire movement or work. It is not designed for the listener to follow, however.

The main forms

Here our concern is perceptible musical form, the structure of a piece of music as it can be grasped by the listener and be an aid to understanding. In the chapters that follow, where we shall be looking at composers and their music in a historical context, and examining a selection of their music, the ways in which the music is organized will frequently be discussed. This will often involve the use of special terms to describe the procedures. We now look at these terms and outline their meaning.

Binary

Binary form means simply two-part form. The term can be applied to anything from a short melody (a folksong, a hymn-tune) to an extended movement, as long as it consists of two sections that in some sense balance each other. In the Renaissance and Baroque periods, dances were often written in binary form. So were Bach's harpsichord pieces in dance rhythm, written to be listened to, not for dancing. These movements tend to follow a regular pattern in key and melody:

melody	A	B :	: A	B
key	T	D :	: D	T

A–opening theme   B–closing theme
T–tonic (or home) key   D–dominant (or complementary) key

Each half of such a movement is repeated, and the listener is always aware of the fresh beginning, with the opening theme heard in a new key, at the start of the second half.

Ternary

Ternary form means three-part form, on the pattern A–B–A (that is, the third part is identical with, or very similar to, the first). This is again a form found in folksongs and hymns, even in children's songs like *Twinkle, twinkle, little star*. The idea of repeating the first part of a piece after a different section is an obvious one, and ternary form has a long history. Composers in the Baroque period wrote many ternary songs or arias: this form is known as the "da capo aria" ("da capo" means "from the head", indicating that the performer should go back to the beginning). The minuet-and-trio movements – usually the third – of Classical symphonies and chamber works are ternary, in that the minuet is repeated after the trio.

Rondo

Rondo form is an extension of ternary. It is a form in which the main section recurs two or more times; its plan, at its simplest, is A–B–A–C–A (longer examples can be shown A–B–A–C–A–D–A or A–B–A–C–A–B′–A, with B′ a variant of B). This form was particularly favored by composers of the Classical period, Haydn, Mozart and Beethoven, usually as the last movement in a sonata, chamber work or orchestral piece. A feature of rondo form is that the recurrences of the A section are in the home key; the episodes (the B, C or D sections) are normally in nearby keys, such as the dominant or the relative minor/major. Here are diagrams of typical rondo movements:

1 melody	A	B	A	C	A
key	T	D	T	M	T

2 melody	A	B	A	C	A	B′	A
key	T	D	T	S	T	T	T

3	*melody*	A	B	A	C	A	D	A
	key	T	D	T	M	T	S	T

T – tonic	D – dominant
M – relative minor	S – Subdominant

Sonata form

Sonata form is the most important form of the Classical and Romantic periods. It came into being soon after the middle of the eighteenth century and remained in use at least to the middle of the twentieth. A sonata-form movement falls into three main sections: Exposition, Development and Recapitulation. This is the ground-plan (there may be an introduction to start with and a coda to end with).

Exposition	Development	Recapitulation
A B	*A/B*	*A B*
T D	various	T T

The *exposition* "exposes", or lays out, the thematic material of the movement. This divides into two groups of themes, *A* and *B*, or two *subjects*, as they are sometimes called. Depending upon the length of the movement – movements in sonata form can last anything between one minute and half-an-hour – each subject may be simply a melody or a group of melodies, or a group of motifs with very little melodic character. Several examples of sonata form are discussed later in this book, with listening notes (they are Haydn, Symphony no. 104, p. 153; Beethoven, Symphony no. 3, p. 174; Schubert, String Quintet in C, p. 193; Brahms, Symphony no. 1, p. 235; and Tchaikovsky, Symphony no. 4, p. 244). They vary in detail, but in all of them the first-subject material is in the main key of the work and the second is in a complementary key, normally the dominant (in a major-key work; in a minor-key one, the relative major). There may be contrast between the themes themselves (some composers tended to use brisk, "masculine" themes in the first subject and gentler, more lyrical, "feminine" ones in the second); but there is always contrast between the keys of the two groups.

The exposition normally ends in the secondary key, and the *development* follows. This generally uses material from the exposition and "develops" it. Themes may be broken up into fragments, and used in dialogue; they may be treated contrapuntally; phrases from them may be repeated at different pitches; they may be used as starting-points for new ideas. The music may go into different keys. Often the development section provides a climax of activity and excitement.

The arrival of the *recapitulation* usually forms the principal climax, with the "double return" to the home key and the music that began the movement. The essential feature of the recapitulation is that, when the second-subject material returns, it is in the home key.

The principle behind sonata form – the presentation of material in two keys, and its later re-presentation all in the home key – runs through many other musical forms in the Classical and the Romantic periods. An important example is sonata-rondo form, of which the plan shown as (2) on p. 46 is an example. There the *B* material is usually presented first in the dominant and second in the home key. Another variant plan, also somewhere between sonata and rondo, takes this form:

material	A	B	A	C	B'	A	(V – various)
key	T	D	T	V	T	T

Ritornello

A standard form of the Baroque period is ritornello form. Like rondo, it is based on a recurring theme; but here the theme is not always in the home key. Here is a typical plan of a concerto-type movement:

orchestra or solo	O	S	O'	S	O'	S	O
key	T	T–D	D	D–M	M	M–T	T

O – orchestra   T – tonic key
S – solo   D – dominant
                       M – relative minor or other key

The orchestra opens and closes the movement with complete statements of its main material, the "ritornello" (O); parts of the ritornello (O') are heard in the course of the movement. The soloist has three main sections to play (in these the music is likely to change key). His material often calls for virtuoso skills. (Examples of ritornello form discussed later in this book are Vivaldi's Concerto op. 3 no. 6, p. 121, and Bach's Brandenburg Concerto no. 4, p. 127.) This formal design is also used in arias. During the Classical period, ritornello form was enlarged by the inclusion of second-subject material, as in sonata form (for a sonata-ritornello movement, the first movement of Mozart's Piano Concerto in G, see Listening Note, p. 165).

Variation, ground bass

Variation form has been used in all periods. The principle is simple: state a theme, then embellish it and elaborate it in various ways. Variation methods were applied to plainsong, as we have seen, in the Middle Ages and the Renaissance. In the Baroque era, the Lutheran composers of northern Europe varied chorale melodies for organ (see p. 109). A type of variation movement used at this period was the ground bass, where a bass pattern is repeated with different music heard above it: a notable example is Dido's lament in Purcell's opera *Dido and Aeneas* (see Listening Note, p. 111).

In the Classical period, composers preferred the purely melodic type of variation. Mozart wrote several sets for the piano. Usually the first two or three variations stay close to the theme, but later ones become increasingly complex and brilliant. In our Haydn example (see Listening Note, p. 155), the theme itself hardly changes but is repeated with different music around it. Beethoven's variations beome more like miniature developments of motifs in the theme than mere melodic elaborations. A particularly interesting set of orchestral variations from the end of the nineteenth century is Elgar's *Enigma Variations*, where each variation portrays the character of one of Elgar's friends. In the twentieth century variation form has been used in fairly traditional ways by such composers as Britten (see Listening Note, p. 42) and Copland, while Schoenberg and Webern have adapted its techniques to their less traditional idioms.

Fugue

The fugue of the time of Bach, its greatest master, represents a late flowering of the techniques used by the polyphonic composers of the sixteenth century. The basic principle of their music is that the voices sing, in succession, the same music to the same words. As they sing at different pitch, one hears each musical phrase several times over, at various levels, as at the opening of Palestrina's *Missa brevis* (see Listening Note, p. 88). The voices seem to imitate one another; this style is often called "imitative counterpoint". The same style was generally used in instrumental music of this period and the Baroque. The word fugue — from the Latin *fuga*, meaning flight or pursuit – was applied to movements of this kind.

Fugues, by Bach and other composers, usually begin with a section in which a *subject* –

26 Opening of the Fugue in C minor by J. S. Bach from *Das wohltemperirte Clavier*, book 1, 1722, autograph manuscript. Deutsche Staatsbibliothek, Berlin.

the theme on which the entire piece is based – is heard, successively, in all the voices (the term *voice* is used, in instrumental music as well as vocal, for the contrapuntal strands of a composition). As each voice enters, the texture grows fuller. In the remainder of the fugue, the subject is likely to be heard several more times; in between there will be passages called *episodes*, usually related to the subject.

Bach used fugue not only in his keyboard music (see Listening Note, p. 129, for one from his "48" – two in each of the keys, major and minor) but also in his chamber and orchestral music (see Listening Note, p. 127, for an example from a concerto). He also wrote fugal choruses in his vocal works. But the most famous exponent of the choral fugue was his contemporary, Handel, in his oratorios (dramatic works on biblical stories: for a fugue from one of his oratorios, see Listening Note, p. 142). Composers long continued to use it in church music, and in other contexts – for example, to round off a set of variations (as in Britten's *Young Person's Guide to the Orchestra*: see Listening Note, p. 42).

Genres

Orchestral music
Symphony

The most important type of orchestral music is the symphony. Symphonies were first composed in the early eighteenth century, when public concerts began. Early symphonies were in three movements, the first and last of them fast, the middle one slow. Later it became usual to add an extra movement, in the rhythm of the most popular dance of the time, the minuet, between the slow movement and the final one.

The Austrian composer Joseph Haydn is often called the father of the symphony. He wrote more than 100 during the second half of the eighteenth century (see Listening Note, p. 153). During the same period, Mozart wrote some 50 symphonies. The mature symphonies of these two men take some 25 to 30 minutes in performance. The next generation is represented by Beethoven, who expanded the form, producing works up to 45 minutes in length (see Listening Note, p. 174). In these Classical symphonies, the first movement – which sometimes has a slow introductory section – is normally in sonata form, and is the intellectual core of the work. Usually the slow movement too is in sonata form, though Haydn often favored variations. The minuet, as we have seen, is normally ternary. The finale is usually in sonata or sonata-rondo form.

The days when composers wrote 100, or even 50, symphonies passed with the eighteenth century. The weightier works of the nineteenth were not of a kind that could be turned out by the dozen. Beethoven's nine came to be regarded as a magic number that until recently no one dared exceed. Schubert completed seven. Schumann wrote four, one called the "Spring", another the "Rhenish", because of their sources of inspiration. Beethoven had earlier written his "Pastoral" Symphony, which reflects his feelings about the countryside. Berlioz, in France, went further; his *Fantastic Symphony* is sub-titled "Episodes in the Life of an Artist" and has a theme running through its five movements that represents his beloved and what happens to her (see p. 211).

The idea of writing symphonies with a story, or "program", attracted several composers. The traditional type was maintained by such men as Brahms, Tchaikovsky and Dvořák (see Listening Notes, pp. 235 and 244). With Mahler, the symphony again expanded; his symphonies mostly involve vocal movements, last an hour or more and are often in five movements. In the twentieth century, Stravinsky wrote two mature symphonies (see Listening Note, p. 292), but the finest body of traditional symphonies comes from Shostakovich, who wrote 15. Some relate to events in Soviet history and some involve singing.

Symphonic poem

The line to which Berlioz's *Fantastic Symphony* belongs turned into a separate outgrowth, the symphonic poem or tone-poem. Liszt wrote several of these, expressing in most of them his reactions to literary or artistic works: *Hamlet*, for example, evokes the Shakespeare character, though one passage describes Ophelia. Several Czech and Russian composers used the genre (Mussorgsky, for instance, in his *St John's Night on the Bare Mountain*), but its leading exponent was Richard Strauss, who wrote several of a very vivid kind, sometimes telling stories in brilliantly descriptive music (see Listening Note, p. 262).

Overture

The overture, originally designed to open an evening in the theater, was much like a small-scale symphony in the eighteenth century. Later, composers wrote overtures for concert use. These are usually like miniature symphonic poems. A good example is Mendelssohn's *Hebrides* overture, inspired by the island scenery off the west coast of Scotland. Many other composers, like Tchaikovsky (*Romeo and Juliet*), have written concert overtures, usually in one movement.

Concerto

The concerto, as an orchestral form, is second only to the symphony. It began as a composition in which a small group of performers was set against a larger group, and developed into the solo concerto – in which one instrument has a solo role, with the orchestra – and the concerto grosso (group concerto) of the early eighteenth century. The Italian composer Vivaldi wrote several hundred concertos, many for solo violin and orchestra. Bach wrote for harpsichord and orchestra, Handel for organ and orchestra; both also composed works of the concerto grosso type. Most are in three movements (fast–slow–fast). Ritornello form is normal for the fast movements.

In the Classical period, the leading concerto composer was Mozart, whose 21 concertos for piano and orchestra are among his happiest works (see Listening Note, p. 165). With the nineteenth century, the concerto increasingly became a vehicle for the virtuoso – first in Beethoven's often stormy concertos for the piano, then in those of Liszt, Schumann, Brahms and Tchaikovsky. The violin concerto too flourished in this period: there are splendid examples by Beethoven, Mendelssohn, Brahms and Tchaikovsky. Most concertos are in three movements, fast–slow–fast. The tradition has continued into the present

27 BBC Symphony Orchestra at the Royal Festival Hall, London.

century. Bartók wrote a concerto for orchestra (see Listening Note, p. 298) in which the concerto form and spirit are evident but there is no single soloist.

Chamber music

Chamber music, though nowadays played at concerts, and much recorded, was not originally intended to be listened to (the term means "room music"). It was composed for the pleasure of those who played it. A common title was *sonata*, which means a piece to be sounded (as opposed to a cantata, to be sung). We have already met the word in the context of sonata form (a form much used in sonatas, but elsewhere too). Taken by itself, the term signifies an instrumental composition, for keyboard alone (the piano sonata: see p. 53) or for an ensemble.

Trio and solo sonata

It was first regularly used for the trio sonata, which came into existence in the seventeenth century. Generally for two melody instruments (like violins, recorders, flutes, oboes) and a bass (or "continuo": see p. 100), it had two streams of development: the church sonata, primarily contrapuntal and in four movements, slow–fast–slow–fast, and the chamber sonata, a group of movements in dance rhythm. Many sonatas were also written for one instrument (usually violin or flute) and continuo.

Violin sonata

These forms fell out of use in the eighteenth century. When the piano became the main domestic instrument, the leading chamber music form was for a time the sonata for piano with violin. Mozart wrote some 30 works of this kind. Beethoven and Brahms used this form and also the cello sonata. Sonatas were written for other instruments too: in the twentieth century Hindemith even wrote a series of sonatas, one for each orchestral instrument with piano.

Ensembles with piano

Related to the sonata for one instrument and piano are works for piano with two, three and four instruments. The piano trio (piano, violin, cello) was a favorite of the main

Classical and Romantic composers. Several of them also wrote piano quartets (with viola added) or quintets (piano and string quartet; Mozart and Beethoven also wrote quintets for piano with wind instruments). Such works are usually in three movements, fast–slow–fast.

String quartet

The most important chamber music form is the string quartet, for two violins, viola and cello. Haydn occupies a central position in its development, as in that of the symphony. He wrote his first string quartets in the 1750s, his last in 1802–3; there are about 70 altogether, containing much of his finest music. He had great influence on Mozart, who composed 26 string quartets. Nearly all these are are four-movement works, usually fast–slow–minuet–fast. Sonata form is used in the first movement, and often in the slow movement and the finale (the latter is often a sonata-rondo). Variation form works well for the string quartet combination and composers often used it, generally for slow movements or finales.

Beethoven wrote 17 string quartets, much expanding the form – from the 25-minute scale of the Haydn-Mozart era to 40 minutes or more. The highly original quartets of his last years mostly abandon the four-movement pattern; one has seven, played without a break. Most of the major Romantic and twentieth-century composers used the form, often for their most personal music.

Other string ensembles

Works for string trio, quintet, sextet or even octet follow essentially the same history as the string quartet. There are string trios by Mozart and Beethoven, but for nineteenth-century composers the trio sound was too thin and it was not until the twentieth that the form was again seriously used. The string quintet has a richer history. Boccherini, an Italian contemporary of Haydn's, wrote over 100, mostly for two violins, viola and two cellos. Mozart wrote six, with a viola rather than a cello as the extra instrument. Schubert's single quintet has two cellos. Brahms also wrote string quintets and, with his love of thick, rich textures, two sextets. Mendelssohn even wrote an octet, for four violins, two each of violas and cellos.

Mixed ensembles

Among the works that include wind instruments are fine quintets from Mozart and Brahms, with clarinet, inspired by the clarinet's particular beauty of tone and its ability to blend with strings. Mixed groups (clarinet, bassoon, horn and strings) are used in the

28 Amadeus Quartet: (*left to right*) Norbert Brainin, Sigmund Nissel, Peter Schidlof and Martin Lovett.

Septet of Beethoven and the Octet of Schubert, following an older tradition of lightweight chamber music. For wind instruments alone there is a considerable eighteenth-century repertory of serenade-type music for the bands of the time, for example two each of oboes, clarinets, bassoons and horns.

Keyboard music

Keyboard music goes back at least to the early Renaissance. Most music from this time was for church use and is built around traditional church melodies. But from the sixteenth century there are also dances and arrangements of popular songs and sacred pieces. This music was designed to be played on any available instrument – the organ (especially for sacred pieces) and the harpsichord or virginals (especially for dance music).

There were several kinds of keyboard work in the Baroque period. One was the contrapuntal piece, often preceded by a piece in a brilliant style, called toccata or prelude (to reach its height in the preludes and fugues of J. S. Bach); these could be for organ or harpsichord. In the Renaissance, dances had often been performed in pairs (usually slow–fast). With the Baroque, it became usual to group them in sets, or "suites", of four or five, often Allemande–Courante–Sarabande–Gigue (in effect, moderate–fast–slow–fast), with an extra one or two (minuet, gavotte or bourrée, for example: for particulars of these dances, see Glossary, p. 350). Bach was the leading composer here, too. In France, a favored type was the "genre piece", music intended to reflect a mood, a person's character or something of the kind (like genre painting of the time). There was also the chorale prelude, for church use in Lutheran Germany; here, as we saw on p. 45, a well-known hymn melody is used as the basis of a piece for organ.

Piano sonata

The word "sonata" began to be used in keyboard music for pieces that do not belong in any of these categories. The leading composer of harpsichord sonatas was Domenico Scarlatti, who wrote over 500 single-movement pieces, some of them in a bold and brilliant style, in the second quarter of the eighteenth century. Soon after that, the sonata became the chief genre of keyboard music. Central figures here were Bach's sons, Carl Philipp Emanuel, working in Germany, and Johann Christian, in London. Haydn wrote more than 50 piano sonatas, Mozart nearly 20, Beethoven 32. Most are in three movements, fast–slow–fast, the first movement in sonata form, the last a rondo or sonata-rondo. Variation form is sometimes used, too.

29 Wind Band of the Prince of Oettingen-Wallerstein: silhouette on gold ground, 1791. Schloss Harburg.

30 The Salle Pleyel, Pari
where Chopin often
played: engraving from
L'illustration (9 June
1855).

19th-century genres

Of nineteenth-century composers, Schubert wrote several sonatas for piano, and Chopin wrote three. But the sonata was not central to the tradition of Romantic piano music. Mendelssohn called his most typical pieces "Songs without Words". For his, Schumann often used literary titles or ones that made some allusion outside music – "Butterflies", for example, or "Carnival Jest in Vienna". Chopin wrote many in the dance forms of his native Poland, like the mazurka or polonaise, and he also used the waltz, the study (or *étude*, designed to highlight some aspect of piano technique) and the nocturne or night-piece. Liszt covered everything: dances, abstract pieces, atmospheric ones, literary ones (based on Petrarch sonnets, for example). Brahms, more traditional, used titles like intermezzo or capriccio, and wrote sonatas and variations in the Beethoven tradition.

Several twentieth-century composers turned back to the sonata, notably two Russians, Scriabin and Prokofiev. The tradition of pieces designed to conjure up an atmosphere suited the French masters of the piano, Debussy and Ravel, and their successor, Messiaen, whose works chiefly evoke religious images or birdsong. But Boulez has written three sonatas, long, intellectual works. Schoenberg, Bartók and Stockhausen have also composed pieces for the piano.

Sacred vocal music
Mass

The central form of sacred music, since the fifteenth century, has been the Mass of the Roman Catholic church. Its early development and its structure are discussed in the next chapter (pp. 61–3). It was used by all the great composers of the polyphonic era (for an example by Palestrina, see Listening Note, p. 88). As we have seen, most composers of this period built their Mass settings around a fixed melody which ran through the work in some way. Later settings of the Mass used instruments and solo as well as choral singing. The Mass flourished particularly in southern Germany and Austria during the eighteenth century, with Haydn and Mozart. Beethoven wrote two, the second on a huge scale that makes it impossible for church use but a profoundly moving evening in the concert hall. There have been other, more recent concert settings, for example Stravinsky's.

Requiem

A special kind of Mass is the *Requiem*, a Mass for the dead. The form became important in the late eighteenth century, the time of Mozart's famous unfinished *Requiem*. A highly dramatic view of death, typical of the nineteenth century, is shown in the colossal scale of Berlioz's *Requiem* and the passion and fire-and-brimstone of Verdi's. Brahms's *German Requiem* is not a true Requiem but a setting of German texts from the Bible about death and consolation. Britten's *War Requiem* intersperses the Latin text with bitter war poems in English.

Motet, anthem, church cantata

Equal in importance to the Mass as a sacred musical form is the motet. Its history begins in the thirteenth century, when words (*mots* in French: hence the name) were added to musical phrases previously sung without text. By the fifteenth century the motet had become a polyphonic setting of a Latin religious text, usually for three or more voices. In the sixteenth century the imitative style was increasingly used, for example in the music of Josquin and Lassus (see Listening Note, p. 85). Towards 1600 a more dramatic style, with contrasts of sound and texture, and instrumental accompaniment, was applied to the motet by composers such as the Gabrielis and Monteverdi.

With the Reformation, the motet was superseded in England by the English-language anthem, used by such composers as Byrd and, later, Purcell. It has a continuing history in Britain and America. In Lutheran Germany the term motet was maintained, but chorales were used rather than plainsong as *cantus firmus*. A leading seventeenth-century motet composer was Schütz. Bach, in the early eighteenth, wrote motets and, more important, sacred cantatas. Some 200 have come down to us, intended for devotional use at Sunday and festival services; they typically consist of a chorus, two or three arias (or a duet in place of one), and a closing chorale, all linked by recitative (see p. 132 for a fuller discussion).

Passion

An important part of the liturgy has been the telling of the story of the crucifixion each Easter. Musical settings of the Passion were often used. In the seventeenth century, Schütz wrote Passions in which the narration and the words of the characters are sung

31 Schütz directing the Dresden Hofkapelle in the palace chapel: engraving from *Geistreiches Gesangbuch* (1676) by his pupil Christoph Bernard (the chapel is shown after its restoration in 1662, by which time Schütz was no longer Kapellmeister).

unaccompanied and the words of groups are sung by choruses. Bach's Passions, the supreme examples, are constructed of narrative (sung in recitative, with contributions from other characters, including Christ), with arias of religious contemplation, vigorous choruses from the populace and other participant groups, chorales (for the congregation) and large-scale choruses at crucial points to give shape and grandeur to the whole.

Oratorio

The telling of religious stories in music has not been confined to the Passion. In the Middle Ages, religious dramas were often enacted in churches with chanted music. At the end of the Renaissance, with the Counter-Reformation, an important new form arose: the oratorio. The word means "prayer hall" and oratorios were designed to be performed there as "spiritual exercise". In early examples, from around 1600, the story is told in a speech-like musical setting with songs from the principal characters and short choruses. But it was with Handel that the oratorio truly flowered. In England, during the 1730s and 40s, he devised a new style of dramatic oratorio with arias, recitatives and choruses that drew on English traditions of choral singing, and created a set of masterpieces (notably *Messiah*: see Listening Note, p. 142). These were not acted but performed in concerts, as were the oratorios of Haydn, Mendelssohn and Elgar, all much influenced by Handel.

Secular vocal music

The most basic of musical activities is singing. The earliest repertories of solo song are those created by the minstrels of the twelfth and thirteenth centuries, like the troubadours of southern France; their songs deal almost exclusively with idealized love for an unattainable beloved (see Listening Note, p.64). In the Renaissance, the most important type was the *chanson*. This term, the French for "song", designates a large, varied repertory of the fifteenth and sixteenth centuries, mostly for three voices. Important composers of the polyphonic *chanson* include Dufay and Josquin (see Listening Notes, pp. 80 and 83).

Chanson

Madrigal

The Italian counterpart of this form was the madrigal. The term applies mainly to a large repertory of the sixteenth and early seventeenth centuries, covering music for any number of voices from one to eight or even ten, but most commonly four or five. It found its poetic inspiration in the verse of the fourteenth-century poet Petrarch.

The madrigal at its height, in the middle and late sixteenth century, embodied imitative counterpoint but had a great variety of texture, with sensitive, often intense expression of the words. Marenzio (see Listening Note, p.91) and Monteverdi are among the most important composers. The form traveled abroad, notably to England, where it found exponents in Byrd and (of the later generation) Weelkes (see Listening Note, p. 94).

Ayre

Another form of song, for one voice with lute or viol, was popular in England: the ayre (or air), cultivated particularly by John Dowland (see Listening Note, p. 97). The Italian equivalent is "aria", the standard term in Italy for song.

Aria

The aria was the main unit in larger vocal compositions, like the cantata or the opera. As we have seen, it took various forms: there were arias on ground basses, arias with several identical verses and by the end of the century arias in an *A–B–A* pattern. This last, the *da capo* aria, the chief form used by Bach in his cantatas and Handel in his operas, was normally in ritornello form. Later, arias began to follow a sonata-form pattern. A new, more dramatic aria type then arose with two sections, slow–fast. This became a standard type in operas of the nineteenth century.

Ensembles

Arias represent the chief opportunities in an opera or any other extended vocal work for the expression of individual emotion. But some situations give rise to joint expressions, by two people – most often lovers, but also (for example) father and child. Here the composer normally provides a duet, like an aria for two people who may sing separately or together or both. Scenes for three, four or more people are not uncommon. There are for example famous quartets in Beethoven's opera *Fidelio* and Verdi's *Rigoletto*, a fine trio

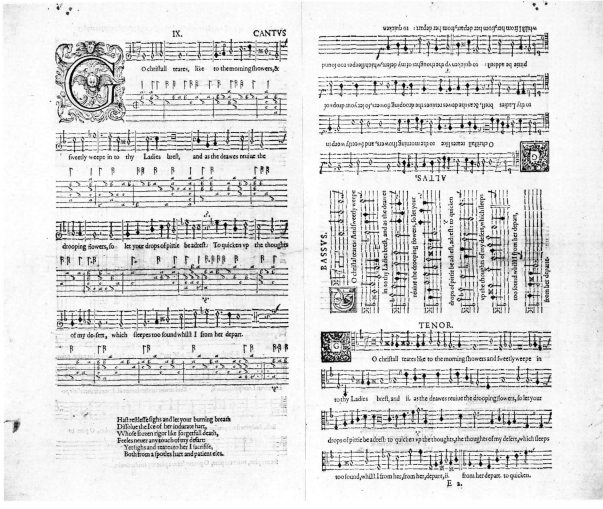

32 "Go christall teares" by John Dowland from his *First Book of Songes or Ayres* (1597). The voice parts are arranged so that the piece can be sung by four singers round a table, or as an ayre by one with lute.

and sextet in Mozart's *Marriage of Figaro* (see Listening Note, p. 161), and a septet of great beauty in Berlioz's *The Trojans*.

Such ensembles may embody dramatic action in a way that arias rarely do. But the chief action in an opera tends to occur not in the lyrical sections but in the narrative or dialogue parts, called recitative. Here the words are sung in a manner best described as conversational, which can be rapid and very lightly accompanied, or can be heightened by a musical setting that conveys strong feeling by exaggerating the inflections of speech.

Recitative

Cantata

Outside the opera house, the main Italian vocal form is the cantata. The term, as we have seen, is a general one. But in the seventeenth and eighteenth centuries it meant a composition for one or two voices and accompanying instruments. Typically, a cantata, like those by Handel, consisted of two or three arias each preceded by a recitative. The theme of almost all these works is love and its betrayal.

In Germany, the great age of song came in the nineteenth century, with the flowering of German literature in the Classical and Romantic eras. Composers found high inspiration in poetry and created the genre known as the *Lied* (German for song: plural *Lieder*). This tradition begins with Schubert, and his new balance is between words and music. He

Lied

wrote over 600 songs, some of them in sequences or cycles that relate a story – an adventure of the soul rather than the body. The tradition was continued by Schumann, Brahms and Wolf. The body of song created in the *Lied* tradition, like that of the Italian madrigal, represents one of the richest products of human sensibility.

The *Lied* tradition is closely linked with the sound of the German language and a particularly German kind of Romantic sentiment. But there are parallels elsewhere, notably in France and Russia.

Dramatic music
Opera

The central form of dramatic music is opera. An opera is a drama set to music, for performance on stage. It may be entirely sung, or there may be spoken dialogue.

Opera as we know it came into existence around 1600, in the courts of north Italy, as an entertainment for a small, aristocratic audience. The first public opera house was opened in Venice in 1637. The leading composer of this early period was Monteverdi, in whose operas musically heightened speech is used for the dialogue, while the characters express their emotions in music of a more lyrical kind.

In Paris, French opera was established by Lully at the court of Louis XIV in the 1660s, with much dance and lavish spectacle. A German opera house was opened in Hamburg, and in London some opera was given in English, but over much of Europe Italian opera was dominant during the eighteenth century. Even Handel's operas, written by a German in London, were in Italian. Most early opera is based on plots from classical mythology or history.

Serious opera became standardized as a succession of arias linked by narrative recitative; it always dealt with heroic topics, with a *castrato* hero and a soprano *prima donna* (first lady). By the middle of the eighteenth century a type of opera that was largely comic was becoming popular. It was written in a faster-moving style, treating ordinary people and their doings rather than gods or heroes. These operas were designed for middle-class audiences and were mostly composed in the audience's native language.

The dominance of the singers – audiences worshipped them then as much as they do now – led to vocal brilliance being rated above dramatic expression. Led mainly by Gluck, whose *Orfeo* was first given in Vienna in 1762, some composers and the poets who wrote their texts gave greater stress to the drama and its expression. During the later eighteenth century, comic opera took in some more serious elements. Mozart's operas, the greatest of the time, illustrate the effects of this fruitful mingling.

The Romantic era saw Germany taking a central role. Wagner was at the climax of the era. In his large-scale works all the arts come together; his operas have a continuous musical texture and elaborate orchestral writing to support the drama, which is usually based on mythology. In Italy, the early part of the century had been dominated by the comic genius of Rossini; later Verdi, with his powerful human drama and his appealing use of the voice, emerged as a figure comparable in stature with Wagner – and more widely admired because of the directness of his music.

France, in the post-Revolution era, produced a type of "grand opera" on national, political or religious themes. Rossini and Verdi contributed to this repertory, and the only Frenchman of true importance was Berlioz. Later in the century the spoken-dialogue tradition gave rise to Bizet's *Carmen* (perhaps the most popular opera ever). A Russian school arose, producing the grandly epic works of Mussorgsky as well as the more conventionally romantic operas of Tchaikovsky.

Italian opera was led into the twentieth century by Puccini, who added to the Verdian tradition more of naturalism and more of sentimentality. Newer ideas came from France, with Debussy's symbolist opera, *Pelléas et Mélisande*, full of subtle hints rather than direct statements. By contrast, the early operas of Richard Strauss and those of Schoenberg and

33 *Orpheus in the Underworld before Pluto and Persephone*: pen and ink drawing with wash by John Michael Rysbrack (1694–1770). Private collection. The Orpheus legend was a popular subject for opera composers.

Berg favor a powerful, even violent, emotional expression. Berg's operas, like those of Janáček and Britten, deal not with the acts of kings or heroes but with the troubles that beset ordinary men and women. Several recent composers have felt that the formal world of opera was unsuited to the needs of musical theater today and have tried to develop musical drama away from the opera house – in the concert hall, on television, in churches and elsewhere.

An important development took place in the later nineteenth century with the growth of *operetta* – light opera, for a large, less intellectual audience. With Johann Strauss in Vienna, Jacques Offenbach in Paris and Arthur Sullivan in London, this soon became a popular genre, treating amorous and sentimental topics, often with a touch of satire. It led to the musical comedy (or "musical"), a form that flourished chiefly on Broadway in New York and in the West End of London in its early days and became in the early twentieth century a vigorous expression of American popular culture (see Chapter XI).

Dance

Music for dance has long traditions. Many operas include ballet sequences; in French ones particularly these may be long and important. Like opera, ballet underwent "reform" in the mid-eighteenth century, moving from a primarily decorative art to a more expressive,

Plate 1 *Opposite* Der
Hiltbolt von Schwangau:
miniature from the
*Manessische
Liederhandschrift,* one of
the major manuscripts of
Minnesang (see p. 64).
German, *c*1320.
Universitätsbibliothek,
Heidelberg.

34 Vaslav Nijinsky as the
Faun in the ballet he
choreographed on
Debussy's *L'après-midi
d'un faune* for the Ballets
Russes, Théâtre du
Châtelet, Paris, 1912:
drawing by Valentine
Gross after designs by
Léon Bakst.

representational one. The Romantic ballet tradition of the nineteenth century culminated in the three great Tchaikovsky works, *Swan Lake*, *Sleeping Beauty* and *Nutcracker*, each a full evening in the theater. This tradition was continued in the twentieth by the dance impresario Diaghilev, who did much to revitalize the art, bringing together leading composers, scenic artists and choreographers; his work gave rise to much new music, above all by Stravinsky, the greatest ballet composer of the period. Meanwhile, the American dancer Isadora Duncan had been revolutionizing the approach to dance in her free representation of intense feeling and her choice of music: she even danced to Beethoven symphonies and operatic music by Wagner. The American John Cage has been the leading composer in recent times in experimental dance.

Chapter IV

The Middle Ages

The history of the music of our own, Western culture – which we should remember is only one of many, by no means the oldest, and only in recent times the most various and complex – may reasonably be regarded as beginning with the cultures in which ours has roots, such as the Jewish, the Greek and the Roman. We know, from (for example) the Bible, with its numerous references to instruments and singing, and from pottery, sculpture and painting, that music played an important part in the life of these peoples. But we have very little idea of what it sounded like. We know something about their instruments but almost nothing certain about what they played on them. There are no musical notations that we can fully understand; and, with the so-called Dark Ages intervening, there is no historical continuity between ancient Greece or Rome and the Europe of the Middle Ages in which our present musical culture has its true beginnings.

Musical history, then, must begin for us around the sixth century AD, when the traditional repertory of church chant, normally passed on orally from one generation to the next, began to be set down and codified. It would be misleading if, through the limitations of our knowledge, the impression were to be given that all music was church music. Rather, all *notated* music at this time was church music: monks were almost the only people who could read or write. We may be sure that even at this date there was music at courts – they were soon to be central to musical culture outside the church – and in the homes of noble families. Humbler people, too, must have sung in their homes, at work and convivially. But it is with the music of the church that our survey must begin – music that emanates from the great Gothic cathedrals and the ancient monasteries, and to be read from the hand-copied books used at their religious services, or, more rarely, from the superb illuminated manuscripts prepared as records or as lavish gifts to kings, popes or princes.

Music of the church

Plate 2 Church service: miniature from a Book of Hours, Paris, 15th century (for Mass music see pp. 54 and 63). British Library, London.

From its earliest years the Christian church has had a place for music. By the beginning of the eleventh century, the form of the church service – celebrating the feasts of the church year, the saints' days and other liturgical occasions – had become more or less standardized in western Europe. Throughout the Christian world the centerpiece of the liturgy was (and remains) the Mass. This ritual re-enactment of the Last Supper was

35 Drawings contrasting "holy" and "worldly" music from a Psalter, possibly from Rheims, 12th century. St John's College, Cambridge

designed to inspire people with the certainty that the spiritual world offered, in contrast to the less certain circumstances of everyday life. Although the Latin text of the Mass was not accessible to most people, those without sufficient education to follow it would be familiar with the ritual and, if they attended a large church, would be affected by its pomp and ceremony and the splendor of its music.

The earliest music in the medieval church was plainsong, or plainchant, sometimes known as "Gregorian" chant through its association with Pope Gregory I (590–604), during whose reign chants used in the Western churches were collected and categorized. For High Mass much of the text would be chanted to music. Some sections, forming the "Ordinary", had the same words on every occasion; others, the "Proper", used different texts according to the feasts of the church year and local custom. The table opposite shows

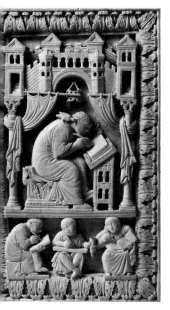

36 St Gregory, the pope
responsible for the
categorizing of plainchant,
and scribes: ivory book
cover, 10th century.
Kunsthistorisches
Museum, Vienna.

Structure of the Mass

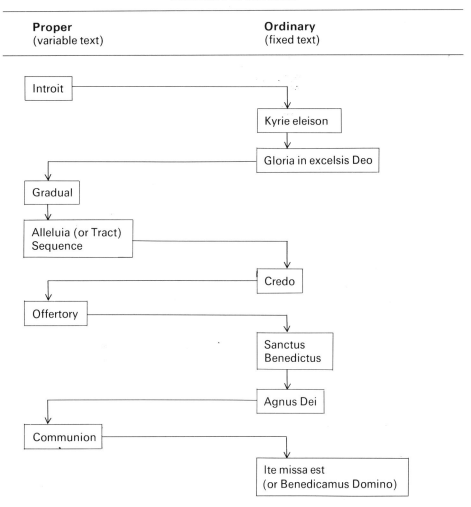

how some of these sections might relate in a typical Mass (spoken text would intervene between these chanted sections).

Plainsong is a single line of text and melody, sung either by the priest or by members of the choir, or by priest and choir in alternation. It has a smoothly flowing, undulating line, often following the rhythm of the text, and falls naturally into separate phrases, with breaks for "punctuation", rather like spoken prose. Some chants have only one note to each text syllable ("syllabic chant"); others have more than one, and sometimes extended groups, to each ("melismatic chant"). A mood of calm assurance, common to much plainsong, reflects the unquestioning confidence that medieval people had in their religion. Plainsong melodies are classified according to mode (the particular pattern of tones and semitones used within an octave; see p. 19). The church modes were of fundamental importance to medieval composers.

The plainsong melodies used in medieval churches and monasteries were first passed down orally from one generation to the next, differing in detail in different communities; they only gradually took on a more or less standard, traditional form that could be notated.

A vast body of plainsong – over 3000 melodies, each with its own significance in the liturgy – survives, and has long played an important part in church music. Besides being sung in its own right, chant has formed the basis of much of the religious music of the Middle Ages and the Renaissance.

Secular song

Music-making in the Middle Ages was not confined to the church. From the end of the eleventh century secular music enjoyed something of a golden age, of around 200 years, among minstrels who traveled between the feudal courts of Europe. At different times and places they were referred to by different names – goliards, jongleurs, scops, gleemen, troubadours, trouvères, minnesinger – but they had one thing in common: the expression of the ideal of "courtly love" through words and music. Their love-lyrics, which often idolized women as beautiful and unattainable, illustrate a side of medieval life directly opposite to the austere spirituality conveyed by the chanting monks.

Among the exponents of this great flowering of secular song, the best known are the troubadours, virtuoso poet-musicians active mainly in Provence, southern France. They wrote their own poetry, not in Latin but in their own language, set it to music and performed it as entertainment at all levels of society, either unaccompanied or with instruments such as the harp, lute or fiddle.

Although they came from a variety of social backgrounds, trouvères (from northern France) and troubadours in particular were often men of high birth – esquires, knights, even kings. Their musical forms take their names from contemporary poetic forms, like *ballade, rondeau* and *virelai*; these are the principal secular vocal forms of fourteenth- and fifteenth-century music.

The songs of the troubadours and trouvères range widely in style and mood: some delicate and restrained, some unadorned, some rhythmic and dance-like (often in triple time). They are usually easy to listen to and directly appealing; and they are highly evocative of the age of chivalry and courtly love. *Chanterai por mon corage* by Guiot de Dijon, who lived at the turn of the thirteenth century, reflects the atmosphere of the crusades to the Holy Land (Guiot himself, a trouvère and a native of Burgundy, went on crusade) (see Listening Note IV.A).

Listening Note IV.A   *Side 1, band 2*

Guiot de Dijon: *Chanterai por mon corage* (c. 1189)

Chanterai por mon corage	I shall sing to cheer my spirit
Que je vueil reconforter,	which I want to comfort,
Qu'avecques mon grant domage	so that with my great grief
Ne quier morir ne foler.	I may not die or go mad.
Quant de la terre sauvage	From the cruel land
Ne voi mes nul retorner	I see no one returning
Ou cil est qui rassoage	Where he is who soothes
Mes maus quant g'en oi parler.	my heart when I hear him spoken of.
Dex, quant crïeront 'Outree',	God! when they cry 'Outree',
Sire, aid és au pelerin	Lord, help the pilgrim
Par cui sui espavantee,	for whom I am so afraid,
Car felon sont Sarazin.	for the Saracens are evil.

This song has three verses. Each is introduced by the flute playing the first phrase.

Time

0:00	flute plays the first phrase (ex. i) accompanied by the lute and rebec		which repeats the melody of the first
0:11	the singer starts the first verse which repeats the melody stated by the flute	2:44	the flute again plays the first phrase of the music to introduce the third and final verse
1:21	the flute plays the first phrase introducing the second verse	2:56	the singer begins the third verse
1:33	the singer sings the second verse,	3:42	this is a repeat of the opening melody, but the accompaniment is thicker, bringing the song to a conclusion.

ex. i

Early polyphony

So far, the music we have looked at has been "monophonic" ("single-sounded"): that is, consisting of a single line of melody. The late Middle Ages saw a development that now seems to have been the most far-reaching in the history of Western music. At a time when the visual arts were beginning to be concerned with depth and perspective, the more learned of musicians – generally the highly educated clerics and the scholars attached to the more sophisticated ecclesiastical centers of Europe – began to have similar ideas, combining two or more melodic lines simultaneously to give "depth" to the music. This style of composition became known as "polyphonic" ("many-sounded").

At first there were only two melodic lines, both based on plainsong, moving in exactly the same rhythm and in parallel, one a 4th or a 5th below the other; later, a third or fourth voice was introduced, an octave below or above the first or second. This rather severe style of early polyphony was known as *organum*.

In the late eleventh century and the twelfth, musicians began to elaborate on this simple style of *organum* by giving the plainsong melody to the lower voice in long, held notes while a second voice above had a freely flowing, "melismatic" line in shorter ones. The lower, principal voice was called the tenor (from the Latin *tenere*, "to hold"). The church apparently encouraged the use of *organum* as long as elaboration did not obscure the meaning of the text.

Léonin, Pérotin   It was natural that the cathedral of Notre Dame in Paris, one of the leading ecclesiastical centers of northern Europe, should be in the forefront of musical development. In the late twelfth century a large group of musicians gathered there, including two whose names we know, Léonin (*c*1163–90) and Pérotin (*fl* 1200). Léonin apparently wrote mainly for two voices, but Pérotin's music was more developed, even more adventurous, often using three or four voices, well-defined rhythms and shorter melismas. His *Viderunt omnes* illustrates this style (see Listening Note IV.B).

Organum illustrates the twofold importance of plainsong in medieval composition: the long tenor notes of the chant, though usually too drawn out to be easily audible as a melody, provide a foundation which is both structural, allowing the composer to devise more inventive upper parts, and spiritual, acting as a reminder of the music's religious meaning. These two functions can be observed to some degree in most of the medieval and Renaissance sacred music that relies on chant. The most effective music that came

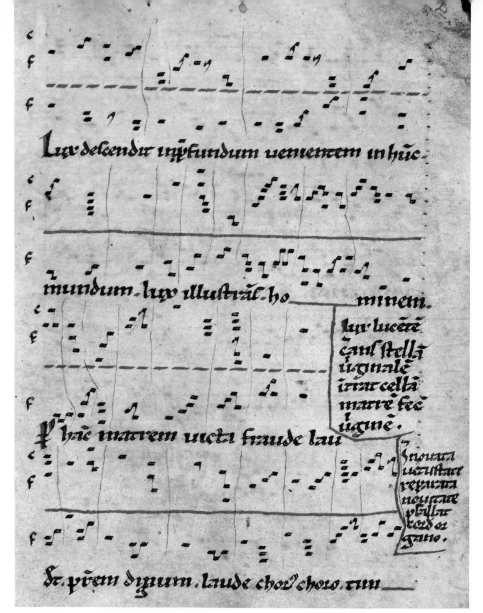

37 Organum "Lux descendit" from a 12th-century manuscript from St Martial. British Library, London.

from Notre Dame, as from Europe's other great ecclesiastical centers, reflected the Gothic architecture that surrounded it – soaring, magnificent and resonant – and it laid the foundation of a polyphonic style that flourished for some 400 years.

Listening Note IV.B Side 1, band 3

Pérotin: *Viderunt omnes* (?1198), opening

Viderunt [omnes fines terrae salutare Dei nostri]   [All the ends of the earth] shall see [the salvation of our God]

Time

0:00	Vi (pronounced "vee")		1:12	-runt
0:47	-de-		2:13	(end)

Only the opening section of this piece of organum is included. The first word, "Vi-de-runt", is treated at great length, with each syllable sung by the upper voices in dance-like rhythms, above a held note on the organ.

The motet

38 Procession of the Blessed (with a positive organ): detail from a Last Judgment scene over the west door of León Cathedral, Spain, 13th century.

Much medieval music is characterized by the same combination of "fixity" and "freedom" as appears in *organum*. Fixity is often present in the form of plainsong, usually in the tenor, which determines the structure and acts as a reference point for the other voices. Freedom is reflected in the freshly composed parts, which may even have a different text (or texts) from the tenor.

During the thirteenth century the most important new form, distinguished by this fixity and freedom, was the motet. It may show a growing interest in worldly matters that both sacred and secular motets were composed, and that sacred and secular texts could be used in the same piece. For example, a Latin liturgical text in one part and a French secular poem in another might be combined with a tenor which retains the notes and Latin text of a plainsong melody. The term "motet" – probably from the French *mot*, "word" – may refer to the added texts in the upper parts. By the end of the thirteenth century the motet had become a sophisticated and complex form, testing the skills and inventiveness of composers. Most of the pieces that survive from this period are for three voices and are by anonymous composers of the Notre Dame school, Pérotin's successors.

Ars Nova

Vitry

Music theorists of the early fourteenth century described this thirteenth-century music as "Ars Antiqua" ("the old art"), for early in the century a new style, which they called "Ars Nova", was gaining currency. Its leader was the French composer and theorist Philippe de Vitry (1291–1361). He was highly regarded by his contemporaries in intellectual and musical circles, for the dozen or so motets he composed and in particular for the famous work attributed to him, a treatise on music entitled *Ars Nova*. This outlined the principles of the new style. During the previous century most "measured" music (as opposed to plainsong, which was "unmeasured") had been in triple meter, which was called *tempus perfectum* (medieval theorists, who were mystics as well as musicians, held 3 – the number of the Trinity – to be "perfect"). Vitry observed that by the early fourteenth century duple meter had become acceptable. He also discussed isorhythm, a structural device whereby rhythmic patterns and units of melody were repeated; and he set out the expanded rhythmic and metrical practices of his day in a system of "rhythmic modes".

Machaut

The most representative figure of the fourteenth century is Guillaume de Machaut (*d*1377), statesman, cleric and poet as well as composer. Born around 1300, probably in Reims, he was secretary to John of Luxembourg, King of Bohemia, for nearly 20 years and probably traveled widely with him in Europe. In about 1340 Machaut returned to Reims as a canon of several major French churches; after King John's death at the Battle of Crécy in 1346, he served various members of the nobility, including Jean, Duke of Berry, and the future King Charles V. Machaut was highly regarded by his patrons as both poet and musician, and for them he supervised the preparation of his works in several beautifully illuminated manuscripts, which present a broad selection of his music unique for a composer of the Middle Ages.

39 Guillaume de Machaut: miniature from a French manuscript, 14th century, Bibliothèque Nationale, Paris.

Guillaume de Machaut   Works
born ?Reims, *c*1300; *died* ?Reims, 1377

Sacred music Messe de Nostre Dame; 2 motets
Secular music 21 motets; over 115 French songs (ballades, rondeaux, virelais) for 2–4 voices – Ma fin est mon commencement; French virelais, lais for solo voice

Machaut's music looks both backwards, to the thirteenth century and the age of chivalry, and forwards, to the fifteenth century and the early Renaissance. Among his wide-ranging output, some early medieval forms such as the isorhythmic motet and the *virelai* for solo voice figure strongly. But Machaut was also a progressive: he wrote extensively in the Ars Nova manner expounded by Vitry and other theorists, and was one of the first to produce polyphonic settings of secular poetry and to write for four voices instead of three. In addition, Machaut was the earliest composer by whom there survives a complete polyphonic setting of the Mass Ordinary. Previously, as we have seen, the texts of the Mass were chanted monophonically; the polyphonic Mass was to be central to liturgical music in the fifteenth century.

Machaut's *Messe de Nostre Dame* is a work of great sophistication and skill. It is for four voices. Four of its six movements (Kyrie, Sanctus, Agnus Dei and Ite missa est) use isorhythm and have a plainsong in the tenor voice, which serves as a framework and as a unifying element. Before each movement of the Mass, one voice gives out the plainsong phrase on which the *cantus firmus* is based; then the others enter with the newly composed polyphony. In the Kyrie (see Listening Note IV.C) the flowing contrapuntal lines, with long melismatic phrases on extended vowel sounds, make the tenor *cantus firmus* barely audible. The Gloria and Credo are in a simpler, note-against-note style, which helps clarify the words of these longer, more involved texts – audiblity of the words was a particular concern of the church authorities at this time.

Machaut's Mass was intended to play a functional part in celebrating the liturgy. It was performed, and can best be appreciated, not as a succession of six polyphonic movements (as on most commercial recordings) but with the polyphonic Ordinary movements interspersed with the chants of the Mass Proper appropriate to a specific feast in the church year (see table, p.63). If we can imagine ourselves listening to the Mass beneath the lofty echoing arches of a great Gothic cathedral – like the one at Reims – it is easy to see how this contrast between the modesty of plainsong and the elaborate grandeur of four-part polyphony can make a most powerful impression.

Listening Note IV.C   *Side 1, band 4*

Machaut: *Messe de Nostre Dame* (?1364), Kyrie I

Kyrie eleison   Lord, have mercy upon us

The Kyrie, the opening movement of the Mass, consists of a passage repeated three times, symbolizing the Trinity and following the plàinsong. This melody (ex. i) is heard in a middle voice, called the "tenor". The upper voices – sung by tenors, in the modern sense – weave a polyphonic texture in free rhythm. In the present performance, the high tenor voice at the top of the texture is supported by a recorder and a fiddle, the second voice by a harp and a reed organ, the third (the one singing the plainsong) by a small organ and a large fiddle, the lowest by a lute and a dulzian (a double-reed instrument of low pitch, like a soft-toned bassoon).

Time

0:00	Kyrie begins	1:59	Kyrie, third time
0:59	Kyrie, second time	2:56	(end)

Machaut's music hints at a smoothness and sweetness, brought about by his use of consonant intervals between the voices, that are lacking in earlier medieval music. It shows a glimmer of the ideals that inspired fourteenth-century Italian painters like Giotto – religious symbolism gradually giving place to a more worldly expression of human feelings. This secularization of the arts may have been related to the series of disasters that rocked Europe in the fourteenth century: the battle over papal authority that led to the papal schism and the "Babylonian captivity" in Avignon; the terrible suffering caused by the plague of 1348; the growing discord between church and state; and the squabbles between the states themselves, particularly in Italy. Yet at the same time there was great artistic activity in secular Italy. It was the era of Petrarch and Boccaccio, and as secular literature flourished so did secular music.

Secular polyphony

Italian polyphony of this period is vigorous and lively. Much of it reflects the pastoral, often lighthearted mood of its texts; a favorite type was the *ballata*, based on a poetic form. Unlike sacred music based on chant, this type of secular composition gives the main melodic material to the upper voice or voices.

Listening Note IV.D   *Side 1, band 5*

Landini: *Ecco la primavera* (late 14th century)

Ecco la primavera	Spring is here
Che'l cor fa rallegrare,	And it fills the heart with joy.
Temp'è d'annamorare	Now is the time to fall in love
E star con lieta cera.	And to be happy.
No' vegiam l'aria e'l tempo	We see the air and the fine weather
Che pur chiam' allegrezza.	Which also call us to be happy.
In questo vago tempo	In this sweet time
Ogni cosa ha vaghezza.	Everything is so beautiful.
L'erbe con gran freschezza	Fresh green grass
E fior' copron i prati,	And flowers cover the meadows,
E gli alberi adornati	And the trees are adorned
Sono in simil manera.	In the same way.
Ecco la primavera . . .	Spring is here . . .

The *ballata* or dance-song was popular for two centuries. Here, the music is played through five times. The first time it is introduced by the instruments, then four verses are sung, the fourth being a repeat of the first.

Time

0:00	instruments play the song through as an introduction	0:45	third verse
0:20	voices sing first verse (ex. i)	0:57	first verse repeated with vigor
0:31	second verse	1:10	(end)

ex. i

Ec - co la pri - ma - ve - ra Che'l cor fa ral leg -

- ra - re, Temp' - è d'an - na - mo - ra - re

E star con lie - ta ce - ra

Landini

The greatest Italian composer of this period was Francesco Landini (c1325–1397). Blind from childhood, he learned to play several instruments, to sing and to write poetry. He spent most of his life in Florence and took part in the main philosophical and religious disputations of his day. He was renowned both as an organist (and organ builder) and as an intellectual. Most of his compositions are polyphonic *ballate* for two or three voices. Many are simple, dance-like settings, such as *Ecco la primavera*, a joyous welcoming of spring (see Listening Note IV.D); others are more complex, but all show his great melodic gift.

40 Minstrels at a wedding feast, with nakers, two shawms, bagpipes, two trumpets, fiddle, and portative organ: miniature from the *Thebiad of Statius*. Italian, c1380–90. Chester Beatty Library, Dublin.

41 *Opposite* Tombstone of Francesco Landini. S Lorenzo, Florence.

Instrumental music

We have seen how poet-minstrels like the troubadours might accompany themselves on plucked string instruments like the lute and harp, improvising melodies to complement and enhance their vocal lines; bowed string instruments like the fiddle were also common. Wind instruments probably included flutes, recorders, shawms (precursors of the oboe, with a double reed) and trumpets, and there was a battery of percussion instruments – cymbals, bells, triangles, drums. Although we do not know exactly how and when these instruments were used, they probably both accompanied and substituted for voices in secular polyphony and were used in dancing. The color and rhythmic vitality of much medieval secular music is enhanced by their judicious use.

Sacred music was more limited in this. Probably the only instrument allowed in church services was the organ, though others might have been admitted for civic festivals and processions. Small, portable (or "portative") organs, which could be slung from a player's shoulders, seem to have been as common as the large, permanent structures that were built into medieval churches.

England

Little is known of earlier medieval music in England; but that country had a special claim to fame in the thirteenth century. There survives in one manuscript an anonymous "round", or canon, dating from about 1250, entitled *Sumer is icumen in*, which represents the earliest known example anywhere in Europe of polyphony for six voices. Its freshness and vitality is typical of much thirteenth- and fourteenth-century English music which, like Italian, was surprisingly "harmonic" in conception, with smooth progressions and intervals (6ths and 3rds) between voices. By the time of England's greatest medieval composer, John Dunstable, the foundations of an English style had been firmly laid.

Dunstable

Born around 1390, Dunstable may have been attached to Hereford Cathedral, and was possibly in the service of the Duke of Bedford when the latter was Henry V's regent in France (1422–35). He died in 1453. His music was highly praised in France and many of his compositions appear in Italian manuscripts.

Dunstable's music has many features typical of the English music of his time. Particularly attractive to contemporary and later European composers was the sonority of his music. There is greater feeling for chords and chordal progression as well as a greater equality among the voices and freer treatment of the *cantus firmus* lines.

Features of Dunstable's style are its lyrical freshness and sheer "singability". The text settings often have one note to a syllable, as in *O rosa bella* (see Listening Note IV.E), a largely chordal setting where the chordal writing and the treatment of musical and textual accents contribute to a particularly sweet, smooth effect. This piece fairly represents the

John Dunstable	Works
*born c*1390; *died*?London, 1453	

Sacred music 2 Masses; Mass movements; over 40 motets and other settings of sacred Latin texts – Veni Sancte Spiritus; Quam pulchra es
Secular music French and English songs for 2–3 voices

42 Emperor Maximilian I surrounded by musicians and instruments: woodcut, 1505–16, by Hans Burgkmair.

English style, though there is some doubt as to whether Dunstable himself wrote it. Contemporary European writers admired the English style, "contenance angloise", which was an important influence on many fifteenth-century composers. Dunstable stands astride our historical boundaries, with one foot in the Middle Ages and the other in a new age – the Renaissance.

Listening Note IV.E   *Side 1, band 6*

Dunstable(?): *O rosa bella* (early/mid-15th century)

O rosa bella, o dolce anima mia,
non mi lassar morire in cortesia.

Ay lasso mi dolente dezo finire
per ben servire, e lialmente amare.

O lovely rose, o my sweet soul,
let me not die in courtly love.

Alas! must I end up being hurt by you,
when I have served and loved you
loyally

O dio d'amore che pena e questa amare
vedi ch'io moro tutt'hora per sta giudea.

O god of love, what pain this love is
See how I am forever dying because of this faithless woman

Soccoremi ormai del mio languire
cor del corpo mio non mi lassar morire.

Save me now from my suffering
Heart of my body, let me not die.

This late example of a *ballata*-type piece illustrates the smooth, sweet English style. (Dunstable's authorship is uncertain but the music is typical of the English style.) It is for three voices; in this performance viols are also used. Note the imitation at the opening (ex. i).

Time

0:00	instrumental "introduction" begins	2:27	voice enters with second voice singing a contrapuntal figure, "O dio d'amore"
0:17	one voice starts the song	3:17	voices are together rhythmically, "Soccoremi"
1:06	"Ay lasso"		
2:06	first verse concludes	3:41	one voice sings an accompanying contrapuntal part
2:08	instrumental "introduction" repeats	4:20	(end)

ex. i

O ro - sa bel - la,   O dol - ce a - ni - ma mi - - a

Chapter V

The Renaissance

The period traditionally known as the Renaissance – the term means "rebirth" – extends from around the middle of the fifteenth century until the last years of the sixteenth. At the time, artists, thinkers, writers and musicians all felt that some kind of corner had been turned, that the darkness and the dogmatisms of the Middle Ages were passing, that a new era was dawning. This new era found much of its inspiration in the ancient classics and their values: hence the idea of rebirth. Such values were particularly focused on human beings, their individuality and their emotions, as opposed to the medieval preoccupation with the mystical and the divine; the concept of "humanism" and its link with the study of ancient Greece and Rome is central to the thinking of the Renaissance. "Academies" began to be founded at which intellectual noblemen gathered to discuss the classics and their implications for the arts of the time. The first was in Florence in 1470; 80 years later, there were some 200, all over Italy.

The visual arts

The Renaissance was essentially an Italian movement, at least in its origins. It produced a uniquely marvelous crop of painters and sculptors in that country – Piero della Francesca, Bellini, Mantegna, Perugino, Botticelli, Leonardo da Vinci, Michelangelo, Giorgione, Raphael, Titian, Tintoretto. In music there is nothing quite of that order; there were few Italian composers of significance until Palestrina, though the Italian courts, centers of artistic patronage, drew an immensely talented collection of composers from the north (mainly north-east France and Flanders, present-day Belgium). Their music shows a different approach from the previous generation's, analogous to that of Renaissance art. There, the stiff, mystical, abstract and highly stylized postures of the Middle Ages began to be superseded by natural, flowing ones, which allow human beings to be seen feeling ordinary human emotions; a man or a woman can be an object of interest in himself or herself, not merely in relation to the divine.

Such a change is not of course sudden; in painting it is already hinted at in the work of Giotto (c1266–1337) and his contemporaries, as it is in the writings of Dante (1265–1321) and, in the next generation, Petrarch and Boccaccio. But the change was not consistent or universal at that early date, and in music (although parallels might be seen in the work of such men as Landini or Dunstable) it is only with the generation of composers active in the late fifteenth century that such a "humanistic" element is regularly found.

In painting, part of this quality is related to the development of the art of perspective; Renaissance pictures have a sense of depth (only the tentative beginnings of this can be seen in medieval ones) and thus a realistic way of relating a person to his or her context. At just the same time, a way of giving music an audible depth was developing. While the

Harmony
and polyphony

medieval composer was content to depend upon such rigid devices as isorhythm – which provides a convenient mechanical framework but has little meaning for the listener beyond that – the Renaissance composer worked in a different way, composing the voice-parts in careful relation to one another, and with lines of more supple character, so as to provide a succession of harmonies. This quickly led to the lowest voice having a slightly different status (and accordingly a slightly different style) from the others: here are the very beginnings of Western harmony, or sense of perspective in music. (It is, by the way, intriguing to note that some 450 years later composers abandoned the traditional ways of handling harmony just as artists were abandoning perspective.) Further, to give their pieces some degree of internal unity, they tended to assign the same musical phrase to each voice, normally in such a way that each sang the same group of notes to a particular group of words. The voices enter successively with the same musical phrase, so that the polyphony becomes increasingly rich and interwoven: this "imitative" technique is the classical style of the Renaissance.

Humanism

This new emphasis on the human being was part of a general move towards the secular as opposed to the sacred, which had dominated life for so long. Power moved in the same direction, away from the church towards kings and princes. These, notably in the city-states of north Italy, were often men of high education and enlightenment, for example in Florence, where the Medici family held sway, or Ferrara, ruled by the Este. Such people were eager to display their power, wealth and taste in lavish entertainments. At their courts secular forms like the madrigal especially flourished, and at Florence in particular the *intermedio*, a mixed entertainment of dance, music of various kinds and poetry was cultivated. At Rome, under the pope, church music remained central, as it also did at

43 Three shawms and a slide trumpet accompanying dancers: detail from the Adimari wedding cassone, Italian, c1450: Galleria dell'Accademia, Florence.

Venice, under civic rule. North of the Alps too there was a strong move towards the secular, notably in England where Henry VIII threw off papal influence; he and later Elizabeth I were important patrons of music, as was Francis I in France. Burgundy, now a part of France but then an independent country which included areas of what are now the Low Countries, had one of the most brilliant of all the courts of the fifteenth century, but its separate history came to an end in 1477.

The Reformation

The biggest change during this period, however, originated in Germany. This was the Reformation. It began as an attempt to rid the Catholic church of corruption and abuse and to "rationalize" religious practice by allowing every man and woman the right to worship in his or her own language. It caused bloodshed and destruction on a vast scale, over many decades, though in the light of history we can see it as an inevitable development of the Renaissance and its modes of thought. Its leader was Martin Luther (1468–1546). To him music was a vital part of worship, and although he greatly admired the Latin works of such composers as Josquin he realized that ordinary people's involvement in religion would be deepened if they were allowed to participate in services rather than listen passively to Latin chant from the clergy or Latin polyphony from the choir.

Luther established a repertory of hymns, or "chorales" (so called because they were to be sung chorally), sometimes drawing on well-known songs, which would be familiar to his congregations, and sometimes composing new melodies himself. Among his own compositions is *Ein feste Burg* ("A stronghold sure"), often called the battle-song of the Reformation (see pp.124 and 132). In the reformed church the chorale largely came to take the place that plainsong had traditionally occupied in the Catholic church, as a basis for newly composed works.

The Lutheran reforms had great influence in Germany, especially the northern and eastern parts, and in Scandinavia. Another reformer, Jean Calvin (1509–64), was more influential in his native France, Switzerland, the Low Countries and Scotland; he was less interested in music than was Luther and advocated the use of psalms in austere, unac-

44 Frontispiece to Antico's collection *Frottole intabulate da sonar organi* (1517).

The Counter-Reformation

45 Facing pages from the *Chansonnier Cordeforme*, Savoy, before 1477. Bibliothèque Nationale, Paris. Among the anonymous French and Italian secular pieces, music by Dufay, Busnois, Ockeghem and Binchois has been identified.

companied versions. In England too the church was reformed, under Henry VIII, and an Anglican church established with congregational participation and use of the English language.

The Catholic church was bound to react to the spread of the Reformation, which by the middle of the sixteenth century had created a hugh schism. What is called the Counter-Reformation had begun by the 1540s: a move by the Catholic church to rid itself of malpractices and to encourage greater piety among the people, involving a revival of Catholic principles and their application in a disciplined way. Music and its use in the church were among the topics discussed in the series of meetings held at Trent, northern Italy, between 1545 and 1563. The Council of Trent expressed concern over the use of secular melodies in church (for example as *cantus firmi* in Mass settings: see p. 45) and the weakening of the traditions of plainsong, and objected to over-elaborate polyphony that might obscure the liturgical words. Virtuoso singing in particular was deplored, and so was the use of instruments other than the organ. In countering Luther and his reforms, the Council were in fact compelled to tread a similar path.

The result was not only music of a new simplicity; the music of the Counter-Reformation is in fact marked by its fervor, its emotional content and its feeling of mysticism. Its greatest composers were Palestrina and Lassus, but the colorful polychoral and ensemble music of the two Gabrielis, Andrea and Giovanni, from Venice, is imbued with the

Counter-Reformation spirit, and so is much music from Spain. The staunch Catholicism of that powerful country, whose empire included most of what is now Belgium, put it in the forefront of the fight against the Reformation.

Printing

It is difficult to imagine how the Reformation could have made any real progress without the invention of printing. Printing was invented (in the West) in the mid-fifteenth century; music printing began in about 1473 and in the last quarter of the century many liturgical music books, for the singing of chant, were produced from woodblocks, carved and inked. It was in 1501 that the first polyphonic music was printed, by Ottaviano Petrucci of Venice, using movable type; this was an anthology mainly of chansons by French and Flemish composers. It must have been a success, to judge by his reprints and his further publications. His methods were quickly copied elsewhere – in Germany, France and England as well as other Italian cities. Until this time, music had circulated only in manuscript, a laborious and costly process; now it became available to a much wider public. The international exchange of ideas that was now possible was important to the dissemination of Renaissance culture.

Petrucci and his followers printed music of all sorts: polyphony, both sacred and secular, instrumental music (including tablatures for the lute – that is, music that tells you not what notes to sound but where to put your fingers for the right ones), and, in the "reformed" countries, hymn books and psalm collections.

This new spread of music and ideas – supported by the idea of "Renaissance man", interested and skilled in all the arts and sciences – made it possible for music-making to become popular among the higher social classes in the sixteenth century. People learned to read music, to sing and play instruments, and a new demand arose for any kind of music that could be performed in the home by a small number of modestly capable musicians. This demand was chiefly met by the new forms of secular song: the madrigal in Italy, and later in England and other parts of northern Europe, in France the chanson, in Germany the polyphonic Lied. The singing of madrigals and similar works came to be regarded as a pleasant domestic pastime. With one voice to a part, it offered an intimate form of music-making – primarily to entertain the performers themselves, and perhaps a few guests, but not a formal audience. The time of the public concert was still a long way off; and we understand music of the Renaissance best if we listen to it with an understanding of the kinds of role in society that it was originally intended to play.

The Franco-Flemish composers

At the court of Burgundy, a rich and splendid cultural environment was nurtured by the patronage of a succession of dukes. The Burgundian ruling family was famed for its political successes and the artistic brilliance of its court, which up to its dissolution in 1477 attracted some of the greatest artists and musicians of the period.

Dufay

Among the composers of the "Burgundian school" was Guillaume Dufay (c1400–1474), the most significant figure of the period. Born near Cambrai in northern France, he spent several years in Italy and traveled extensively. He was thus well placed to achieve a fusion of the late medieval style of his native France and the early Italian Renaissance style, with its literary and humanist associations.

To appreciate the spirit of Dufay's music we have to view it as if looking forward from an earlier, medieval period instead of looking back from the later Renaissance. Perhaps its most striking feature is its relative straightforwardness as compared with the complexities

---

Guillaume Dufay   Life

*c*1400	born in or near Cambrai
1409	choirboy at Cambrai Cathedral
1413–14	clerk at Cambrai Cathedral
*c*1420	in the service of the Malatesta family, Pesaro
1426–7	Cambrai
1428	singer in the papal choir, Rome; established as one of the leading musicians in Europe; developed ties with important courts in northern Italy
1434	*maître de chapelle* at Savoy court
1436	motet performed at the dedication of the dome of Florence Cathedral; canon at Cambrai Cathedral
1437	Este court, Ferrara
1451–8	Savoy chapel
1458	settled in Cambrai; beginning of period of pre-eminence
1474	died in Cambrai, 27 November

Guillaume Dufay   Works

Sacred vocal music 8 Masses – Se la face ay pale; Ave regina caelorum; Mass movements; over 20 motets; hymns

Secular vocal music over 80 chansons (rondeaux, ballades, virelais) for 3 voices – Ce moys de may

---

of some of the late Gothic music that preceded it. Many of Dufay's works first impress the listener for their melodic character.

The *cantus firmus* of his Mass *Se la face ay pale*, for example, it not plainsong but derives from a song Dufay had composed some 20 years earlier. The use of a secular *cantus firmus* in a sacred work became common in the fifteenth century and gives an idea of the degree of "secularization" of liturgical music at this period.

Here the *cantus firmus* appears in the tenor part throughout each movement, acting as a unifying element. Of the other three voices, the top one is predominantly tuneful. Contrast is achieved in several ways, for example by changes of meter and by lightening of the texture – sometimes two of the voices drop out for extended passages, leaving the others to sing in duet fashion, overlapping and imitating each other. This too was common in fifteenth-century Masses. The skillful construction of the Mass *Se la face ay pale* around its *cantus firmus* is a fine technical achievement, yet barely discernible to the listener who is much more aware of the elegance of the melodies, the sonority of the harmonies and the smoothness of the textures.

Dufay was also one of the greatest composers of polyphonic *chansons* in the fifteenth century. His songs range widely and show a new, flexible attitude to medieval forms like the *rondeau* and the *ballade*. His range of expression was wide, and his techniques varied according to the words of each song and the purpose for which it was composed. *Ce moys de may* ("This month of May"), a *rondeau*, shows Dufay in an energetic and carefree vein of invention (see Listening Note V.A). Some of its music has no text written under the

Listening Note V.A

Dufay: *Ce moys de may* (c.1440)

Ce moys de may soyons lies et joyeux	This month of May let us be happy and joyous
Et de nos cuers ostons merancolye;	And banish melancholy from our hearts.
Chantons, dansons et menons chiere lye,	Let us sing, dance and make merry,
por despiter ces felons envieux.	To spite these base, envious creatures.
Plus c'onques mais chascuns soit curieux	Let each one try more than ever
De bien servir sa maistresse jolye:	To serve his fair mistress well:
Ce moys de may soyons lies et joyeux	This month of May let us be happy and joyous
Et de nos cuers ostons merancolye.	And banish melancholy from our hearts.
Car la saison semont tous amoureux	For the season bids all lovers
A ce faire, pourtant n'y fallons mye.	To do so, therefore let us not fail.
Carissimi! Dufaÿ vous en prye	Dear ones! Dufay begs you thus
Et Perinet dira de mieux en mieux:	And Perinet will speak better and better.
Ce moys de may soyons lies et joyeux	This month of May let us be happy and joyous
Et de nos cuers ostons merancolye;	And banish melancholy from our hearts;
Chantons, dansons et menons chiere lye,	Let us sing, dance and make merry
por despiter ces felons envieux.	To spite these base, envious creatures.

This mid-fifteenth-century *chanson* is rhythmically lively, with considerable syncopation. An instrumental "introduction" serves as a divider between the verses.

Time

0:00	instrumental introduction	1:32	instrumental interlude
0:05	first verse begins	1:38	fourth verse
0:42	instrumental interlude – same music	2:16	instrumental interlude
0:48	second verse begins	2:22	fifth verse
1:06	instrumental interlude	2:59	(end)
1:13	third verse		

ex. i

46 *Opposite left*
Ockeghem (presumed to be the figure with glasses) among singers at a lectern: miniature from a manuscript dating from about 20 years after the composer's death. Bibliothèque Nationale, Paris.

47 *Opposite right* Dufay (with a portative organ) with another song composer, Binchois (with a harp): miniature from *Champion des Dames* by Martin le Franc, French, 15th century. Bibliothèque Nationale, Paris.

notes, which suggests that instruments were intended to play with some or all of the voices. These might have included wind (recorders, shawms, crumhorns, sackbuts), plucked and bowed strings (viols, fiddles, lutes) and percussion (drums, tambourines).

Dufay's greatness lies in the wide scope and consistent high quality of his output, which sums up the compositional styles of his time and reflects the increasing flexibility with which medieval forms were being handled. Related to this, and perhaps to a growing secularization, is the personal quality of some of his music, a feature rare in the medieval period but commoner in the years to come. An interesting example, because it makes a musical point, is in the solemn four-voice motet *Ave regina caelorum*. Here Dufay introduces his name into the text, interrupting the traditional words to ask forgiveness for his transgressions in a moving, chromatic passage. We know from his will that Dufay intended the motet to be sung at his deathbed. While the text makes its point, the music creates an

unmistakable mood of penitence. This early example of "mood painting" is a supreme instance of the tempering of austere medieval traditions with Renaissance humanism.

Ockeghem

Of the generation after Dufay, the chief figure is Johannes Ockeghem (*d*1497), another Franco-Fleming. He spent most of his time in Paris as head of the chapel to three successive kings of France. He was widely praised both for his splendid bass voice and for his compositions, and after his death he was much lamented by poets and fellow musicians (see pp. 82–3).

Ockeghem is renowned for his use of intricate contrapuntal devices. But he also had a special gift for long, expressive melody, with phrases in different voices overlapping to avoid cadences and to achieve a continuous fabric of sound – a technique that differed from the shorter phrasing used by Dufay but was to become standard practice.

Johannes Ockeghem   Works
*born c*1410; *died* ?Tours, 1497

Sacred vocal music 10 Masses – Missa cuiusvi toni; Missa prolationum; Requiem;
Mass movements; 10 motets
Secular vocal music over 20 chansons

Another forward-looking element of Ockeghem's style is the greater equality he gives to the voices, extending the lower ones into a deeper register than had previously been common. He also shows an interest in musical illustration of the text, sometimes in a literal sense, such as using an ascending scale for the words "et ascendit in caelo" ("and he ascended into Heaven"), at others creating a musical mood to reflect the textual one. This was to become a significant feature of later Renaissance music.

Josquin

Ockeghem's pupils may have included the greatest composer of the early Renaissance: Josquin Desprez (*c*1440–1521). Josquin was a Frenchman who spent most of his adult life in Italy, including a spell in the papal choir in Rome. Before he left the north Josquin composed in the reserved, sober style of Ockeghem and his predecessors. His experiences in Italy brought him into contact with a more fluent and flexible style. The music from these middle and later periods of his life is regarded as his finest. He was prolific and wide-ranging.

The motet *Ave Maria ... virgo serena*, for four voices, a prayer to the Virgin, provides a good introduction to his music and shows how an apparently simple style can conceal a wealth of ingenuity. The part-writing is mostly imitative, and the general impression is of smooth, flowing lines, transparent textures and sonorous harmonies. The mood, reflecting the text, is of perfect calm.

Josquin's motet sounds different from those of the fourteenth century. The melodies are more flowing and wider-ranging, free of the patterns of plainsong. The rhythms are more varied, less restricted by meter and by such devices as isorhythm. The harmony is richer, intervals are more sonorous and chord progressions more natural. Imitation is an important feature; but its progress is often arrested by chordal sections where the voices move together. Dissonance now has an expressive value of its own and contributes to the effect.

The most significant difference between Josquin's music and that of the Middle Ages is in general approach. Josquin is the first great composer to attempt to express emotion in music in any consistent way. If we listen to almost any medieval motet without reading the text, we are hard pressed to tell from the music alone whether the piece is narrative or reflective, whether its subject is penitence or rejoicing, where the significant points in the text occur, whether it closes optimistically or gloomily. Josquin explored the new, humanistic Renaissance attitude – not only to religious expression but to man's whole approach to his relationship with the outside world. This is typified by his *chanson Nymphes des bois*, a deeply felt lament on the death of Ockeghem (see Listening Note V.B). It is this expressive quality in Josquin's music that places him at the pinnacle of the early Renaissance.

Josquin Desprez		Life
*c*1440	born in north France	
1459–72	singer at Milan Cathedral	
1474	singer at Sforza family private chapel, Milan	
1476–9	in the service of Cardinal Ascanio Sforza, Rome	
1486–99	singer in the papal choir, Rome	
1499–1503	France	
1503–4	director of music to Duke Ercole I, Ferrara	
1504	canon of the collegiate church of Condé-sur-L'Escaut	
1521	died in Condé, 27 August	

Josquin Desprez	Works
Sacred vocal music 20 Masses – Missa pange lingua; Mass movements; over 80 motets – Ave Maria ... virgo serena	
Secular vocal music *c*70 chansons – Nymphes des bois	

48 Josquin Desprez: woodcut from *Opus chronographicum* (1611) by Petrus Opmeer.

Listening Note V.B   *Side 2, band 2*

Josquin Desprez: *Nymphes des bois* **(1497)**

Nymphes des bois, déesses des fontaines,	Nymphs of the woods, goddesses of the fountains,
Chantres expers de toutes nations,	fine singers of all the nations,
Changez voz voix fort clères et haultaines	change your strong, clear, high voices
En cris tranchantz et lamentations.	into searing cries and lamentations.
Car d'Atropos les molestations	For the ravages of Atropos
Vostre Okeghem par sa rigueur attrappe	Have cruelly ensnared your Ockeghem,
Le vray trésoir de musicque et chief d'oeuvre,	the true treasure and supreme master of music,
Qui de trépas désormais plus n'eschappe,	who can no longer escape death,
Dont grant doumaige est que la terre coeuvre.	and who, alas, is covered by the earth.
Acoutrez vous d'abitz de deuil:	Dress yourselves in clothes of mourning,
Josquin, Brumel, Pirchon, Compère	Josquin, Brumel, Pierchon, Compère
Et plorez grosses larmes de oeil:	And let your eyes weep copious tears:
Perdu avez vostre bon père.	for you have lost a good father.
Requiescat in pace. Amen.	May he rest in peace. Amen.

(one voice sings the following throughout)

Requiem aeternam dona ei Domine	Eternal rest give to him, O Lord:
et lux perpetua luceat ei.	and let perpetual light shine upon him.

This *chanson* is in the "old style", using the plainsong "Requiem aeternam" from the Mass for the Dead as a *cantus firmus*. The technique is very smooth, with cadences merged into the musical fabric. Later in the piece the shorter phrases indicate Josquin's more modern style. An extended cadence brings the piece to a conclusion.

Time

0:00	beginning of the motet-chanson "Nymphes des bois"	3:25	"Requiescat in pace, Amen". Note the extended cadence
2:30	"Acoutrez vous"	4:00	(end)
2:56	"Et plorez grosses larmes de oeil"		

ex. i

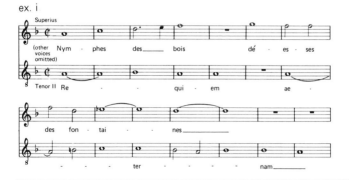

Lassus

The greatest composer that northern Europe produced at this time spent most of his adult life in southern Europe. Orlande (or Roland) de Lassus, or Orlando di Lasso as he was known in Italy, was born in 1532 in the Franco-Flemish town of Mons in Hainaut, an area that had produced a number of famous musicians. As a boy he is thought to have been a fine singer; there is even a tale that he was three times kidnapped for the sake of his beautiful voice. From about the age of 12 he was in Italy. In 1556 he joined the musical establishment of Duke Albrecht V of Bavaria in Munich and soon took over the ducal chapel, where he remained for more than 30 years. He died in 1594.

Lassus continued to visit Italy, and his fame as a composer spread rapidly, not least because his output was immense – over 2000 works. Many of them were published during his lifetime, and he was highly regarded among his contemporaries.

Probably the most versatile composer of his time, Lassus combined the best features of several national styles: the beauty and expressiveness of Italian melody, the charm and elegance of French text-setting, the solidity and richness of Flemish and German polyphony. Like all the best composers, he had something of his own to add – a vivid imagination, with which he made dramatic and emotional responses to the words. That is particularly evident in his motets. His cycle of 12 entitled *Prophetiae sibyllarum* ("Prophecies of the sibyls") was a product of his adventurous youth: in setting the cryptic

49 Opening of Josquin's *Nymphes des bois* ("La déploration de Johan. Ockeghem"), showing the superius and contratenor parts, with the Requiem text in the tenor. Biblioteca Medicea Laurenziana, Florence.

50 Orlande de Lassus:
engraving. 16th century.

statements of these legendary prophetesses he plumbed expressive depths and created, through a striking use of chromaticism, a highly colored style. A typical example is his eight-part motet *Alma redemptoris mater* (see Listening Note V.C).

Lassus was a true man of the Renaissance, whose court appointment and European

Orlande de Lassus	Life
1532	born in Mons
1544	entered the service of Ferrante Gonzaga and traveled with him to Mantua and Sicily
1547–9	Milan
1550	entered the service of Constantino Castrioto, Naples
*c*1551	Archbishop of Florence's household, in Rome
1553	*maestro di cappella* of St John Lateran, Rome
1554	Mons
1555	Antwerp; supervised publication of early madrigals and motets
1556	singer in Duke Albrecht of Bavaria's chapel, Munich
1558	married Regina Wäckinger
1563	*maestro di cappella* of the Bavarian court, for which he provided numerous sacred works; continued making journeys to European musical centers to recruit singers; international reputation firmly established
1574	made a Knight of the Golden Spur by the pope
1574–9	journeys to Vienna and Italy; *Patrocinium musices*, five volumes of sacred music, published
1594	died in Munich, 14 June

Orlande de Lassus	Works

*Sacred vocal music c*70 Masses; 4 Passions; *c*100 Magnificat settings; over 500 motets – Alma redemptoris mater, Prophetiae sibyllarum; Magnus opus musicum; Penitential psalms; Lamentations; hymns

*Secular vocal music c*200 Italian madrigals and villanellas for 4–6 voices; *c*140 chansons for 4–8 voices; *c*90 lieder for 3–8 voices

Listening Note V.C   Side 2, band 3

Lassus: *Alma redemptoris mater*

Alma redemptoris mater,	Gracious mother of the redeemer,
quae pervia coeli porta manes,	who stands at the doors of heaven,
Et stella maris, succurre cadenti	star of the sea, aid the falling,
surgere qui curat populo:	the people who struggle to rise:
Tu quae genuisti, natura mirante,	You who gave birth, by wonder of nature,
tuum sanctum genitorem:	to the Lord almighty,
Virgo prius et posterius,	eternal virgin,
Gabrielis ab ore sumens illud:	who received from the lips of Gabriel that greeting:
Ave, peccatorum miserere.	have mercy on our sins.

This eight-voice motet is an early example of "stereophonic" sound. The choir is divided to give a spatial effect. It is typical of the fervent, colorful Counter-Reformation style.

Time
0:00	"Alma redemptoris mater"	2:08	"Virgo prius" (tenor voice)
0:40	"Et stella maris"	3:46	(end)
1:21	"Tu quae genuisti"		

---

travels ensured that he was very much of the world. His secular pieces show his varied tastes. As well as spiritual madrigals, he set lighthearted pastorals and racy songs in several languages, including rumbustious German drinking-songs, which show yet another side of his personality. His versatility, his humanity and the expressive range covered in his large output mark him as one of the most significant figures of the period.

Italy

Palestrina

Among the composers of church music working at the time of the Council of Trent was Giovanni Pierluigi de Palestrina (*c*1525–1594). He was so well attuned to the spirit of the Counter-Reformation that his music has traditionally been revered as the summit of sixteenth-century polyphony. He took his name from his likely birthplace, Palestrina, a small town near Rome, and his entire life was devoted to the service of the greatest churches of the city.

Giovanni Pierluigi da Palestrina	Life
*c*1525	born, probably at Palestrina, near Rome
1537	choirboy at S Maria Maggiore, Rome
1544	organist at the cathedral at S Agapito, Palestrina
1547	married Lucrezia Gori
1551	*maestro* of the Cappella Giulia, the musical establishment of St Peter's, Rome
1555	singer in the Sistine Chapel; *maestro di cappella* of St John Lateran, Rome
1561–71	*maestro di cappella* of S Maria Maggiore; period of growing reputation and influence
1564	appointed by Cardinal Ippolito d'Este to take charge of music at his villa in Tivoli, near Rome, during the summer
1566–71	music teacher at Roman Seminary; publication of important collections of motets and Masses
1571	*maestro* of the Cappella Giulia
1572–80	plague in Rome: wife and several close relatives died
1577	asked to revise books of plainsong following guidelines laid down by the Council of Trent
1581	married Virginia Dormoli
1594	died in Rome, 2 February

IOANNIS PETRI
Loysij Praenestini in basilica
S. Petri de vrbe capellae
Magistri.
MISSARVM LIBER PRIMVS.

51 Title-page of
Palestrina's *Missarum liber
primus* ("First book of
Masses", 1554), showing
the composer handing his
work to Pope Julius III.

Palestrina owed his early success to the Bishop of Palestrina, who on his election in 1550 as Pope Julius III asked the composer to accompany him to Rome. Palestrina never enjoyed quite the same favor under subsequent popes, but was always comfortably placed at the head of one or other division of the papal chapel. By his mid-30s he had earned a remarkable reputation as a composer and music director. Though attempts were made to entice him elsewhere, he never left Rome.

Like Lassus, Palestrina was extremely prolific. He wrote many secular pieces, but his main energies were spent on church music and he produced over 100 Masses (more than any other composer of the period) and nearly 400 motets.

Palestrina's Masses embrace all the current types of Mass composition. Many are "parody" Masses, where existing pieces are interpolated into the structure of the Mass –

Listening Note V.D   *Side 2, band 4*

Palestrina: *Missa brevis* (1570), Kyrie

Kyrie eleison.	Lord have mercy.
Christe eleison.	Christ have mercy.
Kyrie eleison.	Lord have mercy.

This is a classic example of the Renaissance style of imitative polyphony, with its smooth voice-leading, of which Palestrina is the acknowledged master. Each of the three short sections that make up the Kyrie is based on a single phrase, which can be heard virtually all the time in one or other of the four voices. Ex. i shows the first Kyrie in full, with each imitative phrase indicated.

Time
0:00	"Kyrie eleison"		2:15	"Kyrie eleison"
1:09	"Christe eleison"		3:16	(end)

ex. i

Giovanni Pierluigi da Palestrina   Works

Sacred vocal music over 100 Masses – Missa Papae Marcelli; Missa brevis; 375 motets – Stabat mater; 35 Magnificat settings; 68 offertories; Lamentations, litanies, sacred madrigals, hymns
Secular vocal music c140 madrigals

at that period a standard method. Other Masses are based on a *cantus firmus*, usually plainsong but occasionally secular tunes. Others are freely composed, among them the four-voice *Missa brevis* ("Short Mass") of 1570 (see Listening Note V.D).

The almost legendary reverence in which Palestrina was held began during his lifetime. Much of his music was published and widely diffused. So great was his reputation that in 1577 he was asked to revise the main books of plainsong in accordance with the guidelines laid down by the Council of Trent, a task he never in fact finished. His famous *Missa Papae Marcelli* ("Mass for Pope Marcellus") may have been written to show that the Council of Trent requirements did not rule out beautiful polyphony in the traditional mold.

Unlike Lassus, Palestrina was conservative in his musical outlook. He was close to the center of the Counter-Reformation, so was more restricted in the music he wrote and less free to experiment. This seems to have suited him. Rather than attempt new methods he refined the existing ones. Palestrina was the ultimate master of the "imitative style", the backbone of sixteenth-century polyphony and probably the single most characteristic feature of Renaissance music. At the same time, stepwise melody is essential to Palestrina's style: his lines have no awkward leaps. The phrases tend to overlap, to form a "seamless" texture, in which the equality of voices and their balance give the music a sense of perfect proportion.

The Gabrielis   Venice, a trading city under an elected ruler (doge) rather than a princely family, reached the height of its prosperity in the sixteenth century. It acquired a musical tradition to match its wealth, artistic richness and love of pomp. The doge's basilica, St Mark's, was the center of its ceremonial and musical life. Among the first Italians to hold important posts at St Mark's at this time were Andrea Gabrieli (c1510–1586) and his nephew Giovanni Gabrieli (c1555–1612).

Andrea was a prolific composer of sacred music and of madrigals. His madrigals are lighter in manner than most of those of his contemporaries, less intense and less contrapuntal. In his sacred music he developed an individual style to suit the needs of St Mark's for ceremonial music, and he was quick to see the special possibilities offered by the basilica's architecture: he sometimes divided up his players and singers into groups, stationing them in different galleries, so that the listener would hear music from a variety of directions. This "spaced choirs" technique was not exclusive to St Mark's or to Venice, but developed there in response to the basilica's design and the Venetian love of the grandiose.

Giovanni Gabrieli followed up his uncle's work. In 1587 he published a volume called *Concerti*, "containing church music, madrigals and other works" by himself and Andrea, mainly for opposing groups of singers and players. (This was the earliest use of the word "concerto".) Giovanni used dialogue techniques with even greater freedom and variety, and with more specific and more colorful instrumental writing, as well as a more intense and dissonant style.

Giovanni Gabrieli	Works
born Venice, c1555; *died* Venice, 1612	

Sacred vocal music Symphoniae sacrae (1597, 1615): Mass movements; c100 motets – In ecclesiis

Instrumental music Canzoni e sonate (1615); canzonas, ricercares, fugues, toccatas for wind ensemble

Secular vocal music c30 madrigals

Listening Note V.E   *Side 2, band 5*

Giovanni Gabrieli: *Canzon XIII* (1597), septimi e octavi toni

Gabrieli took advantage of the architecture of St Mark's and wrote antiphonal music. Here we hear representative instruments from Gabrieli's time: cornetts and sackbuts ("brass") to left and right, strings and dulzian (bassoon) in the center.

Time

0:00	full ensemble opens the canzona with the traditional rhythm, long-short-short	1:07	soft group heard again, alternately with small brass group with many antiphonal passages between groups
0:14	small brass ensemble enters		
0:17	"soft-toned" group of strings and dulzian	1:40	string solo
		1:44	cornett solo answers followed by a great deal of antiphonal activity
0:22	brass ensemble enters		
0:29	soft group	2:05	full ensemble, then antiphonal passages
0:33	brass enters – an antiphonal passage follows		
		2:38	small brass ensemble as in the beginning
0:49	full ensemble		
0:53	small brass group takes over	2:52	(end)
1:01	brass group features cornett solo		

The Venetian love of color belongs to music as well as painting. A work like Giovanni Gabrieli's *Canzon XIII* from a collection published in 1597 (see Listening Note V.E), shows him setting three ensembles against one another, sometimes in echo, sometimes in dialogue, and sometimes combining in rich counterpoint. In some respects he belongs – as we shall see – as much to the period we call the "Baroque" era as to the Renaissance, with his emphasis, especially in the works of his last years, on contrast and his development of the concerto-like (or *concertato*) style.

Marenzio

Luca Marenzio (*c*1553–1599) is the chief figure in the later history of the Italian madrigal. His madrigals cover a wide variety of subjects. The best of them combine features of the earlier madrigal with his individual manner for text-setting by word-painting, a notable element in his music. The images of Renaissance poetry inspired him to match specific words or ideas with striking melodic twists and highly colored harmonies.

Luca Marenzio   Works
born near Brescia, 1553 or 1554; *died* Rome, 1599

Secular vocal music c500 madrigals for 4–6 voices – Io partirò; c80 villanellas
Sacred vocal music c75 motets

He was at his most characteristic in somber, dark-toned pieces, and seemed to favor the richness of texture offered by five voices. A violent wrench in the harmony marks the expressive climax of *Io partirò* ("I shall depart"; see Listening Note V.F). Often an idea in the text is reflected in the shape of the melodic line: an ascending scale may illustrate upward flight, short phrases punctuated by rests describe breathlessness or excitement, a falling semitone depicts swooning or death. Marenzio handled these devices with a sensitivity lacking in his less talented contemporaries.

Listening Note V.F   *Side 2, band 6*

Marenzio: *I must depart all hapless* (1581)

I must depart all hapless,
But leave to you my careful heart oppressed,
So that if I live heartless,
Love doth a work miraculous and blessed,
But so great pains assail me,
That sure ere it be long my life will fail me.

This madrigal was composed to Italian words (beginning "Io partirò") and published in 1581. Seven years later, it was included in the English publication *Musica transalpina*, a book of Italian madrigals in English translation; it is the English text we hear.

Time
0:00	"I must depart"	1:02	"Love doth work"
0:05	tenor entry		decorative writing repeated
0:08	bass entry	1:12	"But so great pains" (note
0:14	"But leave to you"		dissonances)
0:25	"So that . . ."	1:26	"That sure ere it be"
0:44	decorative writing on		then repeated contrapuntally
	"Love doth work"	1:47	"That sure ere it be"
0:50	"if I live heartless."	1:58	"my life will fail me."
		2:16	(end)

England

The end of the sixteenth century in Italy witnessed the decline of the madrigal, essentially a Renaissance genre, in favor of a new style which properly belongs to the Baroque era. But the madrigal was not yet dead. Individual pieces had reached England by about 1570, and the genre was taken up enthusiastically there. Printed anthologies of madrigals by Italian composers were circulated in England with translated texts (notably *Musica trans-alpina*, 1588), and soon English composers began to write their own, for there was a wealth of English poetry to draw on. The Elizabethan age set great store by literary and musical accomplishment, and in an environment where domestic music-making flourished the madrigal was bound to thrive.

Byrd

The greatest English composer of the time was William Byrd (1543–1623), often referred to as the English counterpart of Palestrina and Lassus. He was the last great English composer of Catholic church music and among the first of the "golden" Elizabethan age of secular and instrumental music.

Byrd was appointed organist of Lincoln Cathedral at the age of 19 or 20, and remained there for about ten years. In 1570 he joined the Chapel Royal as a singer and soon became its organist. In 1575 he and the composer Thomas Tallis were granted a valuable royal monopoly on music printing in England and on the issue of printed manuscript paper.

Byrd remained in court service for the rest of his life. After a brief period of Catholicism, England returned to Protestantism under Queen Elizabeth and many Catholics feared persecution. The queen tolerated Byrd's Catholic sympathies. He was able to write music for both churches, including three sublime Latin Masses and a large number of motets. For the Anglican church he wrote Services and anthems, usually with the organ or other instruments to accompany the "verse" or solo sections.

Byrd's restraint and expressiveness as a composer of sacred music are shown at their finest in his short four-part motet *Ave verum corpus*. There is a simple beauty about the gentle chording of the voices, a rich warmth as the opening notes of a phrase in one voice are taken up by the others (see Listening Note V.G).

Plate 3 *Opposite* Basse danse, accompanied by musicians in a gallery, at the Burgundian court (see p. 78): miniature from the *Chronique d'Angleterre* by Jean de Waurin, 1470. Österreichische Nationalbibliothek, Vienna.

William Byrd		Life
1543	born, probably in Lincoln	
1563	organist and master of the choristers at Lincoln Cathedral	
1570	appointed singer in the Chapel Royal but did not go to London for two years	
1572	organist (with Thomas Tallis) of the Chapel Royal	
1575	granted, with Tallis, a royal monopoly on music printing; *Cantiones sacrae*	
c1580	absent from London in Harlington during period of persecution of Roman Catholics	
1585	Tallis died, leaving Byrd the printing patent	
1588	*Psalmes, Sonets and Songs*	
1593	moved to Stondon Massey, Essex	
1623	died at Stondon Massey, 4 July	

Listening Note V.G   *Side 2, band 7*

Byrd: *Ave verum corpus* (1605)

Ave verum corpus natum
de Maria vergine:
Vere passum, immolatum
in cruce pro homine:
Cuius latus perforatum
unda fluxit sanguine:
Esto nobis praegustatum
in mortis examine.
O dulcis, o pie, o Iesu fili Mariae
miserere mei. Amen.

Hail, true body, born
of the virgin Mary:
who truly suffered and died
on the cross for mankind:
from whose pierced side
water flowed with blood:
be a consolation to us
at our last hour.
O sweet one, O pious one, O Jesus, son of Mary,
have mercy upon me. Amen.

This motet is one of Byrd's most popular and admired works. It shows his expressive techniques, for example in his telling harmony – at the opening, the G♯ close to a G♮ (ex. i, where these tones are marked x) produces an arresting and poignant effect – heard again at "O dulcis, o pie" (ex. ii).

Time

0:00	ex. i: "Ave verum"	
0:33	"Vere passum"	
1:02	"Cuius latus"	
1:29	"Esto nobis"	
1:53	ex. ii: "O dulcis" (G♯ and G♮)	

2:23	ex. iii: "Miserere mei"
2:55	"O dulcis" (second time)
3:26	"Miserere" (second time)
4:22	(end)

He excelled in elegiac music, but it would be a mistake to imagine that he wrote only somber works. As he grew older he seems to have become more cheerful; both his Latin and his Anglican music included marvelously joyful pieces, like the exuberant six-part anthem *Sing joyfully*, where the overlapping voice-parts ring out like peals of bells.

In his secular music too Byrd encompassed a wide range of texts and moods. Though he issued no volumes of madrigals he did publish two volumes of *Psalmes, Songs and Sonets* (1588 and 1611) and one of *Songs of Sundrie Natures* (1589). He also excelled in instrumental music, both for solo keyboard instruments and for ensemble. Many of the keyboard pieces,

Plate 4 Musicians playing the flute and the lute in a polyphonic chanson (see p. 95): detail from the painting *The Prodigal Son among the Courtesans*. 16th century, artist unknown. Musée Carnavalet, Paris.

William Byrd	Works

Sacred choral music Cantiones (with Tallis, 1575); Cantiones sacrae (1589, 1591); Gradualia (1605, 1607); 3 Masses; Mass movements; Services – Short Service, Great Service; anthems; motets – Ave verum corpus; Anglican liturgical settings
Vocal chamber music Psalmes, Sonets and Songs (1588); Songs of Sundrie Natures (1589); Psalmes, Songs and Sonnets (1611)
Instrumental music fantasias and In Nomines for viol consort
Keyboard music fantasias, variations, dances, grounds for virginals

intended for harpsichord, virginals, spinet or organ, are dance movements or arrangements of popular tunes. His unending inventiveness in keyboard variations and pieces for five-part instrumental "consort" shows how a composer can use his imagination even when working with an existing melody.

Byrd's other music includes songs accompanied by an instrumental ensemble, a peculiarly English genre, and music for viols alone, mostly contrapuntal fantasias and dance movements.

The English madrigalists

Byrd's successors carried the English madrigal to its peak. By the end of the sixteenth century there was a school of English madrigalists; while the public demand was there, new pieces continued to appear in a fever of production.

Among the related forms was the "ballett", a light, dance-like piece, less sophisticated than the madrigal proper, in repeating verses and often with a "fa-la" refrain. Thomas

---

Listening Note V.H   *Side 2, band 8*

Weelkes: *As Vesta was from Latmos hill descending* (1601)

As Vesta was from Latmos hill descending,
she spied a maiden queen the same ascending,
attended on by all the shepherds swain,
to whom Diana's darlings came running down amain.

First two by two, then three by three together,
leaving their goddess all alone, hasted thither,
and mingling with the shepherds of her train
with mirthful tunes her presence entertain.
    Then sang the shepherds and nymphs of Diana,
    Long live fair Oriana!

Weelkes's "word-painting" – his use of music to illustrate individual words – is seen here. In the first line, "hill" is treated in a series of upward phrases, then turned downwards for "descending". The next line counters this with imitations on an upward phrase at "ascending". "Attended on by all" is sung by all the voices; "Came running down amain" is a series of downward-running phrases. The "two by two" and "three by three" lines are sung, respectively, by the voices in pairs and in threes, with all six at "together": and the "goddess all alone" is represented by a solo voice.

Time
0:00	"As Vesta was"	1:22	"leaving their goddess"
0:33	"attended"	1:57	"Then sang the shepherds"
0:50	"to whom Diana"	3:05	(end)
1:13	"First two by two"		

52 Wind band with treble and two tenor shawms, cornett, trombone and curtal: detail of the painting *Procession of the Religious Orders of Antwerp on the Feast Day of the Rosary.* 1616, by Denis van Alsloot. Museo del Prado, Madrid.

Morley (*c*1557–1602) and Thomas Weelkes (*c*1575–1623) were its chief exponents. Morley was a particularly interesting figure, a teacher, a theorist and intellectual, as well as a popular composer. His lively ballett *Now is the month of maying* provides a foil to Byrd's "May" madrigal discussed earlier: here dance rhythms provide the inspiration. Byrd's madrigal is more contrapuntal, and on another plane of seriousness.

In 1601 Morley edited a volume called *The Triumphs of Oriana*, compiled in honor of the queen ("Oriana" herself). Most of the leading madrigalists of the day contributed, each setting the words "Long live fair Oriana" as a refrain. It provides an interesting survey of the English madrigal at the end of the sixteenth century. Thomas Weelkes's contribution, *As Vesta was from Latmos hill descending*, is a good example (see Listening Note V.H); his style was bold and original, very Italian in his approach to the words.

Ensemble music

During the Renaissance, instruments were originally used to accompany voices or, in domestic music-making, to take a voice part. Many instrumental adaptations exist of *chansons* and madrigals. The instruments used would normally be viols or recorders, of various sizes, grouped in families or "consorts". At first, such ensembles played arrangements of vocal pieces; later, music was composed specially for consort, by Byrd and his successors. These were often contrapuntal pieces, but there was also dance music.

The relatively soft-toned instruments, and the lute, were sometimes described as *bas* ("low" or "soft"), while the strident ones were classified as *haut* ("high" or "loud"). The latter included wind instruments such as the cornett, trumpet, shawm (precursor of the oboe) and sackbut (trombone) as well as percussion. They were suitable for playing outdoors, to accompany dancing, in processions or in church ceremonial.

Keyboard music

In the earlier Renaissance there was little distinction between music for keyboard instruments with plucked strings, such as the harpsichord or spinet, and that written for the organ.

Listening Note V.I

Bull: *Coranto "Alarm"*

This brief piece illustrates dance music of the late Renaissance and the English keyboard style. The word "Coranto" is an English adaptation of the dance type known in Italy as the "Corrente" and in France as the "Courante". It is a running, triple-meter dance.

Time

0:00	first section	0:50	repeat, second part
0:14	repeat of first section	1:15	(end)
0:28	second part begins (note suggestion of a trumpet call at the beginning of section)		

When vocal music was transcribed for domestic keyboard instruments, compensation had to be made for the lack of sustaining power. Composers would avoid long notes, dividing them into a number of shorter ones in a decorative fashion. This device was similar to the technique of writing variations, as practiced by Byrd. These features helped establish an independent style of keyboard writing. One of the leading keyboard composers in the late sixteenth century was an Englishman, John Bull (1562–1628), a virtuoso who developed a distinctive and brilliant style (see Listening Note V.I).

Lute music

Like the keyboard, the lute only gradually gained its independence from its traditional accompanying role. But by the end of the sixteenth century pieces for solo lute were being composed and published in a style of their own. There was a special emphasis on fantasias and sets of variations.

The lute was also used to accompany songs like those by Byrd and his successors. It was partly from these that another distinctive English form – the ayre – developed, which took over from the madrigal in popularity at the beginning of the seventeenth century. The ayre's chief melodic interest lay in the top line. It could be performed by several voices or, more commonly, as a lute-song with a solo voice taking the top line and a lute supplying the accompaniment.

Dowland

The ayre's greatest exponent was John Dowland (1563–1626). His extensive travels in Europe earned him a number of important court appointments and brought him international fame as composer, singer and lutenist. He was famous enough for many of his works to be printed and sold in the publishing centers of northern Europe. His ayres were immensely popular, no doubt partly because they could be adapted to whatever performing resources the amateur had at his disposal.

John Dowland   Works

born ?London, 1563; *died* London, 1626

Secular vocal music over 800 ayres for voice and lute – In darknesse let mee dwell, Flow my teares, Fine knacks for ladies; I must complain

Instrumental music Lachrimae for viol consort and lute (1605); fantasias, pavans, galliards, almains, jigs for solo lute

Sacred vocal music psalms and spiritual songs

Listening Note V.J

John Dowland: *I must complain* (1603)

I must complain, yet do enjoy my love,
  She is too fair, too rich in beauty's parts.
Thence is my grief: for Nature, while she strove
  With all her graces and divinest arts
To form her too too beautiful of hue,
She had no leisure left to make her true.

Should I aggrieved then wish she were less fair?
  That were repugnant to my own desires.
She is admired; new suitors still repair
  That kindles daily love's forgetful fires.
Rest, jealous thoughts, and thus resolve at last:
She hath more beauty than becomes the chaste.

This song comes from Dowland's third collection; the words are by the poet and composer Thomas Campion (who also set them). Dowland's setting shows his characteristic vein of melancholy, with its gentle, arching lines and its tendency to drop back into a minor key. The accompaniment is played on a lute, with the bass line reinforced by a bass viol.

Time
0:00 "I must complain"
0:26 a linking passage on the lute occurs after "beauty's parts"
0:31 "Thence is my grief"
1:04 "She had no leisure"
1:21 repeat of last line, first verse
1:40 second verse begins, "Should I aggrieved"
2:04 pause after "to my own desires"
2:09 song resumes with "She is admired"
2:42 "She hath more beauty" – last line of the second verse
2:59 repeat of the last line
3:20 (end)

Dowland's ayres illustrate his ability to match in music the mood and emotion of a poetic text. He was at his best when in somber mood. Some of his ayres show passionate intensity, with uneasy rhythms and colorful dissonances. An example is the gently elegiac lover's plaint *I must complain* (see Listening Note V.J).

The lute-song was a specialized English genre. It represented the last flowering of the Renaissance in England, and when it was at its height, at the turn of the century, new and far-reaching musical developments were taking place in Italy. These innovations herald a new musical era: the Baroque.

Chapter VI

The Baroque Era

The word
"Baroque"

By the "Baroque" era, musicians generally understand the period from roughly 1600 to 1750 – beginning with Monteverdi, ending with Bach and Handel. The word is little more than a convenient label for a period that has a certain degree of underlying unity because of its techniques and its approach to musical expression. "Baroque" comes from the French, and, further back, from a Portuguese term for a misshapen pearl. It was first used in the discussion of art and architecture, mainly by writers at the end of the period itself and usually in a negative, critical way, implying something clumsy, strange and overblown. Musicians adopted it, generally in the sense of confused, over-elaborate and harsh; the generation that followed the Baroque era (as we shall see) were eager to simplify and regularize the language of music and regarded the style of their immediate forebears as extravagant and irregular. Thus the word came into use, both in art criticism and music criticism, for the products of the seventeenth century and the early eighteenth. Nowadays, we still apply the term, but with the broader historical view that we have gained through the lapse of time we do so without any of its original disapproving implications. But the notions of extravagance and irregularity, at least as compared with the music of the periods just before and just after, still have meaning.

The Renaissance emphasized clarity, unity and proportion. But as the sixteenth century moved towards its close, the representation of emotion was seen as increasingly important. Serenity and perfection of form are overtaken by the urgent expression of feeling. In the visual arts this is seen in the forceful, dramatically colored paintings of Caravaggio (1573–1619). We have already seen its beginnings in music, in the madrigals of Marenzio or the ayres of Dowland. The next generation carried it much further.

To create these strong effects, it was necessary to develop a new style. The smooth polyphony of the Renaissance was not adaptable to priorities so different from those of the era in which it had arisen. One of the most important creations of the Baroque was the concept of contrast. Renaissance music is typified by its flowing, interweaving lines, most commonly four or five in number, each of them singing (or playing) music that moved at roughly the same pace. Textures of that kind became increasingly rare after 1600, and when they were used it was almost exclusively in church music – the most conservative area because it was tied to traditional, unchanging liturgical patterns.

Contrast could exist on various planes: loud and soft; one color and another; solo and tutti; high and low; fast and slow (this could occur in two main ways, either a fast-moving part against a slow-moving one, or a fast section against a slow one). All these, and others, had their place in the musical schemes of the new era. Many are represented in the music

The word
"Baroque"

Contrast

of the important transitional composer, the Venetian Giovanni Gabrieli, whose interest in contrast we noted on p. 91. Numerous composers used the *concertato* or *concertante* style – a style with a marked contrasting element, the essence of which was a texture that varied, sometimes with solo voice or voices, sometimes with larger groups. It was mostly applied to sacred music, particularly motets.

The most striking, most violent contrasts, however, were those in the new genre called "monody". This is a kind of solo song, a vocal line that may be very intense with a slow-moving accompaniment for a lute or a harpsichord. The most important exponent of this genre (and to some extent its creator, in his epoch-making publication *Le nuove musiche* – "The new music" – of 1602) was the composer and singer Giulio Caccini (c1545-1618). The vocal line, taking its cue from the words, could vary greatly in pace and in texture, from the simple to the highly embellished; this further contrasted with the static line played by the accompanying instrument. Caccini was a member of the group of musicians, intellectuals and noblemen of Florence (the "Camerata") who had met during the 1570s and 80s with the idea of re-creating what they took to be the ancient Greek ideal of expressing in music the "affect" (or emotional character) of the words. The idea of monody follows up the thinking of that group.

The word "accompany", used above, does not often appear in the discussion of Renaissance music. As a concept, it belongs to the Baroque – it implies, of course, a difference in status between instrumental parts. And in fact the most important unifying

53 Stage design by Francesco Galli-Bibiena (1659–1737) for an unknown *opera seria*. Museo Nacional de Arte Antiga, Lisbon.

Continuo

feature of all Baroque music is the characteristic accompanying part, the basso continuo (or simply continuo). The continuo player, at a keyboard instrument (like the harpsichord or the organ) or a plucked string instrument (like the lute or guitar), was given a bass line, above which figures were usually written to indicate what additional notes he should play to fill in the harmony. Often there were two continuo players, one playing the written line on a sustaining instrument, like the cello, viol or bassoon, the other also supplying the harmony. The kind of texture that the use of continuo implies – a top, melodic line for a voice or instrument, a bottom line for a bass instrument, and a harmonic filling – is typical of the Baroque; often, just as typically, there might be two upper lines, perhaps for a pair of singers or (in a trio sonata) violins. The use of this kind of pattern, and especially the almost invariable presence of the continuo line, shows how central to the Baroque idiom was the idea of a bass line that generated harmony. This was not a sudden development. Throughout the sixteenth century there had been a tendency for the bottom line of the music to become distinct from the other strands of the polyphony. Only with the new Baroque idioms was this distinction fully recognized.

Harmony, cadence, rhythm

Along with these changes came other, related ones. When polyphony was relegated to the status of an old-fashioned method, to be used almost exclusively in certain types of church music, a new way of constructing movements was needed. The emphasis on harmony led towards the use of harmonic goals as stopping-points. These stopping-points, or cadences, would be reached by a sequence of harmonies of some standardized kind.

Linked with these harmonic developments are rhythmic ones. In vocal music, the need to reflect the sense of the words meant that the music was obliged to follow, or even exaggerate, natural speech rhythms. In instrumental music (and some kinds of vocal piece, choral ones especially), dance rhythms came to be used. The bass patterns associated with the regular rhythms of dance music hastened the development of a sense of key, of the music's gravitational pull towards particular tones.

At the same time, new instruments were developing that accelerated these processes, the most important being the violin family. While the viol had a tone well adapted to polyphonic clarity but was weak in rhythmic impetus, the violin – with its clearly defined attack and its capacity for brilliant effect – was suited to music in dance rhythms and to sonatas of a virtuosity comparable with that of the singers of monody. The interchange of vocal and instrumental idioms was a typical Baroque device; it may seem strange that the Baroque should have created these different idioms only to exchange them in its search for novelty and effect.

Passion and grandeur

It is the pursuit of striking effect, above all, that marks out the Baroque era from those immediately before and after. Composers aimed to move the passions (or the "affections", to use their favored word), and not just instantaneously: they tried to sustain the "affect" of a movement – that is, its prevailing emotion – throughout its length. The idea of exciting appropriate emotion was, moreover, closely attuned to the spirit of the Counter-Reformation. There are parallels between music and the other arts. The Baroque emotional extravagance that we find in the grandiose motets of Italy and the other Catholic countries in the early sixteenth century, some of them with multiple choirs and bold harmonic effects, may be seen as analogous to, for example, the new architecture of Rome: this was the period when the huge, overwhelming square and cathedral of St Peter's were built, and also part of the church of St John Lateran. Like the giant Salzburg Cathedral across the Alps, these are designed – in a sense that no Renaissance one was – to make the mere human being who entered them feel puny beside these grand creations that embodied divine mysteries. Similarly, the decorated lines of the music have much in common with the florid ornament found in such buildings with their elaborate statuary – in Rome particularly, where the sculptor Gianlorenzo Bernini (1598–1680) enriched the new churches and public buildings. Further north it was different, for this exuberant spirit was alien to Protestantism: the churches and the music alike are more sober. But the new mercantile spirit encouraged by the reformed faiths found musical outlets too, in the civic musical patronage of the north German cities like Hamburg and Leipzig, for example. It was mainly in the northern lands that a middle-class concert life arose towards the end of the seventeenth century – and in the eighteenth it was the middle classes who lent support to Bach's concerts in Leipzig and to Handel's oratorio performances in London.

Courts, however, remained important centers of musical patronage, along with the church. In Italy, it was the Gonzaga family, the rulers of Mantua, who employed Monteverdi before he worked for the church in Venice. It was the noble Venetian families who opened the earliest opera house to a wider public. Composers like Alessandro Scarlatti, Corelli and the young Handel were supported by the princely families around Rome. Germany suffered the Thirty Years War in the early seventeenth century; after it, in 1648, the country was divided into numerous dukedoms and the like, as well as some "free cities" (governed by city fathers) and church lands (governed by bishops). Many had their own courts, with musical establishments headed by a *Kapellmeister* or "chapelmaster" whose duties included the organization of a choir and instrumental ensemble to provide music for worship and for entertainment. In France and England, each with a central court, musical patronage was based firmly in Paris and London and there was relatively,

Patronage

54 Second day of the *divertissements* celebrating Louis XIV's conquest of the Franche-Comté, held in a garden salon specially created at the palace of Versailles, 1674; engraving after Israel Sylvestre.

Seconde Journée. Concerts de musique, sous une feüillée.   Dies Secundus. Varij musicorum concentus sub frondea.

Opera

little musical activity elsewhere, except in the larger noble and ecclesiastical establishments, until the rise of bourgeois groups late in the seventeenth century.

One of the first creations of the Baroque period was opera. It arose in the first place out of the Florentine Camerata's desire to re-create the ancient Greek drama with music, though it has other ancestors too, for example the lavish court entertainments of the time that used music, dance, drama and speech. The earliest operas were given as court entertainments, but by 1637 there were opera houses open to the public in Venice, and other Italian cities soon followed, notably Rome (where many earlier musical dramas were on sacred topics) and Naples. Most performances were given under the patronage of local noblemen. Around the middle of the seventeenth century, Italian opera was carried abroad, to Paris and Vienna in particular. The first German opera house opened in Hamburg in 1678, under civic patronage. It was royal patronage that promoted opera in Paris, at much the same date. England was a little later; opera there enjoyed royal support but essentially it was run as a commercial enterprise by groups of noblemen.

Monteverdi

The first operas regularly performed today were written by Claudio Monteverdi. Born in 1567 in Cremona, the main Italian center of violin-making, Monteverdi has been described as "the creator of modern music"; in that he represented human emotion in music with a new force and richness there is some truth in it. He was only 17 when his first musical publication was issued. By the early 1590s he had an appointment at Mantua, playing the violin or viol in the duke's group of musicians and in 1601 he became *maestro di cappella* ("master of the chapel") there.

The early years

Monteverdi's early madrigals follow the prevailing trends, moving away from the

Claudio Monteverdi		Life
1567	born in Cremona, 15 May	
1587	first book of madrigals published	
*c*1591	string player at the Gonzaga court in Mantua	
1600	reputation as a composer firmly established	
1601	appointed *maestro di cappella* at Mantua	
1607	*Orfeo* produced in Mantua; his wife, Claudia, died	
1608	*Arianna*; returned to Cremona in a depressed state and tried to leave service of the Gonzagas	
1610	*Vespers* published; began writing sacred music	
1613	*maestro di cappella* of St Mark's, Venice; began reorganizing musical establishment there	
1619	seventh book of madrigals published, including works in more modern style	
1620–25	period of opera composition	
1630–31	plague in Venice	
1632	took holy orders	
1638	*Madrigals of Love and War* (eighth book) published	
1640	*The Return of Ulysses to his Country*	
1642	*The Coronation of Poppaea*	
1643	died in Venice, 29 November	

Renaissance pattern of continuous polyphony and laying more stress on expressing the text. With his fourth and fifth collections he went much further towards an expressive and free style. In polyphonic writing, the words were often unclear to the listener, because the different voices were singing different syllables at the same time. Here, Monteverdi takes care to avoid that, using a new recitative-like technique, preferring group dialogue to imitative writing, and elaborating on crucial phrases in the text by treating them freely. He also made much greater use of dissonance, as an expressive device, than his predecessors had done, and varied the pace at which the music moved to strengthen the emotion at particular points. Not all of this was new, but the imagination and sensitivity that Monteverdi brought to these processes gave them new meaning.

"Orfeo"

The year 1607 saw the performance in Mantua of Monteverdi's opera *Orfeo*. It was given, probably at the court, by one of the learned "academies" – groups of intellectuals, amateurs and artists, characteristic of Italian life at this period. Its theme is the popular one of Orpheus's journey to the underworld to rescue his beloved, Eurydice; this offers a great opportunity for a demonstration of the power of music to move the passions, for in its central scene it is with his singing and his playing that Orpheus procures her release. *Orfeo* combines several features of the music of the time in a powerful way. The choruses are akin to the new madrigal style. The main action is carried out in an expressive dialogue, not unlike monody, treated with a freedom that enabled Monteverdi to mirror the sense of the words – for example by using harsh discords or unexpected leaps to heighten an expression of grief, or varying the pace or the texture to reflect the urgency with which the characters express themselves. One telling moment comes when Orpheus is joyously singing of his marriage, and the tragic news arrives of Eurydice's death: flowing, dance-like rhythms and lyrical lines give way to a halting recitative accompanied with jarring dissonances (see Listening Note VI.A). Orpheus's great plea to Charon to admit him to the underworld is set to richly ornamented music, supported first with two violins, then two cornetts and finally the harp.

Such variety of instruments was unusual. This has been called the first modern use of the orchestra; that is an exaggeration, but Monteverdi was indeed aiming at something new. He listed the instruments he required – two harpsichords, two small wooden organs and a reed organ, a harp, two large lutes, three bass viols, ten violins and two small violins, two instruments like small double basses, four each of trumpets and trombones, two

Listening Note VI.A   *Side 3, band 1*

Monteverdi: *Orfeo* (1607), Act 2, excerpt

Dramatic context: Orpheus is celebrating, with his friends the shepherds, his marriage to Eurydice, whom he has long loved.

Time

0:00	orchestral ritornello
0:11	voice enters – Orpheus sings: "Vi ricorda . . ." (ex.i)
0:38	ritornello
0:52	Orpheus: "Dite all'hor"
1:18	ritornello
1:31	Orpheus: "Vissi già mesto . . ."
1:59	ritornello
2:13	Orpheus: "Sol per te bella . . ." The music slows before the entry of the shepherd
2:46	Shepherd: "Mira, Orfeo"
3:20	Messenger (female voice, recitative): "Ahi, caso acerbo!" (ex.ii)
3:53	Shepherd: "Qual suon . . ."
4:00	Messenger: "Lassa dunque . . ."
4:39	Shepherd: "Questa è Silvia . . ."
5:14	Messenger: "Pastor . . ."
5:38	Orpheus: "D'onde vieni?"
5:55	Messenger: "A te ne vengo . . ."
6:25	Orpheus: "Ohimè . . ." (ex.iii)
6:31	Messenger: "La tua diletta sposa . . ."
6:52	Orpheus: "Ohimè".
7:00	(end)

ORPHEUS

Vi ricorda, o boschi ombrosi,	Do you remember, O shady woods,
De' miei lungh'aspri tormenti	my long and bitter torments,
quando i sassi ai miei lamenti	when the rocks to my laments
rispondean fatti pietosi?	took pity and responded?
Dite all'hor non vi sembrai	Tell me, did I not then seem
più d'ogn'altro sconsolato?	more inconsolable than any other?
Hor fortuna ha stil cangiato	Now fortune has changed
et ha volto in festa i guai.	and has turned my woes into joys.
Vissi già mesto e dolente,	I have lived with sadness and grief;
hor gioisco e quegli affanni	Now I rejoice, and those sorrows
che sofferti ho per tant'anni	that I suffered for so many years
fan più caro il ben presente.	make my present joy the more dear.
Sol per te bella Euridice,	For you alone, fair Eurydice,
benedico il mio tormento,	I bless my former torments;
dopo il duol si è più contento	after grief one is the more content,
dopo il mal si è più felice.	after suffering one is the more happy.

SHEPHERD

Mira, Orfeo, che d'ogni intorno	Wonder, Orpheus, that all around you
ride il bosco e ride il prato.	the woods and the meadows join in laughter.
Segui pur col plettr'aurato	Continue with your golden plectrum
d'addolcir l'aria in si beato giorno.	to sweeten the air on so blessed a day.

MESSENGER

Ahi! caso acerbo!	Oh, bitter event!
Ahi! fat'empio e crudele!	Oh, impious and cruel fate!
Ahi! stelle ingiuriose!	Oh, unjust stars!
Ahi! ciel'avaro!	Oh, avaricious heaven!

SHEPHERD

Qual suon dolente il lieto dì perturba?	What mournful sound disturbs our happiness?

MESSENGER

Lassa dunque debb'io	I am wretched, for now I must,
mentre Orfeo con sue note il ciel consola	while Orpheus with his tones consoles the heavens,
con le parole mie passargli il core.	pierce his heart with my words.

55 Title-page of Monteverdi's *Orfeo* (Venice, 1609).

Questa è Silvia gentile,
dolcissima compagna
della bell'Euridice. O quanto e in vista
dolorosa; hor che sia? Deh, sommi dei
non torcete da noi benigno il guardo.

SHEPHERD

This is the lovely Sylvia,
the sweetest companion
of the beautiful Eurydice. Oh, how her face
is sad; what has befallen? O mighty gods,
do not turn your kindly glances away from us.

Pastor, lasciate il canto,
ch'ogni nostra allegrezza in doglia è volta.

MESSENGER

Shepherd, cease your singing,
all our happiness is turned to grief.

D'onde vieni? ove vai? Ninfa, che porti?

ORPHEUS

Where do you come from? where are you going?
Nymph, what do you bear?

A te ne vengo Orfeo
messagera infelice
di caso più infelice e più funesto.

MESSENGER

To you I come, Orpheus,
unhappy messenger,
of a matter most unhappy and most terrible.

Ohimè, che odo?

ORPHEUS

Alas! what do I hear?

La tua diletta sposa è morta.

MESSENGER

Your beloved wife is dead.

Ohimè.

ORPHEUS

Alas!

ex. i

ex. ii

ex. iii

ex. iii

cornetts and two recorders. Then, at various points, he indicated which ones should play, choosing the color to suit the words and the setting. *Orfeo*, which also includes instrumental dances, must have had an overwhelming effect, with its variety of resource and its intensity of expression. It still belongs in the late Renaissance tradition of courtly entertainments, however; not until the coming of the public opera houses do we find operas treating human characters in a fully human way.

Soon after the performances of *Orfeo*, Monteverdi must himself have longed for the powers of an Orpheus, for his wife Claudia died. It is appropriate that his next opera, *Arianna*, should have as its emotional focal point a great lament. In fact, only the lament survives; the rest of the music is lost. This lament won Monteverdi still greater fame for its passionate expression of grief, and was also published as a madrigal. Later in the year of the work's performance (1608) Monteverdi sought to retire from the service of the Gonzaga family, apparently because of depression and overwork; he was refused. But in 1612 his employer died, and the new duke released him. After a spell in Cremona, he was invited to Venice, the richest and most independent city of Italy, where he accepted the important post of *maestro di cappella*.

Venice

One reason for the invitation may have been that he was already known as a skillful and original composer of church music. In 1610 he had published a collection of music for the Vespers service; it was printed in Venice, dedicated to the pope. Here again Monteverdi draws on new techniques to give the work greater impact: this was all the more revolutionary in that they came from a world of emotional and dramatic music and were not in the accepted church manner. He reserved his most conservative writing for the Mass setting in the collection; this is in the traditional imitative style, carefully and elaborately worked. The treatment is austere, with no madrigal-like illustrative word-setting. This style Monteverdi called the *prima prattica* ("first practice"); the new style he called *seconda prattica* ("second practice"). In the motet movements he moves fully to *seconda prattica*, using a free, ornamental melodic line with the same kinds of expressive dissonance and color as in his operas. Monteverdi's *Vespers* – his most important church work – decisively brought Baroque expressive principles into sacred music.

At St Mark's, Venice, Monteverdi's first task was to reorganize an inefficient music establishment. He engaged new, younger musicians, improved the pay, and brought the music library up to date. He was appreciated and his salary was raised. Venice suffered from an epidemic of the plague in 1630–31; when it passed, Monteverdi wrote a Mass in thanksgiving. A little later, he took holy orders.

Monteverdi turned back to the madrigal in his early Venetian years. The sixth book (1614) includes two long laments (including the one from *Arianna*): his feeling for the effect of harsh, unexpected dissonance gives his laments an often heart-rending force. The seventh book has a much wider range of types, from monodies to duets (some of his most tuneful pieces) and works for larger groups with instruments. An eighth book is divided between "songs of war" and "songs of love". The "songs of war" reflect Monteverdi's theories about the "humors" - linked with early medical ideas – and their representation in music; they use what Monteverdi called the *stile concitato* ("agitated style"), with rapid repeated notes, or fanfare-like patterns, often for several singers together, producing a vigorous, aggressive effect. The battles mentioned in the texts, however, are often symbolic of love and amorous conquest.

These theories, even if curious, lead to some of Monteverdi's most intense and passionate music. In these works, and a further collection issued after his death, the old concept of the polyphonic madrigal gives way to a much freer kind of composition, of any length and for any performers, vocal or instrumental. The eighth book even includes a ballet from his Mantua days and a stage entertainment, *The Combat of Tancred and Clorinda*, which significantly tells of a fight between a crusader and his lover, disguised as a man, giving opportunity for music in both the warlike and (as, at the end, Clorinda dies) amorous vein.

Last years

In his last years Monteverdi turned to opera again. As we have seen, the first Venetian opera houses opened in 1637, and he composed, it seems, three operas before his death in 1643. One is lost and there are doubts about whether all the music in the others is in fact his. The last is *The Coronation of Poppaea*, on the story of the Roman emperor Nero and his lover Poppaea. It is presented as a story about the power of love – Nero's, illicit though it is, for Poppaea – and how it transforms people's lives. Love triumphs over morality, and, with Monteverdi's music to support it, the listener is bound to be won over and to believe that the values of love override all others. Again, Monteverdi harnesses a wide range of styles to drive home his expressive points. Nero and Poppaea sing amorous duets, in the manner of those in some of the madrigal collections. Octavia, the empress whom Nero renounces in Poppaea's favor, sings in the style of the monodists, using Monteverdi's full resource of dissonance to convey her bitterness and grief. The servants take semi-comic roles, to provide relief: they sing frivolous ditties about their love, in the manner of Monteverdi's light, miniature madrigals. There is even a madrigal-like number when the friends of the philosopher Seneca, told by Nero to kill himself, beg him not to die. In the theater, the opera is effective not only because of the musical resource that Monteverdi uses but above all because it is true to life: there are not, as in the mythological operas, characters that are wholly good or wholly evil, but rather a selection of human beings, all flawed, victims of forces they cannot control. Monteverdi's great achievement, here as in his other music, is to realize so powerfully the underlying emotions.

Northern Europe: early–middle Baroque

Schütz

If any composer can be regarded as the north European counterpart to Monteverdi, it is Heinrich Schütz. Like Monteverdi, he wrote nothing but vocal music, though in Schütz's case the sacred far predominated over the secular. This to some extent reflects the differences between German and Italian life; for during much of Schütz's lifetime Germany, as we have seen, was riven by the Thirty Years War, her courts were impoverished, and in times of stress religious observation and consolation were more important than secular entertainment.

Schütz was born in Saxony in 1585. When he was 13, the ruler of Hesse-Kassel, the Landgrave Moritz, stayed at the inn owned by the Schütz family, heard the boy sing, and invited him to join his choir at the Kassel court. Then the Landgrave offered him the opportunity to go to Italy to study with Giovanni Gabrieli. He went in 1609, and soon became a favorite pupil. Schütz became *Kapellmeister* to the ruler of Saxony, at Dresden, in 1618 or 1619. His job involved providing music for major ceremonies, religious or secular, and supervising the musical establishment, the largest in Protestant Germany.

Schütz remained there for the rest of his working life, though he had several spells away, including one in Venice, where he met Monteverdi. His life, however, was unhappy. He lost his wife after six years of marriage, and his two daughters both died before he did. On a professional plane, he had terrible difficulties because of the impoverishment of the Dresden court caused by the war and its aftermath; many of his musicians were dismissed, and those that remained were not paid. So he tried several times to move or retire. Not until 1657, when he was over 70, was he released from daily responsibilities. But he continued composing, and some of his most original works date from his very last years. He died in Dresden in 1672.

Apart from a few early works, Schütz's entire output is sacred. He made less use of the chorale repertory than most German Protestant composers, preferring to compose freely. He wrote numerous psalm settings, some simple, some elaborate; he wrote many motets, some of which he called "sacred symphonies" or "little sacred concertos"; and he wrote works for the major seasons of the church year, like settings of the Christmas story and the Passion.

In some respects Schütz was conservative; many of his motets are in the older polyphonic manner, though they usually have features that show their composer to be familiar with a more modern approach, for example in their variety of pace or their striking treatment of crucial words. Often Schütz used a simple style because he had limited performers at his command. The somber Passion settings of his old age reflect the dark times in which he lived. He has fairly been called the first great German composer.

56 Musical scene including (*left to right*) the musicians Johann Theile, Johann Adam Reincken, and Dietrich Buxtehude: painting, 1674, by Johannes Voorhout. Museum für Hamburgische Geschichte, Hamburg.

Buxtehude

Schütz had a reputation as an organist, but as far as we know he wrote no music for his instrument (or indeed for any other). Yet northern Europe in the seventeenth century was a productive region as far as instrumental music was concerned, keyboard music in particular. The leading northern keyboard composer was Dietrich Buxtehude (*c*1637–1707), who worked in north Germany and regarded himself as Danish. In 1668 he became organist of St Mary's, Lübeck – an important post in a "free", Hanseatic city, ruled (like Hamburg) not by a local princeling but by the city fathers. There he revived an old practice of giving public concerts in the church (*Abendmusik*, "Evening music"). They were widely admired, and when Bach was a young man at Arnstadt he walked hundreds of miles to hear some of them and in particular to hear Buxtehude play the organ.

It is for his organ music that he is mainly remembered. About half consists of chorale preludes, in which a familiar Lutheran hymn is used in some way, and the rest are toccatas and fugues, often in a brilliant, improvisatory style. No composer had a greater influence on the organ music of Bach.

England

The flowering of music in England during the late sixteenth century and the early seventeenth, in the madrigal, the ayre, sacred music, keyboard and ensemble music, lent the country a natural resistance to the extremes of the Italian Baroque. Also against it were the undemonstrative English temperament and the Puritan tendencies of the times. The situation in architecture was similar: the Baroque spirit is rare in England, though it is to be found in St Paul's Cathedral, built by Sir Christopher Wren in London at the end of the seventeenth century in imitation of Italian churches, or in the flamboyant Blenheim Palace, built near Oxford for the Churchill family in the early eighteenth by Sir John Vanbrugh.

In music, English equivalents began to develop of the new Italian genres and styles. The monodic song, whose mannered diction anyway did not suit the English language, found a parallel in a newly florid type of song. The *concertato* motet of the Italians is paralleled by the Anglican verse anthem in which solo verses alternate with passages for the whole choir. Opera was slow to take root, but at court and later in the public theaters a mixed type developed, called "masque", owing more to French courtly entertainments than to Italian opera, including poetry, music, dance and lavish scenery. These came to a decisive end – as did the king himself – in the Commonwealth period from 1649; court and cathedral appointments for musicians were abolished and theatrical events discouraged. The monarchy was however restored in 1660, the year after Henry Purcell was born.

Purcell

Purcell is one of that small group of enormously talented composers, including Mozart and Schubert, who developed rapidly and died young. He was trained first as a choirboy in the Chapel Royal (the king's musical establishment) in London; a song was published as his when he was eight. At 15 he was appointed to tune the organ at Westminster Abbey; at 18 he became a composer to the royal band; and at 20 he was named organist of Westminster Abbey. In 1682 he also became a Chapel Royal organist. He had begun in 1680 supplying music for use in the London theaters, and from then on divided his time between religious music and theatrical, writing songs, chamber music and keyboard pieces too. He died at 36, in 1695, recognized and mourned as a great composer.

Purcell was a highly original composer too. His command of melody was exceptional for its freedom, its readiness to take its rhythm and shape from the sound and sense of the

Henry Purcell	Life
1659	born in southern England
1660s	chorister in the Chapel Royal
1674–8	organ tuner at Westminster Abbey, London
1677	composer to the royal band
1679	organist of Westminster Abbey
1680	fantasias for strings published; composed first "welcome" song and first music for the theater
1682	organist of the Chapel Royal
1683	organ maker and master of the king's instruments
1685	anthem *My heart is inditing* composed for James II's coronation
1689	*Dido and Aeneas* performed in Chelsea
1695	died in London, 21 November

Henry Purcell	Works

Opera Dido and Aeneas (1689)

Other music for the stage 5 semi-operas – King Arthur (1691), The Fairy Queen (1692), The Indian Queen (1695); incidental music and songs for plays

Secular choral music court odes – Come, ye sons of art, away (for Mary II's birthday, 1694); odes for St Cecilia's Day – Hail, bright Cecilia (1692); welcome songs – Sound the trumpet (for James II, 1687)

Sacred choral music c55 verse anthems, c16 full anthems; Te Deum and Jubilate (1694); services

Instrumental music fantasias for strings – Fantasia upon One Note (c1680), 9 fantasias (1680); Sonatas in 3 Parts (1683); Sonatas in 4 Parts (1697); March and Canzona for 4 slide trumpets (for Mary II's funeral, 1695); overture, In Nomines

Keyboard music suites, marches, grounds, hornpipes, dances for harpsichord

Songs   *Vocal duets*

words; harmonically, he was unusually enterprising, with unexpected chords, often to underline a crucial word.

Among his earliest works are some "fantasias" – music for string instruments, probably viols. Their style is essentially that of the Renaissance polyphonists, but more instrumental, with bold rhythms and harmonies, changes of key and contrasts of speed; vivacious music is set against music that is grave in mood. Purcell's other important ensemble works are his trio sonatas. He published 12 in 1683, for the more modern combination of two violins, bass viol and harpsichord or organ. Purcell said that he composed them "in imitation of the most fam'd Italian masters", and although some passages are very like those in the fantasias many others use a more brilliant and up-to-date violin style and the feeling of the music is more harmonic. Ten more were printed after his death.

In the field of sacred music, Purcell was working in a long and conservative tradition. His anthems are mostly in the verse anthem form, and the most characteristic are those that also call for orchestra. Here Purcell tends towards the Italian *concertato* style. The individuality of his contribution lies mainly in the rhythmic life and harmonic boldness of his finest examples, and in the way in which he widened the expressive resources of

Engish church music by using the same kinds of device as in theatrical works (much as Monteverdi had).

As a composer of dramatic music Purcell was particularly gifted. Had he lived longer he might have created a tradition of English opera that could have resisted the international prestige of Italian opera (which, as we shall see, was to be the ruling form in the London musical theater). As it was, he wrote a great many songs and dances to be given in plays, one true opera and a handful of "semi-operas". These last, which include *The Fairy Queen*, based on an adaptation of Shakespeare's *A Midsummer Night's Dream*, are extended entertainments, mainly spoken drama but with musical sections of some substance at several points. In *The Fairy Queen* each of the five acts ends with a group of songs and choruses, some with dances. The music is thinly justified by the action, but revivals have shown that the form works well in the theater, with the music resolving the tensions of the drama.

Purcell's only true opera was composed not for professionals but for a girls' school. This is the miniature masterpiece *Dido and Aeneas* (1689), which relates the story of Aeneas, fleeing from the destruction of Troy, falling in love with Queen Dido of Carthage and then having to leave her when the gods summon him to Italy (his mission is to found a new Troy, which is to be Rome). The music depicts Dido's court at Carthage, a hunt, a coven of witches and a sailors' scene. There are choruses, dances, recitatives and a variety of songs, several using ground bass (see p.48), a favorite scheme of Purcell's and one he handled with particular art. The opera's climax is tragic – Dido's proud dismissal of her lover and her death, which follows her famous lament (see Listening Note VI.B).

Purcell composed everything from bawdy catches to impassioned prayers, intimate

57 Henry Purcell: portrait, 1695, attributed to John Clostermann. National Portrait Gallery, London.

Listening Note VI.B   *Side 3, band 2*

Purcell: *Dido and Aeneas* (1689), Act 3, ''When I am laid in earth''

Dramatic context: Dido, Queen of Carthage, has declared that she loves Aeneas, the Trojan prince who escaped the sack of Troy, and they have married; but the very next day Aeneas is summoned to Italy to fulfill his destiny. He has to leave his new bride, ''One night enjoy'd, the next forsook''. Dido, deserted and humiliated, looks forward to death in this famous lament.

The music: Like many Baroque laments, this song is constructed on a ground bass (see p.48). The phrase shown in ex. i is repeated throughout; its falling chromatic scale, from G to D, is a traditional elegiac device.

Thy hand, Belinda; darkness shades me	When I am laid in earth,
On thy bosom let me rest;	May my wrongs create
More I would, but Death invades me:	No trouble in thy breast;
Death is now a welcome guest.	Remember me, but ah! forget my fate.

(words by Nahum Tate)

Time
0:00	"Thy hand ...", recitative	2:52	instrumental interlude
0:47	orchestra plays descending bass line	2:56	"Remember me"
1:12	"When I am laid in earth"	4:41	instrumental conclusion
1:58	instrumental interlude	5:31	(end)
2:04	"When I am ..."		

ex. i

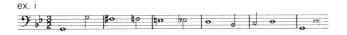

chamber music to ceremonial court odes, fresh melodies and dances to elegiac laments. It is perhaps in the expression of the darker moods, grief, pathos and despair, that he proved himself even in so brief a life the greatest English composer of the Baroque and perhaps of any era.

France

The connections between France and Italy were historically strong. Two French kings had married ladies of the important Medici family from Florence, and these queens had imported Italian artists of various sorts to Paris; it was through this influence that ballet became popular in Paris at the end of the sixteenth century and that the new recitative style arrived (with a visit from Caccini) in the early seventeenth. Italian opera was introduced in the middle of the seventeenth century, with limited success (in spite of a visit from Francesco Cavalli, the leading Italian opera composer of the generation after Monteverdi, in 1660). The time was ripe for the establishment of French opera, for the devising of a style that took account of the French taste for dramatic entertainment, including ballet and giving due weight to the traditions of French theater. The man who accomplished that, paradoxically, was an Italian.

Lully

Giovanni Battista Lulli, born in Florence in 1632, went to Paris in 1646; he was not yet 14. As Jean-Baptiste Lully, he worked as a boy attendant to a noblewoman at court. He became a skilled violinist, guitarist, harpsichordist and dancer, and it was in that last capacity that he met the young king, Louis XIV. His fame grew rapidly and he advanced from one post to another, becoming music master to the royal family in 1662. Ten years later he had consolidated his position by obtaining the sole rights over all dramatic performances with singing. His musical absolutism was on a par with the king's political absolutism.

Lully attained this position largely by clever manipulation. But he did also create a new French dramatic musical style. He wrote mainly ballets at first, including songs that embody an adaptation of Italian recitative to the French language – which lacks the accentuation system of Italian (and most other languages) so falls less naturally into metric patterns. Lully's recitative is constantly changing in meter. In the late 1660s and early 1670s he wrote mainly ballet comedies, working with the well-known dramatist Molière; from then on he concentrated on classical tragedies, working with famous dramatists like Quinault and Corneille. In all these works the music seems restricted, compared with its Italian counterpart, by the rhythms of the language and its vowel sounds (which give little scope for florid singing). But there are also dance scenes and choruses, and the acts generally end with a decorative scene barely relevant to the action. Possibly Lully tailored the new French operatic form as much to his own abilities, or their limitations, as to the French taste. But it worked, and the traditions he laid down lasted long after his death and continued to influence the patterns of French opera for two hundred years or more.

Lully held no official appointment in the royal chapel, but he wrote a certain amount of sacred music, especially motets of a ceremonial kind which seem to praise the magnificence of Louis XIV (whose supposed virtues were hinted at in the heroes of his operas) just as much as that of God. He died in Paris in 1687.

58 Scene from Lully's opera *Phaëton*, first performed at Versailles on 9 January 1683: pen and wash drawing, school of Berain. Bibliothèque de l'Opéra, Paris.

Couperin

The most important and most gifted French composer in the first three decades of the eighteenth century was François Couperin. He was born in Paris in 1668, into a family of organists and harpsichordists. When he was 25, François was appointed a royal organist, and soon was in demand in court circles as a teacher; later he was also harpsichordist in the royal chamber music. He died in Paris in 1733.

Couperin's greatness lies in his perfection of the French chamber and harpsichord music

59 Part of the Table of Ornaments from Couperin's *Pièces de clavecin ... premier livre* (1713).

idioms. His chamber works consist of several sonatas, among the earliest written in France under that title, for two violins (or wind instruments) and continuo, in which he tried to bridge the gulf between the French and Italian traditions. The Italian sonata composers tended to write in a more brilliant and forceful manner, more rhythmic, more contrapuntal than the French, who were chiefly concerned with dance-like rhythms and delicately ornamented lines. He even wrote sonatas in honor of Lully and Corelli (see p. 119), twin masters of the French and Italian styles, and in some of the movements portrayed in picturesque terms the reception of the composers into Parnassus (or heaven). Couperin's other chamber works include music written for the Sunday afternoon concerts that he directed before Louis XIV.

As a harpsichord composer Couperin was unrivaled. He wrote some 225 pieces, grouped in suites according to key and, to some extent, mood. Each has a title: it might be a name of some particular person, or a state of mind, or a familiar institution, or a natural phenomenon like a plant or animal, or indeed anything else. A few simply have dance titles. The pieces are in a sense little portraits, though it would be wrong to take their "meanings" too seriously. Their ornamentation may be seen as analogous to the florid Rococo decoration of French art and furniture of the Louis XIV period and the Regency that followed. Couperin himself may best be compared to Jean-Antoine Watteau (1684–1721) for the refinement of his art and the expression of serious emotion behind a highly polished surface. Many of his pieces are charming, even frivolous, and some are gracefully pictorial; many are pathetic, grave, mysterious or noble.

Rameau

Lully's greatest successor as a dramatic composer was Jean-Philippe Rameau. Born in Dijon in 1683, Rameau began his career as an organist and theorist. He held posts in various cities and settled in Paris only in 1722–3 where he soon published collections of harpsichord music and theoretical books that earned him a reputation as an original and controversial thinker.

As a composer, Rameau's ambitions lay in the theater. But not until he was 50 was his first opera, *Hippolyte et Aricie*, given, at the Paris Opéra. It follows up the Lullian tradition of tragedy; Rameau went on to write several more, and he also composed in the other French theatrical forms, in particular the *opéra-ballet* (which is little more than a series of scenes loosely strung together, with dance playing a large part). When he died, at the age of 81, his last opera was in rehearsal. But he is said to have cared more about his theories than his compositions; he was eager to interpret music in line with the rationalist, scientific outlook of his time.

Jean-Philippe Rameau   Works
born Dijon, 1683; *died* Paris, 1764

Operas (*c*30) Hippolyte et Aricie (1733), Les Indes galantes (1735), Castor et Pollux (1737)
Keyboard music 65 pieces for harpsichord
Chamber music 5 pieces for harpsichord and 2 instruments (1741)
Sacred choral music motets
Cantatas

Although he wrote many further operas, Rameau did not surpass his achievement in *Hippolyte et Aricie*. Following the usual French pattern, it is a five-act opera with an allegorical prologue about the power of love. It is based on Greek mythology and on a play by the classical French dramatist Racine. The plot concerns the adulterous love of Phaedra, second wife of King Theseus, for her stepson Hippolytus, who in turn loves Aricia.

Unlike Italian operas of the time, where there are clear breaks between recitative (where the action takes place) and aria (where a character expresses his or her feelings), French opera has a relatively continuous texture. The recitative imitates the rise and fall of speech in a formal, declamatory manner, while the arias are usually brief and rarely lyrical in character, with no vocal flourishes and little repetition of words.

Rameau is at his most powerful in scenes like the one following Hippolytus's death, which gives scope for the expression of strong feelings. His style, in which – following

Listening Note VI.C   *Side 3, band 3*

Rameau: *Hippolyte et Aricie* (1733), closing scene of Act 4

Dramatic context: While Theseus, King of Athens, is away, his wife Phaedra has fallen in love with Hippolytus, Theseus's son by a previous marriage. Hippolytus loves Aricia and rejects Phaedra, who asks him to kill her and seizes his sword; as he snatches it back Theseus returns. Phaedra allows him to think that Hippolytus was forcing his attentions on her (which Hippolytus is too honorable to deny). Accordingly, Theseus asks his father, Neptune, god of the seas, to punish Hippolytus. Hippolytus is (apparently) killed by a sea-monster sent by Neptune.

The music: The scene is in three sections. First: Phaedra enters and learns the situation from the hunters, who witnessed Hippolytus's disappearance in his fight with the monster; she sings in straightforward recitative. Second: Phaedra gives vent to her feelings; claps of thunder and the shaking of the earth are represented by the orchestra, and her vocal line is freer and more vivid. Third: she returns to a more formal manner of recitative as she addresses the gods.

PHAEDRA

Time		
0:00	Quelle plainte en ces lieux m'appelle?	What complaint calls me to this place?

CHORUS
(huntsmen and huntswomen)

| 0:07 | Hippolyte n'est plus. | Hippolytus is no more. |

PHAEDRA

| 0:14 | Il n'est plus! ô douleur mortelle! | He is no more! oh mortal grief! |

CHORUS

| 0:23 | O regrets superflus! | O vain regrets! |

PHAEDRA

| 0:26 | Quel sort l'a fait tomber dans la nuit éternelle? | What fate made him fall into eternal night? |

CHORUS

| 0:34 | Un monstre furieux, sorti du sein des flots, | A raging monster, rising from the depths of the waves, |
| | Vient de nous ravir ce héros. | Has just snatched the hero from us. |

PHAEDRA

0:48	Non, sa mort est mon seul ouvrage.	No, his death is caused by me alone.
	Dans les Enfers c'est par moi qu'il descend.	It is because of me that he is descending into the underworld.
	Neptune de Thésée a cru venger l'outrage.	Neptune thought he would avenge Theseus's wrong.
1:26	J'ai versé le sang innocent.	I have shed innocent blood.
	Qu'ai-je fait? Quels remords!	What have I done? What remorse!
	Ciel! J'entends le tonnerre.	Heavens! I hear thunder.
	Quel bruit! quels terribles éclats!	What noise! what terrible thunderclaps!
	Fuyons! où me cacher?	I must flee! where shall I hide?
	Je sens trembler la terre.	I feel the earth shake.
	Les Enfers s'ouvrent sous mes pas.	Hell gapes beneath me.
	Tous les dieux, conjurés	All the gods, conspiring
	Pour me livrer la guerre,	To wage war on me,
	Arment leurs redoutables bras.	Arm their redoubtable hands.
2:18	Dieux cruels, vengeurs implacables!	Cruel gods, implacable avengers!
	Suspendez un courroux qui me glace d'effroi!	Hold back your wrath which freezes me with terror!
2:55	Ah! si vous êtes équitables,	Ah! if you are fair,
	Ne tonnez pas encore sur moi!	Thunder on me no longer!
	La gloire d'un héros que l'injustice opprime,	The glory of a hero oppressed by injustice,
	Vous demande un juste secours.	Demands due relief from you.
3:50	Laissez-moi révéler à l'auteur de ses jours	Let me reveal to his progenitor
	Et son innocence et mon crime!	Both his innocence and my guilt!

CHORUS

4:09   O remords superflus! Hippolyte n'est plus!   O vain remorse! Hippolytus is no more!

4:47   (words by Simon-Joseph Pellegrin)

his own theories – a dissonance should sound on every chord, if possible, except the tonic of the home key, lends itself to the expression of anguish (see Listening Note VI.C). By contrast, the other most striking feature of any Rameau opera is the dance music. He brought remarkable originality to the dance rhythms of French music, in his melodies, his harmonies and his orchestration; these pieces are sometimes quirky and angular, sometimes warm and sensuous, always in some way piquant and emotionally suggestive.

60 Interior of the Teatro Regio, Turin, during a performance of Francesco Feo's opera *Arsace*: painting, 1740, by Pietro Domenico Olivero. Museo Civico d'Arte Antico, Turin.

The Italian late Baroque

Alessandro Scarlatti

The early and middle Baroque in Italy were times of experiment and novelty. The late Baroque was a time of ripening and fulfillment. With firmly established forms, composers were encouraged to invent new ideas. Alessandro Scarlatti was the chief representative of vocal music as the middle Baroque moves to the late; in instrumental music Corelli stands for the establishment of the late Baroque ideal and Vivaldi and Domenico Scarlatti its final phase.

61 Interior of a typical Venetian theater in the 18th century: engraving from the satire *I viaggi d'Enrico Wanton* (1749) by Zaccaria Seriman.

Alessandro Scarlatti was one of the most prolific composers of the era. Born in Sicily in 1660, he went to Rome as a boy; he was not yet 20 when his first opera was given there. He worked for several of the wealthy musical patrons in the city. In 1684 he moved (after a family scandal) to Naples, where he became *maestro di cappella* to the viceroy; he remained there for most of his life, composing operas at a phenomenal pace – he claimed that an

opera of 1705 was his 88th stage work – and was busy too writing cantatas, oratorios and other pieces. He died in Naples in 1725.

Scarlatti wrote some 600 cantatas, mostly for solo voice and continuo. The totally free, monody-style setting of the early 17th century had passed; Scarlatti and his contemporaries used a more organized design, usually alternating recitative and aria. Often there would be a section in a style between recitative and aria, suitable for the expression of strong emotion. Most cantatas dealt with the unrequited love of a shepherd for a shepherdess (or vice-versa), so that the music would express such feelings as love and yearning, jealousy and forgiveness.

The move towards more regular patterns is even more marked in operas of the time. In an early Scarlatti opera there may be as many as 60 arias, all quite brief, with recitative in between and occasional ensemble items (usually at the ends of acts). Some of the arias are in *A–B* form, or *A–B–B′* (*B′* being *B* modified). But by the 1690s the *A–B–A* design was standard. This allowed for longer arias, better developed and so better able to convey serious emotion. It also allowed the virtuoso singer, who was becoming increasingly important, to show his abilities in the repeat of the *A* section by adding expressive embellishment. As the individual arias increased in length, so the number of them in an opera decreased.

Those trends are also found in the works of other composers. Scarlatti, however, was the most gifted of his time, with a particularly graceful vein of melody and sensitivity to words. He was important in the development of the opera overture, which by the 1690s normally consisted of three short movements, fast–slow–fast; this was eventually to lead to the symphony of the Classical period.

Corelli

In instrumental music, Arcangelo Corelli had an importance akin to Alessandro Scarlatti's and a reputation unrivaled in his time. Born near Bologna in 1653, he went to study in that city in 1666 and to Rome nine years later, where he quickly became prominent among local violinists and played for the leading musical patrons. He died in 1713.

Corelli published six sets of works: his op. 1 and op. 3 are church sonatas, his op. 2 and op. 4 are chamber sonatas, his op. 5 is a set of violin solo sonatas, and his op. 6 a set of concertos. Each publication contains 12 separate works. The establishment of the slow–fast–slow–fast movement pattern for church sonatas was largely due to Corelli. His style was long and widely regarded as a model for its purity and formal balance. The trio sonatas, for two violins and continuo, strike a classical balance between the instruments and obtain much of their musical momentum through dissonance – the tension helps propel the music onwards. His smooth, graceful melodic style is evident in the op. 5 violin sonatas, which also show the measure of his virtuosity. The concertos are for two violins and cello with a larger string body; in style they are like trio sonatas in which some of the music is played solo and some by a larger group. They are old-fashioned in form compared with the concertos of Vivaldi, but their dignity, integrity and melodic charm (typified by the famous Christmas Concerto, op. 6 no. 8) lend them a timeless quality.

Vivaldi

While Corelli represents the conservative development of the late Baroque concerto, Antonio Vivaldi represents its progressive development. His concertos, which number about 500, are one of the peaks of the Italian Baroque. Vivaldi was born in Venice in 1678, the son of a violinist. He was trained as a priest and ordained in 1703, though on grounds of health he was soon granted dispensation from saying Mass. Meanwhile he had become a skilled violinist and sometimes deputized for his father in the orchestra at St Mark's. In 1703 he obtained his first musical appointment, as master of the violin at one of the

Venetian orphanages, the Hospital of Piety. This was one of four institutions in Venice which took in orphaned, abandoned or poor girls and educated them, and in particular trained them in music. Its orchestra was well known for its skill; several visitors reported on its concerts, during which the girls were discreetly shielded from the audience's view to avoid any impropriety. Vivaldi worked there, with brief breaks, for some 15 years, during which time he wrote many concertos and sacred music for the girls. His reputation grew, in Italy and abroad: he had some of his best concertos published, was sought out by visitors and received commissions to write concertos for performance elsewhere.

Vivaldi's father was involved in opera-house management, and it was probably this connection that led Vivaldi himself into the world of opera – both its composition and its management. He wrote over 45 operas, several for Venice but many for other cities in north Italy as well as Rome and Prague. This involved him in much travel and long periods away from Venice, during which he kept in contact with the hospital and even sent concertos by post. But his appointment was discontinued because of the continual absences. In 1740 he went to Austria, and there he died.

Antonio Vivaldi   Works
born Venice, 1678; *died* Vienna, 1741

Concertos (*c*500) *c*230 violin concertos, *c*70 orchestral concertos, *c*80 double and triple concertos – L'estro armonico, op. 3 (1712); La stravaganza, op. 4 (*c*1713); Il cimento dell'armonia e dell'inventione, op. 8 (*c*1725) [Le quattro stagioni, "The four seasons"]; *c*100 bassoon, cello, oboe and flute concertos
Operas (over 45) Orlando finto pazzo (1714), Giustino (1724), Griselda (1735)
Sacred choral music 3 oratorios – Juditha triumphans (1716); Mass movements – Glorias; psalm settings, motets
Chamber music Il pastor fido, op. 13 (The faithful shepherd, *c*1737: sonatas for 5 instruments and continuo); violin sonatas, cello sonatas; trio sonatas; chamber concertos
*Secular vocal music c*40 solo cantatas

As an opera composer Vivaldi is of modest importance. His church music at its best has great vigor and, like his opera airs, shows the influence of the concerto style; a notable piece is the *Gloria* in D.

It is as an instrumental composer, particularly of concertos, that Vivaldi was – and is today – chiefly famous. Of his 500, close on half are for solo violin; others are for solo bassoon, cello, oboe or flute, and about 150 have more than one soloist or are "orchestral concertos" (i.e. have no solo parts). A few are chamber concertos, without orchestra. The music itself is marked by its sheer energy, its driving momentum and its strong rhythms. Vivaldi's opening themes are nearly always direct and memorable, and their memorability is important because the themes need to be recognized if the form of the music is to be grasped. The Violin Concerto in A minor, no. 6 of the set he published in 1712 as his op. 3, *L'estro armonico* ("Musical fancy"), shows Vivaldi's vigorous style at its best, and illustrates well too his handling of ritornello form, which he normally used for the outer movements of his concertos (see Listening Note VI.D).

Vivaldi wrote a number of "programmatic" concertos – works that tell a story in their music, or at least carry some meaning outside the music itself. There is for example "The Night", with dark and sinister effects (this is a bassoon concerto); and "The Storm at Sea". The most famous of his concertos of this type is the group *The Four Seasons*, which Vivaldi

---

Listening Note VI.D   *Side 3, band 4*

Vivaldi: *Violin Concerto* in A minor, op. 3 no. 6 (1712)
solo violin; strings (1st and 2nd violins, viola, cello, violone), continuo

1st movement (Allegro): Ritornello form, a
The movement begins with an orchestral ritornello, tutti I, using the theme in ex. i. This is
followed by the arpeggiated figure, ex. ii. The solo violin enters playing the theme of ex. i.
Orchestra and solo alternate until the final orchestral tutti closes the movement.

Time	
0:00	tutti I (opening ritornello), a, ex. i
0:13	ex. ii
0:26	solo I, ex. i
0:43	tutti II, a
0:50	solo II
1:14	tutti III (central ritornello), e
1:36	solo III
2:04	tutti IV (final ritornello begins), a
2:09	interruption for solo IV
2:26	tutti V (final ritornello resumes)
2:33	interruption for solo V
2:42	tutti VI (final ritornello ends)
2:55	(end)

2nd movement (Largo), d: solo violin in free, florid style, accompanied by violins and
violas

3rd movement (Presto), a: Ritornello form

ex. i

ex. ii

---

included in a set he published in about 1725 as op. 8, with the fanciful title *Il cimento
dell'armonia e dell'inventione* ("The contest between harmony and invention"). These go
further than the others: their music represents phenomena associated with each season –
birdsong in the spring, for example, summer thunderstorms, harvesting in the fall, shivering
and skating in winter. Yet the basis of the concerto form remains unchanged, for it is in
the solo music (these are violin concertos) that Vivaldi generally depicts the changing
events in the story he is telling.

Vivaldi's gifts had a certain brilliance and waywardness. He brought to the concerto a
new tone of passion, a new vigor, a new awareness of instrumental color and of how to
exploit it. The freshness and clarity of his invention made his concertos attractive and
influential; many composers imitated and learned from them, the greatest being Bach.

**Domenico
Scarlatti**

Domenico Scarlatti, a son of Alessandro, is another composer whose influence and importance are confined to a single form. He was born in Naples in 1685, the same year as Bach
and Handel, and went in 1719 to Portugal where he worked in the royal chapel in Lisbon
until 1728. When the Portuguese princess married the Spanish crown prince, he left for
Madrid, remaining there until his death in 1757.

In Italy, under his father's watchful eye, Scarlatti composed in the standard vocal forms,
in which he produced music of no great originality. We do not know what he composed
in Lisbon because virtually all the music in the libraries there was destroyed in an earthquake
in 1755. In Madrid he seems to have devoted himself to sonatas for the harpsichord, of
which he composed about 550, each a one-movement piece in binary form.

These sonatas are unlike any other music of the time. They demand great brilliance on
the performer's part: the music ranges across the whole keyboard, often moving very
rapidly, with spectacular arpeggio figuration; other devices like hand-crossing, quick
repeated notes, fast scale passages and so on add to the dazzling effect. Scarlatti was clearly
influenced by the sounds of Spanish music: sometimes guitar-like strumming is heard, and
Spanish dance rhythms creep into some of the sonatas. Another feature, perhaps to be
linked with guitar music, is the repetition, many times over, of a brief phrase, producing
an almost nagging effect. Scarlatti's tendency to shift between major and minor is another
Spanish feature. His love of dissonance on the harpsichord, of the jangling sound that the
instrument can make in full chords including dissonant notes, gives his music a special
color. Sometimes this is obtained by the use of "crushed notes", or acciaccaturas, struck
with the chord but instantly released and thus adding bite.

Late Baroque Germany

In the late Baroque period Germany produced two of the greatest of all musical geniuses.
They had careers as different as can be imagined: one as a local organist, the other as an
international opera composer.

Bach

Between the middle of the sixteenth century and the middle of the nineteenth there were
more than 80 musicians in Germany who bore the name Bach. The ancestry of most of
them can be traced back to a Veit Bach, who settled in central Germany around the 1540s.
Seven generations later, eight Bachs were active as professional musicians, mostly church
organists. The last two died in 1845 and 1846. The area in which they chiefly lived was
Thuringia, a reasonably prosperous rural part of central Germany, firmly Lutheran in
faith, governed in small regions by dukes. Musical life flourished at the courts of the local
potentates and in civic institutions – the churches, first, but also the local town bands of
town pipers. The greatest member of the family, Johann Sebastian Bach, was born on 21
March 1685, the son of a town musician of Eisenach (trumpeter and director of the town
band).

Early years

J. S. Bach began his schooling in Eisenach, but when he was nine his mother and father
died and he went to Ohrdruf, where his elder brother was organist, attending a particularly
enlightened school there until he was 15. Then he went north to Lüneburg to a boarding
school, free to needy boys with good voices.

In 1702 Bach left Lüneburg. Appointments as organist at this time were normally open
to competition: Bach applied for one, won, and was offered the post, but the local duke

Johann Sebastian Bach		Life
1685	born in Eisenach, 21 March	
1700	chorister at St Michael, Lüneburg	
1703	organist at the New Church, Arnstadt	
1705–6	visited Lübeck to hear Buxtehude	
1707	organist at St Blasius, Mühlhausen; married Maria Barbara Bach	
1708	court organist in Weimar; prolific output of organ works	
1713	*Konzertmeister* at Weimar court, responsible for providing a new cantata every four weeks	
1717	*Kapellmeister* to Prince Leopold in Cöthen; many instrumental works, including Brandenburg Concertos, violin concertos, sonatas and keyboard music	
1720	Maria Barbara Bach died	
1721	married Anna Magdalena Wilcken	
1723	*Kantor* of St Thomas's School, Leipzig, supplying cantata for the main city churches each Sunday	
1727	*St Matthew Passion*	
1729	director of the *collegium musicum* in Leipzig	
1741	Berlin and Dresden; *Goldberg Variations*	
c1745	*The Art of Fugue*	
1747	visited Frederick the Great's court in Berlin; *Musical Offering*	
1749	B minor Mass	
1750	died in Leipzig, 28 July	

appointed an older man. Bach soon found a position at Weimar, as "lackey-musician" at the secondary court there (a junior post, as a servant with some musical duties). After a few months he obtained an appointment more fitted to his abilities, as organist of the New Church in Arnstadt; this was a minor church, the third in importance there. Bach did not stay long and does not seem to have been particularly content in Arnstadt. Once, in the company of his second cousin Barbara Catharina, he was involved in a fight after insulting a bassoonist; he was reprimanded, and told that his work was unsatisfactory – he got on badly with the choir and failed to rehearse them properly. Soon after, he was granted leave to go to Lübeck – some 250 miles away, a journey he made on foot – to hear Buxtehude play; he overstayed by almost three months, probably to hear *Abendmusik* performances (see p. 109) and possibly so that he could inquire about succeeding the 68-year-old Buxtehude. He was in trouble on his return, not only for his long absence but also for his still unsatisfactory work; the authorities complained that he introduced strange notes and elaborations into the hymns, making them difficult for the congregation to follow. And he was in trouble for bringing a young woman into the church.

Bach was soon looking elsewhere for a post. In the spring of 1707 he competed for the organistship of the St Blasius Church at Mühlhausen, about 35 miles away. He took up the appointment during the summer, and in the fall he was married, to his second cousin Maria Barbara Bach. He stayed there only briefly. The pastor was a strict Pietist who objected to any but the simplest music in church, and the congregation was conservative. Again, this was no place for a young musician whose brain and fingers teemed with new,

Johann Sebastian Bach	Works

Sacred choral music St John Passion (1724); St Matthew Passion (1727); Christmas Oratorio (1734); Mass, b (1749); Magnificat, D (1723); over 200 church cantatas – no. 80, Ein feste Burg ist unser Gott (*c*1744), no. 140, Wachet auf (1731); motets – Singet dem Herrn (1727), Jesu meine Freude (?1723); chorales, sacred songs, arias

Secular vocal music over 30 cantatas – no. 211, "Coffee Cantata" (*c*1735); no. 212, "Peasant Cantata" (1742)

Orchestral music Brandenburg Concertos nos. 1–6 (1721); 4 orchestral suites – C (*c*1725), b (*c*1731), D (*c*1731), D (1725); harpsichord concertos; sinfonias

Chamber music 6 sonatas and partitas for solo violin (1720); 6 sonatas for violin and harpsichord (1723); 6 suites for solo cello (*c*1720); Musikalisches Opfer (Musical offering, 1747); flute sonatas, trio sonatas

Keyboard music Chromatic fantasia and fugue, d (*c*1720); Das wohltemperirte Clavier (The well-tempered keyboard), "48" (1722, 1742); 6 English Suites (*c*1724); 6 French Suites (*c*1724); 6 Partitas (1731); Italian Concerto (1735); French Overture (1735); Goldberg Variations (1741); Die Kunst der Fuge (The art of fugue, *c*1745); inventions, suites, dances, toccatas, fugues, capriccios

Organ music over 600 chorale preludes; concertos, preludes, fugues, toccatas, fantasias, sonatas

imaginative ideas. So when he received an invitation to become court organist at Weimar, the following summer, he accepted – and, as he had done at Arnstadt, handed his old position to another member of the Bach family. He retained his connection with Mühlhausen; as an authority on organs, he was asked to see through the rebuilding he had initiated of the St Blasius instrument.

Weimar and Cöthen

Weimar was jointly ruled by a senior and a junior duke. Bach had previously been employed by the junior; now he was working for the senior, Duke Wilhelm Ernst, and in a much more important capacity. The duke admired his playing and encouraged him in composition. Many of Bach's organ works were written at Weimar, including most of those in the prelude-and-fugue (or toccata-and-fugue) category, in which a fairly free, often brilliant first section is followed by a fugue, along the Buxtehude model, as well as chorale preludes. One chorale prelude of the Weimar period is based on the Reformation hymn *Ein feste Burg* (see also p. 76 and p. 132). The opening of the prelude is typically original, with the melody elaborated and running off into rapid notes. The Arnstadt fathers may not have liked Bach's elaborations on hymns, but clearly the Weimar duke relished his ingenuity, especially as his settings of these chorales so often mirrored the sense of the words associated with them.

Bach was at Weimar until 1717. During his years there six of his children were born, including two who were to become composers, Wilhelm Friedemann (born in 1710) and Carl Philipp Emanuel (born in 1714 – see p. 148). He was active in teaching and in organ and harpsichord construction and repairs. In 1713 he applied for a post as organist at Halle, and was offered the position; but the duke gave Bach a salary increase and promoted him, with the duty of providing a new cantata every four weeks. Soon, however, something seems to have gone wrong. From 1716 there are few cantatas, and none from 1717. At the end of 1716 the old *Kapellmeister* died, and perhaps Bach expected to be promoted again; but he heard that the duke was looking elsewhere (the post was offered to the prolific and popular composer G. P. Telemann, of Hamburg, who declined). So Bach

Plate 5 *Opposite* Consort of viols at the court of Duke August the Younger: detail of the portrait *Duke August and Family, c*1645, by Albert Freyse. Landesmuseum, Brunswick. For German courts, see p. 101.

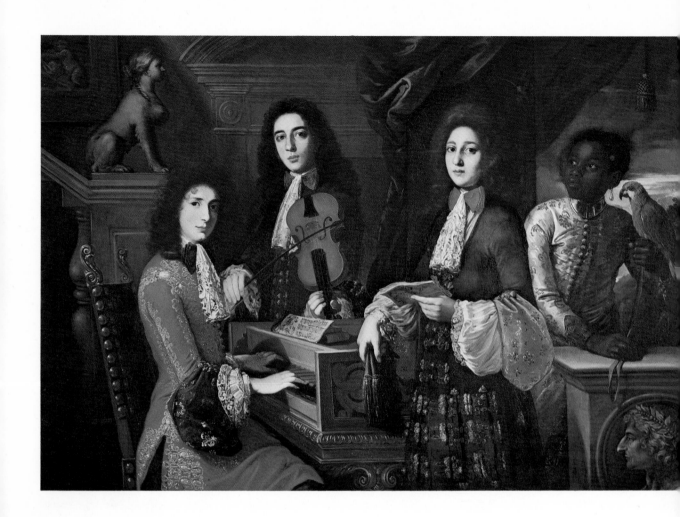

Plate 6 *Florentine Court
Musicians*: painting by
Anton Domenico Gabbiani
(1652–1726). Palazzo
Pitti, Florence. A cantata
with violin and harpsichord
(see pp. 51, 100).

sought a similar position, and was offered one by Prince Leopold of Cöthen. He applied in such strong terms for his release that the duke sent him to prison for four weeks and then dismissed him.

Bach must have been glad to move. At Weimar his employer was a strict disciplinarian who imposed puritanical standards on his employees. At Cöthen, Prince Leopold, a younger man, was a keen music-lover, a good amateur player, and a kind employer and good friend to Bach. By faith he was Calvinist, which meant that music played little part in worship. Bach wrote a few cantatas for special occasions but his chief duty was to provide music for his employer's entertainment and perhaps participation. Bach's life was active and varied. He was in demand for testing new organs, had trips to Berlin to buy a new harpsichord, and was one of the group of musicians (some five out of a payroll of 15) who accompanied Prince Leopold when he went to take the waters at a fashionable spa in Bohemia. It was during the second such visit, in 1720, that tragedy struck the family: he came back to find his wife, Maria Barbara, dead and buried. She was only 36, and left a family of four (two had died in infancy), aged eleven, nine, six and five. At the end of 1721, Bach remarried; his new wife, Anna Magdalena, was a singer at the court, and like his first wife came from local musical stock – her father was a court trumpeter at nearby Weissenfels. She was 20; Bach was 36. The marriage seems to have been happy, to judge by the tales of domestic music-making and the books he compiled for her of simple and tuneful keyboard pieces. It was certainly fruitful: she bore him 13 children, of whom six grew to maturity and two achieved fame as composers (Johann Christoph Friedrich, born in 1732, and Johann Christian, born in 1735 – see p.148).

In the month of Bach's marriage, his employer was also married. Leopold's new wife did not share his love for music, and from this time on Bach found his position at the court decreasing in importance. He had earlier considered leaving Cöthen: in 1720 he had applied for a post as organist in Hamburg, had played in the city (delighting Reincken, the 97-year-old organist of St Catherine's there, with his command of the traditional technique of improvising on a chorale melody), and had been offered the position; but he declined, possibly because a large donation to the church funds seems to have been expected of him.

A new opportunity came up in 1722, and closer at hand, in Leipzig, the largest city near the region where Bach had lived and worked. This was the post of *Kantor* of St Thomas's School, which carried with it the city directorship of music. The duties were heavy, but the prestige was high and the salary good. The *Kantor* was reponsible for music in the city's four principal churches, in two of which regular cantata performances with orchestra and choir were the rule. He also had to supervise other civic musical activities, compose music for special occasions like weddings or funerals as well as regular Sunday services, select the choirs and train the senior one himself, and teach music at the school. Other distinguished musicians applied for this post, and it was first offered to Telemann who however was persuaded to remain at Hamburg. The second choice was J. C. Graupner, *Kapellmeister* at Darmstadt and a former pupil of St Thomas's; but he too withdrew when the Darmstadt authorites offered him a salary increase to stay there. The third choice was Bach.

The instrumental music

Most of Bach's chamber and orchestral works belong to the Cöthen years, as well as much of his harpsichord music. Of these the best known are the Brandenburg Concertos, so called because Bach presented a manuscript of these six works to the Margrave of Brandenburg, who heard him play and asked to have some of his music. Probably they had been written for the Cöthen players.

During his Weimar years, Bach had become interested in the current styles of Italian instrumental music and had made arrangements, for solo harpsichord or organ, of orchestral concertos, chiefly by Vivaldi and other Venetian composers. His own concertos are to some extent modeled on these. He used the Vivaldian type of ritornello form (see p. 120), though he liked – in accordance with German tradition – fuller, more contrapuntal textures than Vivaldi's. He also followed German tradition in another way. While Vivaldi's published concertos (the only ones Bach had access to) were for strings, Bach liked to use wind instruments. He obviously enjoyed experimenting with instrumental combinations, as the layout of the Brandenburg Concertos shows:

no.	solo group (concertino)	tutti group (ripieno)
1	violin, 3 oboes, bassoon, 2 horns	strings, continuo
2	trumpet, recorder, oboe, violin	strings, continuo
3	3 violins, 3 violas, 3 cellos	the same used in unison, continuo
4	violin, 2 recorders	strings, continuo
5	violin, flute, harpsichord	strings, continuo
6	2 violas, cello	the violas used in unison, 2 bass viols, continuo

The schemes for all the concertos are unusual. The first two are the most colorful, with their wind groups: in no. 1 some of Bach's musical ideas are so devised that dialogues between horns, woodwinds and strings help propel the music, while in no. 2 he secures variety by pairing the soloists in all possible combinations. No. 3 departs in another way, by treating the groups of three as solo players, each with different music to play, in the solo sections but having them play the same music, in unison, in the tuttis; the contrast is thus between emphatic tuttis and gentle, multi-strand music in the solo episodes. No. 6 works on a similar principle, and draws a special character from the absence of violins, so that its colors are dusky and veiled. No. 5 represents another important departure. Usually the role of the keyboard in orchestral or chamber music was to play a filling-in continuo part. Here the harpsichord is one of the solo team, and even has a lengthy cadenza in the first movement. The work is one of the earliest keyboard concertos. No. 4 is almost a violin concerto; the two recorders have solo parts, though less important than the violin's virtuoso one. As in Vivaldi's concertos, there are divisions between solo and tutti sections; but the textures are much fuller, and the material is used more rigorously to provide stronger unity and logic (see Listening Note VI.E).

Bach used designs similar to the fugal ritornello type of the Brandenburg Concerto no. 4 finale in another group of works from the Cöthen period, the four "orchestral suites", as they are usually called. (The word "orchestra" may be misleading; the ensemble Bach used, as we have seen from the size of the Cöthen establishment, was small – normally one string player to a part, or at most two or three, so that none of the Brandenburg Concertos needs more than 13 players.) These suites are in the French style, with overtures in the abrupt, arresting, jerky rhythms that the French favored in their theater music; then follows a fugal movement with ritornello features, and a series of dances. These are among Bach's most cheerful and tuneful works; one has a solo part for flute, and two gain a touch of ceremonial splendor from the use of three trumpets and a pair of drums.

For Bach's fugal writing at its most varied, however, we may turn to another important work of the Cöthen years. Around 1722, he began to compose a seies of preludes and fugues for the harpsichord or clavichord, one in each of the 24 keys, major and minor. He called this *The Well-Tempered Keyboard*, for it was partly designed to demonstrate a fairly new principle – that an instrument could be tuned to play effectively in every key.

These 24 preludes and fugues became, by 1742, part of what musicians call the "48", for Bach later wrote a second set. The preludes are of various kinds – some brilliant display pieces, other lyrical and aria-like, yet others contrapuntal or involving patterns of keyboard

Listening Note VI.E   *Side 3, band 5; side 4, band 1*

Bach: *Brandenburg Concerto no. 4* in G (1721)

solo violin, two recorders
1st and 2nd violins, viola, cello, violone, harpsichord

This concerto has solo parts for a violin and two recorders, but the virtuoso violin writing makes it almost like a solo violin concerto.

1st movement (Allegro): Ritornello form; nearly all the figuration is derived from the patterns in exx. i, ii and iii.

Time	
0:00	tutti I, opening ritornello, ex. i, G
0:11	ex. ii
0.20	ex. i, D
0:32	ex. iii, G
1:18	solo I, G–D
1:56	return of idea in exx. ii and iii, D
2:07	tutti II, ex. i, e
2:27	solo II, recorders, e . . .
2:53	. . . continuing with rapid and brilliant violin passage, a, C
3:16	tutti III, ex. i, C
3:41	solo III, violin, with recorders, C–G
4:07	tutti IV, with exx. ii and iii, G
4:28	solo IV, recorders, then with violin, G–b
4:53	tutti V, violins with exx. ii and iii
5:05	ex. i, b
5:25	cadence in b
5:26	tutti VI, final, G: from 5:26 to 6:48 identical with 0:00 to 1:18
6:48	(end)

2nd movement (Andante): free form, based on echo principle.

Time
0:00   opening (ex. iv)
0:06   first echo
0:12   tutti
0:21   second echo
0:51   cadence in e
1:21   cadence in a, followed by faster-moving recorder passage
1:52   beginning of chromatic passage
2:13   cadence in b
2:45   cadence in e; lower instruments take up main theme
3:03   passage for soloists
3:34   cadence on dominant of e, leading directly into third movement
3:43   (end)

3rd movement (Presto): Ritornello-fugue. Ritornello form but akin to a large-scale fugue.

Time
0:00   opening theme, ex. v, viola, G
0:04   theme in second violin
0:11   theme in first violins
0:15   theme in the bass line
0:24   theme in recorders
0:39   extra statement of theme in recorders
0:44   solo voices (violin against recorders in dialogue)
1:08   orchestra enters
1:13   theme in bass line, D
1:36   cadence in e; solo violin passage
2:22   theme in first violins, e
2:26   theme in recorders, then basses
2:51   cadence in b; next episode begins, mainly recorders
3:17   theme in violins, C
3:21   recorders have theme, C
3:33   tutti, theme in violins, G
3:41   soloists alone
3:49   orchestra enters, theme in bass line, D;   full tutti, G
4:40   (end)

ex. iv

ex. v

---

configuration. The fugues embody the richest array of techniques ever assembled. In them, Bach again shows that fugue is not – despite the disciplines it involves – a mechanical process but a live artistic creation. Some are highly complex in their form and development; no. 2 in C minor from Book I is an example of a direct and logical handling of fugal

Listening Note VI.F *Side 4, band 2*

Bach: *48 Preludes and Fugues, I* (1722), Prelude and Fugue in C minor

The prelude is in a brilliant keyboard style.

Time	
0:00	the prelude begins as shown in ex. i. The music follows the same patterns (with changing harmony: ex. ii) until . . .
1:05	. . . presto, played in a free style
1:19	Adagio, begins with a rolled chord, then freely played into the . . .
1:30	Allegro, an arpeggiated figure to the end

The fugue is in three "voices" – three clearly defined contrapuntal lines (which for convenience we may call soprano, alto and bass). They enter in the order A, S, B; in this particular fugue, when any voice is assigned the subject (ex. iii), the other two have material that goes satisfactorily against it. When, for example, the Bass (B) enters with the subject (S), the soprano (S) has the first countersubject ($C1$) and the alto (A) the second ($C2$). The chart below shows how the material is divided between the voices.

Time	0:00	0:05	0:18	0:30	0:43	0:59	1:17	1:27
Soprano	–	S	C_1	S	C_1	S	C_2	S
Alto	S	C_1	C_2	C_2	S	C_1	C_1	–
Bass	–	–	S	C_1	C_2	C_2	S	–
Key	c	g	c	E♭	g	c	c	c

ex. i

ex. ii

ex. iii

writing (see Listening Note VI.F).

Bach wrote other kinds of keyboard music at this period. There are notebooks of simple pieces for his eldest son and his new wife; there are what he called "inventions" and "sinfonias" (exercises in the interchange of material between the hands); and two fine books of dance suites, known as the English Suites (which have long, concerto–like preludes as well as dances) and the French Suites. Each has the four basic dances (Allemande, Courante, Sarabande, Gigue) with an extra one between the last pair.

Before we pass on from the Cöthen years, the chamber music Bach wrote there should be mentioned. His interest in the role of the harpsichord, which we noted in Brandenburg Concerto no. 5, extended to its use in chamber groups. Traditionally, the harpsichord merely supplied continuo harmonies; but in his violin sonatas he assigned it an obligatory right-hand part, usually playing music essential to the texture. He was thus able to enrich the violin sonata form. This is typical. The other notably original contribution came in the sonatas or suites for solo violin or cello – he wrote six for each, with no accompanying part, but managing the distribution of notes so as to imply harmony. This may seem to be the opposite of textural enrichment, yet paradoxically it is not, for the listener is invited to hear in his mind many notes that are barely touched or even hinted at, so that the texture never seems sparse or thin.

Leipzig

Bach moved to Leipzig in May 1723. He must have been pleased to do so. In this thriving commercial city he would be the employee not of a private patron, who could act on whim, but the civic and church authorities; further, his sons could obtain a good education at St Thomas's School. And the musical duties offered more of a challenge than he had faced before.

He set to work in methodical fashion. He had to supply cantatas for performance each Sunday, so he set out to build up a new repertory. Starting in June 1723, in his first year Bach composed a complete cycle of cantatas (about 60 for the church year, allowing for feast days). In his second, he produced another. He embarked on a third cycle, which he took two years to complete. Then followed a fourth, in 1728–9 (we cannot be certain of this as only a handful of the cantatas composed after 1727 have survived). Probably he wrote a fifth cycle during the 1730s and 1740s.

Bach was astonishingly industrious. Soon after he arrived in Leipzig he applied for the restitution of a traditional right of the holder of his post to direct the music at certain services at the university; a dispute ensued, and a compromise was reached. This was only one of numerous quarrels in which he was involved. He was constantly alert for any infringement of his rights or privileges. Later, he was often at odds with the headmaster of St Thomas's School, for example over his neglect of teaching or his absence. The headmaster appointed in the 1730s was an educational reformer whose academic ideals created conflicts with Bach who wanted the brightest boys for musical activities. Even before then Bach, discontent with the resources he had, drew up a strong memorandum about the requirements for "a well-regulated church music".

In spite of his responsibilities at St Thomas's and the other churches, Bach found time to pursue other musical activities. Music was his preoccupation at home as well as at work: there were musical evenings there (his family could provide a vocal and instrumental ensemble) and he spent much time on his sons' musical education. He did other private teaching: several of the best German organists and composers of the next generation were his pupils. He wrote music for instruction, including a second set of 24 preludes and fugues in all the keys and four books entitled *Keyboard Exercise*, with organ chorale preludes and dance suites and variations for the harpsichord. One especially interesting collection forms the second book: here Bach contrasts the Italian and the French styles, publishing side by side an "Overture in the French Manner" and a "Concerto in the Italian Style". The French work consists of an overture in the dramatic, jerky rhythms of the kind Lully used, followed by a fugue and a series of characteristic French dances; the Italian one uses Vivaldian concerto form in its fast movements, with "solo" and "tutti" passages distinguished by contrasting weights of texture and different thematic material. Bach wanted to make clear the differences between these two national styles. But his music never merely imitates that of composers from other countries; it always sounds his own, and sounds German.

Another important side activity of Bach's was his organization of the local musical society. He took up the directorship in 1729, when his period of intensive cantata composition was finishing. The society gave weekly concerts during its seasons – in a coffee-house in the winter, a coffee-garden in the summer. Bach revived his Cöthen instrumental music and supplemented it with new harpsichord concertos and other music for small orchestra. The concerto for harpsichord was a novel idea; never before had the solo role in a concerto been given to a keyboard instrument. Most of Bach's harpsichord concertos are adaptations of violin concertos: he ingeniously rewrote passages that were designed for a string instrument to make them sound well on the harpsichord, and added left-hand parts to enrich the texture. He also wrote multiple concertos – for two, three and even four harpsichords. It must have been difficult to get four harpsichords and four harpsichordists together in a coffee-house music room, with an orchestra, but Bach's delight in rich textures and unusual instrumental effects justified it. In fact, the four (or three, in the triple concertos) rarely play together in counterpoint; more often the music falls into patterns of dialogue, using the kinds of symmetry of which Bach was so fond. He also performed other composers' music at these concerts – suites by his cousin Johann Ludwig Bach, for example, and pieces by the many musicians who visited Leipzig. He remained in charge of the society for about ten years.

62 Thomaskirche and Thomasschule (center), Leipzig: engraving (c1735) by J. G. Schreiber.

**The Leipzig
sacred music**

Bach's central work, however, for the rest of his life, was in the church. One of the first works he had performed on his arrival was the *St John Passion* – a musical setting of the Passion story as related by St John. He followed this up in 1727 with the *St Matthew Passion*, a longer work – it takes around three hours – and one of his greatest achievements. A Passion setting involved a narrator, singers to take the roles of Christ, Pilate, Peter and the other participants, and a chorus to represent the crowd; the narrator would tell the story, in lightly accompanied recitative, and the other characters would sing their own parts. The story was interrupted, for hymns (chorales), to be sung by the congregation at suitable moments for reflection, and for arias of meditation on the religious message of the events described. Bach framed the entire work with large-scale, contemplative choruses.

The Passion form offered him great scope. Much of the recitative is plainly set, the line following the natural rhythm and the rise and fall of the words. But where events of special force or poignancy are described Bach altered the pace or gave an unexpected twist to the line or the harmony. In the chorales he supplied harmony that reinforced the sense of the words, often adding a dissonance for a word or phrase of emotional significance. There is drama in the crowd choruses, where the clamor of the mob is represented in vigorous counterpoint. Bach's finest music in the *St Matthew Passion*, however, is in the arias, where the emotion aroused by the events is expressed in music of great beauty, and in the choruses at the beginning, the middle and the end of the work. These, in large-scale ritornello forms planned with clear and satisfying symmetries, raise the Passion on to a plane of collective, communal experience through the use of the chorus.

Bach wrote three Passion settings for Good Friday performances. His basic work for St Thomas's was the production of a weekly cantata, as we have seen. Probably he wrote as many as 300. They are composed for a small choir (Bach liked to have around 12 singers), with solos for two or three choir members, and an orchestra of strings and organ with up to half a dozen wind instruments. An average cantata lasts between 20 and 25 minutes. The congregation would normally join in the final chorale, which would have words appropriate to the day in the church year. This would, typically, follow an opening chorus and a couple of arias.

The text for the day, and meditations on it by the poet who supplied the words, made a cantata unified as a religious entity. Sometimes Bach and his contemporaries reinforced that unity with a musical one, derived from the chorale melody associated with that text. In the cantatas of 1724–5, particularly, Bach wove the chorale melodies into his music – since these, and the words that belonged with them, were familiar to his congregation, this helped hold their interest and remind them of the religious message. In no. 80, for example, based on the Reformation chorale *Ein feste Burg* (see p. 124), the opening chorus is a fugue on this melody; at its climax the chorale rings out in long notes on a high trumpet. In the next number, a duet, a soprano sings a varied version of the chorale while a bass sings a new melody. And in a chorus different presentations of the chorale are heard in counterpoint.

Last years

Bach often traveled during his Leipzig years, to inspect organs or to perform. Several times he went to Dresden, where he held the title of Court Composer. In 1741 he presented a patron there with a new work, the *Goldberg Variations* (named after the harpsichordist, probably a pupil of Bach's, whom the patron is said to have employed). This, which Bach later published as the fourth and last book in his *Keyboard Exercise*, is his longest and most demanding harpsichord work. All 30 variations are composed to the bass of the theme heard at the start. They dazzle by their virtuosity, move by their depth of expression and fascinate by their elaborate counterpoint. The set includes all the musical forms that Bach had used in his harpsichord music – French overture, fugue, invention, dance movements.

It seems that, in several of his late works, Bach was setting down a lifetime's experience in composition. Another journey he made in 1741 was to Berlin, probably to visit his son Carl Philipp Emanuel, court harpsichordist there. He went back six years later, when his son's employer, King Frederick the Great of Prussia, admired his art and invited him to make up at the piano a fugue on a theme he himself had written (he was a skilled flutist and a composer). Bach did so. When he got home he decided to offer the king a musical collection built around his theme; this he called *Musical Offering*. It includes not only a version of the fugue he had played but also a larger fugue, for six voices (playable on the organ) and a trio sonata for flute, violin and continuo – the sonata was clearly intended to please the flute-playing king, the more so because Bach worked the royal theme into it.

In fugue composition, too, Bach left a monument. He wrote, probably in the early 1740s, a work that he called *The Art of Fugue*. It has fugues of all sorts: simple, inverted, double, triple and quadruple, in the French style, and ''mirror-wise'' – this last meaning a fugue in which all the music could be played as if seen through a mirror (high notes become low ones, upward phrases become downwards, etc). In this austere, abstract work Bach seems to have set down models of his fugal art, for a generation that no longer cherished it.

The work we call the B minor Mass may belong to the same category. Bach wrote a short Lutheran Mass in 1733, dedicating it to the Dresden court. It consists of a Kyrie and Gloria, the first two movements of the traditional Roman Catholic Mass. In the late 1740s he enlarged it into a full Roman Catholic Mass, composing two new movements and adapting a number of others from cantatas and similar works. The B minor Mass was never performed by Bach, and it again seems that in putting it together he was satisfying a desire to create a model example of this ancient and traditional form. Here again, he used a wide variety of forms and techniques, some of them belonging to earlier eras. He even worked plainsong melodies into the texture, as in medieval and Renaissance music; and some movements are in an imitative style without independent orchestral accompaniment, a kind of updated version of Renaissance polyphony.

Bach was in fact regarded in his day as an old-fashioned composer. He was not out of touch with new currents of musical thought. But he chose a more conservative path. He was criticized for his methods – for example, composing music too intricate to be ''natural'' (which to writers of the mid-eighteenth century meant tuneful and lightly accompanied), and asking voices to sing lines as complicated as those he could play on the keyboard. When he died, in the summer of 1750, after a year of poor health and finally blindness, the music he had created could be seen as a summary of the musical art of the Baroque, drawn together with unparalleled inventiveness and intellectual force.

Handel

The other great composer of the late Baroque period, George Frideric Handel, was born in a neighboring province of Germany within four weeks of J. S. Bach, into the same religious faith and a similar social background. While Bach remained in central Germany, and continued composing in the manner traditional to his background, Handel traveled widely and made his career far away from his homeland – and his music reflects his life and the taste of the wider public for whom he composed.

Early years: Germany and Italy

Handel was born in the Saxon town of Halle in 1685. His father, a barber-surgeon, discouraged his musical leanings; he presumably wanted his son to enter a more secure and respected profession and directed him towards the law. As a boy, Handel had to pursue music secretly; he is said to have sneaked a clavichord – a small, gentle-toned keyboard instrument – into an attic where he could practice unheard. When the family

George Frideric Handel	Life

1685	born in Halle, 23 February
1694	pupil of Zachow at the Church of Our Lady, Halle
1702	law student at Halle University; organist of the Calvinist cathedral
1703	violinist and harpsichordist in Hamburg opera orchestra
1705	*Almira* (Hamburg)
1706–9	Italy: Florence, Rome and Venice; contact with the Scarlattis and Corelli; oratorios, operas, many cantatas
1710	*Kapellmeister* to the Elector of Hanover; first visit to London
1711	*Rinaldo* (London); Hanover
1712	settled in London
1717	*Water Music*; director of music to Earl of Carnarvon (later Duke of Chandos) at Cannons, near London
1718	*Acis and Galatea*
1719	visit to Germany to recruit singers for the Royal Academy of Music, of which he was musical director
1723	composer to the Chapel Royal
1724	*Julius Caesar*
1726	naturalized English
1727	anthems for George II's coronation, including *Zadok the Priest*
1729	second Royal Academy established after collapse of first; to Italy to recruit singers
1733	first organ concertos
1735	first Lent series of oratorios in London; *Alcina*
1737	collapse of Handel's opera company (and its rival, the Opera of the Nobility); Handel ill
1739	*Saul, Israel in Egypt*; composed 12 Grand Concertos, op. 6
1742	*Messiah* (Dublin)
1752	*Jephtha*; deterioration of eyesight leading to virtual blindness in two years
1759	died in London, 13 April

visited a nearby court, where his father was court surgeon, the duke heard Handel play and advised his father to let him study music. Handel's house stood close by the city's main Lutheran church, and the boy became a pupil of the organist there, under whom he made rapid progress both as composer and as player. When he was 17 he entered the university, and took a temporary post as organist of the Calvinist cathedral.

A year later, he left Halle for Hamburg, a busy commercial center with a lively musical life. At the opera house there he found employment, first as a violinist and then as harpsichordist; and he made friends with Johann Mattheson (1681–1764), later an eminent composer and theorist. He and Mattheson went to Lübeck in 1703 to hear Buxtehude (as Bach did later: see p.109) and they evidently considered applying to succeed him, being put off, however, by the obligation to marry Buxtehude's daughter. Handel, it seems, was already wedded to an operatic career. His first opera was given at the beginning of 1705 (he was still not quite 20) and his second a few weeks later. The first was a success, the second a failure.

There was only one place where an ambitious young composer keen on opera could study: Italy. He was invited there by a prince of the Medici family, from Florence, where he went at the end of 1706. He spent more than three years in Italy, dividing his time between Florence, Rome and Venice, with a journey to Naples. Opera was forbidden at Rome, by papal decree; but a number of cardinals and princes were noted patrons and at least four of these men commissioned music from Handel or employed him. He wrote two oratorios there, one a setting of the Resurrection story which was spectacularly performed on a stage. He also wrote numerous cantatas – not sacred works, like Bach's, but mostly pieces some ten minutes long for solo voice and continuo consisting of two songs (usually about unhappy love) each preceded by a recitative. Handel quickly developed a new vein of melody suited to the Italian language, which he needed for success in the opera house. These fluent, graceful pieces offer the earliest evidence of the great melodist he was to be. It was in Rome, too, that he composed a group of works for the church, writing in Latin for the Roman Catholic liturgy. His brilliant *Dixit Dominus* shows with its striking, picturesque choral effects and its vigorous, punched-out rhythms that he was already a masterly composer for chorus. Outside Rome, he had two notable successes as an opera composer: in Florence, probably at the end of 1707, and in Venice, in winter 1709–10, when his *Agrippina* was so well received that it was given as many as 27 times.

In Italy Handel met many of the leading composers of the day, among them Corelli, the Scarlattis and Vivaldi. He is said to have engaged in competition with Domenico Scarlatti, whom he surpassed on the organ though on the harpsichord they were adjudged equals. He was much influenced in his composition by Alessandro Scarlatti, whose warm, flowing melodic style was his model. He also met potential patrons, among them several Englishmen who pressed him to go to London; but the invitation he accepted was from the Elector of Hanover, and when he left Italy in 1710 he went to the north German city of Hanover, where he was appointed court *Kapellmeister*.

London: the early years

Handel accepted the Hanover post on condition that he should at once be given a year's leave to visit England. The Elector of Hanover was the heir to the English throne, then occupied by the aging Queen Anne; possibly there was an understanding that Handel would eventually work for him in London. Handel spent his first visit to the English capital in establishing a position for himself. London had a flourishing theatrical life, but opera was not yet a regular part of it. English connoisseurs of music were realizing that if they wanted to hear singing of the kind they had heard in Italy there would have to be an Italian opera house. So they set about founding one. It still exists.

In 1711, Handel composed the first Italian opera written specially for London, *Rinaldo*. It was a huge success, but also started a controversy – for while the audiences were delighted with the singing, the music itself and the theatrical effects (which included ingenious machinery for scene changes and the release of live sparrows for a woodland episode), some London intellectuals mocked at the effects and scorned the idea of opera in Italian, sung by castratos before an English-speaking audience.

Handel went back to Hanover, but by the fall of 1712 he was back in London, having been allowed leave "for a reasonable time". He stayed for the rest of his life. He lived at first at the house of Lord Burlington, a noted patron of the arts, where he met many leading literary men; while he was there he composed four more operas. He began to establish himself at the English court, composing music for a celebration at St Paul's Cathedral and an ode for Queen Anne's birthday. That was in 1713. The queen awarded him a generous salary, but the next year she died, and the Elector of Hanover – Handel's employer – came to London as the new king, George I. Stories have been told of how

George Frideric Handel	Works

Operas (over 40) Almira (1705), Rinaldo (1711), Giulio Cesare (1724), Rodelinda (1725), Orlando (1732), Ariodante (1735), Alcina (1735), Serse (1738)

Oratorios (over 30) Acis and Galatea (1718), Athalia (1733), Alexander's Feast (1736), Saul (1739), Israel in Egypt (1739), Messiah (1742), Samson (1743), Semele (1744), Belshazzar (1745), Judas Maccabaeus (1747), Solomon (1749), Jephtha (1752)

Other sacred vocal music 11 Chandos anthems; 4 coronation anthems; Utrecht Te Deum and Jubilate (1713); Latin church music – Dixit Dominus (1707)

Secular vocal music over 100 Italian cantatas; trios, duets, songs

Orchestral music Water Music (1717); 6 Concerti grossi, op. 3 (1734); 12 Grand Concertos, op. 6 (1740); Music for Royal Fireworks (1749); organ concertos; suites, overtures, dance movements

Chamber music trio sonatas; sonatas for recorder, flute, oboe, violin

Keyboard music harpsichord suites, dance movements, chaconnes, airs, preludes, fugues

Handel, embarrassed at having overstayed his leave, was restored in favor with George I by arranging a serenade for him at a water-party on the Thames. In fact, George had heard music by Handel within days of his arrival and had doubled his salary. But music for a water-party – one is known to have taken place in 1717 – survives and is among the most popular of his works. The *Water Music* borrows from the grand ceremonial style that was particularly favored in France, and consists mainly of dances. An exception is the fanfare-like movement designed to show off the horns and the way they could ring across the water.

About 1717 Handel took a position as resident composer at the house, just outside London, of the Earl of Carnarvon (later Duke of Chandos), a newly rich nobleman with a small musical establishment. He remained there until about 1720, and composed both sacred and dramatic music. The main sacred works are the 11 "Chandos anthems", pieces in the Purcell tradition but with an Italianate melodic style that is expressive and colorful: they reflect the confident, worldly attitudes of the Anglican church of the time. The two dramatic works proved to be of greater importance. One, a setting of the biblical story of Esther, was Handel's first English oratorio. The other was *Acis and Galatea*, a miniature opera on the mythological tale of the love of the shepherd Acis and the nymph-goddess Galatea, and the jealous giant Polyphemus who kills Acis. Probably composed for a handful of singers and a tiny orchestra, for performance on the terrace of a country mansion with gardens, woods and lakes nearby, it has a grace and freshness all its own. Although the artificial pastoral convention is used, the emotions expressed are real and powerful. The first half chiefly consists of love-songs for Acis and Galatea in Handel's fluent, sensuous melodic style and with happy touches of nature imagery; Acis's "Love in her eyes sits playing" (see Listening Note VI.G) is typical of his gently amorous manner. In the second half there is tragedy, but not without humor: the grotesque Polyphemus sings his famous serenade to Galatea's beauty, "O ruddier than the cherry", to the accompaniment of a small, high-pitched recorder. The climax comes in Galatea's final song, where in sublime music she uses her divine powers to turn her dead lover into a spring so that he will live for ever; the soft, throbbing accompaniment of recorders and low, muted violins conveys the tenderness of her emotions and the flow of the "crystal flood" that Acis has become.

The opera ventures

Up to this time, opera life in London had been haphazard and poorly run. A group of noblemen now founded an organization to finance and regularize the hiring of theaters, players, singers, scene designers, composers and so on, and to raise money by selling subscriptions for seats. It was called the Royal Academy of Music (the king's patronage meant that "Royal" could be used). Handel, appointed musical drector, went off in 1719 to the main courts and opera centers of Europe to hear and engage singers. In 1720 the Academy opened; Handel's *Radamisto* was its second opera, performed at the King's Theatre to great applause.

The main triumphs of the Academy were still to come. For the second season, some of Handel's new singers arrived, notably the superb castrato Senesino; his powerful alto voice made him ideal for the heroic roles. In 1723 a new soprano, Francesca Cuzzoni, arrived; her brilliant singing created a sensation. In 1724 and 1725 Handel composed some of his finest operatic music, particularly in *Julius Caesar* and *Rodelinda*.

We may pause to took at the former as an example of late Baroque opera. It is constructed almost entirely of arias, with recitatives between them. The dramatic action takes place in the recitatives; in the arias the characters sing of their emotions. Most of the arias are in the *da capo* form (A–B–A; see p. 56). At the end of each aria the character who has sung it goes off the stage, partly so that he can be applauded without disturbing the action and partly because his aria is a musical and dramatic climax to the scene. There are six main characters: Julius Caesar himself (taken by a male alto, Senesino), the Egyptian queen, Cleopatra (soprano, Cuzzoni), her brother Ptolemy, King of Egypt (another male alto), Cornelia, the widow of Caesar's former Roman enemy Pompey (contralto), and

63 Handel: marble statue, 1738, by Louis François Roubiliac, commissioned for Vauxhall Gardens. Victoria and Albert Museum, London.

Listening Note VI.G   *Side 4, band 3*

Handel: *Acis and Galatea* (1718), "Love in her eyes sits playing"

Dramatic context: The first act of the masque *Acis and Galatea* treats the idyllic, pastoral love of the shepherd Acis and the nymph Galatea; the second deals with the intrusion of the giant Polyphemus who kills Acis. "Love in her eyes sits playing" is sung by Acis in Act 1.

Love in her eyes sits playing,
And sheds delicious death;
Love on her lips is straying,
And warbling in her breath!
　Love on her breast sits panting,
　And swells with soft desire;
　No grace, no charm is wanting,
　To set the heart on fire.
Love in her eyes . . . etc.

(words probably by John Gay, or Alexander Pope)

Time

0:00 orchestral preface, E♭	2:49 Acis: "Love on her breast" (different music), c
0:32 Acis (tenor voice): "Love in her eyes"	3:48 orchestral preface repeated
1:00 orchestral ritornello	4:21 Acis: "Love in her eyes" music as before but the lines are ornamented
1:11 Acis: the first four lines of verse are repeated with different music	6:50 orchestral ritornello brings aria to an end, E♭
2:16 orchestral ritornello, E♭	

64 Scene from Handel's *Flavio*, believed to show Gaetano Berenstadt (*right*), Senesino (*left*) and Cuzzoni: engraving by J. Vanderbank.

her son Sextus (male soprano), and the Egyptian general Achillas (bass – the bass voice was usually reserved to military men). The plot deals with the rivalries of Cleopatra and Ptolemy for the Egyptian throne and their courting of Caesar's help – Ptolemy by treacherously murdering Caesar's Roman rival (whose widow he then pursues) and Cleopatra by attempting to ensnare him with her beauty.

The relative importance of the different singers is shown by the amount of music each of them sings (see the table below). The nature of the music is intended to convey the kind of person each of the characters is. The simplest is Achillas, a soldier, sturdy and direct in all he does, whether military or amorous (he too is drawn to Cornelia). Ptolemy's cruelty and unscrupulousness are more artfully conveyed in the twisting, eccentric lines of some of his music. Cornelia's music is mostly somber, appropriate to a widow from ancient Rome, loyal to her husband's memory; Sextus's is more impetuous in mood, suitable to a loyal son bent on revenge. The most complex characters are Caesar and Cleopatra themselves. Caesar starts with a song of triumph on landing in Egypt, continues with an outburst of fury at Ptolemy's outrage and presumption: his music, sung at high pitch but with a man's lungs and chest cavity, could have immense force: a contemporary described Senesino as "thundering out" his music. Caesar's nobility is conveyed in a scene where, by the urn containing Pompey's ashes, he pays tribute to his former enemy. The wily military man is portrayed in another aria, when on meeting Ptolemy he compares himself to the stealthy huntsman, silent and concealed. In the orchestra there is a special part for the horn, the instrument of the hunt; this is a typical piece of imagery of the kind composers used to add variety and color. His later arias further enlarge the character – a fiery, warlike song when he finds himself betrayed, an expression of grief at supposedly losing his beloved, and a song of triumph in the end (for all ends happily in eighteenth-century opera, with Caesar and Cleopatra united: this is not of course historically true).

character	arias	shorter items	duets
Caesar	8	2	1
Cleopatra	8	1	1
Sextus	5	—	1
Cornelia	3	2	1
Ptolemy	3	1	—
Achillas	3	—	—

Handel's drawing of Cleopatra's character is just as rich. She begins with a spirited, kittenish group of arias, showing her as an ambitious young woman. She begins Act 2 disguised as a serving-maid, trying to entice Caesar with her beauty; Handel stresses the voluptuous side of her personality by providing an exceptionally rich accompaniment, with a harp, a large lute and a viol to add density and color to the orchestra of strings, oboes and bassoon. Now, with the onset of real love, she becomes an emotionally more powerful character, and when she believes Caesar to have been killed she mourns him eloquently. Later, imprisoned by her brother, she bewails her fate in tragic terms, and here Handel uses the *da capo* aria in an unusual way, making the middle section an outburst of rage and determination. Her last aria, when she is freed by Caesar and pledged to him, recalls the style of the earlier ones but with a new breadth to convey the development of her personality.

Not all Handel's operas are as rich or dramatically convincing as *Julius Caesar*. The Royal Academy continued putting them on, but it also continued to lose money, and in 1728 it collapsed. There had been errors of judgment, for example the hiring of another soprano, Faustina Bordoni, which led to the forming of factions and eventually an undignified fight on the stage between her and Cuzzoni. Meanwhile, Handel had been active in other spheres: in 1723 he was appointed composer of the Chapel Royal, and he wrote four anthems for the coronation of George II in Westminster Abbey in 1727 (one, *Zadok the Priest* has been performed at every British coronation since). That year he became a naturalized English subject.

Opera however remained central to him. Handel and the Academy theater manager now decided to put on operas themselves, and started at the end of 1729. Their success was limited. Several operas failed, and their new singers did not much please the audiences. Soon a rival opera organization, known as the Opera of the Nobility and run by a group of noblemen, was set up; from 1733 London, which could not support one opera company, was asked to support two. Not surprisingly, both collapsed, in 1737. By then Handel had composed no fewer than 13 new operas since the closing of the Academy. Two of the finest are *Orlando* and *Alcina*, not on heroic themes but based on tales of magic, with their basis in medieval literature rather than history and giving opportunity for spectacular effects. Handel's interest in opera – or his confidence in the possibility of pursuing it successfully – seems to have faded in the 1730s, and he finally abandoned the form in 1741. By then he had a good idea of the new directions his career was taking.

The move to oratorio

Back in 1718, as we saw, Handel had written two dramatic works to English words. The occasion for them had passed in the 1720s and they had been put aside. But in 1732 *Esther* was privately performed, by friends of Handel's, at a London tavern. Then a professional group, unconnected with Handel, advertised a performance. Without a copyright law,

Handel could not prevent it, but he could – and did – retaliate, by giving a performance himself, adding extra music so that his version would be the most up to date and authoritative. The Bishop of London, however, forbade the acting of the story on stage. A little later, the same happened with *Acis and Galatea* – a performance by rivals, a retaliation by Handel with extra music but no stage action.

The success of these works gave Handel new ideas about his future. In 1733 he performed a new oratorio, *Deborah*, after the biblical story, during Lent, when operas were not allowed. That summer, in Oxford, he gave *Acis and Galatea* and another new biblical oratorio. In Lent 1735 he held an oratorio season in London, and during the intermissions played organ concertos – a new genre. Handel's organ concertos are notable for their brilliance and grandeur, and his performances helped attract audiences.

During the late 1730s, as his interest in opera waned, Handel turned increasingly to other large vocal forms and also wrote a quantity of instrumental works. Some of his earlier ones had been issued in print by the leading London publisher, and now Handel added his finest ones, a set of 12 concertos for strings, op. 6, written in the first place for use at his oratorio concerts. These and Bach's Brandenburg Concertos stand as twin peaks of the Baroque concerto repertory. Handel's are not as consistent in form or style as Bach's, nor as carefully worked out; he composed in broader strokes and depended more on the striking quality of his ideas, his melodic gift and the sheer originality and variety of the music. Some of the concertos have dance movements, some have elaborate fugues, some have large-scale ritornello movements; some movements are not much more than exquisite melodies with accompaniment.

In 1741, Handel was invited to visit Dublin, in Ireland, and give concerts in aid of charities. He accepted, and set about preparing two new works. One was what he called a "Sacred Oratorio", better known as *Messiah*; the other was *Samson*, based on verse by Milton. He arrived there in November, and gave two concert series with great success. The climax was the first performance, on 13 April 1742, of *Messiah*. The hall was full; the ladies had been asked to wear dresses without hoops, and the gentlemen to abandon their swords, so that there would be room for more people. A reporter wrote that "words are wanting to express the exquisite delight it afforded to the admiring crouded audience. The sublime, the grand, and the tender, adapted to the most elevated, majestick and moving words, conspired to transport and charm the ravished heart and ear".

Messiah (not "*The*" *Messiah*) has become not only the most famous and most loved of Handel's works but also the most famous and most loved of choral works in the English-speaking world. Handel was at his most inspired when composing it during six weeks in the summer of 1741. He found fresh stimulus in the familiar biblical words that his friend Charles Jennens had put together for him, and recalled not only the traditions of German Passion music in which he had been brought up but also the melodic grace of his Italian settings (some of the choruses use music he had first composed as Italian love duets) and the grand choral effects that he had inherited from the English tradition through Purcell. Handel's theatrical sense is present in *Messiah*, too, in the music announcing Christ's birth (with distant trumpets and the effect of a choir of angels), in the drama of the Passion music, above all in the grandeur of the most famous number, the Hallelujah chorus: here Handel said that, while composing it, he saw "the great God himself upon his throne, and all his company of angels" (see Listening Note VI.H).

Back in London, Handel seems to have had a clear picture of his future. Opera was now behind him; his main occupation was to give seasons of oratorios and similar works at Covent Garden theater. He was composing now not primarily for the small, aristocratic class with inherited wealth, land and titles, who understood Italian. His new audience was

65 Opening of the aria "Evr'y valley" from the autograph of Handel's *Messiah*, 1741. British Library, London.

a more broadly based middle-class public who, created by the commercial and industrial activity that had already made London the biggest, busiest and most prosperous city in the world, were keen to share the cultural pleasures of the upper classes but were also touched by the religious spirit of the times and thus wanted "improvement" from their pleasures as well as diversion.

Handel gave his new *Samson* (he had not performed it in Dublin) in Lent 1743, with great success. *Messiah*, which followed, was a failure – the singing of biblical words in a theater offended many people and the work became popular in London only when, in 1750, Handel gave performances of it in a chapel for charity. The oratorio seasons continued. At some, Handel experimented – in 1744 he gave *Semele*, not an oratorio but more like an opera, based on an erotic story from classical mythology, set in English with oratorio-like choruses and with no acting. It was a failure; the audiences found none of the moral uplift they were seeking. The same happened the following season with *Hercules*, another classical drama. These two are among Handel's finest works, the former for its portrayal of sensuous love (the well-known "Where'er you walk" comes from it), the latter for its powerful treatment of jealousy. But neither was much liked in Handel's time. The oratorios chiefly admired in Handel's own day include, besides *Saul* and *Samson*, *Judas Maccabaeus* – a rousing, warlike piece that caught the national mood at the time of the 1745 Jacobite rising.

Each of the oratorios relates, in musical-dramatic terms, a story, usually a well-known Bible one. Each singer plays a particular character: in *Saul*, for example, the Jewish king himself is a bass, his son Jonathan a tenor and David an alto. The chorus sometimes represent an army or a populace, sometimes simply provide an external observer's com-

Listening Note VI.H   *Side 4, band 4*

Handel: *Messiah* (1742), Hallelujah Chorus

Hallelujah! Hallelujah!
For the Lord God omnipotent reigneth
The Kingdom of this world is become
    the Kingdom of Our Lord
And of his Christ.
And he shall reign for ever and ever
King of Kings and Lord of Lords
And he shall reign for ever and ever
Hallelujah! Hallelujah!

This chorus, the most famous piece Handel wrote, ends the second of the three parts of his oratorio *Messiah*. His vigorous and triumphal choral style is demonstrated in the opening music.

Time
0:00   orchestral introduction
0:06   "Hallelujah", ex. i
0:25   "For the Lord", ex. ii
1:14   "The kingdom of this world", soft section
1:33   "And he shall reign", fugue, ex. iii
1:56   "King of Kings", top voices sustain
2:10   trumpet
3:31   final "Hallelujah"

mentary. Handel was careful to provide different kinds of music to indicate the character of the group they represented. In *Samson*, for example, the Philistines have tuneful, rhythmic choruses while the Jews have grave contrapuntal ones. Many of the choruses culminate in the praise of God in a brilliant, exuberant vein, influenced by the ceremonial Anglican church music of the time. As in the operas, the main action is in the recitatives, here in English (the new audience expected the words to be comprehensible, in their own tongue), and the arias express the characters' emotions. Although the oratorios were never acted, Handel still thought in dramatic terms; the word books in which the audience could follow even included stage directions.

The last of Handel's biblical oratorios was *Jephtha*, written in 1751. As he composed it his eyesight began to fail; at one point in the score, the chorus "How dark, O Lord, are thy decrees, All hid from mortal sight", he noted in the margin that he had to break off owing to the failure of his eyes. He was able to resume, but by 1753 was virtually blind; he continued to attend performances, and even managed to play organ concertos – at first he relied on his memory, but later had to improvise the solo sections, indicating to the orchestra when they should enter.

A number of enigmas surround Handel. One concerns his personal life. He never married, though was said to have had love affairs with women musicians; but no word of scandal, in an age of gossip, has come down to us. Another, more troublesome, concerns his "borrowings". He often re-used music from an early work in a later one; *Rinaldo*, for example, hastily written when he first went to London, incorporates items from his Italian compositions. But he also used other composers' music. Usually he adapted and rewrote what he used, nearly always improving it and stamping his own character on it. He "borrowed" extensively, throughout his life; sometimes he bought music from abroad and within months was using ideas from it in his own works. That there was an element of deception in all this, and some kind of moral flaw, is clear; yet the individuality, the grandeur and the honesty that shine through his music provide their own answer.

At any rate, Handel was much esteemed by those who knew him. He was quick-tempered, but keenly witty, "impetuous, rough, and peremptory in his manners and conversation, but totally devoid of ill-nature or malevolence", wrote a contemporary. He had a huge appetite. He played in concerts at the homes of patrons in his young days, but gradually withdrew into a life of more privacy. He practiced the harpsichord a great deal; it is said that the keys of his instrument were worn hollow. In his later years, he attended church regularly. He died in April 1759, aged 74. Three thousand Londoners attended his funeral; he was buried in Westminster Abbey.

Chapter VII

The Classical Era

"Classical" is a misused word. Even when it is used correctly, it has several different though related meanings. Its chief misuse these days is when "classical" music is opposed to popular music; there it is intended to include all kinds of "serious" music, irrespective of when or for what purpose it was composed. Here we use the term mainly to denote the music of the period that runs roughly from 1750 to the death of Beethoven in 1827.

Classicism

Why *classical*? That word, strictly, applies to the ancient Greeks and Romans, to "classical antiquity", the two great Western civilizations of early times. Many eras have looked back at "the ancients" and tried to borrow what is best in their cultures. They did so, as we have seen, in the Renaissance, and again at the beginning of the Baroque. But it was the mid-eighteenth century that truly began to rediscover classical antiquity, especially through archeology, and to build up a new picture of its simplicity, its grandeur, its serenity, its strength, its grace, all typified in the newly found and freshly excavated temples of Greece and southern Italy. The remains of Pompeii, for example, were discovered in 1748: artists drew them; engravers copied them, for wider circulation; theorists worked out the principles along which they were designed. Historians and estheticians – the most famous was the German J. J. Winckelmann (1717–68) – studied and praised the works of classical antiquity and put them forward as models for their own times. Creative artists quickly followed: Sir Joshua Reynolds (1723–92), for example, stressed that the highest achievement in painting depended on the use of Greek or Roman subjects and their representation of heroic or suffering humanity, a principle also followed notably in the heroic paintings of Jacques-Louis David (1748–1825), the official artist of the French Revolution. Sculptors used classical statues as the basis for their figures of modern men and women. Classical history, mythology and philosophy came to be increasingly influential, as the opera plots favored at this time show with their settings in ancient times and their identification with the ancient virtues.

Borrowing from the association of merit with the ancient civilizations, people have always regarded the word "classical" as implying a model of excellence. To say that something is "a classic" suggests, whether it be a poem or an automobile, that it is a superior example of its kind, still praised, admired and suitable to be considered a model. We also tend to use the word to imply something about design, for example in the expression "classical proportions", which means proportions that possess a natural balance, without extravagance or special originality, but following an accepted principle of rightness. It is the acceptance of such principles of "just proportion" and natural balance that marks out an important distinguishing feature of music of the Classical period. This was a time when virtually all composers pursued the same basic ideas as to how music should be constructed: the idea of balance between keys, to give the listener a clear sense of where the music was going, and between sections, so that the listener was always correctly oriented within a piece and had a good idea of what to expect of it. Composers could be original less by varying the systems of composition or the outlines within which they worked than by the ingenuity and the enterprise they could exercise to charm or surprise the listener.

It may be said that there was no "Classical period" in music, only a "Classical style", the one in which Haydn, Mozart and Beethoven wrote their masterpieces. In terms of "models of excellence", that is partly true. Yet the styles used by those three men were not created by them alone; others writing at the same time composed in basically the same manner, and all drew on the same traditions. We shall now examine some of the ways in which the Classical style differs from that of the late Baroque, that used by Bach and Handel.

66 St Michael's Square, Vienna, with the Burgtheater (right foreground) and Spanish Riding School behind it: engraving (1783) by C. Schütz.

Rococo, galant

There are a number of intermediate stages between the Baroque and the Classical. As with the term "Baroque" itself, music historians have drawn on other disciplines for words to describe them. One is "Rococo", used by art historians particularly of French decorative work of the late seventeenth and early eighteenth centuries. In French architecture, the strong, severe lines came to be broken or softened by shell-work (*rocaille* in French), and this led to a newly picturesque, elegant, fanciful style. Like all products of French culture and taste, this style traveled rapidly across Europe; it was particularly favored in southern Germany and Austria. Parallels between music and other arts are always dangerous. But there was in music a similar breaking down of larger lines and a growing interest in graceful, detailed elaboration; this also manifested itself, differently and somewhat later, in Germany, Austria and Italy. The Rococo, though not a central development, shows the breakdown of severe Baroque grandeur, essential if a new style was to replace it.

Another term from France, *galant*, has wider implications in the growth of the Classical style. It means "gallant", at its simplest; but its meaning in the arts was richer than that. It implied pleasure, of an undemanding kind, and also a certain elegance and worldliness. Musically, it meant a flowing melodic style, free of the complexities of counterpoint; for a *galant* melody to be heard to maximum advantage it would be lightly accompanied, with a slow-moving bass line that did nothing to draw attention away from the melody. The ideal medium for *galant* melody was the singing voice, in a cantata or an operatic song (preferably on an amorous text); the composer would construct it in simple, regular phrases, answering one another in an agreeably predictable fashion, and the singer would shade the line expressively. Another popular medium was the flute (as opposed to the more old-fashioned and austere recorder), which was specially esteemed for its capacity for elegant and tender shading. The term *galant* could also imply the use of dance rhythms; and it often signified the use of a number of short, stereotyped melodic phrases, akin to graceful bows or curtseys.

The term *galant* came into use, applied to music, soon after 1700. The style it described began to gain currency in the 1720s but prevailed only around the middle of the century, as the generation of Bach and Handel and their contemporaries disappeared and a new one assumed importance. By then, the driving bass lines of the Baroque masters, which could impart so much vitality, were giving way to ones that moved more slowly and served merely to support what went on above them. After the Baroque preference for fugal texture, the top line now came an easy first, with the bass second and the middle ones nowhere. The long, often irregular phrases of Baroque music gave way to shorter ones, usually in two- or four-measure patterns, in which the listener could sense the outcome as he heard the beginning.

The Enlightenment

What were the reasons for these changes in the language of music? A major one is that the climate of thought was changing, with what is called the Enlightenment. The early part of the eighteenth century saw important changes in philosophy, in the wake of the scientific discoveries of Isaac Newton in England and René Descartes in France: rationalism and humanitarian ideals came to the fore, mysticism and superstition faded. The idea of extending culture to the ordinary man and woman – to the middle classes as well as the nobility to whom it had exclusively belonged in the past – was one of the goals of the Enlightenment: human life should be enriched by the arts. In the early eighteenth century, forms of opera arose not for performance in foreign languages and private theaters but in native languages and in public. In France "opéra comique", in which songs were interspersed with spoken dialogue in simple stories about ordinary folk, got decisively under way in the middle 1720s at the Paris street theaters, appealing to a far wider public than could have ventured into the court Opéra. In England, while Italian opera entertained the

London aristocratic audiences, a middle-class public enjoyed, from the 1730s, lightweight operas with spoken dialogue, composed in a simple and tuneful style; these were performed not just in London but all over the country. In Germany, English operas of this kind, translated and given in Berlin and Hamburg around the middle of the century, provoked the development of the native German form, the *Singspiel*. And in Italy, new forms of comic opera appeared in the early part of the century, often in local dialects, in Naples, Venice and other centers. With their popular subject-matter and their catchy melodies, they appealed to a public that found the behavior of the classical and mythological figures of serious opera incomprehensible and their music boring.

Opera was only one of the media that showed this spread of culture. In these years, music publishing became a substantial industry, enabling ordinary people to buy music and sing or play it at home – on the instruments which, with the development of new manufacturing techniques, they could now afford. It became an important social accomplishment for a young woman, especially, to play the harpsichord or the piano; the flute and violin, the other favored amateur instruments, remained on the whole male preserves. Numerous home tutors were published for these instruments in the eighteenth century. Composers, writing for home consumption, were eager to make their music easy enough to play yet interesting enough to play with taste and elegance. This was a factor in the shift towards a more regular melodic style. The amateur was also encouraged to sing the music heard at public entertainments: books of "favorite songs" from the newest operas (in London also those sung at the famous pleasure gardens) were printed and sold while they were fresh in the audience's memories.

It was not only opera that was attracting new listeners. Concert life as we know it began in the eighteenth century. In earlier times instrumental music was chiefly intended for performance at court or for groups of gentleman amateurs to play in their homes. Now groups of people, often both amateurs and professionals, got together to give concerts for their own pleasure (or for their living) and for the pleasure of others who came to listen. In larger cities, where more professionals were to be found, orchestral concerts were regularly given. London and Paris led, and others were quick to follow. The concerts of court orchestras were often opened to a paying public. During the late eighteenth century in particular, concert life developed rapidly; traveling virtuosos went from city to city, organizing concerts in each. Local musicians put on concerts from which they retained the takings. The orchestra as a unit began to take shape. The concept of a public that came to concerts to listen was a novel one, demanding a novel approach to composition; it was more than ever necessary for a piece of music to have a logical and clearly perceptible shape, so that it would grasp and hold the listener's attention. Composers rose to this challenge: above all, the three great men of the era, Haydn, Mozart and Beethoven.

But before we look at the three "Viennese Classical composers" (each spent much of his career in or near Vienna), let us see how some of the other composers of the time contributed to the style and the repertory of the late eighteenth century.

Stamitz

One of the most influential figures in orchestral music of the time was Johann Stamitz (1717–57). He was appointed in the 1740s to direct the orchestra at the court of Mannheim, in south-west Germany. The ruler there, Elector Carl Theodor, was a passionate music-lover, and built up an orchestra that one writer described as "an army of generals". Stamitz, in his 50 or more symphonies for them, exploited their exceptional skill with new kinds of writing. Unlike composers of the Baroque, he made a distinction in style as to what music he gave string and wind instruments to play, and he devised new, dramatic and expressive orchestral effects, used by the "Mannheim School" of composers. This

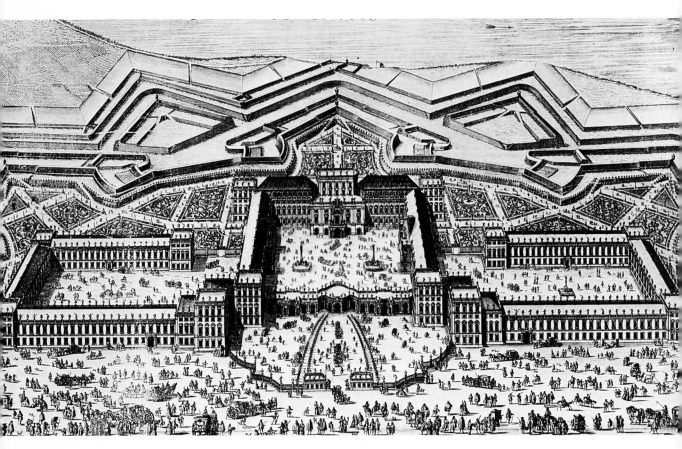

Bach's sons

influenced orchestral writing and musical styles across Europe.

Two of J. S. Bach's sons played important roles in the development of the musical style of the Classical composers. Carl Philipp Emanuel Bach (1713–88) spent much of his career as court keyboard player to King Frederick the Great in Berlin. Later he was music director to the city of Hamburg, with responsibility for the music of the five main churches there. He largely created the north German "sensitive style", in which the conveying of strong emotion is all-important. His most individual music is for the clavichord or piano; it is often rhetorical in tone, with abrupt gestures, expressive chromatic notes and appoggiaturas ("leaning notes") which seem to sigh with emotion. Expressiveness is discussed, as well as matters of technique and style, in his influential *Essay on the True Art of Playing Keyboard Instruments* (1753). His younger half-brother, Johann Christian Bach (1735–82), was quite a different kind of composer. He studied under Carl Philipp, then went to Italy, becoming organist at Milan Cathedral, and then went to London as an opera composer – though in fact he succeeded more in orchestral and chamber music. Where his brother is impassioned, he is graceful and elegant, writing "singing" melodies and using clear, Italian-type forms to please the fashionable public that patronized him. Mozart admired him.

In the world of opera, the Italian serious style was dominant at the middle of the century, with its heroic subjects and its succession of *da capo* arias linked by recitatives. This was partly the creation of the court librettist in Vienna, Pietro Metastasio, whose elegant verse and ingenious plots were calculated to show that virtue was rewarded, and to reinforce confidence in the existing systems, both spiritual and temporal. Comic opera in the audience's native language was beginning, as we have seen, but even for court theaters (at

67 The electoral palace at Mannheim: engraving (1725) after the drawing by the architect Jean Clemens de Froimont.

Gluck

which the public were increasingly admitted) this style was starting to seem too stiff and formal. The most important attempt to break it down came from Christoph Willibald Gluck (1714–87), a Czech by birth, who worked in Italy and Vienna. Collaborating with a poet and a choreographer, he put forward in his *Orfeo ed Euridice* (Vienna, 1762) a new approach. First, it tells a simple, direct story of all-consuming love in place of the usual type of plot with dynastic rivalries, disguises and so on. Second, the music is continuous, with choruses, dances and vocal solos flowing into one another, with no breaks for recitative and no *da capo* arias, and no opportunities for the singers to show off with brilliant, rapid passages. The long scenes and the strongly focused emotion gives *Orfeo* and Gluck's other "reform" operas a new and powerful appeal, and though his ideas were not widely copied they had an effect on opera composers during the rest of the century.

Haydn

When Joseph Haydn was born, in 1732, J. S. Bach had just composed his *St Matthew Passion*; Handel's *Messiah* was still ten years off. When he died, in 1809, Beethoven had written his Fifth Symphony. His long life thus covers a vast series of changes in musical

Franz Joseph Haydn	Life
1732	born in Rohrau, Lower Austria, 31 March
1740–49	choirboy at St Stephen's Cathedral, Vienna
1750–55	freelance teacher and musician in Vienna
1755–9	study with Nicola Porpora; period of great musical development and contact with prominent musicians and patrons
1759	*Kapellmeister* to Count Morzin; instrumental and keyboard works
1760	married Maria Keller
1761	appointed to the service of Prince Paul Anton Esterházy at Eisenstadt
1766	*Kapellmeister* of Prince Nikolaus Esterházy's musical establishment at the new palace at Esterháza; beginning of prolific output of church music, opera, symphonies, baryton music, string quartets, piano sonatas
1768–72	"Sturm und Drang" ("Storm and Stress") period of expressive, passionate minor-key instrumental works
1775–85	concentration on operas
1781	commissions from publishers; String Quartets op. 33 composed "in a new and original manner"
1785	Paris symphonies; beginning of friendship with Mozart
1791	returned to Vienna after Prince Nikolaus Esterházy's death
1791–2	first visit to London, with the concert manager J.P. Salomon; Symphonies nos. 93–8 performed
1792	took Beethoven as pupil in Vienna; String Quartets opp.71 and 74
1794–5	second visit to London; Symphonies nos. 99–104 performed
1795	*Kapellmeister* to the younger Prince Nikolaus Esterházy, composing a Mass each year for Eisenstadt
1798	*The Creation*
1801	*The Seasons*
1803	last public appearance
1809	died in Vienna, 31 May

68 Frontispiece to the first edition of Gluck's *Orfeo ed Euridice* (Paris, 1764).

style. He was central to those changes, and was recognized as such by his contemporaries. Haydn was not a revolutionary: the changes he instituted arose not from a conscious desire for change but from a wish to supply the kinds of music society demanded of him – whether it be the princely family who employed him during most of his working life, or the public who bought his music and went to his concerts. In exercising his skill and his ingenuity to answer these needs, he devised many new ways of putting music together and delighting his hearers.

Early years

Haydn was born in Lower Austria; his father, a cartwright, was fond of music. At eight, he joined the choir of St Stephen's Cathedral, Vienna, and remained there some nine years, acquiring sufficient musical skills to scrape a modest living when he left by teaching, playing the violin or the organ and accompanying. Through accompanying for the Italian composer Nicola Porpora, he learned much about singing and the Italian language, and came into contact with leading figures in Viennese musical life; Porpora also instructed him in composition. His first appointment, around 1759, was as music director to Count Morzin. During these early years he composed sacred works, keyboard pieces and divertimentos – pieces for various combinations of instruments, usually intended to provide easygoing pleasure for listeners and performers.

Esterházy Kapellmeister

In 1761 Haydn was appointed to the service of the Esterházy family. The Esterházys were Hungarians with long traditions of artistic patronage; they owned a castle in Eisenstadt, near Vienna, and in the 1760s built a new palace with an opera house just within present-day Hungary, called Eszterháza. In 1766 Haydn assumed charge of the prince's musical establishment, which included some 15 musicians. He was required to compose exclusively for his employer and to take charge of the music library and the instruments.

Haydn's post was demanding. He was expected to compose in a wide range of media, and in quantity – he was once "urgently enjoined to apply himself to composition more diligently". His music in the late 1760s and early 1770s includes symphonies, divertimentos, chamber music, pieces for the baryton (a viol-like instrument, which Prince Nikolaus Esterházy himself played), operas and church music. He later said: "I was away from the world, there was no one nearby to confuse or disturb me, and I was forced to become original".

The least original works are the divertimentos, the baryton music (though Haydn was

---

Franz Joseph Haydn   Works

Symphonies no. 6, "Le matin", D (?1761); no. 7, "Le midi", C (1761); no. 8, "Le soir", G (?1761); no. 22, "The Philosopher", E♭ (1764); no. 45, "Farewell", f♯ (1772); no. 49, "La passione", f (1786); no. 73, "La chasse", D (?1781); nos. 82–7, Paris Symphonies; no. 92, "Oxford", G (1789); nos. 93–104, London Symphonies: no. 94, "Surprise", G (1791), no. 100, "Military", G (1794), no. 101, "Clock", D (1794), no. 103, "Drum Roll', E♭ (1795), no. 104, "London", D (1795)

Other orchestral music violin and cello concertos; divertimentos, cassations, dances, marches

Chamber music c70 string quartets – op. 20 nos. 1–6 (1772); op. 33 nos. 1–6 (1781); op. 50 nos. 1–6 (1787); op. 54 nos. 1–3 (1788); op. 55 nos. 1–3 (1788); op. 64 nos. 1–6 (1790); op. 71 nos. 1–3 (1793); op. 74 nos. 1–3 (1793); op. 76 nos. 1–6 (1797); op. 77 nos. 1–2 (1799); op. 103 (1803, unfinished); 32 piano trios; string trios, baryton trios

Operas (c11) Il mondo della luna (1777), L'isola disabitata (1779), La fedeltà premiata (1780)

Oratorios Die sieben letzten Worte (The seven last words, 1796), Die Schöpfung (The creation, 1798), Die Jahreszeiten (The seasons, 1801)

Choral music 14 Masses; sacred and secular works

Keyboard music 52 sonatas; variations

Vocal music solo cantatas, vocal quartets and trios, canzonettas, arrangements of British folksongs, canons

ingenious in devising music for the prince's limited abilities) and the vocal items. Church music was inevitably conservative, while the operas tend to follow stock comic patterns.

The string quartets

Haydn reserved his most striking ideas for his chamber works, especially his string quartets, and his symphonies. The quartet was designed for amateur music-lovers who gathered to savor this particular repertory. Haydn's string quartets were not written exclusively for Prince Esterházy but for publication in Vienna, where they enlarged his reputation. He completed six, probably in 1770, then embarked on another set, which he finished the next year; a third followed the year after. Each consisted of six works, the standard publisher's package and a convenient quantity of music for an evening's music-making.

These three sets – numbered opp. 9, 17 and 20 – established the four-movement pattern, with quick outer movements and a slow movement and a minuet in between. They also show a remarkable series of changes in Haydn's musical thinking. Op. 9 radiates the confidence of a composer full of strong, new ideas about how to make a piece interesting – there are ingenious accompaniments, sudden changes of pace in the melodic first violin part, spacious first movements, much fire, many strokes of wit. In the next set this vitality is disciplined; each work is more purposefully organized and holds better together.

The process is carried further in op. 20; moreover, the range and depth of the music are significantly enlarged as Haydn's command increases. The ideas are more fully worked, the moods more strongly defined and sustained, the scale of imagination is larger, and each quartet has a marked character. Several of the last movements are fugues. Haydn, like some other Austrian composers, revived this Baroque form to provide a new kind of finale, exploiting the string quartet as four equal voices and offering a way of writing a fairly weighty movement in a different style.

"Storm and Stress"

The most original quartet in op. 20, no. 5, is in a minor key. A large proportion – some 95% – of works from the third quarter of the eighteenth century were in major keys; the minor was used exceptionally, generally for music of a passionate, angry or sometimes sad character. Haydn composed many symphonies, probably 30 or 40, for the entertainment of the Esterházy family during the 1760s; only one or two are in minor keys. But of those of the early 1770s, almost half are minor. Much German art – literature, drama, painting – was affected during the 1760s and 1770s by what is called the "Storm and Stress" movement, and the Haydn symphonies numbered from 39 to 52 show him departing from elegant, tasteful entertainment music, written to charm his patrons, in favor of music that embodied urgency and strong feeling. The slow movements are slower and more intense, the rhythms less regular, the lines less smooth, and there are sudden changes of pace.

From the mid-1770s Haydn seems to have drawn away from this style. Perhaps his employer found it uncongenial; perhaps it was a passing phase. In any case, it was opera that chiefly occupied him in the ten years from 1775 – not only composing but also arranging, planning the repertory and directing the performances. He wrote several comic operas, but also serious ones. For all the beauty of their music, stage performances show that they lack some vital ingredient as regards dramatic vitality and feeling for character. The symphonies of this period are traditional, expansive, cheerful works, less personal than those preceding; but there is a set of string quartets, op. 33 (1781), which Haydn said were composed "in a new and special manner" – this may concern the dialogue-like style of instrumental writing, but more likely the works' lighter, more polished character.

International figure

Haydn's reputation had been steadily widening. His music had been carried by international music publishers – who in the days before copyright laws could "pirate" any foreign publication they thought they could sell – to the areas served from London, Paris, Amsterdam, Berlin and Leipzig as well as Vienna. From Spain came a request for a church work, for Passion week; from Italy, the King of Naples commissioned concertos for a kind of hurdy-gurdy (like a street organ); from Paris, one of the greatest musical centers, came an invitation to compose six symphonies – to which Haydn responded with nos. 82–7, works of a new originality and brilliance. But the most important contact was with London. He had earlier declined an invitation there, but this time a leading violinist and concert promoter from the city, J. P. Salomon, who heard of Nikolaus Esterházy's death in 1790 and realized that Haydn would be free, went to Vienna to take him back.

This was a great adventure for Haydn, now approaching 60. London, a famous center for commerce, industry and the arts, was the largest city in the world, offering rewards like no other. He was well treated during two long visits: received at court, rapturously applauded, richly entertained, greeted with warmth by his fellow-musicians, honored with an Oxford doctorate of music, taken to choral performances on a scale he had never imagined. And he fell deeply in love with Rebecca Schroeter, the widow of a musician (he had left his wife, a shrewish woman with whom he had never been happy, in Austria).

The London symphonies

For his London concerts Haydn composed 12 symphonies, his greatest achievement in orchestral music. They include works that have since earned themselves nicknames – the "Surprise", with its loud chord to arouse anyone who might doze; the "Clock", with its ticking figure in the slow movement; the "Drum Roll", called after its unusual opening; and the "Miracle", so called because miraculously no one was hurt when at its première a chandelier fell on the audience seats, as all the audience had rushed forward to applaud. The last of the symphonies (for no good reason) is known as the "London", no. 104 in D; it has features that show the directions in which Haydn's music had moved (see Listening Note VII.A).

Listening Note VII.A
Side 5, band 1

Haydn: *Symphony no. 104* in D (1795)
2 flutes, 2 oboes, 2 clarinets, 2 bassoons
2 horns, 2 trumpets; timpani
1st and 2nd violins, violas, cellos, double basses

1st movement: Adagio—Allegro
The movement is in sonata form, with a slow introduction, designed to set the atmosphere for a substantial work.

Time
0:00	slow introduction, d
2:01	exposition, first subject, ex. i, D
2:49	second subject, starting as ex. i with "x", A
3:24	closing theme, ex. ii

Note: entire section repeats back from 0:00 to 2:00

3:48	first subject, D
4:36	second subject, A
5:11	closing theme
5:35	development: uses "y" from ex. i
5:54	uses "z" from ex. ii
6:43	recapitulation: first subject, ex. i, D
7:39	second subject, D
7:54	closing theme, ex. ii

Haydn returned to Vienna a happy man – and a rich one. After a career as a provincial *Kapellmeister,* he had become an international celebrity. He was a simple enough man to take enormous pleasure in his new status as the greatest living composer, at a time when social change had not only raised the standing of the creative artist but also ensured that he could reap the proper financial rewards. The London visits also profoundly influenced the music he was still to write.

The final years

Between his two journeys to London, Haydn spent a year and a half in Vienna (1792–3). His new reputation had made little impact on the Viennese, and he spent much of his time preparing new works for the second visit. Among them are six string quartets. Salomon's concert programs were not purely orchestral, as orchestral concerts are today, but might also include songs, concertos, keyboard music and chamber works. String quartets were now given in the concert room. This affected Haydn's style: most of his earlier quartets begin softly, but the quartets of this group, opp. 71 and 74, and most of his later ones, start with a loud, arresting gesture – essential to quieten a talkative audience.

Haydn had composed several sets of quartets since op. 33. There had been two groups in the late 1780s, and the masterly op. 64 set in 1790, essentially intimate works in the true chamber-music tradition. In the opp. 71 and 74 group the style is more brilliant, with virtuoso writing for Salomon's violin and fuller textures. This more "public" quartet style remained with Haydn in the works of his last years. He was to compose only eight more complete quartets, in the late 1790s, then another half-quartet which he was too weak to

Listening Note VII.B

Side 5, bands 2–3

Haydn: *String Quartet in C,* op. 76 no. 3 (1797)
2 violins, viola, cello

1st movement (Allegro): Sonata form, C

2nd movement (Poco Adagio): theme and variations, G
This movement consists of a statement of a theme, followed by four variations. They are unusual in that the theme itself is unchanged but its setting is different each time.

Time

0:00	Theme in first violin (ex. i)
	(Note: the first and last measures are only half measures)
1:39	Variation I: a duet. the sixteenth-note figure in first violin, melody in second violin (ex. ii)
2:57	Variation II: melody in cello, first violin plays a syncopated figure (ex. iii)
4:30	Variation III: melody in viola, other voices have various figures (ex. iv)
6:06	Variation IV: melody in first violin, slightly varied; other voices supply harmony (ex. v)

3rd movement (Menuett: Allegro): C.

Time

0:00	minuet, first section (ex. vi)
0:23	repeat
0:46	minuet, second section
1:28	repeat
2:11	trio, first section
2:21	repeat
2:30	second section
3:16	repeat
4:03	minuet, da capo, repeat of the first part, first section (ex. vi)
4:26	second section

4th movement (Presto): Sonata form, c–C.

69 Joseph Haydn: portrait, 1791, by John Hoppner. Royal Collection, London.

ex. i

ex. ii

finish. A new self-confidence can be seen in the sheer variety of these quartets. Some are serious and tightly argued, some lyrical, some playful. One of the most popular is op. 76 no. 3, the most famous part of which is its second movement, a set of variations on the "Emperor's Hymn" that Haydn had composed as an Austrian national anthem (see Listening Note VII.B).

The last years of Haydn's creative life, however, were spent primarily on vocal music. Hearing large choirs in London singing Handel's music had inspired him to write sacred choral music. The opportunity came. The new Esterházy prince, Nikolaus the younger, asked Haydn to resume charge of his musical establishment, but with lighter responsibilities. Haydn agreed. His chief duty was to write a new Mass to celebrate the princess's name-day; he wrote six such works in the seven years 1796–1802. He carried the Austrian Mass tradition to a noble climax by integrating its conservative manner with a symphonic concentration and unity – most of the movements have the clear, strong structure that Haydn, with his experience of composing symphonies, had at his command.

Haydn also wrote two extended choral works more directly related to his experience in England. They were oratorios, composed not for church performance or private patrons but for large-scale concert performance before a wide public. These were quite different from his earlier oratorios, emphasizing the chorus rather than the soloists and thus turning the work towards the character of a collective religious celebration. These are *The Creation* (1798), based on *Genesis*, and *The Seasons* (1801), in which the bounties of Nature as provided by God are praised.

Plate 7 *Opposite The Death of Dido*: painting by Guercino (1591–1666) (see p. 111). Galleria Spada, Rome.

Plate 8 *Overleaf Jupiter and Semele:* painting, 1722–3, by William Kent (see p. 141). Ceiling of the King's Drawing Room, Kensington Palace, London.

If there is a single work that summarizes Haydn the man and Haydn the composer, it is *The Creation*. Musically, it embraces his mature symphonic style, but it draws too on Viennese traditions and on English, Handelian ones. And it wonderfully reflects Haydn's grandeur and simplicity of spirit. There are joyous choruses, like "The heavens are telling the glory of God", which ends the first part, in which the creation of the earth is related; the chorus is used to tremendous effect at such moments as "And there was light", with a radiant chord to the final word. There are songs to describe the rolling of the sea, the flowering of the meadows, the flight of birds. In the second part, the creation of living creatures is described, often with illustrative music whose imitations of Nature are both appealing and amusing, as Haydn intended – the cooing dove, the leaping lion, the creeping worm. In the third part Adam and Eve are heard, celebrating the world and their mutual

love. So *The Creation* treats of many topics close to Haydn's heart. Appropriately, it was the last work he heard, at a concert in March 1808; little more than a year later, Napoleon's armies were bombarding Vienna, and indeed Napoleon had posted a guard of honor outside Haydn's house by the time the aged composer died, on 31 May 1809. After his death he was rightly honored as the principal creator of the Classical style.

Mozart

Haydn's greatest contemporary, and the other master of the mature Classical style, was Wolfgang Amadeus Mozart, born at Salzburg in 1756. Both were Austrians; yet their careers were quite unlike, and their music is remarkably different. Born 24 years after Haydn, and dying 18 years before him, Mozart composed a lesser quantity of music, but excelled in every sphere – opera, sacred music, the concerto, the symphony, chamber music.

The child prodigy   Mozart's father, Leopold, was a composer and violinist, and author of an important book about violin playing. By the time he was four Wolfgang could play the harpsichord, and at five he was composing. Before his sixth birthday his father took him from their home city of Salzburg to play at the Elector of Bavaria's court in Munich. Leopold soon devoted himself to fostering what he called "the miracle that God let be born in Salzburg". The next years were spent traveling Europe to exhibit the boy's genius. Leopold saw it as his ordained task to show his child to the world, and was not averse to any financial rewards for doing so. Mozart was put to various tests, like playing the harpsichord with a cloth covering his hands or improvising on themes supplied to him. In 1770 he went on the first of three journeys to Italy, the home of opera; he heard operas by leading composers, took lessons from a famous teacher, received a knighthood from the pope, played at concerts and wrote operas for production at Milan, the first when he was only 14.

When Mozart came back to Salzburg from his last Italian journey, in 1773, he was 17. His compositions were already voluminous. There was sacred music, and also dramatic works, among them two full-scale operas for Italy and shorter Salzburg ones. There were

Wolfgang Amadeus Mozart	Life
1756	born in Salzburg, 27 January
1761	first public appearance; taken by his father, Leopold, to Munich; beginning of career as child prodigy touring European musical centers (Paris 1763, 1765; London 1764–5) playing the harpsichord
1770–73	three journeys to Italy; *Lucio Silla* (Milan 1772)
1773	Vienna; contact with Haydn's music; composed first works that hold a place in the repertory, instrumental music and sacred works for Prince-Archbishop of Salzburg
1775–7	concertmaster in Salzburg; first piano sonatas and concertos
1777–8	visits to Munich, Mannheim, Paris, seeking a post; Symphony no. 31 for Concert Spirituel, Paris
1779	court organist in Salzburg; cosmopolitan orchestral works
1781	*Idomeneo* (Munich); resigned from Salzburg court service; beginning of career in Vienna, playing, teaching and composing for piano
1782	*The Abduction from the Seraglio* (Vienna); married Constanze Weber
1783	concentration on vocal, contrapuntal and wind music; six string quartets dedicated to Haydn
1784–6	highpoint of acclaim in Vienna; 12 mature piano concertos became a freemason
1786	*The Marriage of Figaro* (Vienna)
1787	Leopold Mozart died ; *Don Giovanni* (Prague)
1788	court chamber musician in Vienna; Symphonies nos. 39, 40 and 41 ("Jupiter")
1790	*Così fan tutte* (Vienna)
1791	*The Magic Flute* (Vienna), *La clemenza di Tito* (Prague); died in Vienna, 5 December

Wolfgang Amadeus Mozart

Works

Operas Idomeneo (1781), Die Entführung aus dem Serail (The abduction from the Seraglio, 1782), Le nozze di Figaro (The Marriage of Figaro, 1786), Don Giovanni (1787), Così fan tutte (1790), Die Zauberflöte (The Magic Flute, 1791), La clemenza di Tito (1791)

Symphonies no. 31, "Paris", D (1778); no. 35, "Haffner", D (1782); no. 36, "Linz", C (1783); no. 38, "Prague", D (1786); no. 39, Eb (1788); no. 40, g (1788); no. 41, "Jupiter", C (1788)

Concertos piano concertos – no. 9, Eb, K271 (1777); no. 15, Bb, K450 (1784); no. 17, G, K453 (1784); no. 18, Bb, K456 (1784); no. 19, F, K459 (1784); no. 20, d, K466 (1785); no. 21, C, K467 (1785); no. 22, Eb, K482 (1785); no. 23, A, K488 (1786); no. 24, c, K491 (1786); no. 25, C, K503 (1786); no. 26, "Coronation", D, K537 (1788); no. 27, Bb, K595 (1791); 5 violin concertos; Sinfonia concertante for violin and viola, K364 (1779); concertos for bassoon, clarinet, flute, flute and harp, oboe

Other orchestral music serenades – Serenata notturna, K239 (1776), "Haffner", K250 (1776); Eine kleine Nachtmusik, K525 (1787); divertimentos, cassations, dances

Choral music 18 Masses – no. 16, "Coronation" (1779), no. 18, c (1783, unfinished); Requiem (1791, unfinished); Exsultate jubilate (1773); oratorios, short sacred works

Chamber music 23 string quartets – "Haydn Quartets" (1783–5) – G, K387, d, K421; "Dissonance", C, K465 (1785); "Prussian Quartets" (1789–90); 6 string quintets – C, K515 (1787), g, K516 (1787); clarinet quintet, flute quartets, piano quartets, piano trios, string trios, piano and violin sonatas, piano and wind quintet

Piano music 17 sonatas; rondos, variations, fantasias, works for piano duet and 2 pianos

Vocal music concert arias for voice and orchestra; songs for voice and piano

more than 30 symphonies, mostly about ten minutes long, and about a dozen lighter orchestral works (serenades or divertimentos). Mozart's father had given him composition lessons, but the quick, impressionable boy had learned mainly by listening to other composers' music: the symphonies he wrote during his years in London (1764–5) copy features of the symphonies by J. C. Bach that he heard there, while the Italian symphonies of 1770 use the kinds of theme and texture favored by Italian composers. Later in 1773, Mozart spent ten weeks in Vienna, where his father sought a post for him; there he came into contact with Haydn's latest music, and the quartets and symphonies of the following months show him adopting some of Haydn's techniques.

Most of the music Mozart had written, though astonishing for its fluency and inventiveness, is relatively conventional. His earliest pieces regularly played today belong to 1773–4. Outstanding are two symphonies, one in G minor, K183 (Mozart's works are identified with "K" numbers, indicating their place in the chronological catalog by Köchel), and one in A, K201. The G minor work, departing sharply from the traditional pattern of graceful, entertaining music, has an urgent and agitated tone. Even the last movement, which in most symphonies of this time is a cheerful, high-spirited piece, remains taut and impassioned. This is partly a result of Mozart's choice of a minor key. As we have seen (p. 47), the contrasting, second-subject music in a minor-key work was usually in the major and to most people's ears the change represents a brightening or softening of the mood. But when, as in both fast movements here, the music associated with that brightening or softening later comes back in the minor, the effect is of darkness and seriousness firmly restored. The work in A major stands out in other ways, combining a gentle and refined manner with real passion. Mozart was turning from a gifted child into a composer of high imagination and originality.

Early maturity

By this time, Leopold Mozart was seeking a post for his son. He himself was an employee of the Prince-Archbishop of Salzburg, who in effect ruled the region and employed a "chapel" of instrumentalists and singers to supply music, for worship in the cathedral and entertainment at his palace. Wolfgang, when he was 13, had been taken on as concertmaster, at first unpaid. But provincial Salzburg, Leopold felt, was no place for his son. He could earn a decent living there, but opportunities to prosper through writing operas or playing before noble patrons were few. Moreover, with the recent death of the old archbishop and the appointment of a less easygoing successor, Leopold recognized that leave to compose or perform elsewhere was likely to be restricted.

But none of Leopold's approaches bore fruit. Wolfgang was a difficult person to employ – too young for a senior post, too accomplished for a junior one, and likely to disturb the smooth running of a musical establishment because of his superior abilities and his likely need for extra leave. So he had to remain at Salzburg and produce the kinds of music required. The years 1773–7 saw him occupied with church music and lighter orchestral music. There were also concertos, among them several for violin (Mozart may have played some of these himself: he was a capable violinist as well as a superb pianist) and four for piano, of which the last, K271, was written for a visiting virtuoso and hints at the great things he was later to do in this genre.

In 1777, the Mozarts' patience with Salzburg ran out, and Leopold sent his son away to find worthy employment. He went to Munich, where he was refused a post; to Mannheim, where he was told there was no vacancy; and to Paris. There he met tragedy as well as failure, when his mother, who had traveled with him, died. Mozart disliked the French and was suspicious of their behavior towards him, and his music made no strong impression. It is fascinating to see, in the symphony he wrote for the leading Paris concert organization, how he adapted his style to the local taste. The orchestra, probably the finest in Europe, prided itself on its violins' vigorous and precise attack. Mozart, knowing his symphony would please the audience if he exploited that, began it with a brilliant, dashing scale. Throughout, he used a showy orchestral style of a kind he had not attempted before – there are sudden dynamic contrasts, difficult and exposed passages, powerful tuttis, and in the finale a wittily hushed beginning that delighted its first audience.

While Mozart was in Paris his father, seeing the hopelessness of his quest for a better job, arranged for him to return to Salzburg with a more senior concertmaster's position. This he accepted, without pleasure: he disliked Salzburg's provincialism, felt he was undervalued there, and was frustrated by the limited opportunities. So for most of 1779–80 he was back in his native city, writing church music as well as orchestral works that reflected what he had learned in Mannheim and Paris. In 1780, he was invited to Munich to compose an opera for the court theater. The archbishop let him go and he enjoyed a great success with one of his noblest works, *Idomeneo,* a serious opera on a theme from Greek mythology. He was still in Munich when a message arrived from Salzburg: the archbishop was about to visit Vienna, and Mozart had to go there to attend on him. This was a turning-point. After consorting with noblemen in Munich and playing in Vienna before the emperor, he found himself placed among the valets and cooks at the archbishop's table. Moreover, the archbishop refused him permission to play elsewhere. Angry and insulted, Mozart complained and asked for his discharge; at first it was refused, but eventually he was released, as he wrote, "with a kick on my arse ... by order of our worthy Prince-Archbishop".

The early
Viennese years

Mozart had investigated the possibility of earning a living in Vienna, by teaching, playing and composing and perhaps later with a court appointment. Vienna, Mozart once wrote, was "the land of the piano", and he quickly set about establishing himself as a pianist. He wrote and published piano sonatas and piano and violin sonatas, following these with three concertos. He took on several pupils, assuring a regular income. In 1782 his new opera in German, *The Abduction from the Harem,* was performed. In that year he was married, to Constanze Weber, with whose elder sister, a singer, he had fallen in love five years before.

But the new compositions about which Mozart cared most were six string quartets. They would make him little money, but quartets were for connoisseurs, and he was eager to show a mastery of the genre akin to that of Haydn – to whom, as supreme master of the string quartet, he dedicated them on publication (rather than to a patron who would pay him for the dedication). Mozart composed them slowly, over more than two years; partly because there was no urgency, but partly because their composition posed new challenges, in particular the development of a style and manner exclusively appropriate to the ensemble of two violins, viola and cello.

Listening Note VII.C   *Side 5, band 4*

Mozart: *The Marriage of Figaro* (1786), Act 1, Terzetto
Singers: Count Almaviva (baritone), Don Basilio (tenor), Susanna (soprano)

Dramatic context: Count Almaviva has been trying to seduce his wife's maid-servant, Susanna, who is engaged to his valet, Figaro. He has come to her room to make an assignation; when he arrived, she was (innocently) with the page, Cherubino, who has been in trouble with the Count because of his amorousness. Cherubino hid behind a chair – and when the Count heard Don Basilio (a cleric and music-master) approaching he concealed himself behind the same chair while Cherubino slipped round and sat on it, covering himself with a dress that was draped over it. But in conversation with Susanna Basilio makes remarks about Cherubino's adoration of the Countess, and this – for the Count is a fiercely jealous man – provokes him into revealing himself.

0:00		**COUNT**	key	
0:03	Cosa sento! tosto andate, E scacciate il seduttor.	What do I hear? Go at once and send the seducer away.	B♭	ex. i: the Count expresses his anger
		BASILIO		
0:16	In mal punto son qui giunto, Perdonate, o mio signor.	I have come at a bad moment: Forgive me, my lord.	B♭	ex; ii: Basilio (with a hint of irony and malice)
		SUSANNA (*almost fainting*)		
0:24	Che ruina, me meschina! Son oppressa dal dolor.	Unfortunate me, I'm ruined! I am cast down with misery.	b♭–f	shift to minor at Susanna's anxiety
		COUNT, BASILIO (*supporting her*)		
0:45	Ah già svien la poverina! Come oh dio! le batte il cor!	Ah, the poor girl is fainting! Good heavens, how her heart beats!	F	ex. iii: expression of sympathy
		BASILIO		
1:03	Pian pianin su questo seggio.	Gently to this chair.	F	Close of section; modulating section begins

	SUSANNA (*reviving*)			
1:06	Dove sono! cosa veggio!	Where am I? what is happening?		
1:09	Che insolenza, andate fuor.	How dare you! let me go!	g	Susanna's anger at being handled— and guided to the occupied chair
	COUNT			
1:15	Siamo qui per aiutarti, Non turbarti, oh mio tesor.	We are only helping you; Do not be disturbed, my treasure.	E♭	ex. iii; note expression similar to phrase at 0:45
	BASILIO			
	Siamo qui per aiutarvi, È sicuro il vostro onor,	We are only helping you; your honor is safe.		
1:30	Ah del paggio quel che ho detto Era solo un mio sospetto!	What I said about the page was no more than my suspicion!	E♭– B♭	ex. ii.
	SUSANNA			
1:39	È un insidia, una perfidia, Non credete all'impostor.	It's a trap and a falsehood; Don't believe this deceiver.	B♭	
	COUNT			
1:47	Parta parta il damerino!	This little beau must go away!	B♭	ex. i: the Court's anger
	SUSANNA, BASILIO			
1:52	Poverino!	Poor boy!		
	COUNT (*ironically*)			
1:58	Poverino! Ma da me sorpreso ancor.	Poor boy! But I've found him out again.		
	SUSANNA, BASILIO			
2:05	Come! Che!	How so? what?		
	COUNT			
1:10	Da tua cugina L'uscio ier trovai rinchiuso, Picchio, m'apre Barbarina Paurosa fuor dell'uso. Io dal muso insospettito, Guardo, cerco in ogni sito,	At your cousin's place I found the door locked; I knocked, and Barbarina let me in, looking unusually flustered. My suspicions aroused, I looked, I searched everywhere,	B♭	recitative-like section for the narrative
2:30	Ed alzando pian pianino Il tappetto al tavolino Vedo il paggio	And lifting very gently the cloth from the table there I saw the page!	B♭	ex. ii
2:42	(*he illustrates this with the dress on the chair discovering the page*)			note how *x* (ex. ii) turns upward as the page is discovered
2:45	Ah! cosa veggio!	Ah, what do I see?		
	SUSANNA			
	Ah! crude stelle!	Oh, cruel heavens!		
	BASILIO (*laughing*)			
2:50	Ah! meglio ancora!	Oh, better still!		
	COUNT			
2:54	Onestissima signora! Or capisco come va!	You most virtuous lady! Now I understand how things are!	B♭	ex. i: the Count's anger again, now quiet and menacing
	SUSANNA			
	Accader non può di peggio; Giusti dei! che mai sarà!	Nothing worse could happen; Great heavens! whatever next?		
3:14	**BASILIO**		B♭	part of ex. iii
	Così fan tutte le belle; Non c'è alcuna novità!	All the women are the same; There's nothing new about it!		
3:22	Ah del paggio quel che ho detto Era solo un mio sospetto!	What I said about the page was no more than my suspicion!	B♭	ex. ii: reflecting Basilio's irony

The piano concertos

Mozart's middle years in Vienna reached a climax in the piano concertos of 1784–6. This was the time when the Viennese public recognized and admired his genius as composer and pianist and flocked to his concerts, which he gave during Lent when the theaters were closed. In the 12 piano concertos of these years he greatly enlarged the concept of the concerto. This, as we have seen, was originally a Baroque form, in which solo episodes alternated with orchestral ritornellos. In tune with the thinking of his time, Mozart added to this a Classical-style, sonata-form contrast of keys and thematic material. Others, like J. C. Bach and to some extent Haydn, had worked along similar lines, but only Mozart achieved a satisfying balance of elements, including the soloist's virtuosity. He did this, at least at first, less by using the kinds of detailed working of themes that he applied to the string quartet than by allowing them to multiply. Ideas are linked either by brilliant passage-work (scales, arpeggios etc) or by orchestral tuttis. The relationship between piano and orchestra is subtle. The orchestra states some of the themes, and provides accompaniment and punctuation; the piano re-interprets some of the orchestra's themes, ventures some of its own, occasionally accompanies the orchestra's leading wind players,

71 Scene from Beaumarchais' comedy *Le mariage de Figaro* (1784): engraving by J. B. Leinard after Jacques P. J. de Saint-Quentin. (This is the scene represented in Mozart's opera, in the Act I terzetto: Listening Note VII.C).

has opportunities to show its brilliance, and brings the movement to a climax in a solo cadenza.

Typical of the concertos of 1784 is K453 in G, composed for one of Mozart's pupils, with its lyrical themes, its clear-cut form, its attractive writing for wind instruments and its fluent virtuoso passages (see Listening Note VII.D). For the slow movement the piano has music that is florid, dramatic and rich in expression, often elaborating ideas already heard in the orchestra; in the finale piano and orchestra share the interest evenly in a witty set of variations. No two of Mozart's concertos follow exactly the same scheme. In the later ones he tended to move away from the multiplicity of lyrical themes towards shorter, more motif-like ideas, and this led to music more strongly unified. The two mature concertos in C, K467 (1785) and 503 (1786), exemplify this; the former is also famous for the poetic eloquence of its slow movement with its soaring piano lines, its throbbing orchestral accompaniment and its disturbingly dissonant harmonies.

Also in this later group are Mozart's two minor-key concertos, which are among his supreme achievements; both begin with material that is essentially orchestral in style, which the pianist cannot take up – so in each case the solo entry begins with a new, lyrical theme of particular pathos and gentle beauty. The C minor work especially is outstanding for the wind writing in its slow movement and for its inventive variation finale. There is an analogy between the piano soloist in a concerto and the singer of an operatic aria; it is no coincidence that Mozart excelled in writing for both. It is from this time that Mozart's most famous operas come: *The Marriage of Figaro,* first given in Vienna in 1786, and *Don Giovanni,* given the following year in Prague.

Listening Note VII.D   *Side 6, band 1*

Mozart: *Piano Concerto in G* K453 (1784)

solo piano
flute, 2 oboes, 2 bassoons, 2 horns
1st and 2nd violins, violas, cellos, double basses

1st movement (Allegro): Sonata-ritornello form, G. Typical are the clear form and lyrical
themes. Note the attractive and conspicuous woodwind writing.

Time
0:00	orchestral exposition: opening ritornello, ex. i
0:27	orchestral tutti
1:02	lyrical theme, ex. ii (violins, woodwind echoes)
1:28	sudden shift to E♭
2:05	orchestral tutti, G
2:14	solo exposition: piano, ex. i
3:22	piano, ex. iii, D
3:54	modulations
4:16	piano restates ex. ii, D (woodwind echoes)
5:13	central section: tutti, D
5:37	piano entry
6:11	piano returns to e
6:57	recapitulation: orchestra, ex. i, G
7:16	piano re-enters
7:25	orchestral tutti
7:52	piano entry
7:55	piano, ex. iii and ii, G
9:44	orchestral tutti, shift of key
10:04	piano cadenza
11:24	orchestral tutti to end

2nd movement (Andante): Sonata-ritornello form, C
3rd movement (Allegretto): Theme and variations, G

72 Wolfgang Amadeus
Mozart: silverpoint
drawing, 1789, by Doris
Stock. Private collection,
Switzerland.

The mature instrumental music

Before we look at Mozart's ultimate achievement, as an opera composer, we should survey his mature instrumental music. He wrote in every medium: piano sonatas, some striking and adventurous, others primarily teaching pieces; piano and violin sonatas, where he shifted the balance from its traditional emphasis on the piano (with the violin merely accompanying) towards one in which both instruments had full expressive rein, as well as piano trios and larger works; string quartets (though he never surpassed the achievement of the set dedicated to Haydn) and string quintets; more concertos, including a fine one for clarinet; and symphonies.

The string quintet was uncommon in Mozart's day. He seems to have been specially drawn to it. He wrote two – K515 in C and 516 in G minor – in the spring of 1787, and two more in 1790–91. In K515 and 516 he drew on the opportunities that the extra instrument (a second viola) provided for full and varied textures. The C major quintet, his most spacious chamber work, unfolds in leisurely fashion, allowing for a new richness in its sound, its working of motifs and its range of key in the first movement; its slow movement is like an operatic love-duet for violin and viola, while the finale mixes counterpoint and wit as no composer had done before. Even more admired, perhaps, is the G minor work, for its poignancy and depth of feeling. When he was writing these works Mozart heard that his father, back in Salzburg, was dying.

Mozart wrote few symphonies in his mature years, mainly because piano concertos served better for his public appearances in Vienna. In 1786, however, he composd one for a visit to Prague, and in the summer of 1788 he produced three. The last two, K550 and 551, are in G minor and C, like the quintets, and bear a similar relationship. The G minor work at once shows its originality in the grace and restrained passion of its opening theme, with its throbbing viola accompaniment and its underlying nervous tension. That tension, or urgency, is brought to the surface in the last movement, fiery music which in the central development undergoes a vigorous, harsh contrapuntal treatment. But the finest manifestation of counterpoint in Mozart's symphonic music comes in the C major work. This, called the "Jupiter", stands in a tradition of ceremonial music in C major, as the presence of trumpets and drums in the orchestra and the military rhythms attest. For the finale Mozart returned to the kind of movement he had used in the first of the string quartets dedicated to Haydn – a sonata-type movement infused with fugue. Its themes, short and motivic, are designed for treatment in combination. There are several fugal sections but only at the very end does Mozart show his full hand and combine all the material, drawing the music together in a coda of unique power: a fitting culmination to his symphonic output.

At the time of his last symphonies Mozart was 33. His Viennese career had begun to turn sour. He was no longer in demand as a pianist, and although he had a court appointment it was a minor one with modest rewards. Mozart and his family never starved, and probably could always afford a servant and a carriage; but they had periods of financial difficulty and Mozart was obliged to borrow, in spite of the successes he enjoyed right up to the end of his life as an opera composer. His last year, 1791, was particularly active: during the summer he wrote two operas, one for a popular Viennese theater, the other for performance at Prague during coronation celebrations. Prague was a city Mozart liked; his operas had been warmly received there. But the new work, *La clemenza di Tito*, was only moderately successful in September 1791. Mozart returned to Vienna, where at the end of the month *The Magic Flute* was first given – to increasing applause during October. Meanwhile, he worked on a *Requiem*, which had been requested from him in mysterious circumstances (it was commissioned by a nobleman who wanted to pass it off as his own); later it was said that Mozart thought he was composing it for himself. For in November he became unwell, and after a three-week feverish illness that defied the doctors, and still defies definite diagnosis (it was not poisoning, as has been suggested), he died on 5 December.

The operas

Mozart composed happily and eagerly for every medium, but it was in opera that his chief passion lay. He wrote a school opera, in Latin, when he was 11, and a full-scale comic opera when he was 12. His first great opera, *Idomeneo,* was written when he was 25. That was followed the next year by his German opera for Vienna. The operas, however, which have always stood firmly in the public taste are three: *The Marriage of Figaro, Don Giovanni* and *The Magic Flute.*

Like Shakespeare's comedies, Mozart's comic operas (as these three are) are not simply funny. We have seen (p.149) what Gluck did for serious opera; Mozart did something parallel for comic opera by infusing it with a new humanity and depth of feeling. There were numerous operas in the middle and late eighteenth century about noblemen with too eager an eye for country girls, and in all of them the nobleman is frustrated and virtue triumphs.

That happens, too, in *The Marriage of Figaro* (*Le nozze di Figaro* – it was composed in Italian), but with a difference. For the characters Mozart drew, with the help of his clever librettist Lorenzo da Ponte, and the French playwright Beaumarchais on whose drama it was based, are not the caricatures generally found in the theater but recognizable human beings. Mozart's music gives them life. The songs for Count Almaviva and his neglected wife, for example, are distinct in tone from those for their servants, Figaro and Susanna (the Countess's maid, whom the Count desires); the music tells the listener of their social

73 Stage design by G. Fuentes for the 1799 Frankfurt production of Mozart's opera *La clemenza di Tito.* Institut für Theaterwissenschaft, University of Cologne.

74 Opening of Bartolo's aria in Act 1 scene iii from the autograph of Mozart's opera *Le nozze di Figaro*, completed 29 April 1786. Deutsche Staatsbibliothek, Berlin.

backgrounds and of the sexual tensions that provide the opera's mainspring; and the music for the adolescent page, Cherubino, portrays his youthful, all-embracing sexuality as words cannot. We hear, in the music for the Count, his urgent passion for Susanna and his fury at the idea that his own servant might enjoy privileges that are not open to him. We hear Figaro's cynicism regarding women when he thinks Susanna faithless; and we hear her relishing the thought of joy in her beloved's arms.

Mozart's music does not, like that of most Italian operas of the time, simply present lively tunes with light accompaniments; the melodic line, the suggestive harmony, the rich orchestration carry messages about the emotion behind the words. As in most comic operas, the action is carried in the recitatives and the ensembles; the arias are moments of repose, where a character expresses his or her reactions to the situation. Mozart's ensembles are especially ingenious; the long, elaborate act finales, divided into sections as the nature of the action changes, succeed in propelling the plot forward and sustaining the tension. (See Listening Note VII.C, p.161.)

The Marriage of Figaro was successful in Vienna and Prague, and it was for the latter city that Mozart, again with Da Ponte, wrote *Don Giovanni*. This too deals with the tensions of class and sex: Giovanni is a Spanish nobleman with an insatiable desire for sexual conquests. Ultimately he is consigned to eternal damnation, in a great scene where the statue of a man he has murdered (the man was defending his daughter's honor) comes to sup with him and drags him, unrepenting, down to the flames of hell; this scene drew from Mozart a noble, inexorable setting in D minor. The score is fascinating, too, for its portrayal of Giovanni's victims (or intended ones) – the peasant girl Zerlina, with her simple, pretty tunefulness; Donna Elvira, whom he has betrayed, and whose venom towards him is faintly flavored with the comic, since a scorned woman pursuing her former lover cannot escape concealed laughter; and Donna Anna, the proud young woman whose father he killed and whose passion for vengeance underlies the opera. The contrasting character sketches of Giovanni and his servant Leporello again show Mozart's musical representation of social class. Though still a comic opera, *Don Giovanni* deals with serious issues; but Leporello's presence, and his common-man's comments, wry or facetious, ensure that we do not treat it as tragedy. The last of Mozart's Da Ponte operas, *Così fan tutte* (1790), is an elegant but heartfelt comedy about infidelity.

Italian was the language preferred for operas at the Vienna court theater. Outside court circles, however, German was spoken, and an opera for middle-class audiences had to be in that language. Mozart, happy to write in his native tongue, accepted in 1791 an invitation to collaborate with the theater manager and actor, Emanuel Schikaneder, on a pantomime-like German opera. Since 1784 Mozart had been a freemason, as was Schikaneder, and the text and music of *The Magic Flute* incorporate much masonic symbolism. It starts like a traditional fairy-tale with a heroic prince (Tamino) attempting to rescue a beautiful princess (Pamina) from the clutches of a wicked magician (Sarastro); but it soon becomes clear that Sarastro represents the forces of light and Pamina's mother, the Queen of Night, those of darkness.

The Magic Flute may have a trite and silly libretto. But it is artfully designed to provide many different kinds of music: the Queen of Night's angrily glittering coloratura; Sarastro's and his priests' noble utterances; the popular ditties for the bird-catcher Papageno (sung by Schikaneder) who accompanies Tamino on his quest; the tense trios for the Queen's Ladies and the serene ones for the three Boys or Genii who support Tamino; and the music for Tamino and Pamina themselves, which is direct and intimate as the music of Mozart's Italian operas is not. This is a philosophical opera, about two people's lofty quest for realization and ideal union; with this is contrasted Papageno and his role as a child of nature. The sublimity of the music with which Mozart clothed *The Magic Flute* shows him unmistakably as a true man of the Age of Enlightenment.

Other opera composers

The Magic Flute is a *Singspiel*, a German-language opera with spoken dialogue – indeed it is the supreme example of the genre. Haydn also wrote *Singspiels,* as did many others. Most of these works are simple in style, almost like spoken plays with songs. English operas of the time, which were composed in large numbers, are similar. In both these countries, and even more in France, light opera reflected contemporary social criticism, with its emphasis on the bourgeois values (duty, honesty, kindness, innocence) as against aristocratic unscrupulousness or heartlessness. *Opéra comique* was finding a middle way between the coarse street entertainment in which it had originated and the more pretentious forms of opera still favored at court. Its leading exponent was A. E. M. Grétry (1741–1813), noted for his fluent melodic style and his gentle, very French, expressive charm. Only in Italy was there no opera with spoken dialogue; because of the language's capacity for rapid and rhythmic speech and its musical rise and fall, recitative could serve as well in comedy as in serious opera. In the last quarter of the century its leading exponents were Giovanni Paisiello (1740–1816), composer of a vivacious setting of *The Barber of Seville* that was regarded as a classic, and Domenico Cimarosa (1749–1801), a Neapolitan whose career took him to all the main centers in Italy and then to Russia. His most famous comic opera, *The Secret Marriage,* was given in Vienna in 1792, with such success that the emperor demanded an immediate repeat performance – the only known encore of an entire opera.

Beethoven

It was with the explosion of the genius of Ludwig van Beethoven, at the turn of the century, that the Classical era reached both a climax and a dissolution. "Explosion" is the right word: Beethoven's music embodied a new dynamism and power which not only demanded that it be listened to in different ways but also symbolized the changing role of the composer in society – no longer its servant, required meekly to meet its needs, but its visionary, its hero-figure.

Youth

Beethoven was born in Bonn, on the Rhine, in western Germany. At the court there of the Electors of Cologne, his grandfather had briefly been in charge of the musical establishment and his father was a tenor singer when, at the end of 1770, Ludwig was born. Discovering his exceptional talent in music, his father wanted him to be a child prodigy, a second Mozart, and compelled him to practice long hours. He played in public when he was eight, but his precocity was not of the order of Mozart's. He had instruction on the piano, organ and violin, and at about ten he began more serious studies, including composition with the Bonn court organist. At 13 he was assistant organist, and four years later he was sent to Vienna to study. There he may have had lessons with Mozart; but the trip was brief as Beethoven was summoned home to see his dying mother. From 1789 he had to manage the family, for his father was a heavy drinker. His main court duty was to play the viola in the chapel and theater orchestras. But Bonn was too small for a developing composer; soon after Haydn passed through on his journey from London in 1792, Beethoven was sent to Vienna to study under him.

The lessons were not successful; Beethoven afterwards said that Haydn took little trouble over him, and though Haydn esteemed the younger man he seems to have been unsympathetic to his musical ideas. When Haydn went back to England, Beethoven turned to J. G. Albrechtsberger, a diligent, methodical teacher. Meanwhile, he was establishing himself as a pianist, playing in the salon concerts organized by noblemen in their houses

Ludwig van Beethoven		Life
1770	born in Bonn, baptized 17 December	
1792	studied with Haydn in Vienna	
1795	public début as pianist and composer in Vienna	
1799	publication of Piano Sonata no. 8 in c, op. 13 ("Pathétique")	
1800–02	deterioration of hearing and period of depression	
1802	Heiligenstadt Testament, October	
1803	beginning of heroic "middle period"; Eroica Symphony	
1805	*Fidelio*	
1806–8	prolific composition, mostly large-scale instrumental works, including Symphonies nos. 5 and 6 ("Pastoral") and "Razumovsky" Quartets	
1812	letter to the "Eternal Beloved"; beginning of "silent period"	
1813	beginning of "final period"	
1814	highpoint of popular acclaim in Vienna; last public appearance as a pianist; revision of *Fidelio*	
1815	appointed guardian of nephew Karl	
1818	Piano Sonata no. 29 in B flat op. 106 ("Hammerklavier") completed	
1820–23	compositional activity: late piano sonatas, "Diabelli" Variations	
1823	*Missa solemnis* completed, Symphony no. 9 ("Choral") begun	
1825–6	concentration on string quartets	
1827	died in Vienna, 26 March	

Ludwig van Beethoven   Works

Symphonies no. 1, C (1800); no. 2, D (1802); no. 3, "Eroica", E♭ (1803); no. 4, B♭ (1806); no. 5, c (1808); no. 6, "Pastoral", F (1808); no. 7, A (1812); no. 8, F (1812); no. 9, "Choral", d (1824)

Concertos 5 piano concertos – no. 4, G (1806), no. 5, "Emperor", E♭ (1809); Violin Concerto, D (1806); Triple Concerto for piano, violin and cello, C (1804)

Overtures and incidental music Coriolan (1807); Leonore Overtures nos. 1, 2 and 3 (1805–6); Egmont (1810)

Opera Fidelio (1805, rev. 1806, 1814)

Choral music Mass in D (Missa solemnis, 1819–23)

Piano music 32 sonatas – no. 8, "Pathétique", c, op. 13 (1799), no. 14, "Moonlight", c♯, op. 27 no. 2 (1801), no. 21, "Waldstein", C, op. 53 (1804), no. 23, "Appassionata", f (1805), no. 26, "Les adieux", E♭, op. 81a (1810), no. 29, "Hammerklavier", B♭, op. 106 (1818); 33 Variations on a Waltz by Diabelli, op. 120 (1823); variations, bagatelles

String quartets op. 18 nos. 1–6 (1798–1800); op. 59 nos. 1–3, "Razumovsky Quartets" (1806); op. 74, "Harp" (1809); op. 95 (1810); op. 127 (1824); op. 132 (1825); op. 130 (1826); op. 133, "Grosse Fuge" (1826); op. 131 (1826); op. 135 (1826)

Other chamber music piano trios – op. 97, "Archduke" (1811); string quintets; piano quintet; sonatas for piano and violin – op. 24, "Spring" (1801), op. 47, "Kreutzer" (1803); Octet for wind instruments (1793)

Songs An die ferne Geliebte ("To the distant beloved"), song cycle for tenor and piano (1816); Scottish songs

and making his Viennese public début early in 1795. About this time his first important publications were issued: three piano trios op. 1 and three piano sonatas op. 2.

As a pianist Beethoven, according to reports of the time, had immense fire, brilliance and fantasy, as well as depth of feeling. In no other musical medium could he be so bold or so wholly himself. In these early years, it is in his piano music that he was most free and most imaginative. The first movement of his first published sonata, in the "stormy" key of F minor, shows his new urgency of voice in insistent figures, accented notes and an undercurrent of movement. It is easy to see how different an impression Beethoven was trying to make here from Mozart or Haydn: the assertiveness, the aggression of the unruly young man from the provinces is far from the graceful entertainment offered by the preceding generation.

In his early Viennese days, Beethoven lived on a salary from his Bonn employer, and was accommodated by various noble patrons like Prince Lichnowsky. It was with Lichnowsky that in 1796 he embarked on his first concert tour, to Prague, Dresden and Berlin. And Lichnowsky was the dedicatee of one of Beethoven's most striking works, the Piano Sonata in C minor op. 13, always known as the *Pathétique*. C minor was a key Beethoven favored for serious, dark-toned utterances. One of the op. 1 trios was in that key. Haydn, on seeing it, counseled Beethoven against publishing such a piece, for he found music of this temper alien. There is a C minor string quartet in the set Beethoven wrote – emulating Haydn and Mozart, but also competing with them – in the last years of the century.

His first two symphonies date from 1800 and 1802, but the passionate tone of his other early works is less clear here; it is still the piano sonatas that contain the most striking ideas. There is something original in every one of the 17 he composed up to 1802 – examples (besides the one discussed above and the *Pathétique*) are op. 10 no. 3, where the first and last movements show Beethoven building large structures from motifs of a few notes, with a slow movement profoundly dark-toned, dissonant and pathetic ("portraying a sad state of mind, with every shade of melancholy", said Beethoven of it); while op. 26 embodies a remarkable funeral march, and op. 27 no. 2 is the famous *Moonlight*, whose gently romantic reflectiveness brings a whole new world of feeling into the ambit of the sonata.

The "heroic" period

Beethoven's creative life has traditionally been divided into three periods: his youth and early manhood, with his establishment as a major composer (1770–1802); his middle life (1803–12), in which he handled all musical forms with full command and produced many of his most famous works; and his final period (1813–27), when the personal stresses he underwent are reflected first in the small number of works he produced and second in their intensely serious, often very intimate character. This division makes good sense and relates convincingly with the times of change, or of personal crisis, in Beethoven's life.

During 1802 Beethoven went through a profound depression. It was probably in 1796 that he had first become aware that his ears had become less keen. By 1800 he was aware that his hearing was impaired and also that the condition was worsening and was unlikely to be arrested, still less cured. To Beethoven the composer, it was not a catastrophe. As a gifted and thoroughly trained musician, with a perfect "inner ear", he could hear even complicated music by looking at it, and could write down the ideas that came into his head. (He had never composed at the piano, but rather at his desk, jotting down his ideas in sketch form, then working at them to give them shape and meaning.) But to Beethoven the pianist, it was a disaster. His ideas of a career as a virtuoso would have to be abandoned. So would teaching (an important source of income); so would conducting his own music. And to Beethoven the social man, deafness was a tragedy. He wrote to a friend, in 1801, that he was "living a miserable life. For almost two years I have ceased attending social functions, simply because I cannot say to people 'I am deaf' ". His ability to communicate freely with his fellow men – and with women – was appallingly damaged; he could never hope for a normal social life. As time went on, he became more and more turned in on himself, unable to share his thoughts and his problems with others, growing steadily more odd, more eccentric, probably more aggressive. This was a gradual process. In 1802 he still had several years of concert-giving ahead of him and his social life was not yet a total void. But in October that year, when he was in a village called Heiligenstadt outside Vienna, he wrote a strange "Testament": a kind of will, addressed to his two younger brothers, Carl and Johann, it describes his bitter unhappiness over his affliction in terms suggesting that he thought death was near.

Beethoven, however, came through this depression with his determination strengthened. He wrote, more than once, of "seizing Fate by the throat" and of the impossibility "of leaving this world before I have produced all the works that I feel the urge to write". This readiness to fight back against cruel adversity, is echoed in the "heroic" character of his music of the ensuing years. While nearly all Beethoven's music so far had been "absolute" (that is, had no content outside music), now he wrote large works that carry implications about his attitudes to life. There is, for example, his oratorio *Christ on the Mount of Olives*, of 1803, in which there is clearly some identification between Christ's suffering and that of Beethoven himself. In the opera *Fidelio* (or *Leonore*, as it was at first called), of 1804–5, other aspects of Beethoven's suffering and aspirations are dealt with, as we shall see. The most obvious product of his "heroic" phase, however, is the *Eroica* Symphony.

Plate 9 *Opposite* The bassoonist Felix Reiner, a court musician (p.147), and instruments: detail of a painting, 1774, by Peter Jakob Horemans. Bayerische Staats-gemäldesammlungen, Munich.

Plate 10 *Overleaf* The palace of Eszterháza (the garden front; the opera house is just visible on the left): painting, 1780, by Bartolomeo Gaetano Pesci (see p.151). Országos Müemléki Felügyelöség, Budapest.

Plate 11 *Left* Musicians playing the cello and square piano (see p.147): detail of the painting *George, Third Earl Cowper and the Gore Family* by Johann Zoffany (1733–1810), Yale Center for British Art. The square piano was the most common domestic keyboard instrument in England and the US in the late eighteenth century.

75 Ludwig van Beethoven: pencil drawing, *c*1818, by Carl Friedrich August von Kloeber. Beethovenhaus, Bonn.

The *Eroica,* Beethoven's third symphony, was written in the summer of 1803. At first Beethoven called it "Bonaparte": it was intended as a tribute to Napoleon, the hero of revolutionary France. But the following spring the news arrived that Napoleon had proclaimed himself emperor. Beethoven, angry and disillusioned at what he saw as a betrayal, ripped the title-page bearing the dedication off the score, tore it in half, and wrote on the symphony: "Heroic Symphony, composed to celebrate the memory of a great man".

The most obvious difference between the *Eroica* and any earlier symphony – by Beethoven or anyone else – is its much enlarged scale. A late Haydn symphony takes 25 minutes to perform, the *Eroica* 45. Yet, paradoxically, it does not have long themes: its themes are little more than motifs of a few notes, particularly in the great first movement (see Listening Note VII.E). The principal idea is simply based on the chord of E♭ major; the second-subject material is made up of a series of ideas, none of them exactly a "theme",

Listening Note VII.E   *Side 6, band 2*

Beethoven: *Symphony no. 3* in E♭, *Eroica*, op. 55 (1803)
2 flutes, 2 oboes, 2 clarinets, 2 bassoons
3 horns, 2 trumpets; timpani
1st and 2nd violins, violas, cellos, double basses

This symphony, the clearest product of Beethoven's "heroic" period, is on a larger scale than any before it, yet the themes are short and developed with concentration and power.

1st movement (Allegro con brio): Sonata form, E♭. The main theme is based on a chord of E♭.

Time

0:00	exposition: two chords serve as introduction
0:02	main theme, ex. i, E
0:46	main theme repeated, full orchestra
0:56	second subject begins dialogue theme, ex. ii, B
1:12	rising woodwind theme, ex. iii, B
1:22	violin, ex. iv, B
1:44	woodwind chord theme, ex. v, B
2:21	closing material
2:52	lyric theme (from ex. i)
3:13	development, starts in C
3:39	use of ex. ii, c–c♯–d
4:06	use of ex. iv over ex. i, d
4:16	use of ex. vi, violins, g–c–f–b
4:50	use of ex. ii, A
5:11	fugue-like section
6:07	crashing dissonant chords
6:19	theme, ex. vii, e
6:41	ex. i, C
7:09	clarinets, ex. vii, e
8:40	string tremolos
8:45	horn softly plays ex. i
8:51	recapitulation: ex. i, cellos, E
9:04	ex. i, horn, F
9:14	ex. i, flute, D
9:54	ex. ii, E
10:10	rising theme, ex. iii
10:20	ex. iv
10:42	ex. v
11:18	closing material
11:47	lyric theme
12:09	coda: beginning from ex. i, D –C
12:49	ex. vii, f
13:55	lyric statement of ex. i, horns, E
14:48	from ex. iii, E
14:58	final chords
15:13	(end)

2nd movement (Funeral march, Adagio): Ternary form, c–C–c.
3rd movement (Scherzo, Allegro vivace): Extended ternary form (A–B–A–B–A), E♭
4th movement (Allegro molto): Variation form, E♭

held together by their sheer power and momentum. Most remarkable is the development, in which most of the exposition ideas are thoroughly worked over, often in complex combinations or in alternation, and then the music seems to twist in wilful, perverse directions, landing on a huge, devastating discord, several times repeated: after which, as if chastened, it quietens and a new lyrical theme is heard, in a distant key.

That alarming climax and its softening, and the music that then hesitantly and mysteriously leads back to the recapitulation, provides one of the noblest yet most disturbing passages in Beethoven. The symphony continues in this exalted vein. The slow movement is a somber yet heroic funeral march, with a middle section that in its expressive oboe theme adds sentiment to the mourning. The third is a Scherzo. Haydn, years before, had talked of the need to invent a new kind of minuet, and Beethoven's need to express something less graceful and more violent had led him to this much more rapid triple-meter movement. The finale follows a variations pattern, one that was increasingly to suit his way of thinking. No early listener to this work could doubt that in it Beethoven was redefining the nature of the symphony.

He continued to do so. No. 4 is relatively orthodox, but the next two each break new ground. No. 5, in C minor, begins with the famous motif below said to represent "Fate knocking at the door" (ex. *a*). It is made the more menacing by its persistence: this motif appears throughout the movement, in one form or another. The slow movement is in variation form: like several of Haydn's, it varies two themes in alternation. It is no accident that the rhythm of the second (ex. *b*) corresponds with the rhythm that dominates the first movement.

With the third movement, a dark-toned Scherzo, the link is more explicit, for after a hushed opening statement the horns burst in with the four-note motif (ex. *c*). The movement becomes more sinister, with this rhythm reduced to an uneasy mutter, then to a background rumble. Then the finale breaks in. C minor changes to C major; the ghostly orchestration gives way to a blazing, triumphant sound, enriched by trombones in the middle, a piccolo at the top and a double bassoon at the bottom, as well as bass drum, cymbals and triangle, and the menace of the four-note rhythm is transformed into jubilation (ex. *d*).

In discussing the symphonies of Haydn and Mozart, it is never possible to talk specifically or with certainty about the emotions the music is intended to evoke. Here there can be no doubt. Beethoven's Fifth Symphony begins with a threat, explicit in the music's insistent rhythms and its tone; it ends with a triumph, darkness defeated by light. It is a typical product of Beethoven's heroic phase, and we can scarcely fail to see the work as representing, in Beethoven's mind, his conquering of the forces of adversity around him.

The Sixth Symphony is also representative, but in a different sense; and it tells us something important about Beethoven the man. He called it "Pastoral Symphony". It is about the countryside – or, rather, about Beethoven's reactions to the countryside. There are five movements, the extra one made necessary by Beethoven's plan: I, Awakening of happy feelings on arriving in the country; II, By the brookside; III, Peasants' merrymaking; IV, Thunderstorm; V, Shepherds' song of thanksgiving. Beethoven said that the symphony was "more the expression of feeling than painting". Although the third movement is akin to a peasants' dance (with hints of bagpipes) and the fourth contains representations of rumbling thunder, Beethoven did not intend us to listen to the music as a depiction of events. The *Pastoral* Symphony makes clear that Beethoven loved nature and the countryside. He lived in a large city, but went each spring and summer to stay in some nearby spa or small town and to take country walks. In his time, natural rural beauty was only just beginning to be admired; the previous generation, the age of landscape gardening, had held that unruly nature could be bettered by human art.

Like the *Eroica,* the Fifth and the *Pastoral* are large-scale symphonies; the scope of Beethoven's ideas and the elaboration of their working-out demanded an expanded time-scale compared with what had served for Haydn or Mozart. The same applies to Beethoven's chamber music. His op. 18 string quartets were on the traditional Classical scale, about 25 minutes long. His op. 59 string quartets, of 1806, have a time-span similar to those of the symphonies. There are three, dedicated to the Russian ambassador in Vienna, Count Razumovsky (they are called the "Razumovsky Quartets"). In his honor each was to include a Russian folk melody.

Opera

By the early years of the new century, Beethoven was widely recognized – not only in Vienna – as a leading composer, a highly original one whose latest works were eagerly awaited by connoisseurs and the public and were competed for by music publishers. With an annuity guaranteed by Prince Lichnowsky he could live in reasonable comfort. He was now anxious to prove himself in a new sphere: opera, which offered a composer the richest rewards, both material and in reputation. An opportunity came in 1803, and Beethoven started work; but the opera-house manager (Emanuel Schikaneder, who had put on Mozart's *Magic Flute*) lost his job and plans were abandoned.

76 Autograph sketches for Beethoven's Symphony no. 6 in F ("Pastoral"), 1808. British Library, London.

The next year he had an invitation to write an opera for the Theater an der Wien. He cast around for a plot and libretto; only a topic close to his heart, he felt, could draw from him music that embodied his deepest feelings. He did not have to look far. Since the French Revolution, many operas had been written that appealed to a love of freedom and

hatred of tyranny; many were "rescue operas", having as their climax the last-minute rescue from death of the hero or heroine. Several of the kind had been given in Vienna. A literary friend of Beethoven's prepared for him a libretto using a French story allegedly based on an actual incident: it was called *Leonore, or Married Love*.

Beethoven worked at the opera, to be called *Fidelio*, during much of 1804 and 1805. It is a tale of political oppression, set in a grim prison where the freedom-loving Florestan has been kept in a dungeon for two years by the district governor, Pizarro; his wife Leonore, disguised as a young man (Fidelio), takes a job at the prison, where the jailer's daughter Marzelline falls in love with "him". In the end, Leonore prevents Pizarro from killing her husband by throwing herself between them – and at that instant a fanfare is heard proclaiming the arrival of the Minister of State to inspect the prison and liberate those unjustly detained.

Beethoven had immense trouble composing the work. When it was first performed, late in 1805, it was a failure – though that was partly because it was given before an audience largely of French officers (Napoleon's army had conquered Vienna a week before). Beethoven's friends told him it was too long and began too slowly; he shortened it radically, and it had two performances, but then Beethoven quarreled with the theater authorities and withdrew it. He did not revive it again until 1814, when he had made extensive further changes. It is characteristic of the more mature man that these changes tend to make the opera less the story of two particular people and more a generalized tale about abstract good and evil. The characters may emerge less individually, but the opera's moral force is greatly increased.

One reason why Beethoven found the subject of *Fidelio* so attractive is that it dealt with freedom and justice. Another is that it dealt with a heroic theme and triumph over adversity. A third is that it dealt with marriage. Beethoven longed to marry; at the time he was composing *Fidelio* he was deeply in love with Josephine von Brunsvik. Like his earlier love, in 1801, for Countess Giulietta Guicciardi, it came to nothing. In both cases the young ladies were Beethoven's pupils; in both, the barriers of social class proved unsurmountable. In any case, we cannot know whether Beethoven's passion was recip-rocated. Possibly he never found a woman who could match his lofty image. We may anyway doubt whether a man so violent in his feelings, so absorbed in his art, so unruly and quarrelsome with those around him, was capable of engaging in a stable relationship.

But he continued, it seems, to hope. A document, as strange as the Heiligenstadt Testament, has come down to us. Written in the summer of 1812 and addressed to the "Eternally Beloved", it is a passionate love letter, expressing a desire for total union yet also expressing resignation at its impossibility. It speaks of mutual fidelity, of the pain of enforced separation, of hopes for a life together. It is hard to know what it really means. The evidence points to its having been written with Antonie Brentano in mind. She was a Viennese aristocrat married to a Frankfurt businessman; they and their ten-year-old daughter had known Beethoven for two years, and we know she admired him. But there is little reason to think that she and Beethoven had a love affair or contemplated a life together. We do not even know whether the letter was actually sent. It could well have been the product of an intensive private fantasy about marriage to an ideal, but safely unattainable, woman.

The last period

The year 1812 – critical in European history, with Napoleon's defeat in Russia – was a turning-point in Beethoven's life. In the preceding years he had composed much of the music by which he is chiefly remembered: the fourth to eighth symphonies, the fourth and fifth piano concertos (the latter, the "Emperor", one of his grandest conceptions, with

77 Scene from Beethoven's opera *Fidelio*, in the revival staged at the Kärntnertor Theater, Vienna, in 1814: engraving from the *Wiener Hoftheater Almanach* (1815).

the piano's heroic strivings and commanding assertions), the supremely lyrical violin concerto, chamber music, several fine piano sonatas including the great *Appassionata*. In 1808 he had considered becoming musical director at the court in Kassel of the King of Westphalia; but he was not eager to leave a busy capital city for a small, provincial one and when three of his Viennese admirers banded together to provide him with a guaranteed income he was glad to be able to stay. His career as a pianist was finished. He played his last public concerto in 1808; when he appeared at a charity concert in 1814 he could not hear himself play, and banged in the loud passages while in the soft ones he played so delicately that the notes did not sound.

The years following 1812 have been called his silent years: first, because he composed relatively little; secondly, because he was more than ever cut off by his deafness and became increasingly morose, suspicious and quarrelsome. He drove away all but his most tolerant friends with his aggressive behavior, was unable to keep servants, and lived in perpetual confusion, even squalor. From 1815 he had another great worry: his nephew Karl. Beethoven thought the boy's widowed mother a bad influence and fought in the courts to be appointed guardian. He succeeded, but as guardian was inevitably a failure, and Karl grew up an unhappy and wild young man who felt little of the gratitude or affection that his uncle demanded.

Beethoven's trials, social and personal, had a clear reflection in his music. His deafness prevented his hearing new works by other men, so his own idiom, instead of altering as the years passed, stayed basically the same, only growing more refined and concentrated. His interest in variation form becomes less a matter of elaborating a theme than of probing into it and discovering new layers of meaning. Several of Beethoven's late piano sonatas – he wrote three in 1814–18, three more in 1820–22 – include variation movements of this kind, but the most striking of his piano variations is the set on a waltz of Diabelli. Diabelli, a publisher, sent several Austrian composers a trivial waltz theme, asking each to write a variation on it so that he could publish a set. Beethoven, apparently intrigued by the theme, sent Diabelli 33 variations of intense complexity and technical difficulty.

Another form that increasingly fascinated Beethoven at this time was fugue. In earlier works, like the *Eroica*, he had sometimes used fugue in his development sections. Now he did so more often, and at greater length, for example in the late piano sonatas. Fugue, like variation, gave him a framework for the persistent treatment of a musical idea; in the finale of the op. 106 sonata, in particular, he wrestles endlessly and furiously with what is already a strange theme, turning it upside-down and inside-out. Its angry contortions seem to mirror Beethoven's restless, impassioned personality and the "distressful circumstances" under which, he later said, it was composed.

The final works

The great climaxes to his life's work, however, were still to come: they consist of two choral works and a group of string quartets. One of the choral works was a Mass, begun for performance at the ceremony in which one of his oldest and most trusted friends and patrons, the Archduke Rudolph of Austria, was to be enthroned as an archbishop. Unfortunately it was not finished in time. The other was a choral symphony. In 1817, he had accepted an invitation to write two symphonies for the Philharmonic Society of London and to go there to direct them. He did not do so, but the invitation drew him back to symphonic composition.

In the Choral Symphony, no. 9, many of the trends in Beethoven's compositional thinking were drawn together. The first movement carries to a new extreme the concept of the generating motif: the "theme" at the opening, simply a figure consisting of two notes, is the germ from which much of this long and powerful movement springs. Its derivatives are worked out plainly and openly so that the listener can hear them grow. The main idea of the second movement, a scherzo, is treated in a fugue exposition. The third is an extended double-variation slow movement on the pattern $A–B–A'–B'–A''$ – though the A'' section is as long as the rest of the movement and embodies several freely worked-out variations. This movement shows an intense lyricism typical of Beethoven's late music.

The final movement sees Beethoven for once making the meaning of an instrumental work articulate. Many earlier finales, as we have seen, carried strong hints of extra-musical meaning (like the triumph of the Fifth). But here Beethoven actually provides a verbal text and introduces a chorus and soloists to join in the expression of feelings about humanity and universal brotherhood: in this he echoed the composers of post-Revolution France. The words are from Schiller's *Ode to Joy,* which Beethoven had long admired and had considered setting as early as 1793. The movement is a huge set of variations. In its introduction, the earlier movements of the symphony are recalled; then comes the famous "Joy" theme – first on cellos and double-basses alone, next in fuller orchestral settings. Then the movement seems to begin again, and a bass singer, after declaiming "O friends, not such sounds as these; let us strike up more pleasing ones, full of joy!", sings the "Joy" theme. Thereafter the theme appears in different guises to parallel the sense of the words – military, for example, when the tenor sings of marching to victory over sorrow or tyranny. This long movement, nearly half-an-hour's music, is one of the most difficult and strenuous ever composed: intentionally so, for the sense of striving and effort is an essential part of the message.

Beethoven finished work on the Choral Symphony early in 1824; in May it had its first performance – he was too deaf to conduct and, at the end, sat in utter absorption until a friend told him that the audience were applauding wildly. Afterwards he gave a dinner party for the conductor, the concertmaster Schuppanzigh and his own assistant Schindler, which ended in disaster as Beethoven virtually accused them all of cheating him of money due from the performance. He was as difficult and quarrelsome as ever.

In 1823 Beethoven had accepted a commission from Prince Golitsïn, of St Petersburg, for some string quartets, a form he had not considered since 1810. With the Choral Symphony premières behind him, he set to work. They occupied him for the rest of his creative life and form a personal, intimate counterpart to the public statements of the Choral Symphony and the Mass for Archduke Rudolph. Golitsïn had asked for three quartets; Beethoven wrote three, but still had more to say and produced another two. The three central ones, traditionally numbered opp. 132, 130 and 131 (in that order of composition), are on a new plane of spiritual depth, with the often strange but exalted nature of their ideas, the abruptness of their contrasts, their passion, their emotional intensity. The op. 132 quartet, for example, begins with slow, grave, sustained imitative writing for the four instruments; then the first violin dashes off in rapid music, and the cello presents a brief phrase. The music is eventful, restless and challenging in a new way; and the ideas thrown up in these opening measures are treated later in the movement, followed up, developed and welded into a unity, so that the confusing opening comes to make sense. The slow movement reflects Beethoven's illness during the work's composition: he headed it "Sacred song of thanks to the divinity on convalescence, in the Lydian mode". By using an old church mode, Beethoven gave the music a feeling of antiquity and remoteness from ordinary human experience. His treatment also suggests the sound of a chorale prelude, as if a solemn hymn is being sung in the slow passages. The chorale-like music is presented with two variations, into which small motifs are woven with increasing elaboration; in between come sections marked "Feeling new strength", which portray a revival of vigor and warmth.

In opp. 130 and 131 Beethoven further extended the language of the string quartet. Op. 130, where again the first movement material is presented in diverse scraps, has six movements, including two slow ones of an intense, ethereal beauty quite unlike anything else in Beethoven. For its finale he originally wrote a huge fugue, long, harsh and immensely demanding to listener and player alike; his publisher persuaded him to replace it with a simpler movement as the quartet was too long and difficult. Op. 131 is in seven movements, though they are played continuously and, since they have material in common, seem to form a unity. The first is a slow, sublime figure, the fourth a complex set of variations.

Beethoven finished his last quartet in the fall of 1826. During the preceding summer he had been profoundly disturbed when his nephew Karl tried to commit suicide. Soon after, it was arranged that Karl would join the army. Beethoven and his nephew went, in the meantime, to spend some weeks at the country home of Johann van Beethoven, the composer's second brother. He returned, in haste (after a quarrel, apparently), in December, and was immediately taken ill. The doctors could do little but relieve the symptoms; everyone knew he was dying, and he was sent gifts, among them money from the London Philharmonic Society and wine from one of his publishers. On 26 March 1827 he died, during a thunderstorm; his last action was to raise a clenched fist. Some 10,000 came to mourn at his funeral: he had lived into the age – indeed had helped create it – when the artist was the property of mankind at large.

Chapter VIII

The Romantic Era

Unlike the terms "Baroque" and "Classical", which have little use in ordinary conversation or writing, "Romantic" is a word full of meanings in everyday use. Dictionaries define it as to do with romance, imagination, the strange, the picturesque, the fantastic. In the arts, it is similarly applied – to literature, painting or music in which fantasy and imagination are more important than such classical features as balance and wholeness. Because the Romantic era succeeded the Classical, roughly at the turn of the eigheenth century, it is usual, and convenient, to define the characteristics of Romantic art and especially music by comparison with those of the art of the Classical period.

Romantic art

The most obvious difference between Classical and Romantic music is usually expressed as one of precedence: in the Classical world, form and order come first, in the Romantic, expressive content does. A Classical piece, broadly speaking, has a clear-cut structure which the hearer is intended to perceive as an important part of the musical experience. By contrast, a Romantic piece depends on strong emotional expression, which may be generated by some subtlety or richness of harmony or color, by some dramatic juncture, or a variety of other means; and this is more important to the impact of the work than is its form. While the form of a Classical work was an outcome of the material of which it was composed, a way of giving it logic and order and balance, Romantic artists tended to accept form as an entity in itself and to fill out the traditional Classical patterns with ideas ever more arresting, attractive and laden with emotion, or to vary them as the spirit moved.

The Classical age, then, was one of orderliness, of serenity, taking its models from ancient Greece and Rome; it is no coincidence that the plots of serious operas were taken from classical mythology and history, which stressed the virtues admired in the eighteenth century. That period was called the Age of Reason, or the Enlightenment. In *The Magic Flute*, the three temples that lead to a symbolic heaven are labeled "Wisdom", "Nature" and "Reason"; there is no worshipping Fantasy or Imagination. Yet even then some disquiet spirits had rebelled against the prevalence of the rational and the well proportioned: this disquiet manifested itself in the German "Storm and Stress" movement, in England in "gothick" architecture which attempted to re-create medieval styles (and with them a sense of mystery), and in all Europe an interest in the Orient, with its exotic and fascinating remoteness.

By the turn of the century, interest in the Middle Ages, and things associated with that period, was growing. Now opera plots were often drawn from medieval history or legend, or from such works as the Waverley novels of Sir Walter Scott (1771–1832) which

78 Walpurgis Night scene from Delacroix's illustrated edition (1828) of Goethe's *Faust*.

aimed to recapture an age of chivalry and high romance. Mysticism, the demonic, the supernatural: all these, which had no place in the rationalist schemes of the eighteenth century, began to reassert themselves as a part of human experience.

The most famous and most influential manifestation of these interests is in the *Faust* of the great German writer Johann Wolfgang von Goethe (1749–1832) – in Faust's compact with the devil in his search for immortality and for sensual experience with an idealized woman. Numerous composers wrote works around Faust, Mephistopheles and Gretchen; some also treated the more philosophical second part of Goethe's great work. In the graphic arts similar interest in the dark, nightmarish side of human experience is seen in the works of such men as Francisco Goya (1746–1828), John Henry Fuseli (1741–1825) and William Blake (1757–1827); in music, examples of their strong expression are Schubert's song *The Erlking*, where a boy's soul is snatched away by an evil spirit during a ride through a forest, or the Wolf's Glen scene in Weber's *Der Freischütz*, where magic bullets are cast with the devil's aid, or the Witches' Sabbath in Berlioz's *Fantastic Symphony* with its shrieks and its ominous sounding of the "Dies irae" ("Day of Wrath") plainsong.

Religion and politics, too, form a part of this picture. Catholicism, the faith of the Middle Ages, underwent a new revival; its music, departing from the decorative Rococo that in effect Mozart and Haydn had been content with, acquired a new solemnity and plainness – the restoration of polyphony and plainsong were widely encouraged, and Renaissance church music began to be seriously studied and even used as a model.

Social change

Socially, this was a time of rapid change. With the American Revolution of 1776, a colony for the first time proclaimed its independence from its rulers: this was the first of a series of momentous events. The French Revolution, in 1789, had seen the near-extinction of the ruling classes in France; all the other crowned and noble heads of Europe were trembling. The Napoleonic Wars which raged from the late 1790s up to 1815 created confusion and poverty; meanwhile, the Industrial Revolution was fast gaining momentum and the shape of society was undergoing fundamental and permanent changes, with great cities growing up (often with appalling living and working conditions) and the countryside becoming depopulated. Political or social oppression became a subject susceptible to treatment through artistic protest; obvious examples are found in the poetry of William

Blake (who writes of the "dark, satanic mills") and in his paintings of industrial desolation.

In music, as we have already seen, Beethoven could hymn the brotherhood of man in his Choral Symphony (a type of work which owes its existence to the massive choral "revolutionary hymns" created in the wake of the French Revolution) and for his only opera set a plot concerned with freeing an innocent man from wrongful oppression. Other composers had earlier set the *Fidelio* story, which is only one (if the greatest by far) in a whole tradition of "rescue operas", coming in the first place from France but traversing much of Europe – except those places where a conservative and oppressive monarchy could still suppress such subversive ideas. Other kinds of political theme gained favor, especially in France, where massive spectacles, made possible by advances in theater design and lighting, were especially admired.

Escapism and Nature

Another aspect of Romanticism involved the use of art to escape from the increasingly unpleasant realities of life. One of the precursors of Romanticism, the German writer W. H. Wackenroder (1773–98), talked of the "wonder of music" as the "land of faith ... where all our doubts and sufferings are lost in a resounding ocean". Nature herself offered one escape route. The eighteenth century had paid homage to Nature, but chiefly packaged into beautifully laid-out landscapes, improved by Man from a crude and imperfect original, where idyllic scenes could be relished. Raw Nature was admired rather less; when Dr Samuel Johnson traveled to the Scottish Highlands he took good care to draw the carriage blinds as he was disturbed by the prospect of the hills. The nineteenth century however saw Nature as a huge and mysterious force, beside which Man shrank into insignificance. The paintings of Caspar David Friedrich (1774–1840) illustrate powerfully the impact of Nature on Man, often portraying a solitary man standing in awe or fascination at some wild scene of mists, rocks, turbulent waves or gaunt trees (which sometimes look as if struck by lightning). A musical analogy might be the storm movement in Beethoven's *Pastoral Symphony* or the country scene in Berlioz's *Fantastic Symphony*. The poetry of William Wordsworth (1770–1850) also talks of Man's relation to Nature and its ability to exalt him or fill him with awe.

79 *Winter.* oil painting, 1808, by Caspar David Friedrich (original destroyed). Neue Pinakothek, Munich.

Haydn and Mozart did not, of course, portray Nature in their music (except in Haydn's direct imitations, in his late oratorios, *The Creation* and *The Seasons*). Beethoven did; so did Mendelssohn, for example in his *Hebrides* Overture (where the music unmistakably symbolizes the waves of the Scottish coastal waters) and his "Italian Symphony"; so did Schumann in his "Spring" Symphony and Liszt in his symphonic poems, to cite only a few. Here we find music used to draw pictures, sometimes to depict events (as we shall see, in Liszt's case especially). Or, it may be argued, music does not draw or depict; rather, it can convey the same emotion as do the pictures or the events themselves. The same kinds of analogy came to exist between music and the literary arts; no longer is a song simply a poem set to music but, in the hands of a Schubert or a Schumann, a distillation of the emotion referred to in the words. This alliance between the arts is particularly characteristic of the Romantic era, and it found its ultimate expression in the "total art work" (*Gesamtkunstwerk*) conception of Richard Wagner's mature operas in which music, words, scenery and stage movement combine in a single whole – or at least that was Wagner's objective. This represented the highest ideal of the Romantics, the all-embracing, transcendent artistic experience: its culmination in acts of love and of death, in *Tristan und Isolde*, carries Romanticism to its farthest point, indeed to the farthest points of life itself.

Yet the huge scale of Wagner's operas represents only one side of the Romantic spirit. In the early days of Romanticism, especially, the emphasis is not on the large but the small. Beethoven, the last great classicist and a "pre-Romantic", wrote large-scale music; but the next generation were essentially miniaturists. Schubert's large structures are not always secure; his spirit is conveyed more essentially in his short songs or piano pieces. The greatest poet of the piano, Frédéric Chopin, created miniatures – waltzes, Polish mazurkas, atmospheric night-pieces that he called "nocturnes" – which catch a fleeting series of emotions in a brief time-span. The nature of the music written by these men, and others, rules out extended works; the expression of the moment is too pungent to be accommodated within a large-scale structure.

The music of Chopin and Liszt raises another issue central to the Romantics: technical virtuosity. Virtuoso had long been admired; Bach and Mozart, and many earlier men, were performers of dazzling skill. But now virtuosity attained new dimensions. What in an earlier age might have been thought tasteless and lacking in musical substance became attractive to audiences. Players technically as accomplished as Chopin or Liszt, but not their equals as musicians, toured Europe and America and filled the concert halls. One of particular fame was the Italian violinst Nicolò Paganini (1782–1840), whose cadaverous appearance and phenomenal technical skill led those who heard him to suspect some sinister alliance with the devil. The audiences were larger, and drawn from a wider range of social groups, than those of the eighteenth century. Larger concert rooms – necessary economically – had to accommodate performances less intimate, less refined, more arresting and more immediately appealing than those that had satisfied the previous generation, when art was the preserve of the connoisseur.

Naturally enough, it is to this age that the concept of "artist as hero" belongs. We have already seen the beginnings of it with Beethoven. While a man like Haydn was content to accept the status of a servant – he would not have thought of questioning it – the Romantic composer viewed himself quite differently. He was not simply supplying a commodity to his employer; he was a creator of something valuable and permanent. Haydn would not have expected his symphonies to outlive him; he wrote them by the hundred and regarded them as expendable, to be surpassed and superseded by those of the next generation. During Haydn's lifetime, however, the idea of preserving and even performing the music of the past began to gain currency, and to Beethoven and the

Romantics composition was for posterity. The creative artist was now the visionary –
compare any eighteenth-century composer portrait with the famous one of Chopin (fig.
84) by Delacroix (1798–1863), expressing his agonized Romantic genius – and he saw
himself as the equal of any man. When, in the middle of the nineteenth century, Liszt
came to Weimar, in central Germany, to work for the duke, it was as a friend and an
honored guest, not as an employee to write music to order. In this new context, it is not
surprising that the Romantic composer set a great deal more store by originality. The
Classicist was generally content to confirm with existing standards and models; the
Romantic was always under pressure to assert his individuality.

As we look in more detail at the main Romantic composers and their music, we shall
see various patterns emerge. Among the musical genres they used are most of those of the
Classical era. The symphony becomes larger as composers strive to embody within this
chief orchestral genre the widest possible range of expression. The concerto becomes
increasingly a vehicle for virtuosity, and one in which the "heroic" soloist may battle,
symbolically, against the world (the orchestra) – and triumph. Not surprisingly the most
characteristic orchestral form of the new era is the symphonic poem, in which the music
tells a story, or at least parallels its emotions: Liszt, influenced by Berlioz, is the central
figure in this development. Chamber music, moving from the drawing-room to the
concert hall, acquires a more public character. Piano music moves away from the abstract
sonata towards the genre piece (designed to capture a particular emotion or atmosphere) and
the idealized dance. Opera takes different directions in different countries, but everywhere it
deals with big issues, like the destiny of Man or the destiny of nations. The most
characteristic new genre of the Romantic era is the solo song with piano, as cultivated in
the German-speaking countries (and accordingly known as the *Lied*). Its first great master
was Franz Schubert.

Schubert

If, as the saying goes, "those whom the gods love die young", Schubert was even more
divinely beloved than Mozart; Mozart died at 35, Schubert at 31. Like the elder master,
Schubert, with his prodigious natural gift and his wide range of feeling, seems even at that
modest age to have reached a kind of maturity that escapes many who live far longer.

Franz Peter Schubert was a Viennese by birth, unlike the other three "Viennese Clas-
sicists" (he is often counted as a fourth but more properly belongs to the Romantic age).
Born in 1797, he was the youngest of four surviving sons. His father, a schoolmaster,
taught him the violin, his eldest brother the piano; but he soon overtook them and was
sent to the local organist – who quickly gave him up as he seemed to know all the organist
could teach him. At 11 he became a choirboy in the imperial chapel, which involved
attending the city college, where music was an important part of the course. Schubert
soon became concertmaster of the orchestra, sometimes directing it, and was taught by
the court music director, Antonio Salieri, a former colleague of Mozart's who years before
had given lessons to Beethoven.

Schubert did well in all subjects, but in music he shone brilliantly. Already he was
composing songs and instrumental pieces, including string quartets in which he played
with his father and brothers (his mother died in 1812). He produced numerous composition
exercises and songs in 1813, and also his First Symphony and an attempt at an opera. Later
that year he embarked on training as a teacher.

He continued to compose fluently and enthusiastically, and from 1814 date his first
Mass setting and a fine string quartet. But more important were his songs, one in particular.
Schubert had read Goethe's *Faust*, and was attracted by the scene where Gretchen, at the
spinning-wheel, is thinking about a lover. Written when he was 17, *Gretchen at the Spinning-*

Franz Schubert   Life

1797	born in Vienna, 31 January
1808	choirboy in the imperial chapel, Vienna
1810	studied with Antonio Salieri
1814	*Gretchen at the Spinning Wheel*
1815	schoolmaster; prolific output, especially of songs; *The Erlking*
1816	abandoned teaching; organized first "Schubertiads", evenings with close friends to perform his music
1818	music master to the children of Count Johann Esterházy, Zseliz; first public concert
1818	Vienna; reputation increased and circle of friends widened; *Erlking* published
1822	*Wanderer* Fantasia, "Unfinished" Symphony
1823	first period of serious illness; *The Beautiful Maid of the Mill*
1824	Octet, *Death and the Maiden* Quartet, A minor Quartet
1825	"Schubertiads" resumed; "Great" C major Symphony
1827	*Winter's Journey*; torchbearer at Beethoven's funeral
1828	three piano sonatas, string quintet; died in Vienna, 19 November

---

Wheel already shows the special qualities that mark out Schubert as a songwriter – the ability to depict poetically in his music something non-musical, the spinning of the wheel, and to couple with this the expression of the words, so that the wheel itself seems to express Gretchen's unhappiness.

In 1815, at 18, Schubert became a schoolmaster. He continued to compose, and at great speed. That year saw the composition of almost 150 songs, as well as two symphonies, piano and vocal music. Of the songs, several are to texts by Goethe, by the great classical poet Friedrich von Schiller (1759–1805) and by the pseudo-medieval Scottish poet known as Ossian whose tales of the romantic north fascinated many musicians (he was not actually medieval but a contemporary writing in a mock-ancient manner).

The greatest song of this year was the Goethe setting *The Erlking*. It is of the ballad type, telling a story rather than portraying a mood: a father is carrying his son on horseback through a forest, trying to ward off the evil spirit (the Elf king) who appears to the fevered child and eventually kills him. The pounding piano accompaniment symbolizes first the horse's hooves, but also the intense agitation felt by father and son, while the fiercely dissonant harmony depicts the tragic events and the boy's terror. Schubert's friend Josef von Spaun later told how, visiting Schubert, he found him reading the Goethe poem in high excitement, how he composed the song at great speed and how friends were immediately gathered to hear it – which they did with astonishment and enthusiasm. Its vivid, passionate expression, its feeling of alarm and horror at the confrontation of the innocent child with death and the supernatural, sound a new note in music, different from anything of Mozart or even Beethoven. This is music of the new, Romantic age.

Schubert had always enjoyed music-making in the family home. Now, by 1816, he was building up a circle of friends, young men like Spaun, who took part in "Schubertiads", evenings of performing Schubert's newest music. It was partly for these gatherings of middle-class, artistically aware, enthusiastic young people that Schubert composed. But gradually his reputation widened: a well-known opera baritone, J. M. Vogl, began to sing his songs, with the composer accompanying, in drawing-room recitals during 1817 and the next year one of his songs was published. In summer 1818 he gave up school teaching to become a music master in the family of Count Johann Esterházy (relatives of Haydn's former patrons).

1816 was another amazingly prolific year, again with song at the forefront of his output, though there were also sonatas for violin and piano and the Fifth Symphony, a work of particular charm and warmth of feeling. 1817 was productive too, with a sudden burst of interest in the piano sonata, another symphony, and many songs. Among these are three favorites: the gently grave *To Music*, a setting of words by Schober in praise of the art of music, lovingly and subtly composed in such a way that the "art of music" – a graceful melody and some characteristically expressive harmony – makes the point on its own behalf; the somber *Death and the Maiden*, akin in topic to *The Erlking* but making its effect more simply and darkly as Death invites the Maiden to sleep in his arms; and *The Trout*, where against a lyrical voice melody, a piano figure represents the glittering fish darting in the stream.

The Trout uses one of Schubert's typical methods in making its point. It is a "modified strophic" song (a strophic one being in several verses to the same music). Schubert often set out as if to write a simple strophic one, then, coming to its emotional climax in the final verse, changed the music to arrest the listener's attention by its unexpectedness and to color the crucial words more sharply. One of the factors that dictated Schubert's choice of verses was that an opportunity for this treatment presented itself. He read a great deal of poetry seeking suitable material for setting; he set many fine poets, but also some indifferent ones, for a good song – as he proved – can be made out of quite ordinary verse if its images and structure lend themselves to musical treatment.

80 *Schubert evening at the home of Joseph von Spaun*: sepia drawing by Moritz von Schwind (1804–71). Historisches Museum der Stadt Wien. Schubert is at the piano, with the singer Vogl on his right, and von Spaun on his left.

Franz Schubert   Works

Songs song cycles – Die schöne Müllerin (The beautiful maid of the mill, 1823),
Winterreise (Winter's journey, 1827), Schwanengesang (Swansong, 1828); *c*600
others – Gretchen am Spinnrade (Gretchen at the Spinning Wheel, 1814),
Heidenröslein (Little rose on the heath, 1815), Erlkönig (The Erlking, 1815), Der
Wanderer (1816), Der Tod und das Mädchen (Death and the maiden, 1817), An die
Musik (To music, 1817), Die Forelle (The trout, *c*1817), Der Hirt auf dem Felsen
(The shepherd on the rock, 1828), with clarinet

Orchestral music symphonies – no. 5, B♭ (1816), no. 8, "Unfinished", b (1822),
no. 9, "Great", C (*c*1825); overtures

Chamber music 15 string quartets – a (1824), "Death and the Maiden", d (1824);
String quintet, C (1828); Piano quintet, "The trout", A (1819); Octet for clarinet,
bassoon, horn, 2 violins, viola, cello and double bass (1824); piano trios, violin
sonatas and sonatinas

Piano music 21 sonatas – c (1828), A (1828), B♭ (1828); Wanderer Fantasia, C
(1822); Moments musicaux (1828); impromptus, dances; piano duets – Sonata,
"Grand duo", C (1824), Fantasia, f (1828), variations, marches

Operas Alfonso und Estrella (1822), Fierabras (1823)

Incidental music Rosamunde (1823)

Sacred choral music 7 Masses; *c*30 other works

Partsongs

The middle years

Back in Vienna at the end of 1818, Schubert took rooms with his friend the poet Johann
Mayrhofer. This began a period that was happy and productive and saw his reputation
steadily increase. He composed a couple of theater works; neither was of high quality but
both helped bring his name to notice. In the summer Schubert went to Steyr, 90 miles
west of Vienna, with Vogl, and was commissioned to write a piano quintet – the "Trout"
Quintet, of which the fourth movement is a happy set of variations on his song. The
whole work is permeated with its spirit, captured in the bubbling melodies, beguiling
harmonies and easily brilliant piano writing – which is often high and quick, adding a
glitter to the textures.

His circle of friends continued to widen: it came to include poets, court officials, singers,
the dramatist Franz Grillparzer and the painter Moritz von Schwind who left us a famous
depiction of the kind of friendly gathering to make music known as a Schubertiad. Some
of Schubert's friends got together to have *The Erlking* and other songs published; curiously,
the Viennese publishers were slow to take up Schubert's music, probably because he had
no real reputation as a concert performer. He spent part of the fall of 1819 at a castle in
St Pölten, working on an opera. But he was never very successful as a dramatic composer.

The great outpouring of songs of 1815, 1816 and 1817 had now slowed to a trickle.
Only about 15 date from 1818; in 1819 he wrote about double that number, and each of
the next three years saw the composition of around 15 to 20. Schubert was now putting
more of his personality and his intellectual and emotional concentration into instrumental
music. Two works from the end of 1822 demonstrate this in particular: the *Wanderer*
Fantasia for piano and the Unfinished Symphony. Schubert already had behind him about
a dozen piano sonatas, numerous dances and other shorter pieces, as well as piano duets
(well suited to his convivial musical evenings). This Fantasia is however something new:
it attempts something that composers had scarcely done before, nor even thought of the

need or desirability for doing. Virtually the whole four-movement work is organized around the same theme, stated emphatically at the opening. The slow movement, which gives the work its name, is based on a song, *The Wanderer*, composed six years before. But even this seems to be based on the same theme, or at least the same rhythm. The scherzo is more distantly derived from it, but the finale sounds almost like a fugal continuation of the first movement. This transformation of themes, where the same musical idea is made to acquire a range of different expressive senses, was later to be pursued by such men as Liszt, Berlioz and Wagner. Schubert's idea was chiefly to find a way of bringing unity to an extended work. This matter seems to have troubled him, for with his strong lyrical and harmonic gifts the passing events in his music are of such striking character that they may undermine unity and continuity.

The other remarkable work of late 1822 was the famous Unfinished Symphony. It is unlike any other earlier symphony in its profoundly poetic manner, its mystery and its pathos, as the dark-colored opening shows with its hushed cellos and basses, then throbbing strings over which oboe and clarinet in a strange unison float their theme. Later there is symphonic "argument" of a more usual, Beethovenian kind, but the atmosphere of the work is that of its opening measures, and the slow movement that follows does nothing to contradict that. Schubert started to sketch a third movement, but got no further. Why did he not finish what was potentially so great a work? We do not know; perhaps he put it aside because he had no need of a symphony at the moment, then later could not recapture its expressive world. He never heard it himself.

There may be other, more tragic factors behind his turning away from this symphony, for at the end of 1822 a catastrophe occurred in Schubert's life. There is evidence that, like many men of his time and class, he sometimes visited prostitutes (sexual activity with girls of his own class was unlikely). He now contracted syphilis. There were many treatments and a number of supposed cures, but the disease was not fully understood. Its progress and the treatments he underwent are easy to follow in the light of his friends' surviving comments on his health; for the rest of his life he suffered uncomfortable, often embarrassing symptoms. The disease moved fast, and it was almost certainly of syphilis (not typhus or typhoid fever, as some books say) that he died. The compositions of his remaining years, 1823–8, have to be seen in the light of his awareness of his illness and the suffering he underwent. It may be that some mental association between the composition of the Unfinished Symphony and the contraction of this terrible illness made it impossible for a man of such sensitive temperament to return to the work.

The late years

The year 1823 began with Schubert's return from his rooms in Schrober's house to the family home. The *Wanderer* Fantasia was published early in the year, and Schubert sold several collections of songs to Viennese publishing firms; his reputation was now sufficient to attract publishers' interest.

During the fall he was ill again – possibly he was in hospital in November – but able to work, and the chief product of the late part of the year was the song cycle *Die schöne Müllerin* ("The beautiful maid of the mill"). This is a collection of 20 songs telling a story in which the poet (and thus the singer) is protagonist: he arrives at the mill, falls in love with the mill-girl, enjoys happiness with her, feels anger and jealousy when she turns to another man, and dies. The bubbling of the brook is heard in many of the songs and there is much Nature imagery, designed to reflect the emotion expressed in the words. The choice of topic, with resignation and bitterness at the end, seems appropriate to Schubert's state of mind; though this kind of expression – love and despair, mirrored through Nature – is typical of early Romantic art.

81 Franz Schubert:
pencil drawing by Moritz
von Schwind (1804–71).
Private collection.

In 1824 Schubert returned to chamber music. First came an octet for wind and strings, a happy work in six movements, in the tradition of Beethoven's similar septet and, looking further back, of the late eighteenth-century divertimento. There were also two string quartets, in A minor and D minor. The first is predominantly lyrical, with hints too of the elegiac and the mysterious. The second, more fiery, pushed the medium of the string quartet towards richer, almost orchestral sonorities. After a dramatic and fully developed first movement comes one of Schubert's most imaginative creations: a set of five variations on a theme and a set of harmonies from his *Death and the Maiden* song.

These three masterpieces were written early in 1824; for spring and summer Schubert went again to the Esterházy family in Hungary. His circle of friends in Vienna had dwindled, and for more than one reason he was inclined to sigh for happier, more innocent days. Back in Vienna, he went early in 1825 to live near Schwind, now his closest friend; a new group formed, and Schubertiads resumed. Meanwhile, his music was being performed elsewhere and more was reaching print.

He spent much of the 1825 summer in Upper Austria. It was probably at this time that he composed his last and greatest symphony, known as the "Great C major" (it is usually called no. 9, sometimes no. 7; in fact, counting only the complete symphonies and the Unfinished, it should be no. 8). It is on a large scale; all its ideas are extended and fully worked out. The Andante introduction, with its solitary horn melody, sounds a Romantic voice; a distant horn conjures up favorite Romantic images. But the main part of the movement is more classical – much more so than the Unfinished – in its orderly statements and repetitions, and in the expressive blandness of the material itself, which is better designed for symphonic argument than most of Schubert's ideas. There are moments of Romantic mystery, too. In the first-movement exposition the music, where it might be expected to settle into the dominant key, G major, dips into remote E♭. The sound of soft trombones – instruments used mainly for their effectiveness in loud music – playing a broad melody that gradually seems to guide the music back where it ought to be, is one of the most imaginative strokes in symphonic music. The rest of the symphony is on a correspondingly large scale.

This great symphony, unhappily, is another work that Schubert himself never heard. It lay unknown in the possession of Schubert's brother Ferdinand until 1837, when Robert Schumann found it; the first performance, in which passages were omitted because of the work's length, was conducted by Mendelssohn two years later.

Schubert was back in Vienna by October 1825. More publications appeared, particularly of piano music, in 1826, and his name was gradually becoming better known. It was not a prolific time for composition, but he wrote nearly 20 songs in the year and a fine string quartet, a work of some violence with its rapid changes of mood, tense tremolos, abrupt changes of key and ferocious accents. There is almost a sense of personal pain and anger behind this remarkable, deeply original music.

A similar pain runs through Schubert's main composition of 1827, the song cycle *Winterreise* ("Winter's Journey"). The poems, like those of *Die schöne Müllerin*, are the work of Wilhelm Müller, whose flowing words, attractive imagery and shapely structures made them ideal for Schubert. As in the earlier cycle, the poems tell, largely through analogies with Nature, of desolation and longing; sometimes they refer to rejection in love, to bitter loneliness, to happy memories that have grown sad in recollection, to solitude and misery in a world where everyone else is joyous, to aimless wandering through cold and dark, and ultimately to death. The music is austere; most of the songs are in minor keys, many are slow, and the old warmth and harmonic richness are rare. It is not surprising that Schubert's friends were disturbed at this gloom.

Half the *Winterreise* songs were written early in 1827 (when, incidentally, Schubert was a torch-bearer at Beethoven's funeral), the others in the fall. Although his illness continued to trouble him, composition continued, sometimes at a rapid pace. To late 1827 and early 1828 belong the two fine piano trios, of which the one in B♭ stands out for its vitality and

---

Listening Note VIII.A   *Side 7, band 1*

Schubert: *String Quintet in C* D956 (1828)
2 violins, viola, 2 cellos

1st movement (Allegro ma non troppo): Sonata form, C. This contains lyrical melodies and subtle harmonies, but is almost symphonic in scale and conception.

Time	
0:00	exposition: opening theme, ex. i
1:08	cellos play ex. i below full texture
1:55	second subject, ex. ii, cellos E♭
2:34	ex. ii, violins
3:19	ex. iii, continuation of ex. ii, first violin echoed in viola, G
3:54	ex. iv (later used in dialogue)
4:38	ex. v, closing theme
5:12	development: idea from ex. ii (*x*) followed by ex. v (*y*)
8:35	recapitulation, ex. i, cello (plus violin), C
10:14	ex. ii, A
11.46	ex. iii, C
13:06	ex. v
13:34	coda
13:46	explosive *fortissimo*, b♭
14:04	*x* from ex. ii, C
14.50	(end)

2nd movement (Adagio): Ternary form, E–f–E
3rd movement (Scherzo: Presto): Ternary form, C–f–C
4th movement (Allegretto): Sonata form, C

ex. iii

ex. iv

ex. v

lyrical warmth. There are also several short, attractive piano pieces, published under the titles *Impromptu* and *Moment musical*.

1828, then, began promisingly. Schubert must have been heartened when, in March, a concert exclusively of his music – the only one he gave – took place in an inn owned by the Vienna Philharmonic Society and brought him some useful income. His publishing plans went forward. In September he moved to lodgings with his brother, and within a few weeks produced four major instrumental works: three piano sonatas and a string quintet.

We have seen that Schubert's command of musical design was not as strong as Beethoven's. But a work like the Piano Sonata in B♭ of September 1828, the last and grandest of these three, shows a powerful structure. It is not comparable with Beethoven's partly because Schubert's objectives were quite different from the elder composer's. His gifts, his musical personality, were of another kind – gentler, more lyrical, more concerned with harmonic effect and the quality of texture. His piano music achieved a climax of greatness in these last three sonatas. His chamber music too reached new heights with the String Quintet in C written at much the same time. For this work Schubert specified an ensemble consisting of string quartet plus an extra cello; this allows for greater enrichment of the sound and for the possibility of a low-pitched bass line continuing even when the first cello is playing in its high, tenor register. As in the B♭ sonata, the music is full of lyrical, expansive melodies, subtle and emotionally suggestive turns of harmony, and original effects of musical texture (see Listening Note VIII.A).

This first movement is one of Schubert's great achievements as a lyrical yet symphonic composer. The equally remarkable slow movement contains perhaps the stormiest, indeed blackest music that Schubert wrote, full of angry, dissonant harmonies, supported by tremolos and dislocated rhythms, and in the distant key of F minor. Here the darkest moods of *Winterreise* are expressed in instrumental terms. Then, in the middle of the hectic Scherzo comes a trio section which, instead of the conventional lyrical contrast, offers slow, bleak music, again in remote F minor. The finale is outwardly happier, but (typically) makes much of major/minor alternation, tingeing the music with darkness.

There was reason for darkness, and Schubert probably knew it. He went for a brief walking tour in October 1828, about the time he was working on the quintet, but was weak and exhausted. Curiously, he arranged to take counterpoint lessons from a well-known Viennese theorist during November, and even wrote some exercises. It seems that he never took the lessons; in November he was increasingly weak, often unable to eat, barely able to correct the proofs of the second part of *Winterreise*. Schubert's own wintry journey was over: he died on 19 November 1828. Grillparzer's famous epitaph – "The Art of Music here entombs a rich possession but even finer hopes" – is appropriate enough for a genius who died at 31; but it is typical of its time in failing to recognize that this man's genius had in fact reached full maturity, and that the legacy of his last few years already places him among the greatest of masters.

Early Romanticism in Germany

Schubert has been called a "Romantic Classicist", and the term is a fair one, for his art, however deeply imbued with Romantic attitudes to life, is still rooted in the musical traditions of Haydn, Mozart and Beethoven. There were others in Germany who show a similar mixture in different forms and proportions, but the first who fully embraced a Romantic attitude to his art was Weber.

Weber

Carl Maria von Weber was born in 1786, in north Germany, into a family of musicians (Mozart's wife, Constanze, was his cousin). His first main studies were in Salzburg, under Michael Haydn, Joseph's younger brother. He was not yet 12 when, in Munich, he wrote his first opera. Before he was 18 he was appointed *Kapellmeister* at the theater in Breslau; he tried to institute reforms to improve the level of performances, but made enemies and had to resign. His career then reads like a German travelogue, but in 1813 he was appointed *Kapellmeister* at the Prague opera house. Again he spent much of his energy on reform. But all this time his health was deteriorating. In 1816 he became royal *Kapellmeister* in Dresden where his plans to improve the German opera were often countered by the Italians, whose influence there was strong. Meanwhile, he was at work on an opera for Berlin, *Der Freischütz*; given in 1821, it was a triumph. Weber eventually managed to have it performed at Dresden early in 1822. Soon after, it was given in Vienna, where he was commissioned to write a similar opera. But he chose a grander manner, less suited to his talents, for the new work, *Euryanthe*. He was back in Vienna (where he met Beethoven and Schubert) in late 1823; *Euryanthe*, handicapped by a poor libretto, had a mixed reception.

The strains of these years – he had worked endlessly and the rewards had been slender – had told on him; he had tuberculosis. Then came an invitation to write an opera for London; the fee was large, and he accepted for his family's sake. In London he was warmly welcomed, but grew increasingly weak. The new opera, *Oberon*, was well received (although a piecemeal work, quite unlike the kind of opera Weber really believed in, and with an absurd plot). But his condition worsened and he died, far from home, in 1826.

Weber occupies a special place in the history of opera. He wrote melodies of appealing charm, he had a rich command of orchestral color (as *Oberon* in particular shows), and he had a real sense of how to convey atmosphere and drama. One of his devices was the use of a special theme in connection with a character, which he would alter to convey that character's feelings or behavior. (This technique, as we shall see, was later developed by Wagner.) *Der Freischütz* – the title literally means "The Freeshooter" – is a tale of the supernatural, about a forester who sells his soul to the devil in order to obtain magic bullets, with which he can prove himself a marksman worthy of his beloved, the head

82 The Wolf's Glen scene from Weber's *Der Freischütz*, in the 1822 Weimar production designed by Carl Wilhelm Holdermann: aquatint by C. Lieber.

ranger's daughter. The opera is full of typical early Romantic features: magic bullets, ominous dreams, a bridal bouquet that turns out mysteriously to be a funeral wreath, Nature (in the form of a forest) that both fascinates and alarms, comradely drinking-songs and hunting-songs, and the devil. For the convivial songs Weber uses the style, with a folk-music basis, favored by the many new choral societies that were coming into existence; these help give the opera its pronounced German flavor which so pleased early audiences. But the most characteristic and striking scene is the one in the Wolf's Glen where Max, the forester, makes his compact with the devil. Here Weber enlarges the vocabulary of music. As the scene opens, we hear soft trombones and low clarinets, a hushed *tremolando* on the strings, a chromatically wandering bass line, in sinister harmonies using chords that make the key feeling uncertain. Then there are shrieks on the woodwinds, shouts from an offstage, invisible chorus of spirits, a clock striking midnight, breathlessly quiet music alternating with violent outbursts, and a series of effects of increasing terror follow as the seven magic bullets are cast. The music is not just horrific; Weber was a musical thinker and planner, and the scene has a structure, in terms of pace, key and motif, that makes it the more effective.

Weber was the first composer to write serious music criticism, an activity that shows an awareness of musical issues and their relation to other aspects of life that it would be impossible to imagine in composers of a generation earlier. This selfconsciousness represents another aspect of the Romantic artist's attitudes to his art and society.

Mendelssohn

Weber conforms to the traditional notion of the Romantic artist who struggles through poverty and incomplete recognition, and in the end dies of "consumption". Felix Mendelssohn, emphatically, does not. He was born in 1809, in Hamburg, into a well-to-do upper-middle-class Jewish family, with a well-established cultural and intellectual background. His grandfather, Moses Mendelssohn (1729–86), was an eminent philosopher and a literary man; his father was a banker. The family moved to Berlin where Felix received a thorough education and his precocious musical gifts were encouraged. He wrote six symphonies when he was 12 and seven more in the next two years – Classical in style but with much spirit and individuality as well as great technical polish. When he was only 12, he was taken to meet Goethe, and a warm friendship developed. At 16 he was taken to Paris, where the senior Italian composer Luigi Cherubini (1760–1842), an opera composer much admired by Beethoven, encouraged him to follow a musical career.

Few musicians up to this time had as full a grounding in literature and philosophy as did Mendelssohn. His father's house was the meeting-place of influential writers and thinkers. Lines from Goethe's *Faust* colored his Octet for strings, written when he was 17; the scherzo of this vividly and richly scored work was inspired by a scene involving fairy spirits. More fairies, Shakespeare's from *A Midsummer Night's Dream*, affected another work of this time, his overture for that play. Although in sonata form, it includes music descriptive of incidents or characters in the play – the soft wind chords at the beginning and end hint at the atmosphere of the woodlands where much of the action takes place, rapid motion of high violins unmistakably represents the fairies, a "hee-haw" figure mimics Bottom with an ass's head, while the expressive second subject stands for the youthful lovers. The work is exquisitely scored, with original and poetic effects capturing the spirit of Shakespeare's world.

Mendelssohn's chief teacher, when he was a boy, was also director of the well-known Berlin choral society, the Singakademie. There he had come across choral music by J. S. Bach, which was unfamiliar – performers preferred more recent music. But Mendelssohn saw a copy of the *St Matthew Passion* and asked if he could perform it. In 1829, just over a century after its première, the work was revived for the first time since Bach's own performances. This initiated the long-term revival of Bach's choral works.

Mendelssohn's travels had been mainly in Germany. Now he went to London, where

---

Felix Mendelssohn   Works
born Hamburg, 1809; *died* Leipzig, 1847

Orchestral music symphonies – no. 3, "Scottish" (1842), no. 4, "Italian" (1833), no. 5, "Reformation" (1832); overtures – A Midsummer Night's Dream (1826), Calm Sea and Prosperous Voyage (1828), The Hebrides [Fingal's Cave] (1830, rev. 1832), Ruy Blas (1839); piano concertos – no. 1, g (1831), no. 2, d (1837), Violin Concerto, e (1844); 12 string symphonies

Oratorios St Paul (1836), Elijah (1846)

Chamber music Octet (1825); 6 string quartets; 2 string quintets; piano quartets, cello sonatas, violin sonatas

Piano music Lieder ohne Worte (Songs without words), 8 vols. (1829–45); sonatas, variations

Sacred choral music cantatas, motets, anthems, psalms

Organ music preludes and fugues

Songs   *Partsongs*   *Incidental music*

he was particularly well received, and on to Scotland, where he noted his impressions (and made many accomplished drawings); then, in 1830, he traveled in Italy. These journeys provided him with material for some of his finest works. The Scottish trip suggested musical ideas from which he composed a symphony and an overture. In the Hebrides islands, off the Scottish coast, Mendelssohn had seen Fingal's Cave, and the swell of the waves on the rocky coastline – as well as their more violent buffeting of it in a storm – can be heard in his atmospheric overture. Another musical element in this work, unrelated to Nature, has its source in Mendelssohn's poetic imagination: the distant fanfares of trumpets (or instruments imitating them), hinting at some mysterious presence in the caves or behind the craggy rocks, especially where the instruments echo one another. In all this we see again that part of the Romantic spirit that concerns itself with the observation of Nature.

To the early 1830s – when Mendelssohn was still in his own early 20s – belong many of his finest works. Among them is his "Italian Symphony", written in 1832 shortly after his return from Italy. It reflects the fascination that Italy, with its brilliant, clear skies, its warmth and vitality has always held for artists, like Goethe and Handel, from the colder, cloudier north. The music catches this clarity unmistakably, not only in the dashing, energetic line of the opening theme, heard on violins in octaves, but also in the extraordinary boldness and originality of the accompaniment, rapid repeated notes on the flutes, clarinets, bassoons and horns. The music is always fluent and graceful, yet such was Mendelssohn's technique that he could also give it symphonic coherence. The slow movement, said to draw its main theme from a pilgrim song, is sometimes called a pilgrims' march. The third is closer to minuet than scherzo in its warmth and charm, with a suggestion of distant fairy horns in its middle section; the finale is a rapid movement in the manner of a saltarello, a dance from Naples.

In 1835 Mendelssohn became conductor of the orchestra of the Gewandhaus ("Cloth Hall") in Leipzig, a post he held for the rest of his life. He did much to raise the orchestra's standard and improve its working conditions; he revived music by Bach and Mozart, pressed the claims of Beethoven, still a modern composer, and introduced music by Weber and Schubert, including the "Great C major" Symphony. In the early 1840s he spent time in Berlin, for which he supplemented his *Midsummer Night's Dream* overture with music for other scenes of the play, including the most famous wedding march ever written. Mendelssohn also made journeys to England, where he was immensely popular – he was friendly with Queen Victoria and her German consort, Prince Albert, and much loved by the choral societies which had come to occupy a large place in English musical life. It was for one of these that he composed his oratorio *Elijah*, in the Handelian tradition though adapted to the musical style of the day, which was a huge success. Leipzig, however, remained the center of his activities. In 1843 he founded there what was to be the most famous European music conservatory; in the second half of the century it was the best place for musical study and especially attracted students from abroad.

Among the compositions of these years are two piano trios (the one in D minor is the most sparkling and effective piece composed for the medium) and several string quartets. But his finest achievement was his Violin Concerto, written in 1844, the first of the great Romantic violin concertos. Here Mendelssohn's capacity for appealing, poetic writing found an ideal outlet in the sweet, refined voice of the violin which could draw lyrical and plaintive melodies above the sound of the full orchestra. His adaptation of traditional concerto form to the special character of the work is typical of his mastery: for example in the opening measures, where he dispenses with the orchestral prelude and simply supplies a gentle accompaniment for the violin theme, or in the new role he finds for the cadenza –

formerly the climax at the end of the first movement, now a point of repose to provide a magical link between development and recapitulation. The slow movement is songlike, with a touch of the sentimentality characteristic of the time (present too in some of Mendelssohn's piano music, like the *Songs without Words*); in the finale, those fleet-footed fairies are back in a movement of spirit and brilliantly handled virtuosity.

Mendelssohn seemed, in the mid-1840s, to be at the highpoint of his career and happy in his family life. But the freshness of his youthful works had gone, and for all his unrivaled technical command nothing had quite taken its place. When he returned from his last English journey, in the spring of 1847, he heard of the death of his sister Fanny, who had been particularly close to him. That summer he wrote a string quartet, a passionate work in the dark key of F minor. But he was unwell and in November he died. It is tempting to offer a Romantic interpretation and see his death as an answer to the dilemma of a prodigious genius that never quite discovered the inner resources needed for its fulfillment.

Schumann

If a single composer had to be chosen to represent the features of Romanticism, it should probably be Robert Schumann. He was almost as much a literary man as a musician, and images from literature pervade his music; he was preoccupied with self-expression; he was a miniaturist with a strong lyrical and harmonic gift. And his life embodied Romantic events in abundance.

Schumann's father was a publisher, bookseller and writer, working in the Saxon town of Zwickau when, in 1810, Schumann was born. Stories of his early abilities focus more

Robert Schumann		Life
1810	born in Zwickau, Saxony, 8 June	
1828	law student at Leipzig University but neglected studies in favor of music and literature	
1829	piano lessons with Friedrich Wieck; Heidelberg University	
1830	lodged with the Wiecks in Leipzig	
1831	"Abegg" Variations published	
1832	first trouble with hand, prejudicing his career as a concert pianist	
1834	founded *Neue Zeitschrift für Musik* which he edited for ten years	
1835	*Carnaval*; first serious interest in Clara Wieck, Friedrich's daughter	
1837–9	relationship with Clara interrupted by her long absences on concert tours with her father, who strongly opposed their marriage	
1840	married Clara after court case; nearly 150 songs including *A Woman's Love and Life*, *A Poet's Love*	
1841	orchestral music	
1842	chamber music	
1843	choral music	
1844	toured Russia with Clara; moved to Dresden	
1846	Clara gave first performance of Piano Concerto	
1850	*Genoveva* (Leipzig); appointed musical director in Düsseldorf	
1852	health deteriorated	
1853	met Brahms	
1854	attempted suicide; committed to asylum	
1856	died in Endenich, near Bonn, 29 July	

Robert Schumann   Works

Songs song cycles – Frauenliebe und -leben (A woman's love and life, 1840), Dichterliebe (A poet's love, 1840), Liederkreis, op. 24 (1840), op. 39; c275 others

Piano music "Abegg" Variations, op. 1 (1830); Papillons, op. 2 (1831); Davidsbündlertänze, op. 6 (1837); Carnaval, op. 9 (1835); Phantasiestücke, op. 12 (1837); Kinderszenen (Scenes from childhood), op. 15 (1838); Faschingsschwank aus Wien (Viennese carnival pranks), op. 26 (1840); Album für die Jugend (Album for the young), op. 68 (1848); 3 sonatas (1835, 1838, 1853)

Orchestral music symphonies – no. 1, "Spring", B♭ (1841), no. 2, C (1846), no. 3, "Rhenish", E♭ (1850), no. 4, d (1841, rev. 1851); Piano Concerto, a (1845); Konzertstück for 4 horns and orchestra (1849); Introduction and Allegro for piano and orchestra (1853)

Chamber music Piano Quintet, E♭ (1842); Piano Quartet, E♭ (1842); 3 string quartets (1842); piano trios, violin sonatas

Opera Genoveva (1850)

Choral music Das Paradies und die Peri (1843); Scenes from Faust (1853)

Incidental music Manfred (1849)

Partsongs   *Organ music*

on the writing of poems and articles than on music, though as a boy he was an accomplished pianist. There are also tales of his early love affairs or at least enthusiasms. His literary enthusiasm was above all for the writings of Jean Paul, as the novelist J. P. F. Richter (1763–1825), noted for his richly sentimental but humorous style, was known. In 1828 he went to Leipzig University to study law, but he spent his time in musical, social and literary activity. He composed piano music and songs and took piano lessons from an eminent teacher, Friedrich Wieck (1785–1873), who had a nine-year-old daughter, Clara.

Schumann was not happy in Leipzig, and the next spring he moved to Heidelberg University. It was music he was studying (though not very methodically), rather than law. Eventually he persuaded his mother, with a letter from Wieck to say that he could be a fine pianist if he would work hard, to permit him to turn to a musical career. He came back to Leipzig in the fall of 1830, to live in Wieck's house and study theory as well as the piano. Nothing, however, went according to plan. Wieck, anxious to foster his daughter's career as a child prodigy, was often away on extended tours. The theory lessons were slow to begin and quick to finish. And then Schumann had trouble with his right hand; almost certainly this was due to treatment he had been given for a syphilitic sore – probably he had contracted the disease in 1828 or 1829. His finger was weakened and not fully controllable; a career as a virtuoso pianist was closed to him.

But composition could continue. His first work to be published, a set of piano variations on the name of a girl acquaintance, Abegg (the theme used the notes A, B, E, G, G), appeared in 1831. A similar idea runs through another, larger work, *Carnaval*. Here the "theme" is A, S, C, H (in German A, E♭, [Es], C, B, or A♭ [As], C, B). Asch was the town from which Ernestine von Fricken, a 17-year-old pupil of Wieck's, came; Schumann and she had a love affair but he abandoned her in favor of Clara Wieck, for his interest in Wieck's daughter took a new direction in 1835, when she was 16.

By then, Schumann had embarked on a career in music journalism. In 1834 he had founded the *Neue Zeitschrift für Musik* ("The New Journal for Music"; it still exists), which he edited. His taste was very personal, and though he was quick to spot the talent of such men as Chopin and Brahms, and to praise the special genius of such men as Schubert (on whose "Great C major" he wrote a detailed essay) and Berlioz (whose *Fantastic Symphony* he likewise lauded), he also liked some trivial music and disliked some that we now see to be of high value. His writing however has great spirit and character, and he uttered many penetrating remarks about the nature of music which summarize the musical philopsophy of Romanticism.

In his criticism and his music, Schumann often donned disguises: he wrote under various names, chiefly "Eusebius" and "Florestan" (modeled on characters in a Jean Paul novel). Eusebius represented the lyrical, contemplative side of his character, Florestan the fiery, impetuous side. These names appear as titles in *Carnaval*, the former for a dreamy Adagio, the latter for a vigorous movement marked "Passionato". Other pieces in *Carnaval* are named after the *commedia dell'arte* characters Pierrot and Arlequin, and such others as "Coquette", "Papillons" (butterflies, a favorite image of Schumann's), "Chiarina" (his name for Clara), "Chopin" and "Paganini" (musical tributes to those men). This parade of characters in Schumann's life or imagination ends with a "March of the League of David against the Philistines" – the League of David being Schumann and his friends fighting for true art against the anti-art philistines. This way of putting together an extended composition was typical of Schumann and his time: a collection of "characteristic pieces", each short and simple in form, allowing contrast in mood and texture, without putting strain on the composer to unify the work. The last movement of *Carnaval* uses material from the first and thus acquires a sense of climax and finality.

Among Schumann's piano works of these next years are *Davidsbündlertänze* ("Dances for the League of David"), *Kreisleriana*, fantasy pieces around the character of a mad *Kapellmeister* created by the Romantic writer E. T. A. Hoffmann, and *Kinderszenen* ("Scenes from Childhood"), a series of nursery pictures for young pianists. But affairs of the heart dominated his life. Clara and he wanted to marry, but Clara's father would not hear of it; he took her away and forbade contact between them. In summer 1837 Clara formally

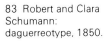

83 Robert and Clara Schumann: daguerreotype, 1850.

agreed to their marriage, though her father continued to thwart it. They were often apart and Schumann was depressed and close to suicide. But in May 1839 they took legal steps to make Wieck's consent unnecessary; not until September 1840, after Wieck had disgraced himself in court, did they marry.

1839 had been a year of strain and Schumann had composed very little. But 1840, when his and Clara's love was realized and consummated, was wonderfully creative. It was natural at this juncture that he should turn to song. He wrote almost 150 in 1840, including several collections ("Liederkreis") and two cycles. One, clearly provoked by his and Clara's situation, tells the story of "A Woman's Life and Love", through falling in love, marriage, motherhood and widowhood; the other, like Schubert's two great cycles, tells of a love that fails. This is *Dichterliebe* ("A Poet's Love"), to words by Heinrich Heine (1797–1856), with whose subtle, often pained poetry with several layers of meaning he felt a natural sympathy. *Dichterliebe* begins with the poet's declaration of love in springtime, moving on to Nature imagery with mention of nightingales' song and flowers, and paralleling the loved one with the image of the Virgin in Cologne Cathedral. But the love is rejected, and the second part of the cycle deals in the poet's exclusion from these joys as he dreams of loneliness on the mountainside and of awaking in his grave, and ultimately he talks of burying his love in a coffin. Schumann was less spontaneous a nature poet that Schubert; he concentrates more on the emotional focal point of a poem than on the details of the text. He was used to conveying the full expressive content of a piece in his piano writing and he continued to do this in his songs. Many of the finest achieve their most powerful moments in a piano solo at the end, when the voice has stopped. And often, during a song, the voice and piano seem to share the expression, as in the opening song of *Dichterliebe* (see Listening Note VIII.B).

Schumann now moved to orchestral music, anxious to attempt the larger forms which until then had defeated him. Clara, perhaps unwisely, encouraged him. In early 1841 he composed a symphony, which Mendelssohn conducted in March; two more symphonic works followed and, for Clara, a movement for piano and orchestra (later to be part of his Piano Concerto).

Married to a concert pianist, Schumann began to feel that he was living in her shadow, and sometimes decided to stay at home rather than travel with her. During such a spell in 1842 he turned to chamber music, and though he was too depressed to compose much when she was away he wrote, soon after her return, three string quartets and three works with piano, of which the Piano Quintet has always been a favorite for the freshness and the romantic warmth of its ideas and the vigor with which it is carried forward. It is essentially the work of a pianist-composer, with piano writing more interesting and effective than the string writing.

In the next year, Schumann turned to choral music, writing a setting of parts of *Faust*. He went on a lengthy tour of Russia with Clara, after which he suffered some kind of breakdown. In the fall he and Clara moved to Dresden, where they spent five years. Schumann had given up the editorship of the *Neue Zeitschrift* but his career as a performer had not advanced. So when in 1849 he was invited to take on the city musical directorship of Düsseldorf he was bound to consider it. He and Clara moved there in September. The early months there were prolific: he wrote his Cello Concerto, the noble "Rhenish" Symphony, with a movement inspired by the grandeur of Cologne Cathedral, and revised an earlier symphony to form the one known as no. 4. But the appointment did not work out well. Schumann's indifferent conducting meant that the orchestra and chorus disliked performing under him. During 1852–3 his health and spirits deteriorated, and though he had another creative summer in 1853 and made a loyal new friend – the young Brahms –

Listening Note VIII.B   *Side 7, band 2*

Schumann: *Dichterliebe* (1841), "Im wunderschönen Monat Mai"

Im wunderschönen Monat Mai, als alle Knospen sprangen, da ist in meinem Herzen die Liebe aufgefangen.	In the most beautiful month of May, as all the buds were breaking, there was in my heart the awakening of love.
Im wunderschönen Monat Mai, als alle Vögel sangen, da hab' ich ihr gestanden mein Sehnen und Verlangen.	In the most beautiful month of May, as all the birds were singing, then did I tell her of my longings and desires.

(words by Heinrich Heine)

Heine's poem is straightforward, telling of the coming of love in the springtime and paralleling it – typically for its time – with the blooming of Nature. Schumann's setting, however, is far from joyous. The key is f♯, predominantly; the voice part alone begins (in each verse) in A – a key Schumann often used for springtime music – and ends in D. But essentially it is the piano, in its prelude (ex. i), its interlude and its postlude, that conveys the true sense, here as in all Schumann's songs; and it begins with dissonance and pathos (see ex. i) and ends the same way. Schumann is not writing about the coming of love but about the unhappy recollection of a love that has vanished.

Time

0:00	piano prelude, ex. i	0:34	"auf-ge-fang-en"
0:14	voice, ex. ii: note	0:38	piano interlude
	expressive	0:48	second verse
	appoggiaturas, x	1:08	piano postlude
0:28	"Herzen"	1:28	(end)

ex. i   Slow, gentle

ex. ii

Im wun·der·schö·nen Mo·nat Mai,   als al·le Knos·pen

sprang·en   da ist in mein·em Her·zen   die

Lie·be auf·ge·fang·en.

it was becoming impossible for him to maintain his directorship.

At the beginning of 1854 Schumann, who had always feared madness, began to have hallucinations. In February he attempted suicide by throwing himself in the Rhine; he was rescued and taken to an asylum. There he lived on for more than two years, having rational spells, but visits excited him and Clara was not permitted to come. His disease finally killed him in July 1856. For years it had affected his perceptions and compositional skills – or so it seems, for the music of his late years lacks the old personal stamp and assurance. But Schumann was the composer of many songs and much piano music in which the spirit of Romanticism is at its most appealing.

Romanticism outside Germany and Austria

The German-speaking countries were the homeland of early Romanticism in music. German nationalism in the late eighteenth century, German poetry, drama and legend (especially as interpreted by Goethe), and German love of the transcendental all went towards ensuring that. In Italy, as we shall see (p. 216), Romanticism took a different direction; in northern Europe, including England, it had no strong manifestation – there were no great Romantic composers there. In the Slavonic countries it was slow to develop, partly because of the social backwardness of their institutions; when it did, as we shall see in Chapter IX, it did so powerfully and distinctively. Yet, for all Germany's pre-eminence, the world capital of Romanticism was Paris. Germany, still not a nation, had rival capitals. Accidents of history had made France more centralized, and Paris the largest and culturally the richest city on the European mainland. Its salons offered unequaled opportunity for aristocratic patronage, and it is to there that men like Chopin and Liszt naturally gravitated – as well as composers like the German-born Giacomo Meyerbeer (1791–1864), the leading figure in the spectacular grand opera tradition that centered on the French capital.

Chopin

The greatest master of the Parisian salons in the early Romantic era was a Pole, by birth and by sentiment. The father of Frédéric (or Fryderyk) Chopin was a Frenchman who had left France in 1787 to avoid army service; he took a Polish wife and settled in Warsaw a few months after the birth of their only son in 1810. Frédéric had a natural gift for the keyboard, improvising and composing dances in the familiar national rhythms; when he was only seven one of his polonaises was published. He often played in aristocratic homes,

Frédéric Chopin	Life
1810	born near Warsaw, 1 March
1818	first public appearance in Warsaw
1822–7	music lessons with the director of the Warsaw Conservatory
1827–9	student at the Warsaw Conservatory
1829	encouraged by noble families in Warsaw
1830	acclaimed in Vienna; toured Germany
1831	Paris
1832	reputation established in Paris after first public concert; became fashionable teacher, member of salon society, popular with noble Polish families, friendly with leading composers, writers and artists
1836	met George Sand; first signs of illness
1837	England
1838	Majorca with Sand and her children; worsening of illness; worked on 24 Preludes
1839	recovered at Sand's summer home at Nohant; Bb minor Piano Sonata
1841–6	summers at Nohant
1847	liaison with Sand ended
1848	Paris Revolution; concert tour of England and Scotland; last public concert in London
1849	died in Paris, 17 October

Frédéric Chopin	Works

Piano music 3 sonatas – c, op. 4 (1828), b♭, op. 35 (1839), b, op. 58 (1844); 4 ballades – g, op. 23 (1835), F, op. 38 (1839), A♭, op. 47 (1841), f, op. 52 (1842); 24 Preludes, op. 28 (1839); Fantaisie-impromptu, c♯, op. 66 (1835); Barcarolle, F♯, op. 60 (1846); nocturnes, polonaises, rondos, scherzos, studies, waltzes, variations

Orchestral music (all with solo piano) piano concertos – no. 1, e (1830), no. 2, f (1830); Variations on "Là ci darem" (1827); Andante spianato and Grande polonaise (1831)

Chamber music Piano Trio (1829); Cello Sonata (1846)

Songs

and he took part in a public concert before his eighth birthday. He was taught music by the head of the Warsaw Conservatory, where he later took a three-year course in theory and composition.

But Warsaw was too small and provincial for a musician of Chopin's potential, as he must have realized when he heard such visiting artists as Paganini. In 1829 he visited Berlin, and then Vienna, where he was well received. He returned to plan an extended concert tour, but there were delays, partly because of political unrest in Europe. His works of this time already show the elegance of line and subtlety of harmony that were to distinguish his music. But he was celebrated in Warsaw chiefly for his treatment of national melodies and rhythms and his absorption of Polish folk traditions into high art.

In September 1831 Chopin settled in Paris, where he quickly became established: he was taken up by patrons, was considered a fashionable teacher, and – being as polished a person as he was a musician – moved with ease in the salons. He did not seek a virtuoso's career, which would not only have made heavy demands on him physically but would also have called for a more flamboyant approach to pianism. He gave fewer than 30 public performances in his entire career; his delicate, veiled, finely detailed playing was heard to better advantage among connoisseurs in a private drawing-room.

84 Frédéric Chopin: detail of portrait, 1838, by Eugène Delacroix. Musée du Louvre, Paris.

Chopin quickly became accepted into the élite artistic society of Paris. His musician friends included Berlioz, Liszt, Meyerbeer and the Italian opera composer Bellini, whose graceful vocal style has its echoes in Chopin's music; he also came to know men like Heine, Balzac and Delacroix, who painted his portrait. He mixed in Polish émigré circles, and may there have met the Countess Delfina Potocka, a notorious beauty; it has been said that they were lovers, but it is doubtful whether Chopin had real sexual interest in women.

Among his music of these years are numerous dances, studies, nocturnes and a ballade. For the dances – not intended for actual dancing – Chopin usually chose the waltz or one of the Polish national types, mazurka or polonaise. Some of the mazurkas, especially, even though transferred from countryside to salon, capture the flavor of the folk-dance rhythm (see Listening Note VIII.C).

The studies (or *Etudes*, the familiar French title) show how real music can be made out of a problem of piano technique. The ballades, more extended, take their name from a supposed narrative content. In them Chopin used broader themes, sometimes assigning to each a particular keyboard texture; the themes are not "developed" in the Beethovenian sense, which would be inappropriate to their lyrically expressive nature, but their recurrences make the formal outlines clear. This is a natural method of constructing a piece for a composer who, like Chopin, worked by improvising at the piano. Further, he usually

Listening Note VIII.C   *Side 7, band 3*

Chopin: *Mazurka no. 45,* op. 67 no. 2 (1849)

This piano piece is in ternary form, in g. The mazurka is a Polish country dance or song, in triple meter and usually with an accent on the second or third beat of the measure. There are various characteristic rhythmic patterns, one of which the present example follows closely; this has the accent shifting between the second and third beats, as can be seen from ex. i.

Time

0:00	first section, first phrase, ex. i
0:12	first section, second phrase, g
0:26	second section, first phrase, B♭
0:31	downward sequence, B♭-A♭-G♭
0:37	second section, second phrase, B♭
0:50	linking passage
1:02	repeat of first section, first phrase
1:15	repeat of first section, second phrase
1:32	(end)

ex. i

added an increasing element of virtuosity during a piece, making each recurrence more of a dramatic event.

It was in the nocturne that Chopin used piano texture most atmospherically. Here his model was the Irish composer and pianist John Field (1782–1837). Most composers for the early piano had exploited its capacity for technical brilliance. Field used a new delicacy of touch; he made the piano sing; and with his left hand he wove a soft texture, using the sustaining pedal to make important bass notes persist. Chopin was able to carry this approach still further; the range of accompaniment patterns is large, and each has its own poetic character. Most involve a singing, finely detailed melody above a gently moving bass part.

The main non-musical event in Chopin's life during the 1830s was his liaison with the woman novelist George Sand. When, through Liszt, they met in 1836, she was 32, legally separated from her husband, author of two novels which questioned social institutions (notably marriage), striking rather than beautiful, respected in literary circles for her progressive thinking. In winter 1838–9 Chopin left Paris with her and her two children for the Spanish island of Majorca. It was a mixed success. For much of their time they were in a disused convent, but it was damp, and Chopin had bronchitis, which must have accelerated the tuberculosis that eventually was to kill him. They returned and went to Sand's country home, where she nursed him back to health. They went to Paris in October 1839, living close to one another but not together; each summer from 1841 to 1846 they went to Sand's country home. This ambiguous liaison, which ended in 1847 when Chopin became involved in her family quarrels, was a source of inspiration to him. Much of his most deeply felt music dates from his years with her, and once they had parted he wrote scarcely another note.

Without Sand's nursing, his health began to fail. Circumstances were against him: the 1848 revolution in Paris left him without pupils or means of support, He accepted an invitation to London, where he played at private concerts and was generously treated; he also went to Scotland, staying with his pupil and passionate admirer, Jane Stirling. He was back in Paris by the end of 1848, and grew weaker. He died in October 1849.

Nearly all Chopin's music is for solo piano. His orchestral works all have solo piano parts; the most important are the two concertos he wrote as a young man in Poland. The works of his time with Sand include dances, ballades, nocturnes and two four-movement sonatas. These demand a new view of the sonata: there is no Beethovenian unity, though one acquires coherence from having been composed around its slow movement, the famous funeral march, which was written first – its dark colors cast a pall on the composition of the rest. The later sonata has much invention and fantasy, and its outer movements show a true, sonata-like purposefulness. Chopin was above all a poet of the piano. But it would be wrong to underrate his range, which extends from the graceful to the grandiose, the tenderly poetic to the tempestuously passionate.

Liszt

The other great pianist-composer of the Romantic era, after Schumann and Chopin, is Franz Liszt: perhaps less fine a composer, but a musical thinker of much importance and a crucial figure in musical Romanticism. Liszt was born in 1811, in Hungary. His native

Franz Liszt	Life
1811	born in Raiding, near Sopron, 22 October
1821	studied the piano with Carl Czerny and composition with Antonio Salieri in Vienna
1822	first public concert, in Vienna
1823	Paris; first tours as an acclaimed virtuoso pianist
1826	first important piano works
1827–30	contact with leading writers and artists in Paris; friendship with Berlioz
1831	deeply impressed by Paganini's violin playing and determined to emulate his virtuosity on the piano
1833	friendship with Chopin; first piano transcriptions
1835	teaching in Geneva; living with Countess Marie d'Agoult (they had three children)
1839	undertook to pay for Beethoven memorial in Bonn; beginning of years of travel throughout Europe and most brilliant period as a flamboyant virtuoso
1844	separated from the countess
1847	beginning of relationship with Princess Carolyne Sayn-Wittgenstein
1848–57	musical director to the Grand Duke of Weimar; made Weimar a leading musical center, conducting new orchestral works and operas, some by Wagner (now a close friend); many orchestral works
1858	resigned Weimar post
1861	Rome
1865	took minor holy orders; religious music
1869–85	divided time between Rome, Weimar and Budapest
1886	died in Bayreuth, 31 July

LISZT és a NÓK.

85 Liszt idolized by female admirers after a concert: caricature from *Bolond Istók* (25 March 1876).

language was German. He studied in Vienna and gave his first concerts when he was 11. In 1823 the family moved to Paris, where Liszt quickly made his mark; he was still only 12 when he made his London début. By the time he was 16 he was a veteran touring virtuoso, and gave up traveling to teach; he also considered entering the priesthood.

Meanwhile, Liszt was moving in Parisian literary and artistic society – his friends included Heine, Victor Hugo and Berlioz, whose music he greatly admired; Chopin's friendship came a little later. In 1831 he heard Paganini and resolved to become his pianistic equivalent. He transcribed works by Berlioz and others for the piano; he believed that any music, for whatever medium it was written, could be performed on the piano just as effectively, and throughout his life made transcriptions – sometimes he went further,

Franz Liszt   Works

Orchestral music Faust Symphony (1854); Dante Symphony (1856); symphonic poems – Tasso (1849, rev. 1854); Les préludes (1854); Hunnenschlacht (The slaughter of the Huns, 1857); Hamlet (1858); piano concertos – no. 1, E♭ (1849), no. 2, A (1849), Totentanz for piano and orchestra (1849)

Piano music Transcendental Studies (1851); Album d'un voyageur (Traveler's album), 3 books (1836); Années de pèlerinage (Years of pilgrimage), 3 books (1837–77); Six Consolations (1850); Sonata, b (1853); Mephisto Waltz no. 2 (1881); Hungarian Rhapsodies, ballades, studies; numerous transcriptions (music by Bach, Beethoven, Bellini, Berlioz, Schubert, Wagner etc)

Choral music St Elisabeth (1862); Christus (1867); Masses, psalms

Songs   Secular choral music

writing fantasies on themes from popular operas, which made excellent recital material as the audiences could recognize the themes and appreciate his brilliant reworkings. He was beginning to compose significant original pieces, too, by the mid-1830s.

Liszt was a glamorous figure, intensely attractive to women. In 1834 he met the Countess Marie d'Agoult; they soon became lovers, and the next year they went to live in Switzerland, Liszt taking up a teaching post in Geneva. Later, they traveled – to Paris, to George Sand's country home, and to Italy, where Liszt found a powerful source of inspiration in art. Their third child was born in Rome in May 1839. Liszt gave many concerts and composed prolifically for the piano; much of his music embodies his impressions of the places they visited, or the artistic associations of those places, for example "The Fountains of the Villa d'Este". Many pieces are headed with poetry, by Byron, Schiller, Michelangelo and others. He later collected these pieces as *Years of Pilgrimage*; some of the music is graphic, like the "Fountains" piece, where rapid arpeggios suggest the flowing water, but most represent Liszt's own emotional reactions to poetry or art, people or places.

The ensuing years were Liszt's busiest. He had committed himself in 1839 to paying a large sum for a Beethoven memorial, and this meant that he had to resume a traveling virtuoso's career. In 1839–47 his program reads like a guide to European travel. Everywhere he was marveled at, fêted and loved. In 1847 he established a new relationship with Princess Carolyne Sayn-Wittgenstein. It was she who persuaded him to give up a virtuoso's life, and he took up an appointment he had been granted in 1842 as honorary music director to the Grand Duke of Weimar, who was eager to re-create the artistic prestige his city had enjoyed in Goethe's time.

Living in Weimar, with Princess Carolyne, he had an orchestra and theater at his disposal. He gave premières of several important operas, notably Wagner's *Tannhäuser*. With the orchestra, he could experiment and to these years belong virtually his whole orchestral output. His symphonic poems are based on ideas from art or literature: *Hamlet*, for example, was inspired by Shakespeare, *Tasso* by a Goethe play (and by Liszt's knowledge of the Italian poet), *The Slaughter of the Huns* by a picture of an early medieval battle. The music is less narrative than expressive of the emotions aroused by the subject; normally there is no attempt to portray events, though the themes may represent aspects of the subject of the work.

The principles are carried further in Liszt's *Faust Symphony* (1854). The first movement is headed "Faust", the second "Gretchen" and the third "Mephistopheles" – "three character studies after Goethe", he called it. But it is more than that, for the treatment of the themes and the ways they are related are linked to the Faust story. At its simplest, the Faust themes and the Gretchen ones intermingle, and the Faust themes are parodied in the Mephistopheles movement. This technique, like those Berlioz had used in his *Fantastic Symphony* (see p. 211) and Wagner's, allows the music to express character development, perhaps even to tell a story in some degree.

Liszt did not regard this as solely a dramatic technique, with meanings outside music. His greatest piano work, the Sonata in B minor, composed in 1852–3 and dedicated to Schumann, uses a similar method: its three movements, played continuously, are largely derived from a single main theme and its offshoots, so that the sonata has a powerful unity. The technique is basically similar to Schubert's in his *Wanderer* Fantasia (see p. 191), though worked with greater intellectual sophistication.

Towards the end of the 1850s Liszt's position at Weimar grew more difficult, partly because there was a new Grand Duke whose interest in music was limited, partly because of Princess Carolyne (who was not divorced from her husband), partly because Liszt's progressive tastes were not echoed by the court – especially his support of Wagner, who was in political disfavor. He finally left Weimar in 1861 for Rome; but his hopes of the princess's securing a divorce were disappointed, and he took minor orders in the Roman Catholic church (though never actually became a priest). His music of this period reflects his increasing religious interests. He gave piano lessons, in Weimar and Budapest as well as Rome. He was estranged from Wagner for a time, because of Wagner's affair with Liszt's daughter Cosima (who was married to the pianist and conductor Hans von Bülow), but they were reconciled and were together in Venice shortly before Wagner's death there in early 1883. His travels continued: in 1886 he was in London and then Bayreuth, where at the end of July he died.

Liszt was a strange mixture: would-be priest, yet with a diabolic streak in his make-up and notorious for his countless illicit love affairs; a composer capable equally of noble invention and cheap effectiveness; a musician who lived by his virtuosity yet was also a searching, adventurous thinker with new ideas about the future of music. Some of those ideas he put into effect, in his notions of thematic transformation and, very strikingly, in the bold harmonies of the dark, austere piano works of his last years. He remains one of the most fascinating of the Romantics.

Berlioz

Among the early Romantic masters the solitary Frenchman, Hector Berlioz, stands apart. He was no pianist, and no purveyor of piano miniatures, but a man with flair, grand ideas and a formidable sense of drama.

Berlioz was born in 1803, not far from Lyons. His father expected him to follow him into the medical profession. But Hector, who played the flute and the guitar, and had jotted down a few compositions in his youth, was bent on a musical career. He went, in 1821, to medical school in Paris, but found dissections and operations hateful. More to his taste were the opera performances he heard, especially those of works by Gluck. He half-heartedly continued medical studies up to 1824, but also studied music and wrote an opera, a Mass and other works. The Mass was performed, and he was encouraged to pursue music. He did. His parents' financial support was now modest, and he scraped a living by writing, singing, teaching and anything else he could manage. He enrolled in 1826 at the Paris Conservatoire, and was now finding his voice as a composer.

In 1827 he went to hear *Hamlet*, in English (which he did not understand); he was profoundly impressed by the play – Shakespeare was to be a lifelong influence – and still more by the Irish actress playing Ophelia, Harriet Smithson, for whom he conceived a powerful romantic passion. He pursued her, and his unruly love for her stands behind his

Hector Berlioz	Life
1803	born in La Côte-St-André, Isère, 11 December
1821–4	medical student in Paris; composition lessons with Jean Le Sueur
1826	entered Paris Conservatoire; first noteworthy compositions
1827	saw *Hamlet* in Paris and developed passion for Shakespeare and Harriet Smithson, the actress who played Ophelia
1830	Fantastic Symphony
1831	to Rome after winning the Prix de Rome at the Conservatoire
1833	married Harriet Smithson
1834–40	period of greatest works, including *Requiem, Romeo and Juliet, Les nuits d'été*; active as a musical journalist
1841	beginning of decline in popularity in France
1842	first concert tour of Europe as a conductor
1844	separated from Harriet Smithson; beginning of increased concert-giving in Europe and of literary activity
1846	*The Damnation of Faust* performed in Paris and poorly received
1848	beginning of period of further tours and less concentrated composing
1852	Weimar with Liszt, who gave a Berlioz Week
1854	married Marie Recio, with whom he had been for 12 years
1856–8	work on *The Trojans*
1863	second part of *The Trojans* performed in Paris with limited success
1862	*Beatrice and Benedict*
1864	health deteriorating
1869	died in Paris, 8 March

Hector Berlioz	Works

Operas Benvenuto Cellini (1838), Les troyens (1858), Béatrice et Bénédict (1862)

Orchestral symphonies – Symphonie fantastique (1830); Harold en Italie (1834), Roméo et Juliette (1839); Grande symphonie funèbre et triomphale (1840); overtures – Waverley (1828); Le roi Lear (1831); Le carnaval romain (1844)

Sacred choral music Grande messe des morts (Requiem) (1837); Te Deum (1849); L'enfance du Christ (1854); motets

Secular choral music Lélio (1832); La damnation de Faust (1846)

Vocal music (solo voice with orchestra) La mort de Cléopâtre (1829); Les nuits d'été (Summer nights, 1841)

first great work, the *Fantastic Symphony*. A more immediate love affair with a lovely young piano teacher, Camille Moke, provided him with the perspective on his passion for Harriet Smithson which he needed to be able to write the symphony. Although Beethoven, whom Berlioz worshipped, was the model, little about the symphony is Beethovenian; it has five movements, and is built around a "program" which Berlioz distributed at performances.

The symphony portrays a musician who, in despair over a hopeless love, has taken opium and is in a feverish, dream-haunted sleep. In the first movement ("Reveries,

Passions") he recalls the emptiness before he met his beloved – a slow introduction, passionate but unfocused and arbitrary, with climaxes that fade into nothing – and then the fierce love that she inspired in him. The beloved is represented by a theme that recurs obsessively. Second, he is at a ball, graceful but later hectic. It is exquisitely scored, with only upper woodwinds, horns, strings and a pair of harps. But suddenly the music takes an unexpected change of key, and the beloved appears, the theme transformed to fit the rhythm of the dance music; as the ball ends, she reappears distantly. The central movement represents a country scene – more literally treated than Beethoven's in the *Pastoral* Symphony with shepherds' pipes, bird-calls and a drowsy languor. Then the music becomes turbulent, and the beloved's theme is heard; finally there is distant thunder, Nature imagery symbolizing unease. The fourth movement and the fifth call on the Romantic preoccupation with death and the supernatural. He dreams that he has killed his beloved and is being marched to the gallows (Berlioz uses cornets and rasping, low-pitched trombones); the beloved's theme is heard as the guillotine blade falls. Then comes a Witches' Sabbath, in which the beloved takes part, her theme vulgarized and grotesque on a high-pitched clarinet. The "Dies irae" sounds on bells, the clatter of skeletons is heard (violinists striking their strings with the wood part of the bow), and all moves to a hectic conclusion.

Shortly before the première of the *Fantastic Symphony*, Berlioz had been awarded a scholarship to Rome (having failed previously because his work was considered too original, he wrote a conventional piece that the examiners would like). But he was unsettled in Rome, and almost returned to Paris, particularly as he heard nothing from Camille, to whom he was betrothed; then he heard that she was to marry someone else, and set off to kill her, her fiancé, her mother and himself – but changed his mind and went back. This inspired in him a sequel to the *Fantastic Symphony*, called *Lélio, or The Return to Life*; that work and one song were the sole products of 15 months in Italy.

Berlioz, back in Paris late in 1832, at once gave a concert with the *Fantastic Symphony* and its new sequel. He arranged for Harriet Smithson to attend, and they were introduced. She could hardly fail to be impressed by the composer who had put his passion for her into this music; soon she reciprocated it, and they were married – contrary to the wise advice of friends and both families – the following fall. They were happy for a time, but by about 1840 had drifted apart. Meanwhile Berlioz was busy with composition and, to earn a living, journalism; he was a brilliant, witty, opinionated and colorful writer. Several important works belong to this period: the symphony *Harold in Italy*, based on a Byron poem; the opera *Benvenuto Cellini*, and the *Grande Messe des Morts* (or *Requiem*), written to a government commission for performance in the large Invalides church.

The *Grande Messe* is on a huge scale. The French, at the time of the Revolution, had encouraged massive musical events to appeal to large audiences. Berlioz's work calls for 16 timpani and brass bands in the four corners of the church, so that in the movement dealing with the last trumpet the listener hears music from all sides, sometimes in turn, sometimes together. The work is not, however, mainly noisy; in some ways it is stark and austere, with thin textures, plain counterpoint, and in the Offertory (which greatly impressed Schumann) the chorus sing in unison on just two notes while the orchestra weaves an increasingly elaborate contrapuntal web. Another striking movement is the Sanctus, with its high, ethereal writing for violins and flutes.

This work was performed in 1837. The next year saw the failure of his *Benvenuto Cellini* at the Opéra, but he extracted from it one of his finest concert pieces, the overture *Roman Carnival* (see Listening Note VIII.D). In 1839 came the "dramatic symphony" on the story of *Romeo and Juliet*. The Shakespeare play had always moved him intensely, especially

Listening Note VIII.D   *Side, 7, band 4*

Berlioz: Overture, *Roman Carnival* (1843)

2 flutes (1 flute, 1 piccolo), 2 oboes (1 oboe, 1 english horn), 2 clarinets, 2 bassoons
4 horns, 2 trumpets, 2 cornets, 3 trombones
timpani, cymbals, triangle, tambourines
1st and 2nd violins, violas, cellos, double basses

This overture is in one sonata-form movement; before the slow introduction is a fast section, designed to set a carnival mood. It provides many examples of Berlioz's colorful orchestration.

Allegro assai–Andante–Allegro vivace; A

Time
0:00	introduction, part 1 (fast section, setting carnival mood)
0:19	introduction, part 2 (slow)
0:28	ex. i, english horn solo, C
1:35	violas, E
2:41	violas and cellos followed by violins, A
4:10	swooping woodwind scales
4:17	exposition: theme, ex. ii, muted violins, A
4:37	continuation phrase, ex. iii, A
4:54	second subject, ex. iv, E
5:29	exposition repeated, different scoring
6:28	development: loud tutti
7:05	ex. i, bassoons, F
7:14	ex. i, trombones
7:22	long crescendo begins
7:36	recapitulation, of second subject: ex. iv, A
7:44	coda: mock fugue on ex. iv
7:56	ex. i, trombones, E♭–A
8:08	ex. iii, full orchestra
8:19	meter changes from 6/8 to 2/4
8:27	brilliant climax based on ex. iv

because of its association with Harriet. For this treatment of it he took a number of crucial scenes, sometimes setting the words, sometimes providing an instrumental representation. The Queen Mab scherzo has fairies even lighter and fleeter of foot than Mendelssohn's; the texture is like the finest threads of gossamer. Among the audience at the first performance, in 1839, was the young Richard Wagner, who was deeply impressed by the work and the artistic ideals behind it.

Berlioz composed a number of concert overtures; most are extremely brilliant, effective orchestral pieces, usually inspired by some literary work. Partly through these, his reputation had begun to travel abroad. Now, in the early 1840s, he wanted to travel himself, especially as his marriage to Harriet was showing signs of strain. His position in Parisian musical life was now acknowledged, but he still felt cynical towards the conservative musical establishment in the French capital. So in 1842 he embarked on the first of a series of concert journeys across Europe, taking with him a singer, Marie Recio, whose lover he had become; he and Harriet were to separate in 1844 and he married Marie ten years later, after Harriet's death. Marie sang in his concerts and for her he orchestrated songs from the *Les nuits d'été* (*Summer Nights*) series, delicate, often exquisite pieces that he had composed in the 1830s with piano.

Berlioz found himself better appreciated abroad than at home. He was a celebrity and his new ideas were welcomed as they never had been in Paris. The point was driven home strongly in 1846. He had composed a major new work, based on Goethe's *Faust*, a "dramatic legend" called *La damnation de Faust* for chorus, soloists and orchestra. When he gave it in Paris he was deeply hurt by the public indifference towards one of his most original and spectacular creations.

Berlioz treated *Faust* rather as he had *Romeo and Juliet*, taking a selection of scenes that appealed to him as material for musical treatment while preserving the broad dramatic design. The first section is set in Hungary; the second deals with Faust and Mephistopheles, with drinking scenes, scenes for soldiers and students, and a graceful sylphs' dance; the third centers on Marguerite (the French usage for Gretchen); and the last has as its climax Faust's consignment to Hell.

Like so many Romantic composers, Berlioz was inspired by the Faust story to some of his finest, most characteristic music. Its opening theme is typical of Berlioz, not only for its sense of longing but also for its curious implications of harmony and rhythm. Most melodies of the eighteenth and nineteenth centuries are conceived within some standard harmonic pattern; Berlioz's often are not. This has something to do with the influence of the French language and its rhythmic structure; but more it is a matter of Berlioz's never having been a pianist and accustomed to the disciplines of harmony that are both trained into the piano learner and acquired under the pianist's exploring, creative fingers. Berlioz's explorations were in the mind, and show freedoms that had no place for men like Schumann or Chopin.

Poetic melodies like these represent one side of this work; others are found in the rousing march, the vivid choruses and ebullient songs, in the exquisite delicacy of the music for the sylphs and wills-o'-the wisp, and in the music of the extraordinary final scenes. Here Mephistopheles takes Faust on a Ride to the Abyss: we hear the pounding of horses' hooves, peasants praying, the wails and shrieks of monsters, as the music strides hellbound with increasing momentum, leading to a Pandemonium scene with a chorus in a made-up language for the inhabitants of hell. Finally Marguerite ascends to heaven to the sound of upper woodwinds, harps and violins. Berlioz was a master of orchestration (he wrote a standard work on the subject) and *Faust* shows him at his most original and effective. And it shows him as the arch-Romantic, his music filled with images of Nature, the

86 *A concert in the year 1846*: engraving by Cajetan after Geiger, based on Grandville's popular view of Berlioz's flamboyant conducting, with a vast orchestra and deafened audience.

macabre and the supernatural, death and redemption, as well as love, both idealized and intensely erotic.

In 1848, the year that Europe (Paris included) was torn by revolution, Berlioz was in London, conducting operas and concerts of his music. In 1852 he was in Weimar, where Liszt put on his *Benvenuto Cellini* and a Berlioz festival, and the next year he met Wagner.

As he grew older, the travels diminished. He continued to write about music – memoirs, travel tales, anecdotes, criticism, textbooks. Opera remained important to him, as a world he had never conquered yet vital because of his veneration of Gluck. Two operas belong to his late years. One, *Béatrice et Bénédict*, based on Shakespeare's *Much Ado about Nothing*, was in his own words "a caprice written with the point of a needle". The other, after the Latin poet Virgil, who for him stood next to Shakespeare, is his great two-part epic *The Trojans*. It had a chequered history and the first part was never staged in Berlioz's lifetime. It is Gluckian in its classical grandeur and its sense of tragic inevitability, and Meyerbeerian in its grand opera spectacle, with crowd scenes dealing with the fates of nations against which the loves and fears of individuals are set in relief. This noble work, drawing together so many of the creative threads that run through Berlioz's life, embodies some of his richest ideas, worked out over a huge canvas, and there is a tragic irony in its failure to secure a performance in his own day.

In the 1860s Berlioz suffered from internal illness, and was much depressed by deaths in his family – Harriet had died in 1854 and Marie in 1862. He struck up a curious friendship with a woman, by then an elderly widow, with whom he had been infatuated as a boy of 12. His Romantic quest for the unattainable was in a sense satisfied. In 1866–7 he undertook some final tours – to Vienna and Russia; he came home weakened, and in 1869 he died. No one did more than this most visionary of the Romantics to widen the scope of musical expression, equally in its means and in its wider objectives.

France after Berlioz

Before we turn to Italian music, we must look at the next generation of French Romantics. Charles Gounod (1813–93) began as an organist and church musician, but his reputation was chiefly made in the opera house, especially with his *Faust*. It is criticized for treating Goethe's work as a peg for a tearful tale, but its lyrical expressiveness and sense of theatrical effect made it for many years the most loved of French operas. In that it was eventually displaced by Georges Bizet's *Carmen*: a failure on its first performance, in 1875 (just before Bizet's death, at the age of 36), but soon recognized as a masterpiece for its powerful portrayal of emotion (especially jealousy and female sexuality), its brilliantly colorful and varied score and its Spanish atmosphere. It brought to the lyric stage a new realism in its handling of passionate feeling.

Italy

The story of Italian music in the nineteenth century is essentially the story of opera, and the story of Italian opera is essentially the story of the music of four men: at the beginning of the century, Rossini; in the early Romantic years, the 1830s and 40s, Bellini and Donizetti; and thereafter Verdi.

Rossini

The life of Gioachino Rossini is a spectacular success story, but with shaded areas. He was born in 1792 (on leap-year day). His main studies were in Bologna. He made his début as an opera composer in Venice, in 1810; two years later his reputation had spread across half Italy. Then he had a triumph at the most famous Italian opera house, La Scala, Milan.

Tancredi, the first of his serious operas, soon followed. Spirited comedy and gentle sentiment give way to a more lyrical and dramatic style. Rossini continued to pursue both. *L'italiana in Algeri* is totally, often absurdly comic, a tale about an Italian girl shipwrecked in Algiers who escapes the desires of the Bey by, with her lover, enrolling the Bey and his men in an imaginary brotherhood and making them helplessly drunk.

Gioachino Rossini   Works
born Pesaro, 1792; *died* Passy, 1868

Operas Tancredi (1813), L'italiana in Algeri (The Italian girl in Algiers, 1813), Il barbiere di Siviglia (The Barber of Seville, 1816), La Cenerentola (Cinderella, 1817), Semiramide (1823), Le Comte Ory (1828), William Tell (1829)
Sacred choral music Petite messe solennelle (1864); Stabat mater (1841); Masses
Secular vocal music Les soirées musicales (Musical evenings, 1835); cantatas, choruses
Chamber music string sonatas

87 Rossini, caricatured by Mailly when the composer was 75, from *Le Hanneton* (4 July 1867).

All Italy had now capitulated to Rossini, except the most important southern center, Naples. For the leading opera house there, San Carlo, he wrote an opera in the fall of 1815 on the story of Queen Elizabeth of England. But before following up its success he had a period in Rome, with far-reaching consequences. First, he wrote a "semi-serious" opera for one theater. While it was still in preparation he arranged to write one for the rival house – a comic opera on a story that had been successful before, that of the *Barber of Seville*. Rossini's choice was risky but successful: not just for the Roman audiences of 1816 – in fact they did not much care for it – but for posterity. No comic opera has ever been as much loved or performed. The music sparkles from start to finish. The plot has familiar ingredients – the old man who wants to marry his ward, the ardent "student" lover who turns out to be a nobleman, the comic old priest-cum-music-master, above all the eager and artful girl who contrives to get the right man in the end. To this collection of characters Rossini brings music that not only makes us laugh – as in the brilliant "patter songs", where the syllables are articulated at a crazy speed, or the ensemble in the Act 1 finale where all stand frozen to the spot with astonishment as they sing – but also touches the listener, with its graceful and gentle sentiment.

This, however, was essentially a comic interlude. His main efforts went into serious works for Naples: an opera on the story of Othello, one on Armida, a sacred one on the biblical tale of Moses. In these Rossini gradually expanded his canvas. The scenes grow longer and more fully developed, the musical textures become more elaborate.

In 1822, the impresario of the Naples opera houses – whose mistress, the singer Isabella Colbran, Rossini married that year – put on a hugely successful Rossini festival in Vienna. Two years later Rossini settled in Paris, becoming the director of the Théâtre-Italien, where he put on operas of his own and by others. Next he conquered the Opéra itself, above all with *William Tell* (1829). This, on a play by Schiller, is a grand historical epic, using the favored French features of ballet and spectacle yet much enriched by its ensembles and elaborate orchestral writing. It is probably his greatest work, but its length and complexity mean that it is rarely performed.

Rossini was 37 when *William Tell* was given. It was his last opera. He needed no more money; he had written an opera to satisfy his deepest artistic ambitions; and he had bequeathed a repertory that would leave laughter echoing round the world's opera houses for decades, even centuries. Why should he compose more operas and open himself up to criticism for being "out of date"? So he retired. He wrote a little more music, some sacred, some instrumental. He lived first in Paris, then in Bologna (1837–55), where he was mostly in poor health, and finally back in Paris. He had separated from Colbran and from the 1830s was cared for by Olympe Pélissier, whom he married in 1846 on Colbran's death. In his last years, restored to Paris and to health, he lived an active social life and composed a little more (including some piano and vocal pieces that he called "Sins of Old Age"); he died, honored by a world grateful for what he had given it, in 1868.

Rossini lived through the early days, indeed the middle ones too, of Romanticism. Yet it is hard to see him as a true Romantic. Most of his operas deal with topics that were familiar on the stage in the Classical era, and there is nothing in his expressive world similar to, say, Weber's exploration of the supernatural, Schumann's literary and poetic inclination, or Berlioz's fevered imagination. Romanticism comes decisively into Italian opera only with the next generation, and even then rather hesitantly. Its two heralds were Vincenzo Bellini (1801–35), whose strength lay in exquisitely shapely vocal lines, and Gaetano Donizetti (1797–1848), a sturdy, professional man of the theater who especially in his operas on Romantic or medieval tales (like *Lucia di Lammermoor*, after Walter Scott) carried Italian opera into the era of full-blooded Romanticism. Donizetti's ability to control dramatic tension, using line, harmony or color, was remarkable, and without him the greater achievement of Verdi would have been impossible.

The operatic masters: Verdi and Wagner

Verdi

Two men dominated opera in the high Romantic era: an Italian, Giuseppe Verdi, and a German, Richard Wagner. Their styles, their methods, their philosophies, even their subject matter differed in almost every imaginable respect, and the differences typify national cultural differences. The operas of these two provide the backbone of the repertory of the world's opera houses, and what they have in common – a search for the profoundest and most telling expression of dramatic truth through music – is of far greater consequence than what separates them.

Giuseppe Verdi was born in October 1813, in north Italy. His main schooling was in Busseto, where he had the classical education normal for a middle-class child, and studied music under the church organist. At 18 he applied for admission to Milan Conservatory, but was refused: he was past the proper admission age and inadequate as pianist and in counterpoint. He studied in Milan nevertheless, then returned to Busseto as town music-master, teaching at the music school and directing concerts. During these years he composed sacred works, choruses and short orchestral pieces.

In 1839 Verdi, ready to venture into a wider world, resigned and moved to Milan.

Giuseppe Verdi	Life
1813	born in Roncole, near Busseto, 9 or 10 October
1832	study in Milan
1835	town music master in Busseto; married Margherita Barezzi
1839	Milan; *Oberto* given at La Scala; his wife and two children died; beginning of period of deep depression
1842	*Nabucco* (La Scala), established Verdi's international reputation; beginning of steady output of operas and travels throughout Europe to supervise productions
1847–9	Paris
1851	*Rigoletto* (Venice)
1853	*Il trovatore* (Rome), *La traviata* (Venice)
1859	married Giuseppina Strepponi, with whom he had already had a long relationship
1860	entered parliament
1867	*Don Carlos* (Paris)
1871	*Aida* (Cairo)
1874	*Requiem* performed in Milan
1887	*Otello* (Milan)
1893	*Falstaff* (Milan)
1901	died in Milan, 27 January

Giuseppe Verdi   Works

Operas Oberto (1839), Nabucco (1842), Macbeth (1847), Rigoletto (1851), Il trovatore (The troubadour, 1853), La traviata (The woman gone astray, 1853), Les vêpres siciliennes (The Sicilian vespers, 1855), Simon Boccanegra (1857), Un ballo in maschera (A masked ball, 1859), La forza del destino (The force of destiny, 1862), Don Carlos (1867), Aida (1871), Otello (1887), Falstaff (1893)

Sacred choral music Requiem (1874); Quattro pezzi sacri (1889–97)

Secular choral music songs

Chamber music String Quartet (1873)

Later in the year his first opera, staged at La Scala, was successful enough to interest the leading Italian publisher and to induce the Scala director to commission further operas. When his next, a comic work, was a failure, Verdi (whose two children and then his wife had just died) went into a depression and resolved to give up composing. He was nursed through it by the Scala director, who found a libretto, on the biblical story of Nebuchadnezzar, to fire him. *Nabucco* was a triumph when, in 1842, it reached the stage; within a few years it had carried Verdi's name to every important musical center in Europe, and then beyond, to America, south as well as north.

Now came what Verdi later called his years in the galleys: years of hard work when composing was drudgery. He wrote not only for Milan but for other Italian cities, London and Paris. Eight further operas date from the 1840s; much the finest is *Macbeth*, after Shakespeare (1847). The somber grandeur of the play appealed profoundly to Verdi, and he matches it in his score. One of its most moving scenes is at the beginning of the last act, where a group of Scottish exiles, who have fled from Macbeth's oppression, are mourning their situation. There is a similar scene in *Nabucco*. When Verdi wrote music of this kind, with a patriotic message, he was really writing about the unhappy lot of the Italians, who had been under foreign – Austrian and Spanish – domination for centuries. Italy was at this time not a country but a geographical region, tied together by language and culture; the move towards union, the Risorgimento, grew stronger and Verdi was deeply committed to it. When he wrote stirring music, its true meaning was understood by his audiences in Italy.

The middle years

With the 1850s, Verdi reached a creative turning-point. Two of his finest and most admired operas come from this time: *Rigoletto* (1851) and *La traviata* (1853). The former, based on a Victor Hugo story, deals powerfully with a seamy side of life: its topics are abduction, seduction and murder at the Mantua court of the sixteenth century. The central character, Rigoletto, is a court jester who mocks the courtiers whom his Duke cuckolds. His own daughter is then abducted and presented to the Duke, for whom in the end she sacrifices her life. Verdi's vivid score conjures up the atmosphere of the court at a ball, touchingly sketches the character of the jester's daughter, and forcefully portrays Rigoletto's thirst for vengeance. The topics treated in Verdi's music make demands quite different from those of earlier opera, and accordingly require a more direct, more earthy, less idealized musical language.

From the same period come *Il trovatore* – famous for its rousing melodies but less persuasive as a theatrical work – and *La traviata*. *La traviata* (literally, the title means "The woman gone astray") represents a side of Verdi, and a side of Romanticism, opposite

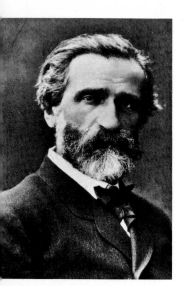

88 Giuseppe Verdi: photograph.

from that displayed in *Rigoletto*. Based on a play set in the "demi-monde" of Paris, it is concerned with true love, in a world where attachments were unofficial and short-term, the heroine Violetta's denial of it as an act of self-sacrifice, and her death from tuberculosis. Here Verdi's triumph lies in the sensitive depiction of many different levels and shades of love, from the frivolous to the intense. The opera ends with the lovers reunited but Violetta dying; as she does, she hears (ethereally, on high violins) the music associated with their love and its beginnings: one of the most moving scenes in all opera.

Verdi's personal life was now on a more secure basis. In his early days in Milan he had been befriended by the soprano Giuseppina Strepponi; they met in Paris in 1847 and soon lived together. They finally married in 1859. Verdi was, incidentally, a non-believer, strongly opposed to what he saw as the oppressive influence of the church; some of this comes through in his operas.

He lived, of course, in oppressive times. When *Rigoletto* was given in Venice, it had to have an anonymous duke as its central figure, not (as in the Victor Hugo original) the King of France; for Rome, the *Macbeth* witches had to be gipsies. Later, an opera involving the assassination of a Swedish king, *A Masked Ball*, had to be shifted to Boston and the king turned into a colonial governor. The censor took a stern view of the politically subversive.

Rigoletto was a huge success on its first performance; so was *Il trovatore*. *La traviata* failed initially, but Verdi made changes and it soon established itself. Then he was invited to write an opera for Paris, and lived there for more than three years. His contact with the French grand opera was fruitful, and the Italian operas of Verdi's next years are infused with grand opera elements. The personal dramas of his earlier Italian operas no longer gave him the scope he wanted. One of his next works (*Simon Boccanegra*, 1857) is a somber piece, concerned with political power in medieval Genoa, the rivalries of the nobles and the plebeians, and a love affair that crosses those barriers. Another, *The Force of Destiny* (St Petersburg, 1862), is a fascinating but rambling opera in which a tragic personal drama – an accidental killing and the vendetta that arises from it – is set against a rich pageant of military and monastic life.

Meanwhile, Verdi had become involved in real-life politics as well as stage ones. In 1860 Italy had thrown off most of her foreign oppressors and achieved nationhood; Verdi deeply admired the chief architect of these developments, Cavour, and agreed reluctantly to enter the new parliament. In 1874 he was honored by election to the senate.

Verdi had regarded himself as retired from composing from about 1860. Each opera thereafter was undertaken simply because he wanted, for one reason or another, to undertake it, often because of the challenge of the subject. One particularly exciting challenge was offered by *Don Carlos*, a French grand opera after the play by Schiller. It touches on all the themes that had appealed to Verdi: nationhood (of Flanders, present Belgium, oppressed by her Spanish overlords and the Catholic church); the rival power of church and state (realized in a duet for two basses, where the Grand Inquisitor tells King Philip II that he must sacrifice his own son); male courage and comradeship; the conflict of generations; and above all love, which has numerous cross-currents and complications. At the center of the opera there is a spectacular scene in which heretics are burned by the Inquisition. The characters are no longer the pasteboard creatures who filled Verdi's earlier operas but real people coping with powerful internal conflicts. There is place in this rich and wide-ranging opera for every kind of music that Verdi could write, and in it he extended himself further.

Plate 12 *Opposite* Hector Berlioz: portrait, 1830, by Emile Signol (p. 210). Villa Medici, Rome.

For his next opera, Verdi chose a simpler, more direct plot: this was *Aida*, first given at Cairo in 1871, celebrating the opening of the Suez Canal. Here again we have the conflicts

"Carmen" 1ᵉʳ acto   E Bertin

89 Verdi's *Don Carlos*: title-page of the first Paris edition, published by Escudier (1867).

Plate 13 Bizet's *Carmen*: stage design by Emile Bertin for Act 1 in the original production at the Opéra-Comique, Paris, 1875 (see p. 216). Bibliothèque de l'Opéra, Paris.

of country and love: the Egyptian general Radames loves the Ethiopian Aida, daughter of his arch-enemy. But there are fewer events, fewer ornaments to the main line of the opera's action, fewer psychological complications: the result is that Verdi had greater freedom to clothe the plot in melodically expansive music. There is still room for spectacle, which provides a context large enough in scale for the personal drama. *Aida* emerges as a perfectly balanced and controlled Italian transformation of grand opera.

Verdi's next major work was not an opera but a *Requiem*. This originated in a proposal for a *Requiem* to commemorate Rossini, to which several leading Italian composers would contribute; this never materialized, but when the poet Alessandro Manzoni died, in 1873, Verdi put the movement he had written towards a new, complete one for Manzoni. Verdi's *Requiem* has been criticized as operatic in style; but the kind of music he wrote for the expression of strong emotion was inevitably operatic and the style finds a proper use here. The *Requiem* had its first performance at a Milan church in 1874. It was repeated at La Scala, and the next year Verdi took it to London, Paris and Vienna.

Last years

If his career as a composer had stopped with the *Requiem*, that might have seemed fitting. There was a precedent, in Mozart. Verdi was close on 70. But his friends knew there was more music in him – none better than his publisher, Giulio Ricordi (who had only to gain from a reawakening of his creative urge). It was Ricordi who hinted at the possibility of a Shakespeare opera, on *Othello*. Verdi's friend the poet and composer Arrigo Boito (1842–1918) produced an *Othello* libretto, and he was duly tempted. He composed it slowly, during 1884–5, and it was given at La Scala in 1887. It is Verdi's tragic masterpiece. Though still firmly within the tradition of operas built up of arias, duets and so on, *Otello* (its Italian title) has more continuity than any of his earlier operas. Verdi wanted to move away from the traditional formality of arias sharply marked off from neighboring items, except where the dramatic context makes it natural. There are "set pieces" in *Otello*, but they arise from dramatic necessity, and the surrounding musical texture is fluid. The orchestration and harmony have a new subtlety and expressiveness.

This was still not the end. In 1889, when Verdi was 76, Boito again tempted him with a Shakespeare text, this time a comedy – a genre Verdi had not touched for more than 50 years, and in which his only previous effort had been a failure. Verdi took up the challenge and *Falstaff* duly came to the stage in 1893, the year he was 80. In method it is akin to *Otello*, but there is even less of formal arias or ensembles and more of dialogue – conversation, exclamation, interjection, laughter. The plot centers on a fat old man who likes to think he is still a dab hand at seduction, but all he achieves is a ducking in the river Thames and a drubbing from a troop of mock fairies in Windsor Forest. There are no real arias, except one for the "Fairy Queen", but the music bounds along at a great pace, little motifs flecking in and out of the gossamer orchestral texture, aria and recitative meeting at some middle point. This wonderfully benign, good-humored piece ends with a fugue – a form Verdi abhorred and could use only as a joke – on an Italian version of Shakespeare's "All the world's a stage": an appropriate ending for the greatest master of Italian opera.

It was very nearly the end for Verdi. He wrote a group of sacred choral pieces, partly experimental in nature, completing them in 1897. That year Giuseppina died; Verdi lived on, in Milan, until 1901. At his burial there was national mourning.

Wagner

Richard Wagner was the greatest German opera composer of his day, the German counterpart to Verdi. He was not merely that. As no one had done before, he changed opera – not just opera, but music itself. Nor just music, but indeed art: the impact of this man, his creations and his thought, left the world a different place. He aroused men's passions, intellectual and emotional, as no artist had done before, nor any since. He has been hailed as a high priest of a thousand philosophies, many of them mutually exclusive, even contradictory. His music is hated as much as it is worshipped. The only issue beyond dispute is his greatness.

Wagner was born in Leipzig on 22 May 1813. The first of many questions surrounding him concerns his paternity: was he the son of the police actuary Friedrich Wagner, his mother's husband, who died six months after his birth, or of the painter, actor and poet

Richard Wagner	Life

1813	born in Leipzig, 22 May
1830	St Thomas's School, Leipzig
1831	Leipzig University
1834	musical director of theater company in Magdeburg
1836	*The Ban on Love* given in Magdeburg; married Minna Planer
1837	musical director of the theater in Riga
1839	Paris; contact with Meyerbeer
1842–3	*Rienzi* and *The Flying Dutchman* acclaimed in Dresden; appointed *Kapellmeister* to Saxon court in Dresden
1848	banned from Germany because of involvement in revolutionary politics; to Weimar (to see Liszt), Switzerland, Paris
1849	settled in Zurich
1850	*Lohengrin* (Weimar); *Opera and Drama*; *Ring* cycle started; began traveling widely as a conductor
1861	revised version of *Tannhäuser* given in Paris to hostile audience
1864	moved to Munich at the invitation of King Ludwig II of Bavaria; began affair with Liszt's daughter Cosima von Bülow
1865	*Tristan and Isolde* (Munich)
1866	set up house with Cosima at Tribschen, by Lake Lucerne
1868	*The Mastersingers of Nuremberg* (Munich)
1870	married Cosima; composed *Siegfried Idyll* for Cosima in gratitude for their son
1871	moved to Wahnfried, a house near Bayreuth
1874	*Ring* cycle completed
1876	first festival at Bayreuth where Wagner had designed an opera house for the *Ring*, which was given its first performance
1882	*Parsifal* (Bayreuth)
1883	died in Venice, 13 February

Ludwig Geyer, a close friend, whom she married soon after? The evidence is ambiguous; all we know is that Wagner was affected by the doubts over his origins. The family moved to Dresden, where Richard attended the leading church school; later he moved to Leipzig. His interests were ancient Greek tragedy, the theater (especially Shakespeare and Goethe) and above all music. He had taken lessons in harmony, piano and violin, and eagerly copied out music by Beethoven for study. He composed a number of pieces and had an overture played at a Leipzig concert. In 1831 he entered Leipzig University to study music, but his chief studies were under the Kantor at St Thomas's. The truth about these early years – and indeed about other parts of his life, too – is not always easy to establish. Wagner left a detailed autobiography, but when his information is checked against other sources it often proves to be wrong; he was inclined to angle the facts, or alter them, to suit his purpose.

At the end of 1832, a symphony of Wagner's had performances in Prague and Leipzig. It was well received, but this was his last substantial instrumental work. That winter he wrote a libretto for an opera, started composing it, then scrapped it; he embarked on another, *The Fairies*, in 1833, and quickly completed it, but it remained unheard until after

---

Richard Wagner   Works

Operas Das Liebesverbot (The ban on love, 1836), Rienzi (1842), Der fliegende
Holländer (The flying Dutchman, 1843), Tannhäuser (1845, rev. 1861), Lohengrin
(1850), Tristan und Isolde (1865), Die Meistersinger von Nürnberg (The
mastersingers of Nuremberg, 1868); Der Ring des Nibelungen (The ring of the
Nibelung, 1876): Das Rheingold (The Rhinegold, 1869), Die Walküre (The Valkyrie,
1870), Siegfried (1876), Götterdämmerung (Twilight of the gods, 1876); Parsifal
(1882)
Orchestral music Siegfried Idyll (1870), Kaisermarsch (1871), Grosser Festmarsch
(1876)
Songs Wesendonk-Lieder (1857–8)
Choral music   *Piano music*

---

his death. His first opera to gain a hearing was his next, *The Ban on Love* (based on a
Shakespeare comedy), which he conducted at Magdeburg in 1836. It had only a single
performance; then the company giving it, which Wagner had been conducting since 1834,
dissolved.

A soprano in this company was Minna Planer; Wagner fell in love with her and in 1836
they were married. The marriage was not at first (nor indeed in the long run) a success,
for Minna left him for another man for several months during 1837. That summer,
however, he was appointed conductor at the theater in Riga, on the Baltic, where she
rejoined him. In 1839 he was not re-engaged; in any case, he wanted to go to Paris, for
the opera on which he was now working, *Rienzi*, was in the grand opera tradition. He
and Minna had to stow away on a ship to evade their creditors. After a stormy journey
by the Norwegian coast, they reached England, and then went on to France; by a
coincidence, Wagner met Meyerbeer in Boulogne during the journey.

Paris and Dresden   In Paris, Wagner scraped a living with hack-work for publishers and theaters. He was
befriended by Meyerbeer and influenced by the music of Berlioz. *Rienzi* was soon finished
and a *Faust* overture composed; he also drafted a libretto on the legend of *The Flying
Dutchman* – it was accepted by the Opéra, but for setting by another composer. With a
recommendation from Meyerbeer, he submitted *Rienzi* to the Dresden Court Opera; it
was accepted, and in 1842 Wagner left for Dresden, where the opera had a triumphant
première in October. Three months later his own setting of *The Flying Dutchman* followed.
Rienzi is an enormously long, grandiose opera, dealing with the rise and fall of a hero of
the people; *The Flying Dutchman* is much shorter and more intense. It treats a supernatural
theme, the haunted Dutchman who sails the seas endlessly until redeemed by a woman's
trusting love. A driving theme and a stormy orchestral texture are associated with the
Dutchman, a gentler theme with Senta, who loves him and saves him; the ghostly music
recalls that of Weber (whom Wagner greatly admired), but the passion and the broad
sweep of the music sound a new note.

After the success of *Rienzi*, Wagner had accepted the post of royal *Kapellmeister* at the
Dresden court. It gave him a security, a place where his music could gain a hearing, and
opportunities to exercise his organizational genius. Yet it was perhaps a curious position
for a man with revolutionary leanings. Wagner had for some time been associated with a
group "Young Germany", a semi-revolutionary intellectual movement, and the reforms
he wanted in the theater had broad social and political implications.

For the moment, he kept clear of active politics. During the 1840s he wrote two more operas, *Tannhäuser* (1845) and *Lohengrin* (1847). The former is concerned with the triumph of a woman's Christian love over pagan sensuality – the theme of redemption again, set in medieval Germany. *Lohengrin* is about a knight of the Holy Grail; again a woman's love and faith are central. In both, Wagner moves away from the concept of opera as songs linked by narrative sections; there are still lyrical numbers, but the divisions are less sharp and the texture more continuous. Much of the narrative music has a semi-melodic character and a supporting fabric of orchestral sound to help convey its sense.

In 1848, Europe's year of revolution, Wagner was caught up in political activity. He was involved in anarchical propaganda, and although publicly he had supported the monarchy he firmly sided with the rebels when in 1849 Dresden was the scene of turmoil. To escape arrest he fled to Weimar, where he sought Liszt's help, and then to Switzerland and safety. Germany was closed to him for 11 years. Soon he went to Paris, where he met and almost eloped with a young woman he had known from Dresden. Meanwhile, *Lohengrin* had its première, in Weimar; its limited success provoked Wagner into thinking more deeply about new forms of opera. He wrote an important book, *Opera and Drama*, in 1850 – his basic statement about the relationship of music and theater. Wagner was a prolific writer; over the years he had written numerous essays, criticisms, theoretical studies and polemical articles. One is called *The Artwork of the Future*; another, notorious one is his bitterly anti-semitic *Judaism in Music*, some of it a merciless attack on Meyerbeer (who had generously helped him).

The middle years

Wagner spent most of the 1850s in Switzerland, active in the musical life of Zurich but expending most of his energies on a new, great conception. This started as an opera based on the mythological story, from the Nordic and Germanic sagas, of the hero Siegfried. He began with the idea of an opera on Siegfried's death, but then prefaced it with another, on the young Siegfried. These were to become *The Twilight of the Gods* and *Siegfried*. Then he planned a third opera to precede these, telling an earlier part of the story, *The Valkyrie*, and finally yet another, prefatory work, *The Rhinegold*. Thus he wrote the text in reverse order, but he composed the music forwards, and more than 20 years elapsed between the first part of *Rhinegold* (at the end of 1853) and the conclusion of *Twilight of the Gods* (at the end of 1874).

Two other works of more normal dimensions, were composed while this huge work, *The Ring of the Nibelung*, was in progress: *Tristan and Isolde* and *The Mastersingers of Nuremberg*. *Tristan*, written in 1857–9, was stimulated by a love affair he had with Mathilde Wesendonck, the wife of a silk merchant in Zurich who was one of Wagner's most generous patrons. Wagner set some of her poems to music and clearly identified their illicit love with that of the lovers in this new work, the greatest of all love operas. He was part-way through the third *Ring* opera, *Siegfried*, when the need to write *Tristan* intervened. And before he had finished *Siegfried* he paused again, to write *The Mastersingers*. These pauses were not made purely for personal or artistic reasons: his publishers would not accept the *Ring* – its huge length made it commercially unattractive – but would pay him well for an opera of normal length. He was chronically in debt and needed the money.

There were other interruptions. In 1860, he was in Paris, revising *Tannhäuser* to suit French tastes. When the new version was performed, it was literally shouted down – not simply a matter of Wagner's music, but a political protest against the Austrians who had supported the performance. Still, Wagner's prestige was enhanced by his having the work given at the Opéra, and that soon led to his being allowed back into Germany. In that year, 1862, Wagner and Minna finally parted. Wagner conducted concerts in London in the 1850s, Vienna and Russia in the early 1860s. But the crucial event of the early 1860s, which made possible the achievements of Wagner's late years, was an invitation to Munich from the young King Ludwig II of Bavaria. This inaugurated patronage from Ludwig on a scale that cleared Wagner's debts, provided him with a regular income, permitted him to compose the music he wanted to and eventually to found a festival for its performance.

Munich, Tribschen, Bayreuth

Wagner moved to Munich in the summer of 1864, having slipped out of Vienna earlier in the year to avoid imprisonment for debt. He was generously treated by Ludwig, but the Bavarian politicians mistrusted his influence at court and his freedom with Bavarian money. Moreover, he became the center of scandal when it was known that he was having an affair with Cosima von Bülow, daughter of Liszt and wife of Hans von Bülow whom Ludwig, at Wagner's request, had appointed to a post as royal musician. The affair had Bülow's connivance. The next April, on the day Bülow conducted the first rehearsal of *Tristan and Isolde*, their first child was born; she was christened Isolde.

Tristan was produced in June, but as the singer of Tristan died it had only four performances. At the end of the year, Ludwig was obliged to ask Wagner to leave Munich. In 1866 Wagner and Cosima set up house by Lake Lucerne in Switzerland, and two years later she finally came to live with him. Meanwhile, he completed *The Mastersingers*, which had its première in Munich in June 1868. His once-progressive political stance had now taken a sharp turn to the Right and towards a ferocious German nationalism.

Wagner remained in Switzerland until 1872; he had married Cosima, who had borne him two more children, in 1870. He completed the third *Ring* opera, and the first two were given at Munich in 1869 and 1870. The fourth was drafted early in 1872. By then, Wagner was hard at work on his plans for a new opera house, designed particularly for the *Ring*. This was to be at the small town of Bayreuth. Wagner and his friends devised fund-raising schemes, but had little success, and only through Ludwig's intervention in 1874 could the plans be carried through. At the end of that year, the last of the *Ring* operas was completed.

The first Bayreuth Festival took place in the summer of 1876. It was an artistic triumph, but a financial disaster; once again the Bavarian treasury bailed him out. Now Wagner started work on a new opera, a "sacred festival drama" to be called *Parsifal*; this occupied him up to the beginning of 1882 – he was working more slowly now, troubled by his health. He also spent time traveling in Italy. *Parsifal* had its first performances at the 1882 Bayreuth Festival. Wagner went back to Italy to recuperate; he had decided to write no more operas and to return to the symphony. But in February 1883, in Venice, he had a heart attack and died. A few days before, his father-in-law, Liszt, had visited him and had been seized by the idea of composing a piano piece about a funeral procession with a gondola. Wagner's body was conveyed by gondola to the railway station, then by train to Bayreuth, where he was buried in the garden of his house.

Wagner's mature operas

We saw how Wagner was beginning to move away from traditional conceptions of opera towards a new, powerful unity, mainly through the use of recurring themes with particular dramatic associations and a more continuous musical texture. These ideas are carried further in his mature operas – or music dramas, as he preferred to call them. The idea of recurring themes was not new. Several composers had used an already-heard theme later in an opera as a reminder of a person, an event or a state of mind, as we saw in Verdi's *La traviata*. Before that, Weber had used recurring ideas with sharper dramatic point: for example, themes heard in association with a particular character and re-heard to hint at his presence. The kind of thematic transformation used by Berlioz and Liszt, in orchestral music, is similar.

Wagner drew all these ideas together, and combined with them a Beethovenian sense of the way in which developing themes can support a large symphonic structure. He made the *leitmotif* ("leading motif") his basic way of linking music and drama. In his mature works, some kind of brief theme is associated with every significant idea in the drama: people, objects, thoughts, places, states of emotion and so on. These ideas are related in character to what they portray, as some examples – taken from the *Ring*, which has over its four evenings a huge corpus of *leitmotif* material – can readily show (*a–d*): these four

a. the forging of the metal

b. the sword   c. the horn call

d. love theme

ideas represent respectively the forging of metal, the brave idea of a sword to redeem the world, the hero Siegfried's horn-call and a love theme. They are not simply "labels", designed to draw attention to something happening on the stage. They may stand for much larger concepts. Thus the *leitmotif* used for the ring – forged from gold from the Rhine, and capable of bestowing power on its possessor – has also been described as standing for the purpose of the psyche or the self, and the one used for Loge, god of fire, can be interpreted as representing libido or primal energy from the unconscious. Further, a *leitmotif* may develop and change to signify development and change in what it stands for. For example, the joyous cry of "Rhinegold!" heard from the Rhinemaidens, custodians of the gold (*e*) acquires a dark flavor when the gold, stolen from them, is being forged (*f*).

90 Richard Wagner: photograph.

e. (Moderato)   f. (Lively)

Rhein - gold! Rhein - gold!

The *leitmotif*, as Wagner used it, offers the composer great opportunities for the subtle treatment of ideas. It may, for example, be heard in the orchestra to represent an unspoken thought of a character on the stage. It may tell the audience something unknown to those on the stage, like the identity of a disguised character or the motives behind some action. It may establish a connection with some earlier event. A number of *leitmotifs* may be combined, to show links between ideas. Many are in any case thematically related where the ideas they stand for are connected. Sometimes the relationships become clear only as the music and the drama progress – (*g*), for example, shows a motif associated with passion and agitation which is clearly linked with the love theme of (*d*).

g. (Fast)

91 Wagner's
Götterdämmerung: stage
design by Joseph
Hoffmann for the first
performance, Bayreuth,
1876. Richard-Wagner-
Museum, Bayreuth.

There are no "songs" in the *Ring*. The musical texture is made up of an enriched narrative and dialogue (characters almost never sing simultaneously); the orchestra supplies commentary and explanation. The work is enormously long: *Rhinegold* plays continuously for about two-and-a-half hours, *Valkyrie* and *Siegfried* each around five hours (including intervals) and *Twilight of the Gods* six. The network of *leitmotifs* holds this structure together, and Wagner supports it in two main ways: first, through his superb sense of theater, which enables him to give each act a powerful shape; and second, through his clever building-in of musical recapitulations. In *Valkyrie*, for example, Wotan, chief of the gods, tells his daughter the Valkyrie (warrior maiden) Brünnhilde of the events portrayed in *Rhinegold*; in *Siegfried* there is a "riddle scene" in which earlier events are discussed; and in *Twilight of the Gods* there is a lengthy prologue in which the Fates discuss what has happened in the world above, and a Funeral March for Siegfried in which the events of his life are recalled. In these, Wagner draws together the musical material associated with the events discussed. As the work proceeds – and particularly in the last part of *Siegfried* and *Twilight of the Gods*, written after the long break when Wagner composed other operas – the musical fabric becomes thicker, but that makes good dramatic sense as the plot does too.

The *Ring* is Wagner's greatest achievement. It has even been claimed, not unreasonably, as the greatest achievement of Western culture, so huge is its scale, so wide-ranging the issues it deals with, so profoundly unified is it. In basing it on ancient sagas, Wagner believed, as others have done, that the truths embodied in myth have meanings beyond literal interpretation. The story is about gods, dwarves (Nibelungs), giants and humans; it has been read (and performed) as a manifesto for socialism, as a plea for a Nazi-like racialism, as a study of the workings of the human psyche, as a forecast of the fate of the world and humankind, as a parable about the new industrial society of Wagner's time. It is all of these, and much more too. It touches at some point on every kind of human relationship and on numerous moral and philosophical issues. It is inevitably the focus of all debate on Wagner's greatness and the meaning of his works.

It does not, however, embody all of Wagner. The other three operas of his full maturity each go uniquely far in a particular direction. *Parsifal*, in which acts akin to Holy Communion are portrayed on the stage, treats in a Christian context the theme of redemption which runs through all his works (the *Ring* included). The theme of *Tristan and Isolde* is sexual love, expressed with the full force of the language Wagner was devising in the 1850s: the same narrative style as he used in the *Ring*, though here warmer and more lyrical, and the same large orchestra, though here treated in a richer and more sensuous way.

Above all, Wagner here extended the expressive capacity of music by developing a style more chromatic than anyone had attempted before. Chromaticism, since the time of Monteverdi and even earlier, had been recognized as a means of heightening emotion. Then, it generally operated within a clear sense of key, which it would contradict only momentarily; but with Wagner it was used so freely, and in so many simultaneous layers, that it loosened the sense of key or even broke it down altogether. This had long-term implications, as we shall see in later chapters; in *Tristan*, it led to a sense of instability, for as soon as the listener feels that the music is moving in one direction, that direction is contradicted.

There are similar procedures in the *Ring*, but they move more slowly and less restlessly. The melodic style of *Tristan* enhances the restlessness: the sense of passionate yearning that permeates the opera is conveyed partly through the chromatic dissonances and the way they demand to be resolved – the notes seem to press urgently onward, and often upward. The famous opening measures, with the enigmatic "Tristan" chord (as it is known), have two notes (see Listening Note VIII.E, ex. i) demanding to move upward in this way; later, Wagner uses this device in different instruments at the same time, not merely to make the effect more strongly but also to give a sense of harmonically shifting sands. This applies above all to the second act of the opera, virtually a continuous love scene, touching on every emotion from the gentlest and tenderest to the most fiercely passionate. At the end Tristan dies, at the instant of reunion with Isolde; she then dies too, a "Love-Death", by

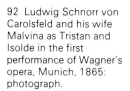

92 Ludwig Schnorr von Carolsfeld and his wife Malvina as Tristan and Isolde in the first performance of Wagner's opera, Munich, 1865: photograph.

Listening Note VIII.E   *Side 8, band 1*

Wagner: *Tristan und Isolde* (1865), Prelude
3 flutes, 2 oboes, english horn, 2 clarinets, bass clarinet, 3 bassoons
4 horns, 3 trumpets, 3 trombones, tuba
timpani; harp
1st and 2nd violins, violas, cellos, double basses

The prelude to *Tristan und Isolde* sets the mood for the opera with its treatment of some of
the main motifs, those which express the main theme of the work – passionate yet hopeless
yearning. The most famous is the one heard at the opening, ex. i, representing the mutual
longing of the lovers, Tristan and Isolde; the chord marked *x* is the so-called "Tristan chord"
(difficult and ambiguous to analyse in terms of traditional harmony).

Time

0:00	statement and repetition of ex. i
1:48	last two tones repeated
2.01	upward extension
2:10	ex. ii, cellos
3:26	ex. iii, violins
3:51	ex. ii, oboe, clarinets, and horn
4:16	linking theme, ex. iv, violins and oboes alternately
4:56	more animated section
5:16	ex. v, oboe
5:28	theme, ex. v, clarinet and horn
5:53	development of ex. ii, woodwinds
6:57	climax of section
7:03	ex. vi, violins
7:58	ex. ii, cello
8:46	ultimate climax
8:53	fragments of ex. ii, violins
10:19	recollections of ex. ii
11:07	ex. i, english horn and oboe, again in bass clarinet
11:36	clarinet
11:48	last phase of prelude

ex. i

ex. ii

ex. iii

ex. iv

ex. v

ex. vi

(mf)

his body – the ultimate, transcendental act of love being union in death.

Tristan, Isolde, Wotan, Brünnhilde, Siegfried: these are not people you meet every day. They are not meant to be "real" people, but ideal embodiments of human qualities. Wagner did however write one opera about real people, *The Mastersingers of Nuremberg*. Here he abandoned myth in favor of history – German history, of course – setting the opera in the sixteenth century and in a famous center of Germanic art, one of the homes of the Mastersinger tradition of the Renaissance. The characters in this work, a comic opera though in its way deeply serious, are worthy citizens of Nuremberg, including one historical figure, the cobbler-musician Hans Sachs; another is in effect Wagner himself. The hero is Walther von Stolzing, a noble poet-musician who loves the daughter of a rich mastersinger and hopes to win her hand by victory in a song contest. At first he is derided for his strange song, which breaks all known rules, but ultimately he triumphs, helped by Sachs's explanation that art cannot be constrained by old rules and that true genius creates new ones. The analogy with Wagner's view of his role, as extending through his genius the laws of music, needs no emphasis.

The Mastersingers does not follow *Tristan* into the world of harmonic complexity, nor does it follow the *Ring* into that of motivic elaboration. The work is distinguished by the warmth and good humor of its music, the expressiveness of its themes, and the richness with which they are interwoven. Perhaps taking a cue from its setting in a great age of polyphony, *The Mastersingers* contains some of the most fluent and sumptuous polyphonic writing of the nineteenth century. In it Wagner created some memorable characters, like Sachs the benign and generous cobbler, Beckmesser the foolish and pedantic town clerk (whom Wagner identified with his critics), and the lovers Walther and Eva. It shows Wagner's humor and humanity as no other work does, and the world would be poorer without it.

After Wagner

Wagner's impact on the art of music was such that no one could ignore him. Some conservative spirits stood aside, finding his music noisy, pretentious, dissonant and uncomfortably sensual – "the music of the future", to use Wagner's own, partly ironic term. Among composers, he had a number of direct followers, even outside the German-speaking countries. These men's work will be considered, along with that of others of the post-Wagner generation, in the next chapter. Here it remains to consider one composer, 20 years younger than Wagner, who was generally (though misleadingly) regarded as a rival or opponent of Wagner's, and who may be seen as a true heir to the tradition of Bach, Beethoven, Schubert and Schumann: Johannes Brahms.

Brahms

Johannes Brahms was born in Hamburg in 1833, the son of a double-bass player; his mother was older than his father by 17 years. At seven he started piano lessons, made rapid progress, and in his early teens was sent to a leading Hamburg pianist and composer. He was soon playing in taverns around the Hamburg dock area and making arrangements of music for his father's group. At 15 he gave his first solo recital. In the 1850s, on tour, he met the eminent violinist Joseph Joachim (1831–1907), Liszt (with whom he felt himself out of sympathy) and Robert and Clara Schumann. Schumann drew attention to him in

Johannes Brahms	Life

1833	born in Hamburg, 7 May
1848	first piano recital; earned living playing in taverns etc
1850	concert tour with the violinist Reményi during which he met the violinist Joachim, who became a close friend, and Liszt
1853	met Schumann who proclaimed his genius in a periodical article
1854	to Bonn to see Clara Schumann, to whom he became passionately devoted; first piano works
1857	Hamburg; piano teacher and conductor of the court orchestra at Detmold
1859	founded and conducted ladies' choir in Hamburg
1860	signed a manifesto opposing the "new music" of Liszt
1863	conductor of the Vienna Singakademie
1864–71	freelance teacher in Vienna; piano and chamber works, *German Requiem*
1872–5	conductor of Vienna Philharmonic concerts; *St Antony Variations*
1876	completed First Symphony, started in 1855
1877–9	Second Symphony, Violin Concerto
1879	awarded many honors; *Academic Festival Overture*
1881	rift in friendship with Joachim; offered Meiningen court orchestra to try out works
1883	Third Symphony
1885	Fourth Symphony
1891	met the clarinetist Richard Mühlfeld who inspired four works
1897	died in Vienna, 3 April

an enthusiastic article. Soon after his return to Hamburg, Brahms heard of Schumann's breakdown and went to be near him – and near Clara, for whom he developed a romantic passion which remained with him, at a calmer level, all his life. Brahms never married.

Brahms's main compositions in these years were principally for the piano, and include a sonata in F minor which shows, in its mixture of the passionate and the contemplative and in its rich, often dark-toned textures, the direction his genius was taking. He also wrote songs. In the late 1850s he spent some months each year at the small Detmold court, where he could work with an orchestra. For this group he composed two light orchestral works (serenades); he did not feel ready to write a symphony. He tried embarking on one, but then decided to use the music in his Piano Concerto in D minor, a work of extraordinary fire and originality.

Original it may have been, but still firmly in a tradition of purely musical expression: Brahms had no interest in changing the nature of expression in music, or lending it non-musical implications, as did Liszt, Berlioz and Wagner. Works of the 1860s include his piano *Variations on a Theme by Handel*, which continues the Beethoven variation tradition with its individually characterized series of variations, in a sequence that imposes a strong, broad shape to the work, with a powerful fugue forming a climax of complexity and virtuosity. Each variation follows the outline, melodic or harmonic, of Handel's theme, but each has a texture and rhythm of its own and several develop particular phrases from the theme, giving the music a symphonic quality and coherence.

Coming up to the age of 30, Brahms now looked for wider recognition; and when he saw the post of conductor of the Hamburg Philharmonic concerts about to become vacant he hoped to succeed to it. But he was passed over. He had in fact left Hamburg shortly before, to make himself known in Vienna; now he decided to stay in the Austrian capital, where he became director of the Singakademie in 1863. This was a choral society which often sang unaccompanied, and Brahms was accordingly drawn to study earlier music. He remained only one season, however; he could make a living by playing, and he also did some teaching.

Brahms later considered taking a formal appointment, but preferred to remain freelance except in the period 1872–5 when he conducted the Vienna Philharmonic Society concert series. All that he really wanted to do was compose. He was a slow and intensely self-critical composer; he consulted his friends, especially Joachim and Clara Schumann, about new works, and was always ready to revise them – he destroyed much that he wrote, held pieces back from publication, and was often indecisive over the form a piece should take. In 1864, for example, he completed a piano quintet: he had started it as a string quintet and then converted it into a two-piano sonata before he settled on its final form. Other compositions of this time include piano and chamber works and songs; there was no orchestral music between 1860 and 1874, when he wrote the popular and attractive *St Antony Variations.*

But he did produce a major choral work, the *German Requiem.* He had begun it many years earlier (again unsure of what form it should take), and resumed soon after his mother's death in 1865. It came before the public in piecemeal fashion – three movements in 1867, six the next year and the complete seven in 1869. It is not a traditional Roman Catholic *Requiem* for the dead but a series of settings of biblical texts, in German, that speak of death, mourning and comfort. It is predominantly slow in tempo and veiled in color. But the message of comfort is always there; it is worth noting that the three movements that begin in the minor mode all end in the major, in light and reassurance instead of darkness and threat.

The first symphony

In 1876 Brahms at last felt ready to give his first symphony to the world, which had been waiting for it impatiently. He had begun its composition as far back as 1855, but had

---

Johannes Brahms   Works

Orchestral music symphonies – no. 1, c (1876), no. 2, D (1877), no. 3, F (1883), no. 4, e (1885); piano concertos – no. 1, d (1858), no. 2, B♭ (1881); Violin Concerto (1878); Concerto for violin and cello (1887); Academic Festival Overture (1880); Tragic Overture (1881); St Antony Variations (1873); serenades

Chamber music 2 string sextets (1860, 1865); 2 string quintets (1882, 1890); 3 string quartets – c, a (1873), B♭ (1876); Piano Quintet, f (1864); 3 piano quartets (1861, 1862, 1875); 3 piano trios (1854, 1882, 1886); Clarinet Quintet (1891); violin sonatas

Piano music sonatas – no. 1, C (1853), no. 2, f♯ (1852), no. 3, f (1853); rhapsodies, intermezzos, ballades, capriccios, variations; piano duets – Liebeslieder Waltzes (1874, 1877); Hungarian Dances (1852–69)

Choral music Ein deutsches Requiem (A German Requiem, 1868); Alto Rhapsody (1869)

Songs Vier ernste Gesänge (Four serious songs, 1896); over 180 others

Partsongs   *Organ music*

moved even more slowly than usual, conscious of the role he had come to occupy in people's minds as heir to the Beethoven tradition, and anxious to be worthy of so weighty a responsibility. He cast it in the traditionally somber key of C minor, and began with a slow introduction in which the main ideas of the first movement are foreshadowed. This grand, solemn, uncompromising music contains figures which acquire a sharper character when presented in faster tempo and in different combinations and relationships. Brahms was endlessly inventive in exploring the possibilities of even simple ideas, and often built entire movements out of them; they may be turned upside-down, for example, interwoven or changed in pace. His broad scheme here is like those of Beethoven, and as in many of Beethoven's mature works there is further development in a coda. Brahms, however, ends the movement on a note of contemplation rather than Beethovenian heroic triumph (see Listening Note VIII.F).

But the heroic triumph was there, even if the tragedy and the storms to be weathered are longer than Beethoven's and more obviously dark. Brahms's slow movement is a contemplative, lyrical interlude which ends with a solo violin adding a voice of special eloquence – a departure for a symphony, where so personal an expressive tone is rare. Instead of a scherzo, there is a relaxed, gentle-toned piece; he preferred this type to help offset the long, sometimes violent music of his outer movements.

Brahms begins his finale with music as grave and intense as that of the first movement, though now there are electrifying passages of string pizzicatos, dramatically accelerating, providing an air of excitement and expectancy: and suddenly the C minor darkness gives way to C major, and a noble theme rings out on the horn, with shimmering strings and soft trombones, soon to be followed by a chorale-like idea on trombones and bassoons. But the great moment, in a sense the climax of the symphony, comes when the introduction draws to its close, the textures clear, and the theme at which the earlier music hinted finally appears – a gloriously long-breathed melody, sober yet full of nobility.

Brahms's audiences had expected a symphony they might call "Beethoven's Tenth", and this clinched it: the theme has an obvious resemblance to the "Joy" theme in the finale of Beethoven's Ninth. But Brahms's treatment is different from Beethoven's. Beethoven's finale is a set of variations, but Brahms's theme is unmistakably intended as the main idea of a sonata-form movement. Elements from this and other themes are used in a variety of ways, and the links provide an underlying unity. Brahms's skill in making the same ideas appear in different guises and senses gives his music its tautness and strength.

The completion and successful early performances of his symphony seem to have released something in Brahms. Now he felt ready to fulfill his destiny as an orchestral composer. His Second Symphony, gentler and more relaxed than his First, was written the following year, 1877. The next year he wrote his Violin Concerto, for Joachim: another extended and spacious work, it taxes the soloist severely (a "concerto *against* the violin", said Joachim), and in doing so it surpasses even the Beethoven concerto in its heroic effect as the violin struggles against the orchestra.

One of the few surviving private orchestras in Europe at this time was at the Duke of Saxe-Meiningen's court. Its director was Hans von Bülow. Since hearing Brahms's First Symphony – and since the time of his break with Wagner – Bülow had come to see Brahms as the custodian of the tradition stemming from Beethoven, and he offered Brahms the use of the orchestra to try out his works.

This encouraged Brahms to pursue orchestral composition. In 1883 he completed his Third Symphony, in 1885 his Fourth. The Fourth, which was to be his last, illustrates in its finale Brahms's application of a principle of form which he had met in his research on earlier composers, like Bach, whom he admired: the ground bass. The music is held

Listening Note VIII.F   *Side 8, band 2*

Brahms: *Symphony no. 1 in C minor* op. 68 (1876), first movement
2 flutes, 2 oboes, 2 clarinets, 2 bassoons, double bassoon
2 horns, 2 trumpets; timpani
1st and 2nd violins, violas, cellos, double basses

1st movement (Un poco sostenuto–Allegro). The slow, somber introduction contains the main idea from which this large-scale sonata-form movement is constructed.

Time

0:00	slow introduction: ex. i (note figures x^1, x^2, y and z, which occur either way up), c
0:35	ex. iii, woodwinds and pizzicato strings
1:48	ex. i, g
2:05	oboe solo
2:46	exposition: main theme, ex. ii (from x and y in ex. i), c
3:00	ex. iv (based on ex. iii)
3:21	ex. v
3:41	transitional material
4:17	second subject, ex. vi – based on x^1 (ex. i and ii) and y (ex. v), E♭
4:29	oboe theme, E♭
4:39	oboe dialogue with clarinet
4:53	clarinet with horn dialogue
5:09	closing material, tutti on z (and y)
5:44	development: material from ex. i
6:04	flute and oboe, c♯
6:26	tutti on z, f
6:42	alternate winds and strings
7:17	quiet passage on x^1, c
8:14	z and x^2, loud tutti, c
8:34	recapitulation, ex. ii, c
8:49	ex. iv, c
9:09	transition
9:36	second subject, ex. vi, C
9:48	oboe theme (from 4:29)
10:12	clarinet and horn dialogue, C
10:28	closing material, z
10:58	coda: dialogue between winds and strings
11:19	quiet passage on x^1 (as 7:17)
11:45	Meno Allegro ("less fast"), on x^1 (similar to opening)
12:35	(end)

2nd movement (Andante sostenuto), E: Ternary form

3rd movement (Un poco Allegretto), A♭: Ternary form

4th movement (Adagio – Allegro non troppo), c—C: Sonata form with slow introduction

ex. i

together by a theme constantly repeated, sometimes conventionally in the bass, and sometimes tucked away inside the melody and the harmony.

Brahms's last orchestral work followed in 1887: a double concerto for violin and cello. He had always loved the cello – in his first sextet for strings, written back in 1859–60, he had given it three of his most glorious themes, some soaring, some serene, and he also wrote two cello sonatas. When he heard Dvořák's Cello Concerto he wished that he had composed such a work himself. The Double Concerto's first movement is in Brahms's most austere vein, but the slow middle movement is scored and harmonized with luxuriant richness and the finale turns again to the gipsy echoes from Brahms's youth.

Meanwhile, chamber music and songs had flowed steadily from Brahms's pen. About 1890, he heard the clarinetist Richard Mühlfeld at Meiningen and decided to write some music for him, including a Clarinet Quintet (1891) in which Brahms revels in the variety of soft and rich colors in the ensemble of clarinet and strings. This is another highly organized work, in which themes are constantly being reshaped and given new meaning.

In these late years Brahms returned, after more than ten years, to piano music. In 1892 he wrote four sets of short, independent pieces with titles like Intermezzo or Capriccio, some fiery and brilliant but mostly reflective, subtle and fanciful, and all written with the serene mastery of the mature composer. Virtually all his life Brahms had composed songs, up to 1886; and here too he turned back at the very end, writing in 1896 a set that he called *Four Serious Songs* – to biblical texts, concerned, as in the *German Requiem*, with death and consolation. These are somber music, dark-toned and powerful, written when he knew that death was near; his earlier songs are closer to the traditions of Schubert and Schumann, though with hints of German folksong in many of them.

The *Four Serious Songs* were Brahms's last composition. He was only in his early 60s; but in spite of the universal recognition accorded to him in his late years he had suffered from the deaths of many friends. In 1896 he developed cancer of the liver, and next spring he died. Brahms was no revolutionary, and an innovator only in an unobtrusive way (though a way that was eventually to have a profound influence on later composers); his principles were classical, yet in his music a warm, truly Romantic spirit is unmistakable beneath the often gruff and austere surface.

Chapter IX

The Turn of the Century

The Romantic era is usually seen as continuing up to those critical years around 1910–13, just before the outbreak of World War I. But we can distinguish between its beginnings, the time of such men as Chopin, Schumann and Berlioz, and the post-Wagnerian period. In the last chapter we dealt principally with composers who preceded Wagner or stood apart from him (like Verdi and Brahms) because they had found their musical language before they felt Wagner's impact. Of the composers considered in the present chapter, virtually all were affected by Wagner, even those who rejected him: men active chiefly between the 1870s and World War I.

Essentially, this is the era when composers, in face of the breakdown of the traditional tonal system, sought new ways of developing the language of music. It was not, however, mainly because of Wagner that the composers of Russia and eastern Europe chose the directions they did. The middle of the nineteenth century was a time when the peoples of many European countries became increasingly aware of their national identity. Partly this

Nationalism

was because of the growing interest in the past and in the meaning of national traditions. But it was also linked with political developments, as the traditional rulers were forced to give way to more democratic forms of government and as groups bound by language and tradition threw off foreign domination.

Belgium and the Netherlands (or Holland) became kingdoms in 1830, Italy in 1861, Germany an empire in 1871. Others, still under foreign domination, found a new awareness of their traditions: the Czechs and Hungarians, for example, began to cherish their folksong and literature although German was generally the language of the ruling classes. In these countries and in Poland and Russia, the traditions of cultivated music had largely been Italian and German, but now composers began to set words in the tongue spoken by the majority. In doing so, they tried to incorporate features of their national folksong traditions – not only did such melodies fit with the rhythms and the rise and fall of the words, but they also had an appealing familiarity. Economic factors played a part: with industrialization, larger population centers were developing, and from what had been a rural peasant class a middle class was forming, ready to go to concerts and opera houses.

The composers of Russia – not all, for the greatest, Tchaikovsky, stood somewhat apart – formed the most prominent group of nationalists, using folksong liberally. This was a period when other arts flowered in Russia, with the poet Pushkin at the beginning of the century and the writers Tolstoy, Chekhov and Dostoyevsky later. The Czechs called more on the rhythms of their native language than on folk melody; as part of the Austro-Hungarian empire, they had deep roots in the Germanic (and Italianate) central European tradition. Northern Europe too had long had links with Germany, but Grieg was not the only composer to draw on local folk music. Spanish composers at the end of the century also drew strongly on local traditions.

The increase in national consciousness was not confined to the periphery of Europe. Brahms, as we have seen, used German folksong, and Wagner was deeply aware of his German identity. Verdi was equally alive to his as an Italian. But in these countries, and in France, the traditions of art music were strong and individual enough for the use of folksong to be neither necessary nor manageable. In Britain, the predominant taste was Germanic, though eventually a folksong movement was to assert itself. In the United States, art music traditions, which essentially were imported from Europe, were diverse though again mainly German. Louis Moreau Gottschalk (1829–69) drew on Afro-American and Hispanic elements, but the best-known American composer of the century, Edward MacDowell (1860–1908), was fully cosmopolitan in his musical language.

Exoticism

The use of national features could be something more than national assertion. The Russian composer Rimsky-Korsakov wrote a *Spanish Caprice*, using the colors and the rhythms of Spain, and a work *Sheherazade* hinting at the music of the Middle East. This was part of a widespread movement towards the mysterious and the exotic. Other composers looked beyond Europe: Debussy, for example, sought inspiration in the gamelan music and the gongs of Indonesia, which he heard at the Paris Exhibition of 1889, and wrote an Egyptian ballet (he also composed Spanish-colored music, like many Frenchmen), while Puccini looked still further afield – to Japan, China and the American Wild West – in search of new colors and ideas.

There are parallels in the visual arts, for example in the inspiration sought by Paul Gauguin (1848–1903) in the South Pacific. Here there was also an element of escape from the sophistication and artificiality of Western society in favor of a "return to Nature", to which there could be no exact analogy in music, although the composers who used folksong had similar feelings. A close parallel between music and painting, however, may

Impressionism, Symbolism

be drawn between Debussy and the French Impressionists, such as Claude Monet (1840–1926) and Camille Pissarro (1830–1903): Debussy used washes of color and vague, suggestive harmony in place of clear-cut themes, and relied on dreaminess and sensory impression. Arguably he is even closer to the Symbolist school, including such painters as Gustave Moreau (1826–98), and the poet Stéphane Mallarmé (1842–98), who wrote the poem that gave rise to his most famous work, *L'après-midi d'un faune*.

Two other French writers should be mentioned: Honoré de Balzac (1799–1850) as the initiator of a new realism that arose out of Romanticism and Emile Zola (1840–1902) as perhaps its most powerful exponent. Balzac represents the reaction against the idealistic, imaginative, fantastic side of Romanticism. His closest equivalent in the visual arts was Gustave Courbet (1819–77). The realism of Bizet's *Carmen*, discussed on p. 216, provides

Realism

a close musical parallel. Realism (*verismo* in Italian), which has strong political overtones in its readiness to face up to social evils (rife in these times, the heyday of industrialization) as well as psychological realities, can also be seen as part of the reaction against the exalted emotions of Verdi's operas and grand opera generally, and against the unreality and loftiness (even if symbolic) of Wagner's world. It had a powerful influence on opera composers, especially Italian ones, who encountered it in the writings of the novelist Giovanni Verga (1840–1922).

The first important *verismo* composer was Pietro Mascagni (1863–1945), whose *Cavalleria rusticana* ("Country chivalry", 1889) tells a tale of infidelity and revenge in a Sicilian village; a one-act work, it is usually coupled in the theater with *Pagliacci* ("Clowns", 1891) by Ruggero Leoncavallo (1859–1919), a similar tale in a context of a traveling theatrical troupe. Puccini is not generally regarded as a *verismo* composer, and he is much more than that; but there are elements of the same kind of realism in his depiction of the life of impoverished artists in Paris in *La bohème* and in the wanton cruelties of *Tosca*. Several other Italians took similar paths; so did Germans and Frenchmen, but fewer of their operas are still performed

Richard Strauss, the most important opera composer in central Europe in the early decades of the twentieth century, had little to do with realism, although the first two of his operas to have entered the repertory (*Salome*, 1905, and *Elektra*, 1909) embody brutality and lust of the kind that the *verismo* composers relished. They might perhaps be called psychological *verismo* operas in that they explore with an attempted realism some basic aspects of the human psyche, using a biblical story (as interpreted by Oscar Wilde) and a classical one. This interest in underlying motives shares something with the contemporary work of Sigmund Freud (1856–1939) – whose links with Mahler, briefly his patient, are possibly even stronger. Strauss moved away from the violence of these early operas. After *Elektra* he wrote *Der Rosenkavalier*, which deals with love affairs in eighteenth-century Vienna, treated with wit and high sophistication. There are parallels here with the *fin de siècle* ("end of the era") decadence of the *art nouveau* movement and with the daring, sexually allusive drawings of Aubrey Beardsley (1872–98) – an art that plays with art.

Strauss nevertheless lies firmly in the central European tradition, for he was more *enfant terrible* than revolutionary. So too does Mahler who, for all the influence he had on the next generation, expanded the framework of the Romantic symphony, as Bruckner had done in the previous generation. He expanded it not only, like Bruckner, to accommodate symphonic development on a Wagnerian scale but also to express a wide range of extra-musical ideas – culminating, in the colossal Eighth Symphony, with philosophical concepts drawn from Part II of Goethe's *Faust*. This expansion of resources that we see in Bruckner, Strauss and Mahler is characteristic of the closing phase of an era. It is tempting, and only partly an over-simplification, to regard such works as the last desperate, passionate, dying cries of the central Romantic tradition.

Russian nationalism

Apart from the products of the eccentric genius Mikhail Glinka (1804–57), Russian music before the middle of the nineteenth century was provincial. Then various factors combined to change matters. The conditions for music in Russia improved in the 1860s with the foundation of the Imperial Russian Music Society, the St Petersburg Conservatory and the Moscow Conservatory. There was the stimulus of Berlioz's visit in 1867. Also diatonic harmony had become so complex that it could incorporate the modalities of Russian folk music and liturgical chant. And there was the emergence of a highly gifted generation of creative individuals, of which one was Tchaikovsky.

Tchaikovsky   Pyotr Ilyich Tchaikovsky was born in 1840 in the Vyatka province, where his father was a mining engineer and factory manager. His mother had a French grandfather, but his attraction to things French has normally been connected with his having been taught by a French governess. In 1848 the Tchaikovskys moved to St Petersburg, where the future composer was educated at the School of Jurisprudence (1850–59). During this time, and particularly after his mother's death in 1854, he began to compose seriously, but on leaving the school he was obliged to take a post in the Ministry of Justice. In 1863 he became a full-time student again, at the St Petersburg Conservatory, where his composition teacher was the young and energetic director Anton Rubinstein (1829–94).

Rubinstein was cosmopolitan, concerned for the standard genres and conservative in his musical taste. The young Tchaikovsky was naturally influenced by his views, and in 1866 wrote a symphony sub-titled "Winter Daydreams". But in the winter of 1867–8 he

Pyotr Ilyich Tchaikovsky	Life
1840	born in Kamsko-Votkinsk, Vyatka province, 7 May
1850–59	student at the School of Jurisprudence, St Petersburg
1859–63	clerk at the Ministry of Justice
1863–5	studied with Anton Rubinstein at the St Petersburg Conservatory
1866	professor of harmony at the Moscow Conservatory; First Symphony
1868	met Balakirev and his group of nationalist composers ("The Five") but did not join their circle
1870–74	nationalist compositions, especially operas, attract attention
1875	Piano Concerto no. 1
1876	began correspondence with Nadezhda von Meck, a wealthy widow who helped him financially
1877	married Antonina Milyukova but separated after a few weeks; emotional breakdown
1878	Fourth Symphony, *Eugene Onegin*, Violin Concerto; resigned from Moscow Conservatory; beginning of period of creative sterility but increasing popularity in Russia
1885	*Manfred* Symphony
1888–9	toured Europe as a conductor
1890	Nadezhda von Meck ends correspondence and allowance; beginning of deep depression
1891	USA
1893	Sixth ("Pathétique") Symphony; died (?suicide) in St Petersburg, 6 November

Pyotr Ilyich Tchaikovsky   Works

Operas The Voyevoda (1869), The Snow Maiden (1873), The Oprichnik (1874), Vakula the Smith (1876), Eugene Onegin (1879), Mazeppa (1884), The Queen of Spades (1890)

Ballets Swan Lake (1877), The Sleeping Beauty (1890), Nutcracker (1892)

Orchestral music symphonies – no. 1, "Winter Daydreams", g (1866), no. 2, "Little Russian", c (1872), no. 3, "Polish", D (1875), no. 4, f (1878), no. 5, e (1888), no. 6, "Pathétique", b (1893), Manfred (1885); piano concertos – no. 1, b♭ (1875); Violin Concerto (1878); Francesca da Rimini (1876); Hamlet (1888); overtures – Romeo and Juliet (1869), 1812 (1880); Italian Capriccio (1880); suites, variations

Chamber music Souvenir de Florence, string sextet (1890); string quartets; piano trio

Choral music cantatas, services

Piano music   *Songs*

came into contact with Mily Balakirev, who was already at the head of a group of composers known as "The Five" (see p. 245). Balakirev held opposite views: he was adamantly Russian and attracted to picturesque symphonic poems. Recognizing Tchaikovsky's talent, he was eager to make him a sixth member of the circle, but two factors prevented that. The first was distance: the Five were based in St Petersburg, whereas Tchaikovsky was now teaching at the new conservatory in Moscow. The second was a natural solitariness on the part of Tchaikovsky, who seems already to have sensed that his homosexuality isolated him.

Nevertheless, Balakirev had considerable sway in encouraging nationalism in Tchaikovsky and that nationalist streak found expression in his now rarely-heard early operas. However, the other early work written under Balakirev's influence was one of the most popular concert pieces and Tchaikovsky's first mature achievement: the "fantasy overture" *Romeo and Juliet* (1869).

The theme of fatal love had an obvious significance to Tchaikovsky. It was one to which he returned in his later illustrative pieces with a literary basis: *Francesca da Rimini* (after Dante, 1876), *Manfred* (after Byron, 1885) and *Hamlet* (after Shakespeare, 1888). But equally characteristic is the musical style of *Romeo and Juliet*: its vivid orchestration, its frankly emotional themes and its adaptation of sonata form to justify and control a dramatic construction with two strongly characterized ideas in unlike keys (in this case B minor and D♭ major). Tchaikovsky's music does not belong in the Haydn–Beethoven–Brahms tradition of development, but his way of cross-cutting between dissimilar themes, intensifying differences of tonality and texture, provides a new concept of development, just as his apotheoses are effective replacements for recapitulation. These features are found in the symphonic poems or descriptive overtures of Liszt and Berlioz. But *Romeo and Juliet* made them more violently effective, and also prepared the way for a reintegration of symphonic-poem techniques into the four-movement symphony without programmatic support.

Tchaikovsky first attempted this in his Second Symphony (1872), which uses Ukrainian folksongs, and then again in his Third (1875), called the "Polish". But both these works suggest he was suppressing his dramatic instincts (they come out in the strongly characterized middle movements), and his best orchestral piece of this period was one where drama could be central: his First Piano Concerto (1875). It is significant here that an obvious structural "fault" – the failure of the famous opening tune to reappear – has not held the work back, for the real function of the opening is not to state a theme but to propose a style, in which piano and orchestra are rivals in emotional and dynamic power as each in turn takes on the responsibility of melodic outburst. In his first ballet, *Swan Lake* (1877), Tchaikovsky delighted in the opportunity to write exquisitely illustrative music without thought of large-scale form. It was a fairy-tale musical world to which he was to return in two later full-length ballets, the magnificent *Sleeping Beauty* (1890) and his masterpiece of orchestral brilliance, *Nutcracker* (1892).

Meanwhile, in the real world Tchaikovsky's state was not so happy. He became convinced that marriage could release him from the homosexual inclinations about which he felt so guilty. When a certain Antonina Milyukova wrote to him in the spring of 1877 with a confession of love he was prepared to see where it might lead – especially when he found himself in much the same position as the hero of the opera he was just beginning, *Eugene Onegin*. Onegin repulsed his admirer and came to regret his folly; Tchaikovsky accepted the attentions of Antonina, but the outcome was the same. They were married on 18 July, less than three months after that first letter; by October they were permanently separated.

Tchaikovsky's emotional perturbation during these months is documented in his letters to his brother Modest and his distant patron Nadezhda von Meck, who gave him financial and (by correspondence) moral support on condition they never meet. But the intensity of his feelings comes out in his music, above all his Fourth Symphony, which also reveals his artistic maturity. The first movement, in particular, shows his mastery of form as a vehicle for the dramatic confrontation of sharply featured yet still companionable themes. The device of the motto theme, which appears in all four movements to make it clear that the symphony is a single experience, was adapted from Berlioz's *Fantastic Symphony* and was common in late nineteenth-century music. Less common was the close derivation of other subjects from the motto theme (see Listening Note IX.A).

Tchaikovsky thought of his themes in terms of their expressive character. According to a program for the symphony which he sketched for Mme von Meck, the motto theme is the voice of fate, "which prevents the impulse to happiness from attaining its goal". The first subject represents the misery of the individual; the second finds him discovering solace in daydreams; and the third speaks of an imagined happiness. But always after this third subject the motto theme enters to give the lie to easy contentment. The effect of this the second time, at the end of the recapitulation, is to leave the music open-ended: the coda, following directions indicated by Beethoven and Berlioz, is now so much a second development that it seems to require a second recapitulation, and so the cycle might continue.

This provides a musical, as well as an expressive excuse for the recurrence of the fate motto in the subsequent movements, as if continuing unfinished business. Both the middle movements are relatively lightweight. In the second, according to Tchaikovsky's program, the protagonist loses himself in nostalgia, and in the third he seeks oblivion in wine, though in both he is recalled by the summons of fate. The finale, a rondo on folktunes, is a recall to seriousness, and again Tchaikovsky makes an expressive point by structural means, since the movement opens with a newly strengthened version of the scherzo's opening.

Tchaikovsky completed the work, early in 1878, towards the end of a long stay in western Europe, where he had gone to get over his marriage. It was a productive holiday, for he also finished *Eugene Onegin* and saw the ballet *Sylvia*, of which the music by Léo Delibes (1836–91) greatly impressed him and left its mark on his own *Sleeping Beauty*. Towards the end of this period he enjoyed the companionship of the handsome young violinist Josif Kotek (1855–85) in Switzerland, and wrote for him his Violin Concerto in D.

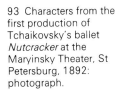

93 Characters from the first production of Tchaikovsky's ballet *Nutcracker* at the Maryinsky Theater, St Petersburg, 1892: photograph.

Listening Note IX.A   *Side 9, band 1*

Tchaikovsky: *Symphony no. 4* in F minor op. 36 (1877–8), first movement
(andante sostenuto, moderato con anima)
2 flutes (and piccolo in later movts), 2 oboes, 2 clarinets, 2 bassoons
4 horns, 2 trumpets, 3 trombones, tuba; timpani (and bass drum, cymbals, triangle in 4th movt)
1st violins, 2nd violins, violas, cellos, double basses

This movement follows the standard sonata-form outline but only partly uses its principles. The motto theme heard at the outset appears throughout the work and from it other themes are derived.

Time	
0:00	motto theme, ex. i, horns and bassoons, echoed by trumpets harmonized
1:19	exposition: principal theme, ex. ii, violins
4:36	transition
5:13	second theme, ex. iii, clarinets accompanied by another theme in cellos, ex. iii
6:17	closing theme, ex. iv
8:47	development
12:08	recapitulation: principal theme, ex. ii
12:35	second theme, ex. iii
13:44	closing theme, ex. iv
15:35	coda: restatement of motto theme
16:33	faster tempo
17:55	(end)

2nd movement (Andantino): Ternary form, b♭
3rd movement (Scherzo: Allegro): Ternary form (strings pizzicato throughout; trio sections for woodwind and brass groups), F
4th movement (Allegro): Rondo form, F

Tchaikovsky returned to Russia in April 1878 and in October resigned from the Moscow Conservatory, since he could now live on his allowance from Mme von Meck. His marriage was over (divorce followed in 1881) and outwardly his life was peaceable. These were not, however, the conditions under which he worked best, and for the next few years he produced relaxed suites instead of symphonies, grand epics (*The Maid of Orleans* and *Mazeppa*) instead of strong, intimate dramas like *Onegin*.

The ending of this period was announced by *Manfred* (1885), where Tchaikovsky again followed a plan of Balakirev's, this time for a four-movement symphony based on Byron's verse drama. No doubt he recognized himself in the hero, doomed to roam the mountains in a hopeless attempt to expiate nameless sins, and the symphony bears comparison, both in its structure and in its expressive character, with its F minor predecessor. So too, still more so, does the Fifth Symphony in E minor (1888), where the problems of integrating a motto theme are overcome when the finale converts the motto from an anxious probing into a march of triumph. The opera *The Queen of Spades* (1890) is also about a man accursed by fate and cut off from normal social life.

The suggestion in all these works – though not directly in his sumptuously escapist ballet *The Sleeping Beauty* – is that Tchaikovsky was not able to live at peace with himself in the way suggested by the works of the early 1880s. His Sixth Symphony in B minor (1893), for which his brother Modest suggested the descriptive title "Pathétique", makes this clear. Here he refused the lures of peasant jollity and the triumphal march accepted in the last two symphonies and instead made the finale a great Adagio, sinking into an inevitable depression. Again his urge to self-disclosure produced a new kind of musical structure, for this was the first great symphony of the nineteenth century to end with a slow movement.

Three days after its first performance, on 28 October 1893, Tchaikovsky – according to testimony recently smuggled out of Russia – was brought before a court of his peers from the School of Jurisprudence and accused of bringing it into disrepute by his homosexual proclivities; a nobleman had complained of his relationship with a nephew. The sentence was that he should kill himself. Whether this is wholly true remains uncertain. We do know that he died a week later, whether because he took arsenic in obedience to such a decree, or because (according to a traditional tale) he caught cholera from drinking untreated water, no one can be sure.

The Five

If Tchaikovsky can be compared with Tolstoy in conceiving his art in classical Western terms, the group known as "The Five" belong with Dostoyevsky as men rebelliously different, individual and Russian. They were Mily Balakirev, Modest Mussorgsky, Nikolay Rimsky-Korsakov, Alexander Borodin and César Cui.

Balakirev

Mily Balakirev (1837–1910), with no advanced musical education, was suspicious of its value for others, and it pleased him that Borodin, Rimsky-Korsakov and Mussorgsky had no more musical training than any boy of their period and (upper or middle) class. Similarly, technique was regarded as a potential enemy to genuineness of expression. Balakirev is best known for his orientally-colored pieces (*Islamey* for piano and *Tamara* for orchestra).

Borodin, Cui, Mussorgsky and Rimsky-Korsakov took lessons with Balakirev and by 1867 were regarded as a group around him, when the critic Vladimir Stasov, a champion of their music, coined the nickname "The Mighty Handful" for them. This was the period of their great masterpieces when they were mighty indeed.

Mussorgsky

Boris Godunov alone would be enough to establish Mussorgsky's place as the outstanding composer of this group. He was born in 1839 in Karevo, the son of a landed family, and educated at the Guards Cadet School in St Petersburg. Though he toyed with composition and was a polished pianist, there is no evidence that he regarded music with much seriousness until in 1857 he met the composers Dargomïzhsky (1813–69) and Cui, and then Balakirev, with whom he took lessons. He resigned his army commission and in 1859 went to Moscow, where he was powerfully struck by the remnants of ancient Russian culture (St Petersburg was more recent, an Enlightenment city). Among his works of the next few years there are strikingly individual creations, like the *Intermezzo symphonique in modo classico* for piano (1861) with its melody in Russian peasant style, but also exercises in sentimental trivia. The inconsistency was to remain characteristic, as was Mussorgsky's difficulty in finishing larger works.

Partly the problem was one of time. The liberation of the serfs in 1861 reduced Mussorgsky's income from the family estate, so he was obliged in 1863 to take a government post. But also he seems to have become intermittently alcoholic after his mother's death in 1865. A further difficulty was that he was in search of expressive means for which there were few precedents. He was attracted to the art of old Russia, as represented musically in the chant of the Orthodox church and in folksong, and he was excited by Dargomïzhsky's exploration of musical realism: capturing in song quirks of speech and nuances of expression, without much care for melodic shapeliness, harmonic coherence or metrical stability.

Mussorgsky began to achieve the naturalism he wanted in his songs, usually through placing each in the voice of an incisively sketched character, in a style of pungent irony. The song thus becomes like a miniature operatic scene. Many of his greatest are in cycles that are almost intimate operas, like *The Nursery* (1870), an unsentimental view of childhood with words by the composer.

This cleared Mussorgsky's path to opera. In 1868 he quickly set the first act of Gogol's comedy *The Marriage*, which gave him the diverse peasant characters and the irony he had proved he could handle in his songs. The same year he began his masterpiece *Boris Godunov*, based on Pushkin's play, which in its first version was finished the next. But it had to be several times revised, and was long best known in a version by Rimsky-Korsakov designed to increase its effectiveness. Nevertheless, *Boris Godunov* remains an eccentric opera – a study of the guilt-ridden tyrant tsar in separate frames of action and narrative rather than in dramatic continuity – and a certain roughness and crudity of style do not seem out of place.

This opera provided Mussorgsky with opportunities for great splendor in his ancient Russian style, using old modes and the sounds of great bells. It also gave him the chance to explore highly contrasted varieties of musical character, from the saturnine, possessed tsar himself to his lively children, or from a solemnly chanting monk to a vulgar, folksong-singing pair of itinerant friars. Boris's great monologues in the second act best show Mussorgsky's attention to verbal rhythm and meaning, as well as his readiness to create expressive effects in the orchestra.

Mussorgsky's only important later works were songs and the suite for piano *Pictures at an Exhibition*, where his skills as a musical illustrator went into creating equivalents for images in the paintings and drawings of his friend Victor Hartmann; the suite has several times been orchestrated, notably by Ravel. Mussorgsky's last years were ones of sporadic work on his two operas, interleaved with bouts of depression and alcoholism, though also with periods when he was able to function quite normally. He died in St Petersburg just a week after his 42nd birthday.

94 Chaliapin as Boris Godunov in Mussorgsky's opera: photograph.

Borodin, Rimsky-Korsakov

The career of Borodin (1833–87) was not unlike Mussorgsky's: although he composed two fine string quartets and two-and-a-half symphonies (no. 2 an expression of the principles of The Five in orchestral terms), his central work was an opera, *Prince Igor* – a grand historical pageant, full of exotic oriental touches, which it fell to Rimsky-Korsakov to edit and publish.

The two remaining members of The Five, Rimsky-Korsakov (1844–98) and Cui (1835–1918), were both much more productive, though slighter creative figures. Rimsky's *The Maid of Pskov* was in the historical genre, but several of his other operas, including above all *The Golden Cockerel* (1907), were fantasies of magic and the supernatural that gave the excuse for the spectacular effects in which he excelled. The more human characters in these operas are surrounded by music in folk style, while the magical elements are depicted in terms of chromaticism. Rimsky's orchestration is unusually varied and brilliant, as it is also in such orchestral works as *Sheherazade* (1888) and the *Spanish Caprice* (1887). His *Principles of Orchestration*, posthumously published in 1913, remains one of the standard texts on the subject and, taken with his music, suggests the influence he must have had on such pupils of his as Stravinsky and Prokofiev.

Later Russians

Apart from the orchestral splendor and modal usage passed on by Rimsky-Korsakov, the direct effect of The Five on subsequent composers was slight. The next generation was dominated by Sergey Rachmaninov and Alexander Scriabin (1872–1915). Scriabin, an outstanding pianist like Rachmaninov, was a progressive who gradually abandoned conventional forms and tonality, seeing music as an agent of spiritual enlightenment. Rachmaninov, who worked largely in the standard genres, had no more pretensions for his art than that it should please and stir.

Rachmaninov

Sergey Rachmaninov was born in Semyonovo in April 1873 into a family of failing fortunes. He studied at the conservatories in St Petersburg and Moscow, graduating from the latter in 1892. He then began a career as a concert pianist while also composing: his popular Prelude in C♯ minor dates from the year of his graduation, his First Symphony from three years later. This period of confidence was brought to an end by a calamitous performance of the symphony in 1897, after which he virtually abandoned composition until he produced his Second Piano Concerto (1901), whose immediate success restored

---

Sergey Rachmaninov   Works
born Semyonovo, 1873; *died* Beverly Hills, 1943

Orchestral music piano concertos – no. 1, f♯ (1891), no. 2, c (1901), no. 3, d (1909), no. 4, g (1926); symphonies – no. 1, d (1895), no. 2, e (1907), no. 3, a (1936); The Isle of the Dead (1909); Rhapsody on a Theme of Paganini for piano and orchestra (1934); Symphonic Dances (1940)

Piano music sonatas – no. 1, d (1907), no. 2, b♭ (1913); Preludes, op. 23 (1903), op. 32 (1910); Etudes-tableaux, op. 33 (1911), op. 39 (1917); Variations on a Theme of Corelli (1931)

Choral music Liturgy of St John Chrysostom (1910); The Bells (1913)

Operas Aleko (1892), Francesca da Rimini (1905)

Songs Vocalise, op. 34 no. 14 (1912)

Chamber music Cello Sonata (1901); piano trios

his creative self-image. With its passionate and lyrical melodic style, rich harmony and its brilliant piano writing it has always been among his most popular works. More quickly followed, including two operas which he conducted at the Bolshoy Theater, Moscow (1904–6).

In 1909 Rachmaninov made his first tour of the USA and then returned to live in Russia. Many works date from the next few years, among them solo piano pieces and choral works. After 1917 his nostalgia was joined by a deep sense of dislocation from his homeland. He and his family left Russia after the October Revolution and settled in the USA. There he became a professional pianist.

Composition was laid aside until in 1926 he wrote his Fourth Piano Concerto, a rambling work that underwent several phases of revision without being made the equal of the Second or the hugely demanding Third. It was followed by several major works in which he reviewed his earlier style from an American standpoint of brilliance and detachment. The *Paganini Rhapsody* for piano and orchestra (1934), the Third Symphony (1936) and the *Symphonic Dances* (1940), first performed by the Philadelphia Orchestra, were written with the precision of American orchestras in mind. Sometimes, especially in the *Symphonic Dances*, the nostalgia becomes part of the musical substance, with themes from earlier works: this happens in the *Dances* with a subject from the First Symphony and quotation from a church work. Rachmaninov died at his home in Beverly Hills in 1943. His piano and orchestral music represent the Westward-looking Russian romanticism that Tchaikovsky had brought to its peak a generation and more before.

East European nationalism

The assertion of national identity through music, and particularly by the use of traditional, folk elements in art music, became important in all the leading countries of eastern Europe during the later nineteenth century. In Poland and Hungary national opera traditions were begun. In Bohemia (now part of Czechoslovakia), closer to the older centers of European musical life (indeed including some of then), national aspirations asserted themselves particularly strongly just after the middle of the century – and in Smetana and Dvořák there were composers of international stature to exploit them.

Smetana

Bedřich Smetana was born in 1824 in the Bohemian town of Litomyšl, where his father, who played the violin, was a brewer. He gained his musical education piecemeal, but earned a living in Prague in the 1840s as a piano teacher while producing a large quantity of trivial piano music. It was not until after a meeting in 1858 with Liszt, one of his heroes, that he wrote his first important works.

Smetana had been brought up as a German-speaker, and had first used Czech only in 1856; he now mastered his national language and in 1861 used it for an opera, *The Brandenburgers in Bohemia*. Given the mood of the time, the opera, on a theme from his country's history, was assured success, and he swiftly followed it with a spirited comedy of Bohemian peasant life, *The Bartered Bride*. This tuneful and appealing work is Smetana's best-known opera (he was later to write two more).

From the 1870s date his cycle of six symphonic poems, *My Country*, based on the countryside, the history and the legends of Bohemia. The best known of these is *Vltava*, which traces in music the course of the country's main river. The music represents first a forest rill (on flutes), then a mighty stream (a broad violin theme, with its roots in folk music); next it moves through the forest, where a hunt is heard, to a village where a wedding is being celebrated (with a mixed march and polka); then the river is seen by moonlight (soft strings and woodwinds), and eventually it passes stormily through rapids and streams majestically on to Prague (a noble, crowning tutti: the music moves from minor to major).

Meanwhile, Smetana's more personal thoughts went into a string quartet (1876), subtitled "From my Life" and consisting of a musical autobiography in four movements. The finale begins as a rustic dance, but it breaks off and Smetana introduces the whining high E that had racked his inner ear during his approaching deafness (which had forced him to resign as conductor of the Prague Provisional Theater). The illness (syphilis) that caused the deafness killed him, in 1884; he received the funeral of a national hero.

Dvořák

By the time of Smetana's death, his example had been followed by others, notably Antonín Dvořák. Dvořák's father was a butcher. He studied at the organ school in Prague (the organ schools were centers of general music education in Bohemia). Then he worked as a viola player, being Smetana's principal in the Provisional Theater orchestra, where he played in the first performance of *The Bartered Bride* and in a concert conducted by Wagner. Smetana and Wagner were the main, and confusing, influences on his early music, though from the first he was intent on writing in the conventional genres of symphony and string quartet. His Third Symphony (1873) won an Austrian national prize and brought him to the notice of Brahms, whose encouragement may well have contributed to his rapid creative development at this relatively late stage.

But Brahms's example was important too. Dvořák dedicated a quartet to him, and made sure the outer movements were in orthodox sonata form, but, as Smetana had done, he introduced a polka instead of the scherzo. He also used Slavonic rhythms in his first mature symphony, no. 6 in D (1880), and in a string quartet, where the second movement is headed "Dumka" and the finale has the rhythm of a Czech leaping dance. The *dumka*

Antonín Dvořák	Life
1841	born in Nelahozeves, 8 September
1857	Prague Organ School
1863	viola player in Prague Provisional Theater Orchestra, from 1866 under Smetana
1873	married Anna Cermáková; organist of St Adalbert, Prague
1874	Third Symphony won Austrian National Prize
1878	Slavonic Dances published; encouragement from Brahms and first international recognition
1884	first of nine visits to England, where he became extremely popular and where several works (e.g. Eighth Symphony, *Requiem*) were first performed
1891	professor of composition at the Prague Conservatory; awarded many honors
1892–5	director of the National Conservatory of Music, New York; "New World" Symphony, "American" String Quartet, Cello Concerto
1895	director of the Prague Conservatory
1898	beginning of concentration on opera
1904	died in Prague, 1 May

Antonín Dvořák   Works

Orchestral music symphonies – no. 1, c (1865), no. 2, B♭ (1865), no. 3, E♭ (1873), no. 4, d (1874), no. 5, F (1875), no. 6, D (1880), no. 7, d (1885), no. 8, G (1889), no. 9, "From the New World", e (1893); Slavonic Dances (1878, 1887); Slavonic Rhapsodies (1878); Symphonic Variations (1887); Nature, Life and Love (1892); Violin Concerto (1880); Cello Concerto (1895); symphonic poems

Operas The Jacobin (1897), Rusalka (1900)

Chamber music 14 string quartets – no. 12, "The American", F (1893), no. 13, G (1895), no. 14, A♭ (1895); Piano Quintet, A (1887); piano trios – Dumky, op. 90 (1891); 3 string quintets; string sextet, 2 piano quartets

Choral music Stabat mater (1877); St Ludmilla (1886); Mass (1887); Requiem (1890); Te Deum (1892); choral songs

Piano music Dumka (1876); Humoresques, op. 101 (1894); piano duets – Slavonic Dances (1878, 1886)

Songs

was a lament which Dvořák often interpreted as a melancholy song incorporating bright dance sections: this happens in the six *dumky* that make up his fine Piano Trio in E minor (1891). Another *dumka* appears among the 16 Slavonic Dances (1878 and 1886), which were published in orchestral and piano duet versions which popularized Dvořák's music.

The proof that a Bohemian style could appeal outside central Europe came in 1884 when Dvořák first conducted his music in London – to immense acclaim. Commissions came for choral works and a new symphony for the Philharmonic Society of London (no. 7 in D minor). Then came a request from further afield, when he was invited to direct the National Conservatory of Music in New York. Apart from one holiday at home, he spent 1892–5 in the USA.

There he took an interest in the music of black Americans and Indians. Some of his American research went into his works, including his Ninth Symphony in E minor, "From the New World", and his F major string quartet, "American" (both 1893). However, what he extracted from his New World sources was a vein of pentatonic melody – that is, based (largely) on a five-note scale (rather like the black keys on a piano) – which is so widespread in folk music that it could equally have been east European. Dvořák accommodated this element within the diatonic system.

The main themes of the string quartet are pentatonic; those of the "New World" symphony slightly less so, but still bring a new idiom into the realm of symphonic music. The well-known theme of the slow movement evokes the nostalgic world of black American song; but again Dvořák's treatment presses it into the mold of the post-Brahmsian symphony. He made this kind of theme very much his own. In the Cello Concerto that he wrote in his last months in New York – perhaps the finest concerto for that eloquent instrument – several themes have this pentatonic leaning, but the music is as Brahmsian as anything Dvořák produced.

Back in Bohemia, Dvořák devoted his final years mostly to opera, ranging from folktale comedy to high Wagnerian tragedy by way of the fairytale fantasy of his dramatic masterpiece, *Rusalka* (1900). He died in Prague in 1904.

Dvořák's influence was so deep on his Czech successors that even Leoš Janáček, born in Moravia (central Czechoslovakia) in 1854, composed in the Bohemian style of his elder

Janáček

contemporary for much of his life. His early music is of slender value but his last ten years saw the composition of four great operas, mostly on highly unconventional topics, as well as a Mass, a Sinfonietta and two string quartets.

There were musical reasons for this late flowering: one may be the influence of Stravinsky, though the no less important influence of Mussorgsky had long been felt. And there was a personal one; the intense emotion Janáček experienced when he conceived a strong attachment for a married woman, Kamila Stösslová, the imagined heroine of his late operas. Also, his late music can be seen as attaining the distinctive Moravian character he had been looking for all his life.

The Moravian quality of Janáček's music is on one level a matter of accentuation. He notated the rhythms and pitch inflections of people's speaking voices, and used the experience in creating, Mussorgsky-like, a variety of operatic characters distinguished by their vocal behavior. It was in an opera with a Moravian village setting, *Jenůfa* (1904), that he emerged as an independent composer, discovering a realistic way of handling people in emotional conflict. To a listener from the West, used to the languages of a smoother rhythmic structure, Janáček's music often sounds jagged and violent; in the operas this is

95 *Opposite* Part of an article on Dvořák's Symphony no. 9 in E minor ("From the New World") from the *New York Herald* (16 December 1893) after its first performance in the Carnegie Hall a few days earlier.

96 *Right* Čapek's design for the lawyer's office in Janáček's opera *The Makropoulos Case*, first performed 18 December 1926. Moravské Muzeum, Brno. The opera was based on a play by the artist's brother.

Leoš Janáček   Works
born Hukvaldy, 1854; *died* Moravská Ostrava, 1928

Operas Jenůfa (1904), The Excursions of Mr Brouček (1920), Katya Kabanova (1921), The Cunning Little Vixen (1924), The Makropoulos Case (1926), From the House of the Dead (perf. 1930)
Choral music Mass (1908); Glagolitic Mass (1926); cantatas, male-voice choruses
Other vocal music The Diary of One who Disappeared (1919); songs
Orchestral music Taras Bulba (1918); Sinfonietta (1926)
Chamber music string quartets – no. 1, "Kreutzer Sonata" (1923), no. 2, "Intimate Letters" (1928); Youth, wind sextet (1924)
Piano music

---

stressed by his orchestral writing, where he often obtains harsh, strongly characterized effects by using instruments at the extremes of their compass.

In achieving this kind of realism, Janáček also learned from Moravian folk music, which encouraged him towards a style of short melodic phrases, baldly repeated or juxtaposed, each phrase normally being identified with its own orchestral coloring. In instrumental works whole movements are constructed from repeated figures in this way. In opera Janáček uses his brevity to color conversation. Long solo passages (or "arias") are rare. Instead, there is a quick crossfire of different characters, different kinds of music.

Janáček spent most of his life in the Moravian capital of Brno, where he taught and wrote acute, often fanciful articles for a newspaper. Most of his extraordinary late music, however, was composed back in his home village, and he died in the nearby town of Moravská Ostrava in 1928.

Vienna

The Bohemia and Moravia of Smetana, Dvořák and Janáček was until 1918 part of the Habsburg empire, ruled from Vienna, and to some extent the very existence of a Czech national style depended on composers keeping their distance from so richly endowed a musical capital: Dvořák in particular was very conscious of that, and resisted commissions to write for Vienna. However, there was no single Viennese style. Brahms was to be heard in the concert halls and the younger Johann Strauss in the ballrooms, but there were others, whom the conservative Viennese public took less readily to their hearts: Bruckner, Wolf and Mahler.

Hugo Wolf (1860–1903) was an outspoken music critic who heaped praise on Wagner at the expense of Brahms. He was influenced by Wagner's harmony and declamatory style in the songs that form the bulk of his output. But his penetrating search for character, for the particular "voice" of a song, for psychological insight, belongs very much in the Vienna of Freud.

Plate 14 *Opposite*
Puccini's *Tosca*: scene by Hohenstein from Act 1 in the original production at the Teatro Costanzi, Rome, 1900 (see p. 275). Commemorative postcard.

Bruckner

Anton Bruckner, also neglected and even despised in Vienna for his Wagnerism, drew something quite different from the master of Bayreuth: symphonic breadth. Born in 1824 in Ansfelden, near Linz, he was the son of a schoolmaster-organist and began by following his father's profession, notably at the monastery of St Florian near his home village. From 1855 to 1868 he was organist at Linz Cathedral. He studied harmony and counterpoint by correspondence with the Viennese teacher Simon Sechter and then had lessons locally. In 1863 he encountered Wagner's music through a performance of *Tannhäuser* in Linz, and soon began to write works that are characteristic: his First Symphony, in C minor, and large-scale Masses. All, however, were subsequently revised. Bruckner always lacked confidence in his mastery and meekly accepted criticism, even the uncomprehending criticism that persuaded him to make damaging cuts in his broad structures.

In 1868 he was appointed Sechter's successor at the Vienna Conservatory, where he remained to the end of his life with a band of disciples (including Mahler, who never actually studied with him) while his music attracted scorn. Apart from a few choral works, he devoted himself to the symphony, and perfected his approach to the form. Beethoven's Ninth gave him the outline – a monumental opening movement, a profound Adagio, a driving scherzo in sonata form and a cumulative finale; Wagner provided the time-scale and some of the harmony (in his later symphonies he used a quartet of Wagner tubas, the instruments Wagner had designed for the *Ring*). But Schubert was his nearest predecessor in matters of form. His sonata allegros often have three groups of subject matter rather than two and, like Schubert's, tend to substitute repetition in a different key for development.

The result is wholly original. Bruckner's long apprenticeship as a church musician, and his devotion to the Catholic faith, imprinted the ecclesiastical modes into his musical nature, and the individuality of his harmony often results from modal inflections. Similarly, his treatment of the orchestra in large homogeneous blocks suggests the work of an organist manipulating stops, though this style of instrumentation enabled him to achieve colossal effects with an orchestra of modest proportions for the period. Only in his Eighth Symphony, in C minor (1887), the last he completed, did he introduce a harp and expand the woodwind from double to triple; and nowhere did he use the unusual woodwinds (piccolo, English horn etc) or the additional percussion prized by Wagner, Mahler and Strauss.

His greatest originality lay in his conception of time. Long-held notes (often in the form of string *tremolandos*) and sequences of continuingly repeated figures create effects of stillness not otherwise to be found in Western music before Messiaen, and generally his structures are static rather than dynamic. Where Brahms was making development more central to his music, Bruckner was insisting on statement, on the symphonic treatment of objects that are essentially stable.

Plate 15 *The Golden Cockerel* by Rimsky-Korsakov, title page of the first edition of the vocal score (Moscow, 1908). See p. 247.

Anton Bruckner   Works
born Ansfelden, near Linz, 1824; *died* Vienna, 1896

Symphonies "no. 0", d (*c*1864), no. 1, c (1866), no. 2, c (1872), no. 3, d (1877), no. 4, "Romantic", E♭ (1874, 1880), no. 5, B♭ (1876), no. 6, A (1881), no. 7, E (1883), no. 8, c (1887), no. 9, d (1896, unfinished)

Choral music Requiem (1849); Masses – no. 1, d (1864), no. 2, e, with woodwind and brass (1866), no. 3, f (1868); Te Deum (1884); cantatas, motets

Chamber music String Quintet, F (1879)

Organ music   *Piano music*   *Partsongs*   *Songs*

That sort of form suits the themes of great length and solidity, rooted in basic tonal elements (triad and arpeggio), that are most characteristic of Bruckner. The opening of the E major Seventh Symphony is typical in its unfolding of a long melody over a *tremolando* accompaniment. The exposition is long and straightforward, introducing three themes, and the "development" explores them in different keys. The "recapitulation" is not the affirmative arrival it might be in a Beethoven or Brahms symphony, but the completion of a giant arch, with a return to the open diatonicism with which the symphony began. The whole work is an arch on a still greater scale, for at the end of the finale the opening motif comes back to add splendor to the conclusion.

Bruckner's next symphony, no. 8, goes further in the confirmation of unity: the ending of the last movement brings back the principal themes not only of the opening Allegro but also of the Adagio and the Scherzo. It is for such feats of construction and symmetry, as well as for their aura of sanctity, that Bruckner's symphonies have been aptly compared with great medieval cathedrals. He dedicated his Ninth Symphony, whose finale he did not live to complete, "to the King of Kings, Our Lord". He died peacefully in 1896.

Mahler

Mahler followed Bruckner in expanding the dimensions of the symphony, but his aims and methods were entirely different. Where Bruckner's symphonies are interpretations of one ideal, Mahler's are stages in a spiritual autobiography. Only three of his, like all Bruckner's, are four-movement cycles for orchestra (nos. 1, 6 and 9). The number of movements may be larger (five in nos. 2, 5, 7 and 10; six in no. 3) or smaller (two in no. 8). Mahler extended the range of the symphony by adding voices: solo women's and choral voices in nos. 2–4 and a mass of soloists and choirs in the symphonic oratorio that is no. 8, sometimes known as the "Symphony of a Thousand".

Gustav Mahler	Life

1860	born in Kalischt (now Kalište), 7 July
1875–8	Vienna Conservatory
1880	*The Song of Sorrow*; conductor at Bad Hall summer theater
1881–3	conductor at Laibach and Olmütz
1883–5	opera conductor at Kassel; composed *Songs of a Wayfarer* after unhappy love affair
1885–6	conductor of German Opera, Prague
1886	conductor of New State Theater, Leipzig
1888	met Richard Strauss, who became a lifelong friend; conductor of the Budapest Royal Opera
1891–7	conductor at the Hamburg State Theater; Second, Third and Fourth Symphonies
1897	baptized Roman Catholic; conductor of the Vienna Court Opera and, with gifted colleagues, was responsible for one of its most brilliant decades
1902	married Alma Schindler; beginning of period of intense composition
1907	elder daughter died; Mahler diagnosed to have heart disease
1908	conductor of the Metropolitan Opera, New York, spending summers in Europe composing
1909	conductor of New York Philharmonic Orchestra; *The Song of the Earth*
1911	died in Vienna, 18 May

97 *Opposite* Mahler conducting: silhouettes by Otto Böhler.

Gustav Mahler   Works

Symphonies no. 1, D (1888), no. 2, "Resurrection", c (1894), no. 3, d (1896), no. 4,
G (1900), no. 5, c♯ (1902), no. 6, a (1904), no. 7, e (1905), no. 8, E♭ (1906), no. 9,
D (1909), no. 10, f♯ (1910, unfinished)

Songs (with orchestra) song cycles – Lieder eines fahrenden Gesellen (Songs of a
wayfarer, 1885), Kindertotenlieder (Songs for the death of children, 1904); Des
Knaben Wunderhorn (Youth's Magic Horn, 1893–8); Das Lied von der Erde (The
song of the earth, 1909)

Choral music Das klagende Lied (The song of sorrow, 1880)

Gustav Mahler was born in 1860 in the Bohemian village of Kalischt. The family soon
moved to Iglau, where he came into contact with military bands, folksongs, café music
and salon pieces, storing memories that were to be revived in his symphonies. He learned
the piano and composed, displaying enough talent to gain admission to the Vienna
Conservatory, where he studied from 1875 to 1878. He remained in Vienna, attending
lectures at the university, working as a music teacher and writing a cantata, *Das klagende
Lied* (1880).

It is immediately characteristic of the mature composer. The style of Romantic medi-
evalism and nature-poetry comes from nineteenth-century German opera, and the harmonic language has the chromatic intensity of *Tristan*, then little more than a decade old.
Mahler's use of the orchestra is already independent, showing his preference for sharp-
edged textures in which threads of melody and accompaniment stand out. Even the themes
bear comparison with those of later works, as does the subject, which is death, with all its
associations of sorrow, inevitability, absurdity and guilt.

In 1880 Mahler began a conducting career that led him to important posts in the opera
houses of Prague, Leipzig, Budapest, Hamburg, Vienna and New York. He became one
of the outstanding conductors of his day, unstinting in his demands on players and singers.

Mahler's First Symphony was completed in the mid-1890s, when it had been reduced
from five movements to four and changed from a symphonic poem into a work in more
traditional form. That it was first a symphonic poem suggests the importance of Richard
Strauss to the young Mahler, less as an influence than as a champion, though soon the two
men were forced into the position of rivals for the torch of the great tradition.

Mahler's First Symphony uses themes from his song cycle of the same period *Lieder
eines fahrenden Gesellen* ("Songs of a wayfarer"). This was something Schubert had done
in several of his later chamber works, but in Mahler's case the introduction of a song
theme hints at a psychological program underlying the music, and in his next three
symphonies such programs become explicit, since songs are included. They use texts from
Des Knaben Wunderhorn ("The boy's magic horn"), an early nineteenth-century collection
of real and imitation folk poetry. Mahler also made independent settings of the *Wunderhorn*
poems, whose naivety was a perfect vehicle for his music, so much more ironic, complex
and inquisitive.

The Second and Third Symphonies use other verse too. The grand choral finale to no.
2 sets an ode on resurrection by Klopstock: a work that begins with a movement filled
with doubt ends in gigantic optimism. The Third, according to its original program, is
an ascent through the realms of existence. Its huge first movement, lasting for half an
hour, is followed by five movements in which the composer listens in turn to meadow
flowers (a delicate minuet), forest animals (a scherzo), the night (the contralto song, with
words by Nietzsche), bells (with angel choirs of women and boys) and love (Adagio). The

Fourth, of more normal dimensions, ends with the soprano singing of the delights of heaven.

While this work was in progress, Mahler was baptized into the Catholic church, though apparently for practical rather than religious reasons: his Jewishness was an obstacle to gaining an appointment in Vienna, where he became director of the Court Opera later the same year.

In 1902 he married Alma Schindler (1879–1964), the daughter of a painter and later, after Mahler's death, the wife successively of an architect (Walter Gropius) and a novelist (Franz Werfel). He embarked on a period of intense creativity, and though his conducting duties left him only the summers in which to compose, by 1905 he had completed three new symphonies. Again there were associated volumes of songs including the *Kindertotenlieder*, setting five of the 400 or so poems that Friedrich Rückert wrote on the deaths of his two children for voice and orchestra.

Much of this music – the symphonies as well as the songs – seems to convey Mahler's feeling of being pursued by fate, represented in the immense finale of the Sixth Symphony by the crushing blows of a hammer. In his own life the doom was prophetic rather than actual. At the Vienna Opera he was staging radically new productions, and he became the proud father of two daughters. It was in 1907 that life caught up with his art. His elder daughter, like Rückert's children, died, and he himself was diagnosed as having a heart condition.

In the fall of that year Mahler conducted his last operas in Vienna. Although his years at the Court Opera had been among the most distinguished in its history, they were not untroubled and his ideas often met with resistance. Meanwhile, he had been invited to conduct at the Metropolitan Opera in New York, which he did for two seasons, though the outlook of the company, with its emphases on Italian opera and star singers, was alien to him. When in 1909 he was offered the conductorship of the New York Philharmonic, he resigned from the Metropolitan. It was during his second season there that he contracted his last illness. Mahler introduced many new works to·New York in his concerts with the orchestra (86 in all), but neither his programs nor his manner were popular, and his departure was little regretted.

If Mahler's music of these later years – indeed of all periods – is unmistakably intro- spective, it appears to speak also of a wider impending tragedy: that of Imperial European culture, in which he had come to hold a prominent place at Vienna, and that of musical language. For his confrontation with death, explicit in the *Kindertotenlieder* and implicit in the Sixth Symphony, is a confrontation too with the dissonance and chromaticism that were threatening the extinction of tonality – not only in Mahler's music but also at exactly the same time in Strauss's and Schoenberg's. His responses to the threat were manifold. Highly characteristic is a tone of poignant nostalgia, present even in the music he was writing as a teenager, but focusing now on the remembrance of the lilting simplicity of the *ländler*, the country cousin of the Viennese waltz. Nostalgia in Mahler, however, is normally combined with a fierce irony, as in the Scherzo of the Fourth Symphony, a *ländler*, with its mistuned solo violin. A more regretful sort of nostalgia is often connected with themes from the Rückert settings to which Mahler looks back in his slow movements, notably the Adagietto of the Fifth Symphony and the Andante of the Sixth, which both include motifs from the Rückert sets.

While slow movements and scherzos thus contemplate the purer lyricism and the easier diatonicism of an earlier age (specifically that of Schubert), the outer movements of Mahler's symphonies tackle the contemporary problems of an expanded tonality. A strong meter is often needed to guarantee forward motion, and in many cases Mahler recalls the military music of his boyhood: both the opening movement and the finale of the Sixth Symphony, for instance, are largely fixed to march rhythms. The main theme of the opening movement is typical in its urgent dynamism and wide leaps.

Mahler follows the outline of sonata form, but his music no more operates in a sonata manner than does Bruckner's, though the reasons are opposite. Where Bruckner's music is about statement and symmetry, Mahler's is all development and thrust, so that his recapitulations are usually much transformed or followed by new developments in a coda. The symphony takes on a narrative aspect, as it had for Berlioz and Tchaikovsky, but Mahler manages to do without a motto theme as his central character: instead there is a basic motivic connection among the themes of a symphony and a powerful expressiveness that marks them all as autobiographical. One result of the narrative conception is what has been called "progressive tonality". Bruckner's music circles around a stable home key; Mahler's journeys in most cases from one to another, for emotional narratives cannot be expected to end where they began.

As narratives, Mahler's symphonies are filled with picturesque detail: the music of café and barracks, the sound of herdbells in the Alps (nos. 4 and 5), the serenades of guitar and mandolin (no. 7). His search for color and at times for emphatic weight, produced a great

98 ″Longing for Happiness″: section from the *Beethoven Frieze* by Gustav Klimt, first shown at the Secession's 1902 exhibition. Österreichisches Galerie, Vienna. The figure of the knight (whose features resemble Mahler's) also appeared as Klimt's contribution to the volume of tributes to Mahler published by Paul Stefan in 1910.

Listening Note IX.B   *Side 9, band 2*

Mahler: *Das Lied von der Erde* (1909), "Der Trunkene im Frühling"

tenor solo
piccolo, 2 flutes, 2 oboes, E♭ clarinet, 2 B♭ clarinets, 2 bassoons, double bassoon
4 horns, trumpet; harp
1st violins, 2nd violins, violas, cellos, double basses

This is the fifth movement of a symphony consisting of six orchestral songs, alternately for tenor and contralto. All six have words from *Die chinesische Flöte* ("The Chinese Flute"), a volume of Chinese poetry adapted into German by Hans Bethge.

Time	Der Trunkene im Frühling	The spring-time drunkard
0:00	Wenn nur ein Traum das Leben ist warum denn Muh' und Plag'!? Ich trinke, bis ich nicht mehr kann, den ganzen lieben Tag!	If life's only a dream why all this fuss and bother!? I drink till I'm full the livelong day!
0:42	Und wenn ich nicht mehr trinken kann, weil Kehl' and Seele voll, so taund' ich bis zu meiner Tür und schlafe wundervoll!	And when I can't take any more, when body and soul are full, I stagger back home and sleep like a top!
1:18	Was hör' ich beim Erwachen? Horch! Ein Vogel singt im Baum. Ich frag' ihn, ob schon Frühling sei.– Mir ist als wie im Traum.	What do I hear when I wake up? Hist! A bird sings from a tree. I ask him if it's springtime yet. To me it's like a dream.
2:09	Der Vogel zwitschert: Ja! Ja! Der Lenz ist da, sei kommen über Nacht! Aus tiefstem Schauen lauscht' ich auf,– der Vogel singt und lacht!	The bird twitters: yes, yes! Spring's here: it came overnight! I listened for it closely, the bird sings and laughs!
3:09	Ich fülle mir den Becher neu und leer' ihm bis zum Grund— und singe, bis der Mond erglänzt am schwarzen Firmament!	I fill my glass again and drink it to the dregs, and sing till the moon comes up in the black heavens!
3:44	Und wenn ich nicht mehr singen kann, so schlaf' ich wieder ein.– Was geht mich denn der Frühling an!? Lasst mich betrunken sein!	And when I can't sing any more, I go to sleep again. So what's the point of spring!? Just let me be drunk!

Time	
0:00	introduction, note ex. i rhythm
0:07	voice enters, first verse, ex. ii
0:42	second verse, varied repeat of the first
1:18	third verse, slower tempo
2:09	fourth verse, original tempo returns
3:09	fifth verse
3:44	final verse
4:26	(end)

This fifth movement functions as a scherzo in the whole *Das Lied von der Erde*, which has the following plan:

I Tenor solo: vigorous allegro
II Contralto solo: slow movement with chamber orchestration
III Tenor solo: moderately quick movement of light character
IV Contralto solo: lively movement
V Tenor solo: quick comic movement
VI Contralto solo: long, slow finale.

ex. i

ex. ii

enlargement of the orchestra, and though to some extent this was prompted by Strauss, Mahler generates an utterly different sound-world. Moreover, in his later works there is an increasing concentration on small groups, so that the large orchestra becomes a source of many different chamber ensembles: even the "Symphony of a Thousand" has its moments when the forces are measured in handfuls.

Fearing to embark on a Ninth Symphony, which had been for Bruckner and Beethoven their last, Mahler wrote a symphony in the disguise of an orchestral song cycle and called it *Das Lied von der Erde* (1909; see Listening Note IX.B). Setting Chinese poems in translation, the music has naive Chinese color in its use of metal percussion and pentatonic motifs, but it is much more a work of European sensibility, not least in the long song of farewell with which it ends. The same atmosphere of melancholy departure provided the emotional character for the whole of the Ninth Symphony (1909), though the unfinished Tenth (1910) would appear to have been working towards a much more positive close. Judgments have to be cautious, because Mahler left this work at quite an early stage of composition when he died, in Vienna, in the spring of 1911.

Strauss

Four years younger than Mahler, Richard Strauss also composed early, but unlike Mahler, whose genius was not fully recognized until the 1960s, he enjoyed public acclaim almost from the first, so that for more than 60 years he was regarded as the outstanding German composer.

Richard Strauss was born in Munich in 1864, son of the principal horn player in the Court Orchestra. He began to compose when he was six and had lessons from musicians associated with his father's orchestra. He never attended a conservatory, though spent two terms at Munich University before the success of his music emboldened him to devote himself to composition.

At this time he veered towards the more classical stream, represented by Mendelssohn and Brahms. But while embarking on his conducting career at Meiningen (1885–6) and Munich (1886–9 and 1894–8), he became a follower much more of Wagner and of Liszt. Symphonies and quartets were replaced by symphonic poems, beginning with the "symphonic fantasy" *Aus Italien* ("From Italy", 1886) and continuing with seven more such works. There was also a first opera, the Wagnerian *Guntram* (1894), but this was not a success, and Strauss's reputation became that of a composer of symphonic poems and of songs (he never wrote chamber music again).

The symphonic poems were played all over Europe and in the USA almost as soon as they were composed. They show Strauss's inventiveness as an orchestrator and his skill in creating musical narratives based on themes which combine strong character with an openness to variation. To some extent these were Mahler's strengths, but where Mahler's music seems to be speaking of himself, Strauss was at his best when telling stories about others. When he is writing about imagined heroes in *Don Juan* (1889), *Macbeth* (1888), *Till Eulenspiegel* (1895) or *Don Quixote* (1897) he is writing about facets of himself, but the choice of a character gives his music an objectivity at the opposite extreme from Mahler's subjectivity.

The two composers had different approaches to form. Where Mahler's sonata movements push towards continuity, drawing the listener into the musical process, Strauss preferred rondo and variation forms in which elements of sectionality and repetition allow a more considered viewpoint.

The difference is apparent too in their use of illustrative detail. Mahler's café and mountain episodes are allusions. But Strauss delighted in making self-sufficient musical pictures, such as the passage in *Don Quixote* where he depicts the bleating of sheep in discordant *tremolandos* on clarinets and brass. This work also shows his ability, surpassing that of Liszt or Berlioz, to move his themes through a diversity of musical atmospheres while keeping them recognizable. It is sub-titled "Fantastic Variations on a Theme of Knightly Character" and is marked out as a set of symphonic variations, while being at the same time a cello concerto. *Don Juan* is a sonata-form movement, with episodes. *Till Eulenspiegel* is a rondo. The last of his short tone-poems (the later ones are much longer), it is arguably the most brilliant – Strauss readily identified with a hero ready to cock a snook at authority (see Listening Note IX.C).

It was not a large step from these "theatrical" symphonic poems into opera. *Salome* (1905) and *Elektra* (1909) each are in a long single act which projects a world of emotions at high pitch, backed by music of corresponding harmonic extremity. Strauss showed himself the contemporary of Mahler in his highly complex, often virtually atonal harmony, as well as in his use of a large and varied orchestra. It even seemed possible that after *Elektra* he would be obliged, like Schoenberg at the same time, to relinquish tonality altogether.

Instead, he wrote *Der Rosenkavalier* ("The Cavalier of the Rose", 1911). This has sometimes been regarded as the gesture of a conservative, even as the escape-act of a musician unwilling to grapple with contemporary issues. However, the highly sophisticated, sentimental and humane comedy of *Der Rosenkavalier* is just as much a product of its time as Schoenberg's *Erwartung*. The latter's plunge into atonality is mirrored in Strauss's opera by an artificial diatonic masquerade in which the Vienna of Maria Theresa vibrates to the waltz rhythms of a century on. *Der Rosenkavalier* initiated one of the most fruitful partnerships in the history of opera, for now Strauss was fully collaborating with Hofmannsthal, not simply setting a pre-existing play of his (as he had done in *Elektra*). The combination of the highly cultivated Austrian poet and the practical, theater-bred Bavarian musician worked well. Though they irked each other at times, they went on to create four more operas over the next two decades: *Ariadne auf Naxos, Die Frau ohne Schatten* ("The Woman without a Shadow"), *Die ägyptische Helena* and *Arabella*. The relationship ended only with Hofmannsthal's death in 1929.

These later Strauss–Hofmannsthal operas form a diverse group: two whimsical interpretations of Greek myth (*Ariadne* and *Helena*, neither attempting anything like the near-hysteria of *Elektra*), a symbolist fairytale (*Die Frau ohne Schatten*) and another sophisticated Viennese comedy (*Arabella*). Only *Ariadne*, in which Strauss used a chamber orchestra of just 37 players, has gained a regular place in the repertory. The story of Ariadne and Bacchus – the opera within the opera –is a high-flown, poetic exploration of love which is effectively deflated by the presence of *commedia dell'arte* characters doing their act.

Listening Note IX.C   *Side 10, band 1*

Richard Strauss: *Till Eulenspiegels lustige Streiche* **op. 28 (1894–5)**
piccolo, 3 flutes, 3 oboes, english horn, clarinet in D, 2 clarinets in B♭, bass clarinet in B♭, 3 bassoons, double bassoon
4 horns in F (4 horns in D ad lib), 3 trumpets in f (3 trumpets in D ad lib), 3 trombones, tuba timpani, triangle, cymbals, bass drum, side drum, large ratchet
16 1st violins, 16 2nd violins, 12 violas, 12 cellos, 8 double basses

The title is usually translated as "Till Eulenspiegel's Merry Pranks": the work is a tone poem on a satirical trickster of German legend. Strauss described the piece as in rondo form, and there are some signs too of sonata structure, while the transformation of themes is an example of variation.

Time	
0:00	opening phrase, ex. i
0:14	main motif for Till, ex. ii, horn
0:58	another Till motif, high clarinet
2:20	quiet passage begins episode depicting Till riding into the market-place
3:48	Till's second joke, based on ex. iii
5:06	Till's amorous mood followed by anger of his rejection, from ex. i
6:54	Till mocks professors, ex. iv
8:18	faster and jollier, then mysteriously shadowy
9:27	Till's main horn theme (ex. ii) stated again, akin to recapitulation but continues to develop
11:45	drumroll represents Till's being brought to trial, answered by Till's perky clarinet phrase (ex. iii). As he is executed his soul takes flight
13:25	epilog recalling opening
14:30	(end)

If *Ariadne auf Naxos* is an opera about opera, so are two of Strauss's later works, *Intermezzo* (1924) and *Capriccio* (1942, his last). *Intermezzo*, with a libretto by the composer himself, is a dramatization of his own marital life. *Capriccio* is an allegory about the rivalry between words and music in opera. The Countess, the central character, has to choose between a poet and a composer as rivals for her love, and at the end of a gentle, supremely accomplished work her difficulty remains unresolved.

Richard Strauss	Life

1864	born in Munich, 11 June
1882	Munich University; Serenade for 13 wind instruments performed; beginning of period of prolific output
1885	assistant conductor of the Meiningen Orchestra; international recognition as a composer
1886–9	conductor at the Munich Court Opera
1889	Weimar; *Don Juan* established him as the most important young composer in Germany
1894	married Pauline de Ahna; conductor at Munich Court Opera
1895–8	prolific years, especially of orchestral music (including *Till Eulenspiegel, Thus spake Zarathustra, Don Quixote, A Hero's Life*); conducting tours of Europe
1898	conductor of the Royal Court Opera, Berlin; turned to opera composition
1905	*Salome* (Dresden) causes scandal
1904	conducted first performance of *Symphonia domestica* in New York
1909	*Elektra* (Dresden), the first of many successful collaborations with the librettist Hugo von Hofmannsthal
1911	*Der Rosenkavalier* (Dresden)
1919–24	joint director of the Vienna State Opera: output diminishing
1929	Hofmannsthal died
1933–5	appointed (without consultation) president of the Nazi state music bureau but removed for collaborating with a Jewish librettist
1942	*Capriccio* (Munich); beginning of period of concentration on instrumental works
1945	voluntary exile in Switzerland
1948	*Four Last Songs*
1949	died in Garmisch-Partenkirchen, 8 September

Richard Strauss	Works

Operas Salome (1905), Elektra (1909), Der Rosenkavalier (The cavalier of the rose, 1911), Ariadne auf Naxos (1912), Die Frau ohne Schatten (The woman without a shadow, 1919), Intermezzo (1924), Arabella (1933), Capriccio (1942)

Orchestral music symphonic poems – Aus Italien (1886), Don Juan (1889), Till Eulenspiegels lustige Streiche (Till Eulenspiegel's merry pranks, 1895), Also sprach Zarathustra (Thus spake Zarathustra, 1896), Don Quixote (1897), Ein Heldenleben (A hero's life, 1898); Symphonia domestica (1903); Eine Alpensinfonie (1915); Metamorphosen for 23 strings (1945); horn concertos – no. 1, E♭ (1883), no. 2, E♭ (1942); Oboe Concerto (1945)

Choral music Deutsche motette (1913)

Songs Four Last Songs, with orchestra (1948); c200 others

Chamber music

Piano music

Strauss intended *Capriccio* to be his last work: he was 78 when it was first performed, in Munich in 1942, at the turning-point in World War II. Unlike many of his colleagues, he remained in Germany after 1933, and even foolishly allowed his name to be used to add spurious prestige to the Third Reich. Retirement from composition was not so easy. He returned to the forms and genres of his youth: concertos for wind instruments, works for a Mozartian serenade ensemble and, for strings, *Metamorphosen* (1945), an elegy for the Germany that was being destroyed in bombing raids. Strauss ended the sequence with the

99 *The Stomach Dance* (or *Dance of the Seven Veils*): ink drawing, 1893, by Aubrey Beardsley, one of his illustrations to Oscar Wilde's *Salome*. Fogg Art Museum, Cambridge (Mass.).

HUGO·VON·HOFMANNSTHAL–RICHARD·STRAUSS: OPERA·BUFFA·

BÜHNENBILD·FÜR·DEN·I·AUFZUG·DAS·SCHLAFZIMMER·DER·FELDMARSCHALLIN·

100 Richard Strauss's *Der Rosenkavalier*: stage design by Alfred Roller for Act 1 in the first performance, Dresden Court Opera, 26 January 1911.

conscious farewell of the *Four Last Songs* for soprano and orchestra (1948), and died at his Bavarian home in September 1949, before those songs had been heard.

Northern Europe

Strauss's near-contemporary Jean Sibelius (1865–1957) was responsible for the main Nordic extension of the symphonic tradition, following the Bohemian extension achieved by Smetana and Dvořák. He was not the first Scandinavian to make an international reputation: the Norwegian Edvard Grieg (1843–1907) had already established a reputation in Germany, England and the USA, chiefly through his piano miniatures, which drew on Norwegian folk traditions, but also for his atmospheric music for Ibsen's play *Peer Gynt* and his popular piano concerto, which was admired (and performed) by Liszt. Of Sibelius's contemporaries, the Dane Carl Nielsen (1865–1931) shared his devotion to the symphony; he wrote symphonies of great force and individuality, distinguished for driving rhythms and the angular quality of his themes and harmonies.

Sibelius

Jean Sibelius was born in 1865 into a Finland that was part of the Russian empire and remained so until after the revolution of October 1917. His family belonged to the Swedish-speaking minority, but he went to a Finnish-speaking school in his home town of Hämeenlinna. He showed aptitude as a violinist and composer, and hoped to become a violin virtuoso (his D minor Violin Concerto of 1903 was a memorial to those lost hopes). In 1885 he went to Helsinki to study law, but gave up after a year to devote himself to composition studies, followed by further study in Berlin (1889–90) and Vienna (1890–91).

He had composed mostly chamber music, but on his return to Helsinki he wrote *Kullervo*, a choral symphony on stories from the Finnish national epic. Its première in Helsinki in 1892 established him as the country's leading composer. That position was his for the rest of his life, guaranteed by a succession of symphonic poems on Finnish myths interspersed among the great pillars of his seven symphonies. The first two still contain evidence of his admiration for Tchaikovsky, but the broad melodies and slow harmony have few parallels outside Bruckner. Where Bruckner's music is essentially stationary, however, Sibelius's grows by organic development of the basic motifs, a technique used with assurance for the first time in his Third Symphony (1907), a work of classical discipline and grace.

The Fourth (1911) shows his technique employed intensively, within a harmonic world as dissonant as that of the contemporary late works of Mahler. The central matter of the musical argument is the tritone, that interval most at odds with the major-minor system. Almost everything in the work can be related to this interval, and the argument is continuous, despite the presentation of the music in four distinct movements.

Continuity is taken further in the Fifth Symphony, in the "heroic" key of E♭ (1915). The Seventh (1924) is at last continuous and conveys an entire symphonic experience, with its elements of slow movement and scherzo, within a single movement. After this Sibelius wrote an incidental score for Shakespeare's *Tempest* (1925) and a symphonic poem, *Tapiola* (1926), but practically nothing for his remaining 30 years.

There may have been personal reasons. His heavy drinking has been blamed. But it is equally possible that he had achieved his ideal of a seamless, all-embracing symphonic development in his Seventh Symphony and could conceive of no way forward. Sibelius lived on, celebrated at home and abroad, and died at his house near Helsinki in 1957.

101 *Symposium*: group portrait, 1894, by Akseli Gallén-Kallela, with (*right to left*) Sibelius, the conductor Robert Kajanus, Oskar Merikanto and the artist. Private collection.

102 Elgar conducting a recording session at the Gramophone Company's City Road studio, London, January 1914: photograph.

Elgar

The rise of Sibelius and Nielsen in the Nordic countries was paralleled by that of Elgar in England, also in the 1890s. Edward Elgar was born near Worcester in 1857, the son of a piano tuner and music retailer. He had no formal training in music, but from his mid-teens was able to make a living as a violinist, organist, bassoonist, conductor and music teacher. And all the time he was composing. Until 1890 he wrote little that is remarkable, but his firm conviction of his worth led him to move to London, to try his luck. He had some salon pieces published, but there was no interest in more ambitious works, and after little more than a year the Elgars returned to home ground.

During the next few years Elgar built the foundations of a personal style, deriving from the symphonic Brahms and the more spiritual Wagner, in a sequence of cantatas that enjoyed much success among English choral societies. One of them won him a commission to write an oratorio for the Birmingham Festival of 1900. The result was *The Dream of Gerontius* (1900), a setting for soloists, chorus and orchestra of Cardinal Newman's poem on death and transport to heaven. This, with the *Enigma Variations* for orchestra (1899), brought the long-hoped-for breakthrough. Within 18 months of its première the oratorio had been heard in the USA and in Germany, where Elgar was congratulated by Strauss as "the first English progressivist"; the variations too were widely played.

These variations owe their nickname to the heading "Enigma" Elgar placed over this theme, which he remarked "went with" some other melody; the puzzle has never been satisfactorily resolved. After the theme come 14 variations which form something akin to a condensed symphony: the ninth is a big slow movement and the last is headed "Finale". At the same time this is a set of character variations in the manner of Strauss's *Don Quixote*, though the scoring shows more allegiance to Brahms than to Strauss. The work is dedicated "to my friends pictured within", each variation being a portrait of someone from Elgar's circle, beginning with his wife and ending with himself.

During the next dozen years Elgar composed copiously. There were two symphonies, a violin concerto and a radiant work for string quartet and string orchestra, the Introduction and Allegro. There were numerous songs and partsongs, and two more oratorios, *The Apostles* and *The Kingdom*. Elgar was heaped with honors, including a knighthood in 1904, and in 1912 he moved again to London, under very different circumstances from those of 1890. Little new was composed. The "symphonic study" *Falstaff*, a richly imagined portrait of the Shakespearean character and Elgar's most Straussian work, appeared in 1913. During the 1914–18 War he wrote patriotic and theatrical scores, then turned to chamber music. But his eloquent Cello Concerto in E minor (1919), run through with nostalgic feeling for a past era, was a leave-taking.

As with Sibelius, there may have been personal reasons for his creative retirement: the death of his wife in 1920 has often been thought at least a contributing factor. But it seems that he recognized too the change brought about by World War I. The culture that gave rise to the Romantic symphony had gone. Elgar returned to the rural midlands of his birth. He frequently conducted his music and recorded a large part of it. These recordings, with Strauss's, are the first in which a major composer has been able to leave an audible account of his intentions. He died in Worcester in 1934.

France

Elgar's creation of an English symphonic style was not matched by any similar development in France. Franck's influence was strong on works written in the 1880s and 1890s but petered out as a deliberately anti-symphonic manner was developed by Claude Debussy. Meanwhile the areas of greatest achievement were opera and, particularly, song. Among opera composers, Jules Massenet (1842–1912) was the most popular and wide-ranging: his two most admired works, *Manon* (1884) and *Werther* (1892: after Goethe – rather a long way after), are intimate dramas of sentiment. In the area of song the outstanding figure was Gabriel Fauré (1845–1924), a sensitive and graceful song-writer who also composed much fine piano and chamber music and a *Requiem* of exceptional gentleness and subtlety.

Debussy

Fauré's late development made him effectively a contemporary of Debussy, who also began to find himself through a response to new poetry: to Verlaine in many early songs and to Stéphane Mallarmé in his orchestral prelude to the poet's *L'après-midi d'un faune* ("The afternoon of a faun", 1894).

Claude Debussy, born at St Germain-en-Laye in 1862, studied as a pianist and composer at the Paris Conservatoire (1872–84). As winner of the Prix de Rome, he spent two years in the Italian capital, but was unsettled there and returned with relief to Paris, where he

Claude Debussy	**Works**

Orchestral music Prélude à "L'après-midi d'un faune" (Prelude to "The afternoon of a faun", 1894); Nocturnes (1899); La mer (The sea, 1905); Images (1912)

Operas Pelléas et Mélisande (1902)

Ballets Jeux (Games, 1913)

Piano music Suite, pour le piano (1901); Suite bergamasque (1905); Estampes (1903); Images (1905, 1907); Children's Corner (1908); Preludes, 2 books (1910, 1913); Studies (1915); two pianos – En blanc et noir (In white and black, 1915)

Chamber music String Quartet (1893); Cello Sonata (1915); Sonata for flute, viola and harp (1915); Violin Sonata (1917)

Incidental music Le martyre de St Sébastien (1911)

Songs Fêtes galantes (1891, 1904); Chansons de Bilitis (1898); c60 others

Choral music La damoiselle élue (The chosen maiden, 1888)

Claude Debussy	Life

1862	born in St Germain-en-Laye, 22 August
1872	entered the Paris Conservatoire to study the piano and (from 1880) composition
1880–81	summers in Russia as pianist to the family of Madame von Meck, Tchaikovsky's patron, with whom he toured Europe
1885	to Rome after winning the Prix de Rome at the Conservatoire
1887	Paris
1888	heard Wagner's music at Bayreuth
1889	impressed by Javanese music, heard at the World Exhibition in Paris
1890	beginning of "Bohemian" years and friendships with literary figures
1894	*Prelude to "The Afternoon of a Faun"*
1897	married Rosalie (Lily) Texier
1901	music critic of *La revue blanche*
1902	*Pelléas et Mélisande*; reputation as a composer established
1904	beginning of prolific period; left wife to live with Emma Bardac; Lily's attempted suicide caused scandal
1905	*La mer*; daughter born; growing international acclaim
1908	married Emma Bardac
1909	first signs of illness
1913	concentration on stage works and projects; *Jeux*
1914	depressed by illness and outbreak of war
1915	Studies for piano, *In White and Black*; two sonatas
1918	died in Paris, 25 March

lived for the rest of his life. Around this time his music began to acquire an individual, often modal character, as may be found in the first Verlaine settings and in the cantata *La damoiselle élue* ("The chosen maiden", 1888), on a poem by Dante-Gabriel Rossetti. Visits to Bayreuth in 1888–9 and an encounter with Javanese music quickened his artistic progress. Only a very few works are fully Wagnerian; his experience of Wagner simply convinced him of the need to approach music differently. In oriental art he found clues towards a modal understanding of harmony, a delight in decoration and an avoidance of symphonic continuity; its essence pervades much of his output.

Equally strong is Debussy's appeal to Greek culture. The search for a new esthetic freedom in an imaginative re-creation of the Orient or of ancient Greece was important to artists in Paris in the 1890s and 1900s. It may be seen in the Symbolist poetry of Mallarmé, in the novels of Debussy's friend Pierre Louÿs and in the paintings of Gustave Moreau; and it was this strand in French culture to which Debussy most belonged. There are parallels with the Impressionists: in the vagueness of his shapes, the subtlety of his coloring and the novelty of his forms. But his friendships were all with literary men rather than painters, and his works testify to the importance of literature to him.

It was a work of literature that released his first orchestral masterpiece, the *Prélude à "L'après-midi d'un faune"*. Mallarmé's poem concerns the erotic reverie of a faun, and Debussy's music adopts not only the poem's atmosphere but also its form, with lazily contemplative outer sections and a more active middle. As such it is not so much a prelude

Listening Note IX.D   *Side 10, band 2*

Debussy: *Prélude à ''L'après-midi d'un faune''* (1894)
3 flutes, 2 oboes, english horn, 2 clarinets in A, 2 bassoons
4 horns, 2 harps, antique cymbals in E and B
1st violins, 2nd violins, violas, cellos, double basses

The work is based on the poem by Stéphane Mallarmé describing subtly and suggestively the amorous daydreams of a faun on a warm afternoon. On some levels there is a close fit between music and poem (for instance, Debussy wrote as many measures as Mallarmé had written lines), but in other respects the relationship is more one of evocation.

Time	
0:00	*Très modéré* (''very moderate'') – main theme, ex. i, solo flute
0:57	repeat of ex. i with orchestral support
2:05	two short developments of ex. i, solo flute
3:30	variant of ex. i, clarinet
3:58	*En animant* (''becoming animated'') – further variant of ex. i, solo oboe, opens a middle section
4:29	*Toujours en animant* (''more animated'') – above process brought to a climax and then stilled
5:02	*1er mouvement* (''original speed'') – activity begun again by solo clarinet
5:24	*Même mouvement et très soutenu* (''the same speed, very sustained'') – new theme in D♭, ex. ii
7:20	*Mouvement du début* (''speed of the opening'') – ex. i, flute
7:58	repeat of previous section, theme now on solo oboe
8:41	*Dans le 1er mouvement avec plus de langueur* (''at the original speed with more languor'') – repetition of ex. i, two flutes
10:21	*Très lent et très retenu* (''very slow and held back'') – final echo of ex. i
11:05	(end)

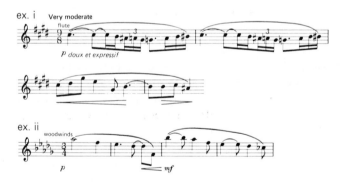

to a poem as a musical equivalent.

The first essential feature is the importance of instrumental color. The opening melody is unmistakably a theme for the flute, and it works effectively on other instruments (oboe and horns in the last part of the work) only if its rhythm and key are changed. The gentle loosening from key centers is also very Debussyan. The initial flute phrase falls through a tritone C♯–G and returns, marking out especially the Lydian or whole-tone scale G–A–B–C♯. Throughout Debussy's music the whole-tone scale is a prominent melodic and harmonic feature, permitting through its symmetry a rapid movement among distantly related keys (see Listening Note IX.D).

Debussy naturally returned to the old modes when his poetic reference was medieval (e.g. in the piano prelude *La cathédrale engloutie*, "The submerged cathedral") and when it

103 Golaud and Mélisande in a scene from the first production of Debussy's opera *Pelléas et Mélisande* at the Opéra-Comique, Paris, in 1902.

was Greek (e.g. in the song cycle *Chansons de Bilitis*). However, the modes were not used exclusively to evoke another time and another place. Rather they were natural allies, like the whole-tone scale, for a composer who worked largely with triadic harmonies while moving them with freedom from the rules of the diatonic system.

The achievement of a new musical language caused Debussy trouble. In the middle section of the prelude to *L'après-midi d'un faune* he had not been able to write quick music without reversion to diatonic practice, and for several years he completed little. But around the turn of the century he produced outstanding and fully accomplished works in every genre that interested him: song (the *Chansons de Bilitis*), orchestral music (the *Nocturnes*), piano music (the suite *Pour le piano*) and opera (*Pelléas et Mélisande*, 1902). After this breakthrough Debussy worked more quickly and confidently, producing the symphonic sketches *La mer* ("The sea", 1905) and the orchestral *Images* (1912), as well as an abundance of piano music, including two sets of *Images* (1905–7) and two sets of *Préludes* (1910–13).

Of the earlier group of works, the *Nocturnes* find Debussy closest to his painter contemporaries. The title is intended to refer not to Chopin but to Whistler, whose coloring of grays and highlights Debussy sought to re-create in music, in three movements depicting clouds, holiday festivities and sea enchantresses. On the other hand, *Pelléas et Mélisande*, his only completed opera, is necessarily a literary work. In it he set a play by the Belgian Symbolist Maurice Maeterlinck, who was trying, through fairytale allegory and an extremely reticent kind of dialogue, to portray the inner mysteries of his characters. Music can only assist in the projection of mental processes beyond words − Debussy's music above all, with its release from the logic of diatonic harmony and its suggestion of dream-states.

Like characters in a dream, the people of Debussy's opera belong in a world largely unexplained (their kingdom is "Allemonde", or all the world) and their hopes, fears and motivations are only glancingly expressed. And so although the basic action of the piece is the most banal emotional triangle (Mélisande, married to Golaud, falls in love with his half-brother Pelléas; Golaud kills Pelléas; Mélisande dies as well), Maeterlinck's discretion and Debussy's obliqueness give it a haunting atmosphere entirely new to opera. It was a difficult work to follow. Debussy subsequently worked on a variety of theatrical ideas but nothing was finished.

Meanwhile the piano pieces of 1903−13 contain in miniature much that is most characteristic of Debussy: the use of the church modes and the whole-tone scale, a delicate flexibility of rhythm, a feeling for the resonating qualities of the instrument and a release from developmental form (most works are static in structure, either of ternary (A−B−A) design or based on ostinato patterns).

Even the three substantial movements of *La mer* depart from convention, in ways suggested by their titles. The first, "From dawn to midday on the sea", is concerned with the growing clarity and power of its main theme, from complex textures where the strings may be divided into 15 parts to the forceful tuttis of the close. The last similarly uses vague and direct music, but in alternation: a "Dialogue of the wind and the waves". In between, the "Play of the waves" is a scherzo where thematic outlines and instrumentation are subject to constant change, to create Debussy's ultimate achievement in free form. All the movements thus use the variability of the sea as a metaphor for music in perpetual motion.

The orchestral *Images* do not make up a coherent cycle in the manner of *La mer*. "Ibéria" is a contribution to the large repertory of Spanish music by Frenchmen; "Gigues" and "Rondes de printemps", are more abstract in expression and are exercises in a favored technique of viewing a folktune through a haze of ostinatos and decorations.

Debussy's last orchestral score, written for the Diaghilev season that included Stravinsky's *The Rite of Spring*, was the ballet *Jeux* (1913). It was quite new in conception. Like the centerpiece of *La mer*, but on a larger scale, it is music of perpetual change, worked on a few thematic suggestions that never appear twice in quite the same form. The tendency to complexity in the orchestral textures renders the ideas difficult to grasp and hold in the memory; the effect is of a continuous fluidity. In expressive terms, this is music where feeling is no less serious for being capricious.

Illness and the outbreak of war depressed Debussy's creativity but in 1915 his compositional spirits were revived by a commission to edit Chopin's piano works, and he added to his own a set of 12 *Etudes*. These are a remarkable, and remarkably mixed, group. Most concentrate on some aspect of keyboard technique indicated by their titles, but they are also studies in compositional style. "For opposing sonorities" is an unusual instance of free form springing from oppositions of clear and succinct musical ideas. Perhaps most startling is the final "For chords", a study in clear-cut syncopation. Like other composers of his time, Debussy had been fascinated by ragtime, to which he had alluded in the "Golliwog's Cake-walk" from the piano suite *Children's Corner*. But here he reacted as well to Stravinsky, whose *Rite of Spring* had stolen the thunder of his *Jeux* in the 1913 ballet season.

Debussy's final project was a set of six sonatas for different ensembles, looking back to the chamber music of Couperin and Rameau, and proudly signed "Claude Debussy, musicien français": wartime patriotism had made him conscious of being French. Only three were composed: one for cello and piano, one for flute, viola and harp and one for violin and piano. He called the Cello Sonata "Pierrot angry with the moon", and its quick changes of mood (avoiding anything like normal cello expressive writing) have the irony of a character study. In the trio sonata, by contrast, the character is that of his orchestral scores. The Violin Sonata is fantastical in the manner of its cello companion.

Debussy made his last public appearance in the première of the Violin Sonata, in Paris in May 1917, and wrote no more music; having been troubled by rectal cancer for many years, he died in Paris the following March.

Ravel

Maurice Ravel, born in the Pyrenees in 1875, took a different approach from Debussy. Trained as a pianist, he was impressed by the virtuosity and splendor of Liszt, who, much more than Debussy, is the main influence on his piano works *Jeux d'eau* (1901) and *Miroirs* (1905). Debussy's importance was rather to give him the elements of an orchestral style: his *Shéhérazade* for soprano and orchestra (1903) owes much to *Pelléas*. Once Ravel had assimilated his influence, as he had by the time he wrote his orchestral *Rapsodie espagnole* ("Spanish Rhapsody", 1908), he was creating music quite different from Debussy's. Their use of modes and the whole-tone scale is often similar, but Ravel's ideas tend to be more sharply etched, his textures precise and his forms correspondingly clear, often with a great deal of repetition (this he carried to the ultimate in his famous *Boléro* of 1928, which repeats the same tune in a continuous orchestral *crescendo*).

Ravel orchestrated most of his piano works, and also made the most commonly played orchestration of Mussorgsky's *Pictures at an Exhibition*. Bright and highly accomplished, his orchestration suggests a creative mind that thrived on artifice, and indeed Ravel enjoyed exploring in each work a particular musical character: the Hispanic, the childlike, the Baroque.

Ravel's most productive period was before World War I, when he composed an hour-long ballet for Diaghilev, the ancient Greek story of *Daphnis et Chloé*, and the fairytale ballet *Ma mère l'oye* ("Mother Goose"). He was living in Paris, where he had been a student at the Conservatoire from 1889 to 1895; a man of independent means, he held no appointment, nor did he teach or perform much in public, except during a tour of the USA in 1927–8. His piano suite *Le tombeau de Couperin* is in a neo-classical style of sparer texture and more severe harmony but some of his later orchestral works take a topical interest in jazz. After five years of illness, in 1937 Ravel died in Paris.

Italy

The age of Debussy in France, Mahler in Austria and Elgar in England was in Italy the age of Puccini, whose operas dominated the Italian stage from the first production of his *Manon Lescaut* in 1893 to his death 30 years later.

Puccini

Giacomo Puccini was born in 1858 in Lucca, where his father was of the fourth generation of Puccinis to have served the republic and the church as composers. Giacomo, five when his father died, studied with local teachers with a view to taking on the family responsibilities, but when he was 17 he saw *Aida* and determined to be an opera composer. He therefore went to the Milan Conservatory. In 1883 he wrote his first opera, on a tale of supernatural enchantment. It had some success when given in Milan in 1884, and on the strength of it the astute publisher Giulio Ricordi initiated an association with him that was to continue throughout Puccini's life. He then tried his hand, less successfully, at a tragic opera after an Alfred de Musset book.

Puccini found the way forward pointed by his junior, Pietro Mascagni, whose one-act *Cavalleria rusticana* (1889) introduced a new kind of opera, dealing with contemporary life in a naturalistic and full-bloodedly emotional way – what, as we have seen (p. 239), is called *verismo* opera. Puccini was not truly a *verismo* composer: his operas are not set in the (then) present; many have exotic locations; only a few have elements of the "realistic" world of feeling. But the heightened emotional condition of *verismo* opera is very much a feature of his works.

The first of his operas that shows the influence of the *verismo* school is *Manon Lescaut* (1893), the story of tragic love that Massenet had set nine years before. Here he proves himself a superior musician to any of his Italian contemporaries (and to Massenet) through his command of musical-dramatic resource: among all music of the period, only Mahler

104 Puccini (seated) with the librettist Luigi Illica, a few months before the composer's death: photograph.

Giacomo Puccini   Works
born Lucca, 1858; *died* Brussels, 1924

Operas Le villi (1884), Edgar (1889), Manon Lescaut (1893), La bohème (1896), Tosca (1900), Madama Butterfly (1904), La fanciulla del West (The girl of the golden West, 1910), Il trittico (1918) [three one-act operas: Il tabarro (The cloak), Suor Angelica, Gianni Schicchi], Turandot (posthumous, 1926)
Choral music   *Instrumental music*   *Songs*

provides a parallel case of Wagnerian harmony being carried to such expressive extremes and of special instrumental effects being used to intensify the feeling. The work was a great success.

Puccini did well not to attempt to repeat it. *La bohème* (1896), a tale of aspiring artists and their loves in the "bohemian" world of mid-century Paris, is a softer, more sentimental piece, much of it in a light-hearted, conversational style, but with a deeply touching final scene where – as in Verdi's *La traviata* – a girl dies of tuberculosis, reconciled with her lover. Here Puccini used the pentatonic scale as a source of strikingly memorable orchestral ideas, and as a means of penetrating the civilized surface of the major-minor system to a more raw, coarser musical and expressive world.

La bohème is Puccini's most popular opera, but his next two, *Tosca* and *Madama Butterfly*, run it close. *Tosca* (1900), set in reactionary Rome when the cause of freedom seemed to depend on the successes of Napoleon, attacks the emotions in its scene where the tenor hero is tortured by the police as information is extracted from his lover (the singer Tosca); Puccini's music seems almost to twist the thumbscrews. Another spectacular scene ends the first act, where the police chief Scarpia is seen devising a scheme, during a church service, to force Tosca to become his lover; the conjunction of religious and sexual emotion is characteristic.

Scenes like these show Puccini's remarkable sense of theater: a sense manifested in his command of color, motif (and especially its use for raising dramatic tension) and harmony. His use of pentatonic melody, often in short, irregular phrases, has no role in expressing location in *Tosca* (perhaps it helps convey the intense, melancholy emotion that so often belongs to his characters), but it does do that in the ensuing works. *Madama Butterfly* (1904), set in Japan, incorporates some real Japanese melodies, but also has a good deal of pentatonic music to convey its oriental exoticism. Most of Puccini's heroines are "little women", who suffer and die for their limitless love. One such is Madam Butterfly, the Japanese girl duped by an American naval officer into marriage, then deserted; his capacity to compel the audience's emotions in sympathy with his heroines is particularly striking here. It happens in his next opera, *La fanciulla de West* ("The Girl of the Golden West"), set in California in the gold rush; to Puccini the Far West was just as exotic as the Far East. His later operas, which include a "triptych" written for the Metropolitan in New York (and containing his only comedy, *Gianni Schicchi*, a slightly macabre piece set in medieval Florence) and *Turandot*, a savage drama set in China, show him enlarging his harmonic and orchestral style, influenced by Strauss and especially Debussy. But none of these has ever challenged in appeal *La bohème*, *Tosca* and *Madama Butterfly*. He died in 1924, leaving *Turandot* unfinished.

Chapter X

Modern Times

The story of modern music begins, essentially, in the years leading up to World War I. These years saw the composition of numerous works rooted in the past: the symphonies of Mahler, Sibelius and Elgar, or the operas of Strauss, Massenet and Puccini. But they saw too a number of works, by younger men, that struck a new – and harsher – note. The most famous, or notorious, of them was Igor Stravinsky's *Rite of Spring*, which caused a riot on its first performance. There are also several by Arnold Schoenberg, his students Alban Berg and Anton Webern, and Béla Bartók.

Violence

Such works did not merely carry further the breakdown of tonality and an increase in dissonance. There is in them a deliberate element of violence and distortion, a renunciation of traditional ideas of the beautiful and expressive. Bartók's *Allegro barbaro* involves ferocious, ugly, "barbaric" pounding of the keyboard. Stravinsky's ballet sets new levels in dissonance and rhythmic energy, of a "primitive", disorienting kind. Schoenberg's *Pierrot lunaire* for speaker and chamber group inhabits a world of nightmare fantasy, macabre and absurd, with hints of cabaret music. The traditional concertgoer was meant to be offended and disturbed from his complacency; and he duly was, just as the traditional art-lover was infuriated by the art of the time.

Artists of all kinds were seeking a more truthful, more expressive way of treating the realities of human existence in the harsh, dissonant world of the twentieth century than a photographic realism could offer. Vincent van Gogh, back in the 1880s, had intentionally altered, even distorted, reality in line with his feelings. His methods were pursued by such Expressionist painters as Oskar Kokoschka (1886–1980) and Wassily Kandinsky (1866–1944) – Kandinsky's move towards abstraction invites analogy with Schoenberg's towards atonality. Equally an analogy may be drawn between Stravinsky and early Cubism, particularly as represented by Pablo Picasso (1881–1973), with whom Stravinsky collaborated. Another fascinating parallel with musical developments of the time is suggested by the prose of James Joyce (1882–1941), which relinquishes the traditional priority of meaning in favor of pattern and allusion.

France – with Paris still the artistic capital of Europe, and the natural home for an expatriate Russian like Stravinsky – and the German-speaking countries led in most of these new developments. But the wind of change blew everywhere. In America, Charles Ives was composing pieces with irrational juxtapositions of musical ideas and deliberately distorted harmonies. Soon Edgard Varèse was to arrive in the country with his revolutionary ideas about musical sounds, partly based on the noise-world of an industrial, urbanized society. In Italy, the Futurists – a movement including visual and literary artists as well as musicians – were thinking along similar lines; one of this group of machine-age artists spent years devising an ingenious series of "noise-intoners" – musically a dead end, but a symptom of the times, comparable perhaps with Dadaism.

Atonality

With the abandonment of tonality, with the work of Schoenberg and his disciples early in the twentieth century, it became necessary to devise new methods of musical structure. In these "atonal" works, Schoenberg, Berg and Webern found themselves drawn to use complex forms of imitation between voices or instruments. It is out of this necessity and their reaction to it that Schoenberg's 12-tone system (see Chapter III, p. 45) began to be devised. It was codified in the mid-1920s, but not widely used outside Schoenberg's circle for more than 20 years, and even then its use was not long sustained. It did however give rise to more complex forms of serialism: Schoenberg's method applies serial processes to pitch, but others later carried the principle further and applied it to such elements of music as rhythm, dynamics and tone-color. Pierre Boulez is among the one-time "total serialists".

Neo-classicism

At the end of his life Stravinsky adopted serialism; but his earlier work, once past his strongly Russian phase (to which *The Rite of Spring* belongs), is primarily "neo-classical". "Neo-classicism" is used in music to describe those works of the first half of the twentieth century that look back beyond the Romantic era to the Classical, the Baroque or earlier for inspiration or for technical procedures. Others, notably Prokofiev, have drawn on classical forms in their instrumental music; in opera Stravinsky's *The Rake's Progress*, with its strong Mozart echoes, is outstanding among neo-classical works. Paul Hindemith, whose music is notably tidy in its forms and techniques, and unromantic in feeling, has also often been called a neo-classicist.

There were other significant influences on music around and after World War I. The folksong interests of the previous generation persisted, but had changed in focus. Men like Ralph Vaughan Williams in England and Béla Bartók in Hungary were collecting folksong on a methodical, scientific basis. Bartók researched not only in his native country but in neighboring regions, and used folksong in his music, to reinvigorate it rhythmically after the sluggish, mechanical rhythms of some late Romantic music.

There was a social, or political, element in this too, aimed at bringing music out of the drawing-room and even the concert hall into a wider realm and giving it contact with a broader, less sophisticated public. One way of doing this was to introduce elements from the folk or traditional music of the people. In the USA, where folk-music traditions were relatively recent, composers like Aaron Copland and George Gershwin also drew on native jazz traditions.

Totalitarian regimes

The political events of the first half of the twentieth century had much influence on music. They always have: composers employed by royal or noble patrons have been expected to compose music to the greater glory – and the perpetuation in power – of their masters, and we should not expect a state to exercise any lesser rights over those it pays to provide its music. States can, however, change their attitudes, as Soviet Russia did in her early days. After the revolution in 1917, Stravinsky had no wish to work in Russia. Prokofiev, out of sympathy with the new regime – and fairly certain that it would be out of sympathy with him – left, though the pull of his native land later proved irresistible. Initially, the Soviet regime encouraged experimental music; later, with Stalin in charge and intellectuals increasingly under pressure, experimentation was discouraged, experimental composers were removed and their works banned. Music was required to be optimistic in spirit and appealing to large audiences, as well as encouraging self-sacrifice and effort on behalf of the community. Prokofiev and Shostakovich were ready to accept these principles without regarding them as improper attacks on artistic freedom (always a relative concept); but they were often troubled by official disapproval of particular works.

At the opposite end of the political spectrum lies the music of Nazi Germany and Austria in the 1930s and 40s. Here, in another kind of totalitarian society, other (and no less ruthless) forms of censorship were applied. Music that challenged the existing order, like Kurt Weill's settings of texts by Bertolt Brecht, was not permitted, and here too experimentation was regarded as degenerate. Forward-looking composers (and not only Jewish ones like Schoenberg and Weill) fled the country; most who remained and were approved have faded into obscurity, and with them their music.

The dust has now begun to settle on the first half of the twentieth century, and it is growing easier to see what lies in common between the various composers of the time. But it is too soon for us to establish much of a perspective on music since 1950. Many composers pressed further the movements of the preceding years, like the "total serialists" and the Soviet bloc composers who developed a popular, patriotic vein that often drew on folksong. But after World War II, as after World War I, the younger generation strove to find fresh means of expressing in their music the ethos of their times, dominated by new and alarming technologies and the uncertainties to which they gave rise.

Electronics

One technological development of the war years particularly important to musicians was tape recording: not only for performance but also for composition. A composer could now conceive and execute a piece without depending on performers to interpret it. At first this was chiefly done with sounds from everyday life, like traffic noise or rustling leaves. With tape recording, the sounds could be manipulated – speeded up, slowed down, superimposed, played backwards, given an echo, and so on. The term *musique concrète* was used for "compositions" of this kind. Later, these techniques were applied to musical sounds, notably by Stockhausen in *Gesang der Jünglinge* ("Song of the youths" – it uses the biblical story of the three boys in the fiery furnace), which is made up from a tape of a boy singing a hymn, and in America by composers at the influential Columbia-Princeton center. With the advent of the synthesizer a large range of sounds could be generated and processed electronically, giving the composer a new comprehensiveness of control over how his music would sound.

Random music

Not all composers wanted that kind of control. Some preferred the opposite. Even in the electronic world, a device called the ring modulator was sometimes used which would distort the sound in ways that could not always be predicted. Some composers combined a pre-existing tape with live music-making, while others used electronic devices to introduce deliberately random elements into their music. In this area the most influential and revolutionary figure is the American composer John Cage. Cage has questioned all the assumptions on which our musical culture is based: he has proposed the elevation of noise and silence to the level at which we hold music, has opposed the idea of the formal concert in favor of musical "happenings", and has used in his compositions such elements as radio receivers randomly tuned to produce crackles and snatches of haphazard speech or music.

Many of Cage's suggestions have been followed up by younger men. In the turbulent late 1960s and early 70s, especially, audiences earnestly (though sometimes impatiently) listened to such events as a player on an amplified cello sounding one note continuously for two hours, perhaps with occasional accompaniment from others using instruments or noise-makers. In terms of traditional artistic values such events meant little; but they served to sharpen one's awareness of the nature and the effects of sound.

Other composers of this period moved along similar lines. Some, wanting to extend the performer's role, abandoned traditional notation in favor of symbolic ones which the player could interpret as he felt inclined; nothing is "wrong" and anything that reflects the player's feelings, on seeing the music, is "right". A piece of music might even be presented to the player as a piece of prose, to which he would react by playing something. Many composers, however, were attracted to the idea of random elements in a less extreme form - in a string quartet by Lutoslawski, for example, the players are asked to improvise on given phrases until the first violinist gives a signal to move on, and in a Stockhausen piano piece the player is required to make decisions, while he is performing, on which sections he will include and in what sequence.

There are limited analogies in the other arts. Some modern poets have had their works printed so as to leave the reader free to choose the sequence of sections. The graphic arts do not embody the time element vital to such procedures, but there are obvious parallels between the art of Jackson Pollock (1912–56), who let paint fall at random on canvases lying on the floor, and Cage's music.

There has, understandably, been a reaction among composers against the experimentalist generation. Several have found what might be called a neo-Romantic idiom in which, without denying the more recent past, traditional values are affirmed. Others have looked, in these times of rapid world communications and ethnic mixing, to non-Western cultures for fresh inspiration – to the *ragas* of Indian music, for example, with their quality of timeless meditation, or to the strangely mystical clangor of gongs in the gamelan music of Indonesia. Still others have sought a coming-together with rock music, a notion that is particularly attractive because it implies an ending to the social and intellectual divisiveness hinted at by the existence of different music systems and the different publics that support them. Certainly it seems that music is at a crossroads; but then, looking back through this book, it is hard to escape the conclusion that it nearly always has been.

The Second Viennese School

One area in which music has most conspicuously changed since 1900 is that of harmony. The change, once it came, came fast. In the nineteenth century composers had introduced an ever greater variety of chords and an ever faster rate of harmonic change. The major-minor system had been threatened in Wagner's *Tristan and Isolde* (see p. 229). In the music of composers otherwise as different as Richard Strauss, Debussy and Mahler, there began to be times when the pull of the tonic was so weak as hardly to be felt at all. To keep their music going, composers had to use ever larger orchestras and bigger forms, as in Mahler's symphonies; the alternative was the almost atonal miniature. In 1908, the decisive break to atonality was made by a slightly younger composer, who was to establish himself as a dominant influence on twentieth-century music: Arnold Schoenberg (1874–1951).

Schoenberg

Schoenberg was a reluctant revolutionary. He was born in Vienna in 1874, when Brahms was working there, and remained devoted to the Viennese tradition as expressed in the music of Haydn, Mozart, Beethoven, Schubert and Brahms. He saw himself not as overturning that tradition but as perpetuating it, continuing a natural process of development. Just as Brahms's harmonies were more complex than Haydn's, Schoenberg's had to be more complex than Brahms's. But the aims stayed the same. Music must unfold with logic, stating its themes, developing them and recalling them. And the vehicle for the most profound musical thinking would have to be chamber music. A good half of Schoenberg's output falls into this category.

Schoenberg started violin lessons when he was eight and was soon composing. Because the family was not well off, there was no opportunity for him to study as a composer; he

Arnold Schoenberg	Life

1874	born in Vienna, 13 September
1890	began working in a bank; contact with musicians including Alexander von Zemlinsky who became a lifelong friend and musical influence
1899	*Transfigured Night*
1900	conducted choirs, orchestrated operettas; began work on *Gurrelieder*
1901	married Mathilde Zemlinsky; Berlin
1902	composition teacher at the Stern Conservatory, Berlin
1903	Vienna; began giving private composition lessons, Alban Berg and Anton Webern being among his pupils; met Mahler
1908	composed first atonal pieces: Piano Pieces op. 11, *The Book of the Hanging Garden*
1910	his latest works greeted with incomprehension; mounted exhibition of his Expressionist paintings
1911	Berlin; published harmony treatise
1912	*Pierrot lunaire*
1913	*Gurrelieder* first performed in Vienna
1915	Vienna; joined army as volunteer
1918	founded the Society for Private Musical Performances
1923	first serial works: Piano Pieces op. 23; his wife died
1924	married Gertrud Kolisch
1926	composition teacher at the Prussian Academy of Arts, Berlin; period of prolific composition
1933	left Germany because of Nazi anti-semitism; emigrated to the USA, to Boston
1934	moved to Hollywood because of health; took private pupils
1936	professor at the University of California at Los Angeles; Violin Concerto, Fourth String Quartet
1944	health began to deteriorate; left professorship
1951	died in Los Angeles, 13 July

had to leave school and work in a bank. So he developed the vigorous enthusiasm and offbeat attitudes of one who has learned his art for himself: there would be no betrayal of the Viennese tradition's ideals, but nor would there be any compromising of the new musical ideas that came rushing into the young composer's mind.

Only at the end of the 1890s did he start writing music he considered worthy. *Transfigured Night*, a symphonic poem for string sextet, was the first instrumental score he acknowledged. It was also the first of his works to create a scandal. In combining program music with orthodox form and medium, the sextet brought together the Wagner–Strauss tradition and that of Brahms. It brought *Tristan*-style harmonies into chamber music. For Schoenberg's contemporaries that was unacceptable; the Composers' Union in Vienna declined to perform it. *Transfigured Night* set the pattern of his music in its heavy emotional load and its density of feelings in conflict, achieved through a web of polyphonic lines that strain out of the harmony.

By this time Schoenberg had left the bank and was earning his living by conducting

105   Arnold Schoenberg: self-portrait, 1910. Arnold Schoenberg Institute, Los Angeles.

choirs and orchestrating operettas. In 1901 he moved to Berlin, where he had a job as a musician at a literary cabaret. He took his most Wagnerian work, the *Gurrelieder*, a sort of concert opera of furious passion and tragic destiny which he had composed in 1900–01. He returned to Vienna in 1903 and soon began giving composition lessons privately. Among his first pupils were Alban Berg (1885–1935) and Anton Webern (1883–1945). Both were to stay close to him for the rest of their lives. The presence of such sympathetic colleagues might well have contributed to the speed with which Schoenberg's music now developed. *Transfigured Night*, in effect a one-movement symphony, was soon followed by a string quartet where the thematic development is pursued through music embracing the conventional four movement-types; the absence of a justifying program helps make the expressive contortions still more intense.

The same style is continued in the First Chamber Symphony (1906), which again plays continuously through sections that correspond to the normal symphonic movements. Again, the music is made tonal only with severe strain; this contributes to the sense of turmoil in so much of Schoenberg's music. For example, one main theme here is a sequence of 4ths, which immediately strikes out from any given key: as first sounded by a horn it is D–G–C–F–B♭–E♭, pulling the music round from F major into the home key of E♭ major, but creating a dangerous precedent in hopping so freely among distant tonalities.

This work brings us Schoenberg as the unheeded prophet, pointing out that the tonal system was about to collapse just when others were creating within it giant monuments (Mahler, for instance, was at work on his Eighth Symphony). Against that trend, Schoenberg's piece is scored for 15 soloists, a crack team who can tackle the dynamism and complex counterpoint more effectively than could larger forces. Significantly, Schoenberg wrote no "normal" symphonies but preferred to bring the genre within his favored sphere of chamber music.

His next chamber work, String Quartet no. 2, completes the move into atonality. After two tonal movements, the third has little feeling of key and the finale is wholly atonal until its drawn-out final settling into the work's home key of F♯. The revolution was momentous – as momentous as that of Sigmund Freud (1856–1939) in psychology, and for similar reasons. Schoenberg and Freud both pull the carpet out from under our feet,

Arnold Schoenberg   Works

Operas Erwartung (Expectation, 1909), Die glückliche Hand (The blessed hand, 1913), Von heute auf morgen (From one day to the next, 1929), Moses und Aron (1932, unfinished) [dates are of composition]

Choral music Gurrelieder (1900–01); A Survivor from Warsaw (1947); Die Jakobsleiter (1922, unfinished)

Orchestral music Pelleas und Melisande (1903); 5 Pieces, op. 16 (1909); Variations (1928); Violin Concerto (1936); Piano Concerto (1942); 2 chamber symphonies

Chamber music Verklärte Nacht (Transfigured night, 1899) for string sextet; 4 string quartets; string trio; wind quintet

Vocal music Das Buch der hängenden Gärten (15 songs, 1909); Pierrot lunaire (1912); cabaret songs; c75 others

Piano music 3 Pieces, op. 11 (1909); 6 Little Pieces, op. 19 (1911); 5 Pieces, op. 23 (1920, 1923); Suite, op. 25 (1923)

Unaccompanied choruses   *Canons*

106 The Kolisch Quartet rehearsing Berg's *Lyric Suite* in the presence of Schoenberg (right, standing) and the composer (center back) before its first performance in Vienna, 8 January 1927: drawing by Benedict Dolbin. Meyer Collection, Paris.

show that accepted certainties (the major-minor system, moral categories) may be artificial. Freudian, too, is the analysis of extreme emotional states of Schoenberg's first fully atonal works. Among these are the short opera *Erwartung* (1909), a monologue for a woman seeking her lost lover in a wood, and *Pierrot lunaire* (1912). The use of a key had always given music a feeling of direction. Without it, the creation of satisfactory instrumental forms was harder: that is one reason why Schoenberg at this time preferred to use words to give him structural backbone.

Schoenberg's high moral seriousness and his restless search for the indefinable are linked with religious searching in the work that should have crowned this period but was never completed, the oratorio *Jacob's Ladder* (1917–22). Schoenberg had been brought up an orthodox Jew, but was no longer practicing (he made a formal return in 1933, soon after he had been ejected from Berlin on Hitler's rise to power). A Jewish sense of the divinity, urging mankind to a perpetual search after truth, underlies *Jacob's Ladder*. The same feeling pervades the later opera *Moses and Aaron* (1932), again concerned with the thorny road to God and again significantly unfinished. For though *Jacob's Ladder* was interrupted because of the war, the real reason for its incompleteness is the impossibility of adequately describing the soul's eventual union with God.

Pierrot lunaire shows us instead the soul lost. The 21 brief poems speak of alienation, uncertainty, madness and disquiet. They draw from Schoenberg a particular musical world of shifting values: ambiguous sound – the soloist's "speech-song"; ambiguous genre, between cabaret and concert hall, opera and chamber music; ambiguous harmony, hovering around keys or other marks of stability. The cabaret element is important. Perhaps Schoenberg was remembering his experiences in Berlin a decade before (*Pierrot lunaire* was written during a second period of residence there from 1912 to 1915). Cabaret, too, provides the background for what Schoenberg called the "light, ironic, satirical tone" of

---

Listening Note X.A   *Side 11, band 1*

Schoenberg: *Pierrot lunaire* (1912), "Mondestrunken"
reciter, flute, violin, cello, piano

This is the first of 21 settings of poems from Albert Giraud's collection *Pierrot lunaire* in the German translations of Otto Erich Hartleben. The words are delivered in what Schoenberg's preface calls a *Sprechmelodie* ("speech-melody", also referred to as *Sprechgesang* or "speech-song"): the idea is that the notated pitches should be sung, but that the voice should immediately change to a speaking character.

Mondestrunken	Moondrunk
Den Wein, den man mit Augen trinkt,	The wine one drinks through opened eyes
giesst nachts der Mond in Wogen nieder,	pours down from the moon at night in waves,
und eine Springflut überschwemmt	and a spring tide overflows
den stillen Horizont.	the still horizon.
Gelüste, schauerlich und süss,	Desires, terrible and sweet,
durchschwimmen ohne Zahl die Fluten!	arrive countless in those floods!
Den Wein, den man mit Augen trinkt,	The wine one drinks through opened eyes
giesst nachts der Mond in Wogen nieder.	pours down from the moon at night in waves.
Der Dichter, den die Andacht treibt,	The poet, lost in his devotions
berauscht sich an dem heilgen Tranke,	grows dizzy on the holy drink,
gen Himmel wendet er verzückt das Haupt	and heavenwards turns in ecstasy
und taumelnd saugt und schlürft er	and staggering sucks and sips
den Wein, den man mit Augen trinkt.	the wine one drinks through opened eyes.

This, like every other poem set in the work, is a rondeau: i.e. the first two lines of the first stanza become the last two lines of the second, and the final line of all repeats the first.

Time
0:00	movement begins, ex. i, piano ostinato
0:03	voice enters
0:18	"stillen Horizont"
0:21	flute begins ostinato
0:29	ostinato alternates between flute and piano
0:38	voice enters for second verse
1:02	final verse opens with sudden *forte*
1:36	(end)

ex. i   Moderate

---

the work, for all its savagery, macabre humor, isolation and hopeless nostalgia. The whole thing presents itself as an image of nightmare fantasy, not the real thing that had seemed to be dredged up in the earlier atonal works (see Listening Note X.A). Those earlier works had enjoyed the freedom to abandon, with tonality, all other kinds of order and symmetry; by contrast, in *Pierrot lunaire* a certain fixity begins to come back, in metrical regularity, in clear formal structure and in contrapuntal cunning.

Gradually he evolved the basic principles of 12-tone serialism, which was intended not so much as a system as an aid to extended composition without tonality. We have already seen (p.45) something of how it works and the possibilities it offers. For Schoenberg, serialism made it possible again to compose in the large instrumental forms, and so the appearance of the new method came with a certain neo-classicism typical of the 1920s. A notable early example is the Piano Suite (1923), Schoenberg's first wholly serial work. As he insisted, "one uses the series and then one composes as before".

This was a period of preparation for the opera *Moses and Aaron*. Its biblical theme was close to Schoenberg's heart as man and musician: it is the insoluble problem of communicating the most important truths. Moses' tragedy is to be a prophet who perceives divine truth but lacks the means to tell it; Aaron's curse is to be articulate but blind, so that he inevitably distorts and even destroys his brother's vision. The whole opera, nearly two hours of music, is based on a single series. Serialism was the most appropriate technique for the work, since its possible forms are infinite, just as Jehovah is infinite: the voice in the burning bush, heard at the start of the work, is only one representation.

Schoenberg felt himself to be more a Moses (a prophet) than an Aaron (a communicator – though he was able to admire such Aarons of the musical world as George Gershwin). He had known ridicule since the rejection of *Transfigured Night*, and it had scarcely abated. An attempt to create a sympathetic, semi-private environment for the performance of new music in Vienna had had some success in 1919–21, but it foundered, and in Berlin, where Schoenberg moved in 1926 to teach composition at the Prussian Academy of Arts, racial intolerance was mixed with musical. When he left in 1933 he went first to France and then to the USA.

In 1934 he settled in California, his home for the rest of his life. This late period was one of continued teaching, both of private pupils (among them John Cage) and of students at the University of Southern California. These were the years too of Schoenberg's most complex and coherent serial works. He extended his serial practice to take command of large spans, even feeling confident enough to go back to his earlier technique of combining several movements into one.

The religious nature of his quest also became fully apparent during his American years. There was a liturgical piece, *Kol nidre*, for rabbi, chorus and orchestra (1938), and at the end a set of "modern psalms", setting his own words. But these too, like all his most profoundly spiritual works, were not to be finished: at his death in 1951 he had left the first of them in mid-air, on the words "and still I pray".

Berg

If testimony to Schoenberg's powers as a teacher were required, one only need look at the example of Alban Berg. Born in 1885 into a wealthy family, he had dabbled in composition from his teenage years, but until he came to Schoenberg in 1904 he had written nothing but songs and had only the merest acquaintance with real compositional technique. Four years later, he could write a single-movement Piano Sonata of Mahlerian dimensions. His development was astounding.

Equally astounding was Berg's hankering after a past he had only recently come to understand – unlike Schoenberg, who had been playing chamber music from his boyhood. His String Quartet (1910) is atonal like Schoenberg's contemporary scores. Its combination of novelty with nostalgia was to remain distinctively Berg's.

In 1912 he set some tiny, quizzical poems by his friend Peter Altenberg for soprano and orchestra. This is one of the most extraordinary first orchestral scores in musical history, filled with new, exactly imagined gestures in five very short movements. The Three Pieces for orchestra of 1915 are different again: leaning more towards Mahler than Debussy, broad and developed whereas the songs are fleeting.

During the war Berg spent more than three years as a soldier, an experience that revived his earlier interest in making an opera out of Georg Büchner's play *Woyzeck*. Like everything else he wrote, this first opera (called *Wozzeck*) is a work of direct emotional involvement and of conscious pattern-making: one scene is a passacaglia, the whole second act a five-movement symphony. On another level, the musical materials are similarly

Alban Berg   Works
born Vienna, 1885; *died* Vienna, 1935

Operas Wozzeck (1925), Lulu (1937)
Orchestral music Chamber Concerto (1925); Violin Concerto (1935)
Chamber music String Quartet (1910); Lyric Suite, for string quartet (1926, later orchestrated)
Songs 4 Songs, op. 2 (1910); Altenberg Songs, with orchestra (1912); *c*75 others
Piano music Sonata (1908)

diverse. A D minor Adagio, salvaged from an unfinished symphony, expresses feeling as in the old tonal tradition. There are also parodies of café music in the manner of Mahler, stretches of speech-song out of *Pierrot lunaire* and exercises in brutal constructivism. What makes it possible to use so wide a range of styles is the diversity of the opera. Some characters – notably Wozzeck's mistress Marie, but also the humble, surly, much abused Wozzeck himself – engage the sympathies of the audience, while others, like the strutting Captain and the manic Doctor, are pure caricature. The world of *Wozzeck* is one in which humans are at the mercy of inhuman forces. It could have come only at a time when music and the world seemed to have run out of control. It was also much the biggest of the works created by Schoenberg and his pupils at this period and after its first performance (Berlin, 1925) it began to be performed widely and so to guarantee its composer an income.

Berg's next work was the Chamber Concerto for piano, violin and 13 wind instruments (1925), a piece riddled with "three-ness" to honor the trio of Schoenberg, Berg and Webern. His new style gained a certain clarification from his adoption of serialism, which he used in part of his *Lyric Suite* for string quartet (1926). The passionate intimacy of this music is sustained at a high pitch, high enough to invoke *Tristan* in the finale.

Berg began his second opera, *Lulu*, in 1929; it was not quite finished when he died in 1935. Drawing on two plays by Frank Wedekind, pioneer of sexual candor in the theater, he fashioned his own libretto in three acts. In the first half of the opera Lulu is on the ascent, rising through connections with men to become the wife of the wealthy Dr Schön. In the second half, after she has shot Schön, her fortunes fall, through prison, harlotry and cheap prostitution to death at the hands of Jack the Ripper (roles are neatly doubled, so that Jack is identified with Schön). But this is not a simple morality. Lulu, like Wozzeck, is more prey than predator. She is the spirit of natural woman, and her destruction is inevitable in a civilization that can exist only by the suppression and perversion of the urgings of raw sex.

By the time of *Lulu*, conditions were starting to deteriorate in Vienna, where Berg lived all his life. After 1933 *Wozzeck* was banned from German theaters; this placed him in financial difficulties. He also interrupted work on the opera to complete a Violin Concerto, marked by something of the musical and emotional atmosphere of *Lulu*, and, like all his finest works, looking through the tawdry surface to what Berg saw as the sensual essence of human existence.

Webern

Anton Webern's background was not so different from Berg's. He came from a middle-class family, arrived in Schoenberg's classes with a clutch of juvenile compositions of no great merit and left as the composer of a big instrumental piece. This, his orchestral *Passacaglia* (1908), is already typical in its brevity, its thinnesss of texture, its close organization and its urgent climaxes. But Webern had enjoyed an education in musicology at

Anton Webern   Works
born Vienna, 1883; *died* Mittersill, 1945

Orchestral music Passacaglia, op. 1 (1908); 6 Pieces, op. 6 (1909); 5 Pieces, op. 10
(1913); Symphony, op. 21 (1928); Variations, op. 30 (1940)
Choral music Das Augenlicht (Eyesight, 1935); cantatas
Chamber music 5 Movements for string quartet (1909); 6 Bagatelles for string
quartet (1913); 3 string quartets (1905, 1929, 1938)
Vocal music George Songs, op. 3 (1909), op. 4 (1909); Rilke Songs, op. 8 (1910); ·
Jone Songs, op. 25 (1934)
Piano music Variations, op. 27 (1936)

the University of Vienna, which affected his intellectual approach to composition.

He was naturally disposed towards serialism, which he brought to an extreme concentration and calculation. His Symphony (1928) is scored for a small orchestra; there are only two movements, the first in sonata form but also a four-part canon, the second a set of variations that pivots halfway, then the music goes backwards and ends as it began.

Webern's music is an architecture of polyphonic lines, playing constantly on the tiniest motifs (six notes in the case of the symphony) and closely organized in instrumentation, rhythm and dynamic level. At the start of the symphony, for example, instrumental coloring divides separate parts in the same way, drawing attention to units of two or four tones.

It took Webern a while to achieve this refinement. After leaving Schoenberg's class in 1908 he took short-lived and unsatisfactory conducting jobs, while closely following his teacher's development within his own briefer manner. This was the period of such

---

Listening Note X.B   *Side 11, band 2*

Webern: *Six Bagatelles* op. 9 (1913), no. 4
string quartet

The Six Bagatelles, a miniature string quartet, all consist of tiny phrases, ostinatos and single chords and are very short. The whole movement is *pianissimo*.

Time
0:00   first phrase, ex. i, second violin
0:12   first violin
0:23   accompaniments precede melody
0:42   (end)

ex. i

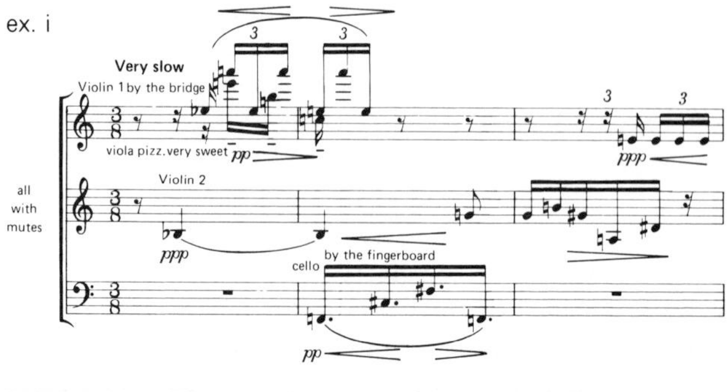

107 Anton Webern: black chalk drawing, 1918, by Egon Schiele. Private collection.

miniatures as his Six Bagatelles for string quartet (1913), each occupying only a small page of score (see Listening Note X.B).

In 1918 Webern settled near Schoenberg in Vienna, where he lived for the rest of his life. During the 1920s and early 1930s he held conducting appointments, but gradually he lost his posts as the Nazis gained control of Austria. Meanwhile he was writing his serial compositions, including not only the instrumental pieces but also a series of settings of verses by Hildegard Jone; the nature symbolism and tremulous mysticism of her work obviously struck a chord in him. There were two sets of Jone songs and three little choral works, all responding to her imagery with eagerness disciplined by the mechanics of serialism. He was working on a further Jone cantata in 1945 when he was shot in error by an American soldier.

The radical alternative

Stravinsky

In terms of creative achievement and influence, Igor Stravinsky (1882–1971) stands with Schoenberg as one of the two dominant figures in twentieth-century music. His influence has probably been the greater, for where Schoenberg's principal effort was towards continuing the Austro-German symphonic tradition, Stravinsky interested himself in radical alternatives. Revolutionary change has been more a feature of music in this century than has evolutionary growth.

The difference in temperament is partly to be explained by a difference of background. Though Stravinsky spent much of his life in France, Switzerland and the USA, he was very much a Russian composer with a Russian's hesitancy over Western values. His independence from the central tradition went far beyond that of Tchaikovsky and Mussorgsky, both influences on him. Another strong influence was Rimsky-Korsakov, with whom he had lessons.

His work took off with two short orchestral pieces performed in St Petersburg in 1908–9. They echo the French music that impressed Stravinsky at the time (including Debussy's), but are full of a youthful brilliance in handling the orchestra. They caught the attention of one member of the audience, Sergei Diaghilev, who at once commissioned Stravinsky to orchestrate pieces by Grieg and Chopin for a ballet season in Paris in 1909. This was the beginning of an association that bore immediate fruit. Three ballet scores took Stravinsky into a new understanding of the art: *The Firebird* (1910), *Petrushka* (1911) and *The Rite of Spring* (1913).

If *The Firebird* still shows several directions Stravinsky was not to take, *Petrushka* is his first wholly individual creation. Interestingly, the central character is a Russian equivalent of Pierrot. It might be supposed that Stravinsky, like Schoenberg, was looking for a puppet figure who could display human emotions more intensely than any real human being; Stravinsky found his in the tale of a doll brought to wretched life just as Schoenberg found his in poems for spoken song. But the comparison points up the differences as well as the similarities. Stravinsky's score is flamboyant in gesture, brilliant in color and crisp in outline. It makes no pretence at Schoenberg's constant development. Instead, Stravinsky cuts from one idea to another to give his music a kaleidoscopic quality. Lacking long-term growth, the score can accommodate a great variety of material. It includes Russian peasant-style dances and more intimate mime sequences in which Petrushka's dual nature is expressed in the superimposition of opposed keys.

The Rite of Spring takes all the novelties of *Petrushka* suddenly to a giant extreme. Scored for a very large orchestra, it is a dance-play of spring festivities in pagan Russia, ending with the sacrifice of a virgin in a tearingly self-destructive dance. This also completes a musical revolution as profound as Schoenberg's at the same time. Just as Western music had hitherto been dependent on concepts of mode or key, so its rhythmic foundation had depended on meter, an underlying stable pattern of beats. Stravinsky dispenses with that in the most overwhelming sections of *The Rite of Spring*. Rhythm here is much more a matter of single impulses and short motifs built into irregular sequences. The emphasis on

Igor Stravinsky	Life
1882	born in Oranienbaum (now Lomonosov) 17 June
1901	law student at St Petersburg University but chiefly interested in music
1902	met Rimsky-Korsakov, who became his mentor
1906	married Katerina Nossenko
1908–9	*Scherzo fantastique* and *Fireworks* acclaimed in St Petersburg and heard by Diaghilev, who commissioned music from Stravinsky, starting a long association with the Ballets Russes
1910	*The Firebird* (Paris) secured him an international reputation
1911	*Petrushka* (Paris)
1913	*The Rite of Spring* – riot in Paris theater
1914	settled in Switzerland
1917	Revolution made it impossible for him to return to Russia; *The Wedding* completed
1920	France; *Pulcinella*, the first of his "neo-classical" works, performed
1921	first European tour with Ballets Russes
1925	first American tour as conductor and pianist
1927	*Oedipus rex*
1935	second American tour
1937	*The Card Party* (New York) led to several American commissions, including the "Dumbarton Oaks" Concerto
1939	professor at Harvard University; his wife died
1940	married Vera de Bosset; settled in Hollywood
1945	naturalized American
1946	Symphony in Three Movements first performed in New York
1948	Robert Craft became Stravinsky's aide
1951	*The Rake's Progress* (Venice)
1957	*Agon* (New York)
1958	began international conducting tours
1962	well received in Russia
1966	*Requiem Canticles*
1971	died in New York, 6 April; buried in Venice

rhythm is enhanced by the unchanging harmony, instrumentation and dynamic level, and through their restless alteration the rhythmic units give a powerful sense of pulse. The pulsating dances are set off by introductions to each part in which rhythmic detail is lost in seamless polyphony. Even so, it is the new, violent rhythm of *The Rite of Spring* that was immediately admired or detested by Stravinsky's contemporaries. The first performance, in Paris on 29 May 1913, was the occasion of one of the greatest riots in the history of the theater, with audience reaction to match the noise from the pit.

The outbreak of World War I the next year severed Stravinsky from Russia. He set up home with his wife and children in Switzerland, and in exile his thoughts turned to Russian folk traditions. He had decided that his next ballet for Diaghilev would be on a Russian peasant marriage. Though the score of *The Wedding* was outlined by 1917, it took another six years to find the right orchestration. He settled on a small percussion orchestra, led by four pianos, to join the chorus – an efficient, quick-moving, machine-like ensemble for music that jumps freely among different repeating patterns geared to an unchanging pulse. In this respect *The Wedding* is a development of one rhythmic principle from *The Rite*. It shares with its predecessor its ritual solemnity, heightened at the end by a characteristic reference to bells.

The most important of Stravinsky's other works from his time in Switzerland is a smaller-scale stage work, *The Soldier's Tale* – a short play with musical interludes and

108   Igor Stravinsky: drawing by Pablo Picasso, Paris, 31 December 1920. Private collection.

Igor Stravinsky   Works

Operas Oedipus rex (1927), The Rake's Progress (1951)

Ballets The Firebird (1910), Petrushka (1911), The Rite of Spring (1913), Pulcinella (1920), The Wedding (1923), Apollon musagète (1928), The Fairy's Kiss (1928), Jeu de cartes (The card party, 1937), Orpheus (1947), Agon (1957)

Music-theater The Soldier's Tale (1918)

Orchestral music Symphonies of Wind Instruments (1920); Concerto "Dumbarton Oaks" (1938); Symphony in C (1940); Symphony in Three Movements (1945); Violin Concerto (1931); Ebony Concerto for clarinet (1945); Concerto for strings (1946)

Choral music Symphony of Psalms (1930); Mass (1948); Cantata (1952); Threni (1958); A Sermon, a Narrative and a Prayer (1961); Requiem Canticles (1966)

Vocal music (with ensemble) Pribaoutki (1914); Abraham and Isaac (1963)

Chamber music Duo concertante for violin and piano

Piano music Sonata (1924); two pianos – Concerto (1935); Sonata (1944)

Songs

dances. Breaking with established genres was just one expression of Stravinsky's breaking with tradition.

But he soon began to find ways of re-using the past. Diaghilev's next project for him was based on pieces by Pergolesi. What he provided in *Pulcinella* was not merely an orchestration: the music is newly imagined for a modern chamber orchestra, the harmony changed to add piquancy, the scoring revised to heighten contrast and character. The ballet sounds more like real Stravinsky than an eighteenth-century retrieval. It was, he said later, a confrontation with himself "in the mirror of the past"; it opened the way to neo-classicism.

There is hardly a major work of Stravinsky's after 1920 that does not refer to the music of other composers. Yet in his hands neo-classicism is not an appeal to timeless principles of form but a way of showing how much things have changed.

Stravinsky had now settled in France, having left Switzerland in 1920. But his works were still intensely Russian: this was the period when he was giving *The Wedding* its final scoring and writing *Mavra*, a short comic opera to a Russian libretto. A striking tendency in these works is that the strings have little importance. Stravinsky prefers the mechanical exactness of the piano and the harder outlines of wind instruments. The two are brought together in his Concerto for piano and wind (1924), where classical forms and Baroque counterpoint are the scaffolding for music of modern verve and aloofness.

The return to the full orchestra came in *Oedipus rex* (1927), the last of Stravinsky's works written for Diaghilev. This is not a ballet but an "opera-oratorio". Describing it thus, Stravinsky calls attention to the manner of staging he envisaged. The characters stand like statues on plinths, and the musical-dramatic action is recounted by a narrator in modern evening dress, speaking in the language of the audience and so associating himself with them rather than with the myth itself, which is retold in Latin. Everything conspires to convert the play into a monument, which the audience is invited to observe but not become involved in: the language is alien and ancient, the action deliberately artificial. So too is the music, where Stravinsky draws on the manner of Handel and Verdi.

If the oratorio aspect of the work carries a hint of sacred music, it would not be unexpected. In 1926 Stravinsky rejoined the Russian Orthodox Church, and wrote a setting for unaccompanied chorus of the Lord's Prayer in Church Slavonic. This was

Listening Note X.C   *Side 11, band 3*
Stravinsky: *Symphony in C* (1940), first movement (moderato alla breve, based on sonata form)

piccolo, 2 flutes, 2 oboes, 2 clarinets, 2 bassoons
4 horns, 2 trumpets, 3 trombones, tuba; timpani
1st violins, 2nd violins, violas, cellos, double basses

This work is in the mold of the Classical symphony but uses unconventional material.

Time	
0:00	exposition: the first four measures, ex. i, state germinal material
0:37	first subject, ex. ii, oboe
1:50	strings take up a staccato of repeated tone figure
2:20	cadence
2:26	second subject, ex. iii, horns
3:13	second subject, ex. iii, violins
3:44	development: after a measure of silence
3:59	ex. ii, G, oboe
4:20	ex. ii, e♭, oboe
4:33	ex. ii, C, flutes
4:49	oboe then violins
4:59	e♭, ex iv, violins and viola
5:08	tutti
5:40	recapitulation: second subject
8:39	coda, ex. ii, clarinet and flute
9:15	(end)

2nd movement (Larghetto): Ternary form, F, leading to
3rd movement (Allegretto): Ternary form, G.
4th movement (Largo-Tempo giusto): partly a sonata-form basis, but also drawing on first movement material, C.

followed by the Symphony of Psalms for choir and orchestra, in three movements, each setting a Latin psalm. Solemn in tone, lacking violins lest they are too expressive, the Symphony of Psalms is a sort of liturgy for the concert hall. It also marks a stage on Stravinsky's path back towards the Austro-German tradition, against which everything he had written in his maturity had been a reaction.

A "real" symphony emerged a decade later in the Symphony in C (1940), in four movements but typically neo-classical in its unconventional treatment. This is not a symphony in C like those of Mozart or Beethoven. It goes through the proper motions: a first movement with sections like those of sonata form, a slow movement, a scherzo and a finale. But this is only the outline, and its skeleton nature is made clear by the unsuitable nature of the material. Stravinsky does not develop his ideas but alters them; continuity is not an aim. The first movement, despite its sonata form, is a patterning of two tiny motifs that are constantly viewed afresh. The idea remains restless, and lends itself admirably to Stravinsky's non-developing, constantly varying music (see Listening Note X.C).

One effect of harmonic changelessness, as in *The Rite of Spring*, is to draw attention to the rhythm. Stravinsky's neo-classical music, reintroducing a background of stable meter, is full of such "motor rhythms" where the pulsation is divorced from harmonic movement. The rest of the symphony shows the same dislocations of rhythm, which gives it an oddly

109   Picasso's stage design for Stravinsky's *Pulcinella*, first staged at the Opéra, Paris, 15 May 1920: Musée Picasso, Paris.

balletic flavor and has helped to make this work and other of Stravinsky's neo-classical scores suitable for dancing. Having reached maturity as a ballet composer, he seems to have found strongly marked rhythm an indispensable part of his thinking. Here his music is a sprightly dance even when, in the slow movement, it is concerned also with florid, song-like lines for solo instruments.

Between the Symphony of Psalms and the Symphony in C Stravinsky had taken French citizenship. However, the outbreak of World War II caused him to move to the USA, where the last two movements of the Symphony in C were composed. In 1940 he settled in Hollywood, finding, like Schoenberg, that the Californian climate suited him. The two were near neighbors for a dozen years, though it seems they set eyes on each other only once, at a funeral.

Stravinsky was no stranger to America. Several of his works had been commissioned by American patrons, including a concerto (*Dumbarton Oaks*) for chamber orchestra, a modern re-creation of the spirit and manner of Bach's Brandenburg Concertos (1938). Moreover, he had used the specifically American genre of jazz in several of his works, with many further allusions helping to give an edge of streamlined modernity to his music.

Stravinsky was keenly aware of what he was worth, and not averse to taking on any compositional task if the money was right. He was involved with various film projects, though none materialized. After 1945, when he became an American citizen, Stravinsky showed his financial canniness by making new versions of many of his works, thus re-establishing his claim to copyright in them. He created three major works to crown the three decades of neo-classicism: an austerely beautiful Roman Catholic Mass for chorus and wind instruments (1948), the ballet *Orpheus* (1947) and the opera *The Rake's Progress* (1951). For the opera he set a libretto on an eighteenth-century subject, alluding to the world of Mozart's comic operas and even incorporating recitative with harpsichord accompaniment.

After this, his largest work, Stravinsky suddenly began to move in two new directions at the same time, even though he was nearly 70. He developed an interest in medieval and Renaissance music. He also began to investigate serialism, to which his own style had seemed utterly opposed. He had the opportunity to acquaint himself with the music of Schoenberg, Berg and Webern through his friendship from 1947 with the young American conductor Robert Craft, his musical assistant and tireless chronicler.

Most of Stravinsky's serial compositions are sacred or intended as funerary tributes. There was a last mixed-media dramatic piece, *The Flood*, a laconic telling for television of the Noah story in narration, song, dance and orchestral imagery. There was also a sequence of epitaphs for distinguished literary friends, including Dylan Thomas, T. S. Eliot and Aldous Huxley: Stravinsky had always maintained the Diaghilev habit of keeping the company of stars. His last memorial, however, was to himself, and it took the form of a typically compact and austere Mass for the Dead, the *Requiem Canticles* (1966). This was sung at his funeral, which he directed was to take place in Venice, scene of the first performances of *The Rake's Progress* as well as the *Canticum sacrum*, and last resting place too of Diaghilev.

Eastern Europe

Schoenberg and Stravinsky, like Brahms and Wagner in an earlier age, seemed to offer clear alternatives to their contemporaries: either to ground their music in the past, or to make a clean break. In art, however, no either/or can ever be clear-cut, and it is notable that several of the greatest composers of the first half of the twentieth century found a way to steer a middle course.

Bartók   Béla Bartók (1881–1945), Hungarian by birth, followed a career loosely matched by the history of his country. During his youth, Hungary was a part of the Habsburg Empire, ruled from Vienna, and Bartók was influenced by the Austro-German tradition from Haydn to Strauss (with a nationalist dash of Liszt). But in 1904 he discovered that the peasant music of Hungary had little to do with the gipsy fiddle-playing that Brahms and Liszt heard in Hungarian restaurants and put into their dances. Bartók set about using true folk music in his creative work. He had first to collect and study it.

Folk music had for Bartók a purity and naturalness that gave it a special legitimacy, and he based his own music on it in melody, rhythm, ornamentation, variation technique and so on. Bartók learned not only from his fellow Hungarians but also from Romanians, Slovaks, Turks and north African Arabs. All these, with their different modalities and rhythmic styles, contribute to the richness of such a work as String Quartet no. 2 (1917),

Béla Bartók	Life
1881	born in Nagyszentmiklós, Hungary (now Sînnicolau Mare, Romania), 25 March
1899	Budapest Royal Academy of Music; began career as concert pianist and started composing
1902–3	influenced by hearing Richard Strauss's music; *Kossuth*
1905	met Zoltán Kodály, with whom he began collecting Hungarian folk music
1906	first folk-music collection published
1907	professor of the piano at the Budapest Royal Academy
1909	married Márta Ziegler
1917	*The Wooden Prince* produced in Budapest, the first of his works to be received favorably
1918	*Duke Bluebeard's Castle*; established as an international figure
1920	toured Europe as a pianist
1923	*Dance Suite* composed to mark the union of Buda and Pest; divorced; married Ditta Pásztory
1926	*The Miraculous Mandarin* causes stir; First Piano Concerto
1934	commissioned by the Hungarian Academy of Sciences to publish folksongs
1940	emigrated to the USA
1942	health deteriorated
1943	Concerto for Orchestra
1945	died in New York, 26 September

Béla Bartók   Works

Opera Duke Bluebeard's Castle (1918)

Ballets The Wooden Prince (1917), The Miraculous Mandarin (1926)

Orchestral music Kossuth (1903); Dance Suite (1923); Music for Strings,
Percussion and Celesta (1936); Divertimento for strings (1939); Concerto for
Orchestra (1943); piano concertos – no. 1 (1926), no. 2 (1931), no. 3 (1945);
violin concertos – no. 1 (1908), no. 2 (1938); Viola Concerto (1945)

Chamber music string quartets – no. 1 (1908), no. 2 (1917), no. 3 (1927), no. 4
(1928), no. 5 (1934), no. 6 (1939); Contrasts for violin, clarinet and piano (1938);
Sonata for solo violin (1944); rhapsodies for violin and piano; duos for two violins

Piano music 14 Bagatelles (1908); Allegro barbaro (1911); Suite (1916); Sonata
(1926); Out of Doors (1926); Mikrokosmos vols. 1–6 (1926–39)

Choral music Cantata profana (1930)

Unaccompanied choruses   *Songs*

Folksong arrangements

one of the first in which almost everything seems to spring from folksong. Clearly, though, Bartók had also learned from his great contemporaries, Debussy, Stravinsky, perhaps Schoenberg.

This work came in the middle of a cycle of theater pieces, an opera (*Bluebeard's Castle*), a ballet (*The Wooden Prince*) and a mime drama (*The Miraculous Mandarin*). All show the same awareness of folk music and of current developments in Paris and Vienna. All are unusually self-revealing for a composer of an unusually reserved personality. The opera,

110   Bartók transcribing folksongs from an Edison phonograph, *c*1910.

dedicated to his young wife, is almost too blatantly a warning: in it Bluebeard's young wife Judith demands to know all the secrets of his heart and thereby loses all chance of happiness with him, for what she discovers appals her. Bluebeard's mysterious concealments are symbolized as a row of seven doors, and the music is in effect a sequence of vivid tone-poems depicting Bluebeard's bloodstained jewels, his procession of former wives or his other secrets, linked by dialogue which finds a Hungarian operatic style by way of folksong.

After World War I, Bartók abandoned his field trips to collect folksongs: he had enough material in his sketchbooks and on phonograph cylinders. He devoted himself to organizing what he and others had gathered, analyzing styles of folksong within any one culture, the influences between cultures, and the ways in which tunes were varied. Through this he gained a formidable understanding of musical variation, always one of his favorite techniques. His music of the 1920s and 30s is based on the constant variation of small motifs.

A case is his Music for Strings, Percussion and Celesta (1936), a four-movement piece for two chamber orchestras of strings and percussion, one including piano and celesta, the other xylophone and harp. This grouping provides varied and precise sounds. Though his own instrument was the piano, Bartók was a challenging but knowledgeable writer for strings, introducing new effects in his quartets and orchestral works; he also gave unusual attention to the percussion. Equally characteristic is the form of the Music for Strings and its dependence on variation. The principal idea of the first movement reappears at the climax of the dance-like finale, taken from four solo violas to full strings and from chromatic darkness into abundant diatonic light. This theme also turns up in the other two movements; the work is bound by similarity of material into a tight slow–fast–slow–fast structure.

That kind of form, alternating slow music with quick rhythmic dancing, is to be found also in String Quartet no. 3. Still more typical are palindromic structures. String Quartet no. 4 (1928), for instance, has the pattern Allegro–scherzo–slow movement–scherzo–Allegro. The outer movements share themes and the scherzos are distinguished by character and by their unusual sound – the first is muted, the second all plucked.

In addition to his studies, Bartók worked as a piano teacher, first at the conservatory in Budapest where he had studied. This is one reason why he produced educational music, including the six volumes of *Mikrokosmos* (1926–39), which range from elementary exercises to big pieces for concert performance by virtuosos. The latter are also well catered for by Bartók's other piano works, mostly written for his recitals and concerto appearances during the 1920s and 30s. Along with Stravinsky, Bartók was a pioneer of the percussive piano, his music suggesting hammered precision rather than a smooth, singing style. This concept of the piano was fully developed by the time of the stamping *Allegro barbaro* (1911) and remains vital in the later solo works and concertos, as well as in the electric tension of the Sonata for two pianos and percussion (1937).

By the early 1920s, Bartók was a composer of world renown. He must have been aware that his complex native language would be an obstacle to the wider appreciation of any vocal works, and concentrated on instrumental music. His preference seems also to answer deeper needs: his secretiveness, his irony, his liking for rules and his wish to balance reflection with activity. He found instrumental forms better fitted to his structural thinking, and preserved harmonic centers with only a hint of traditional tonality. There is a similarity here with the Stravinsky of the 1930s, also a composer mostly of instrumental music.

Like Stravinsky, and like Schoenberg, Bartók left Nazi Europe for the USA. His American years were overshadowed by leukemia and financial hardship. The money problem was partly alleviated by a grant from Columbia University enabling him to study

Listening Note X.D

Bartók: *Concerto for Orchestra* (1943), first movement (andante, allegro vivace; sonata form with slow introduction)
3 flutes/piccolo, 3 oboes/english horn, 3 clarinets in B /bass clarinet, 3 bassoons
4 horns, 3 trumpets in C, 2 tenor trombones, bass trombone, tuba; timpani, cymbal, harp
1st violins, 2nd violins, violas, cellos, double basses

The whole work shows Bartók's brilliant and colorful orchestration within a symmetrical, five-movement structure.

Time

0:00	introduction, a pentatonic arch, ex. i, cellos and basses
3:03	exposition; first theme, ex. ii
3:18	second theme, a variation of the first
3:46	third theme, ex. iii, related to the first
4:01	*Tranquillo*, second subject, ex. iv, solo oboe
5:16	development: develops the first theme
5:46	second subject
6:22	first theme
6:24	second subject used again, then treated in canon
7:10	recapitulation: first theme, ex. ii, heard briefly
7:20	second subject
8:36	coda: first theme, ex. ii, tutti
8:51	third theme, brass
8:56	(end)

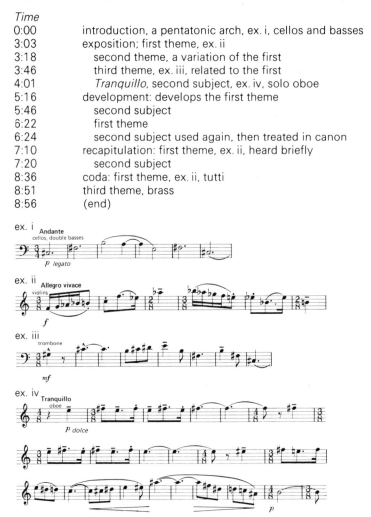

ex. i

ex. ii

ex. iii

ex. iv

a huge archive there of Yugoslav folk music. Despite the difficulties, his American works display a great deal of exuberance and a new simplicity of harmony and construction.

It would be possible to see Bartók's music as becoming steadily more inward-looking and chromatic, reaching an extreme around the time of String Quartets nos. 3 and 4. Thereafter there is a more diatonic feel and a more relaxed style, this change being marked already by the time of Piano Concerto no. 2. In America this process continued, with a further piano concerto and especially the boisterous Concerto for Orchestra (1943). This work, with its brilliant orchestral style, is another example of mirror symmetry grounded in a structure of five movements (see Listening Note X.D).

Prokofiev

While Bartók's nationalism was primarily a matter of reaching his ethnic roots through folk music, for the Russians of his generation the assumption of a national identity has been politically essential. The career of Sergei Prokofiev (1891–1953) shows this clearly. His early music, often wild and uncontrolled, reflects vividly Russia on the threshold of the 1917 Revolutions. In 1918 he left the new Soviet Union, but he did not sever his links. Starting in 1927, he made return visits, confirming an enthusiasm for the Soviet state that had already been expressed in some of his works. In 1936 he returned definitively, and had to contend with the increasingly tight cultural policy of Stalin's Russia: the condemnation of anything that did not speak optimistically to the masses.

Prokofiev was inevitably affected by these changes, but at an early stage had established a musical personality that could flourish in any circumstances. By the time his studies were complete, in 1914, he had several published works to his credit. He had established a reputation as a flouter of convention, with a vein of bitter irony. He attracted the attention of Diaghilev, but enjoyed a less fruitful relationship with the great impresario than did Stravinsky. A project for the Ballets Russes in 1915 was *Chout*, in a favorite Prokofiev mode of fantastic comedy and keen satire, but war held up its production until 1921.

Political developments also upset Prokofiev's operatic plans. His first full-length opera, *The Gambler*, was being rehearsed when the February 1917 Revolution broke out, and so this powerful, violent adaptation of a Dostoyevsky novel was not staged until 1929. In a quite different style was a piece in which he opened a door into the world of Haydn: his *Classical Symphony* (1917). Antedating Stravinsky's first neo-classical works, this symphony is in four short movements emulating eighteenth-century form, gracefulness of pattern and lightness of orchestration.

But Prokofiev did not move into a neo-classical period. His next major work was another opera, *The Love for Three Oranges* (1921), composed after he had left Russia and settled briefly in the USA. The plot, exceedingly complicated and almost entirely

---

Sergey Prokofiev   Works
born Sontsovka, Ukraine, 1891; *died* Moscow, 1953

Operas The Love for Three Oranges (1921), The Fiery Angel (1928), The Gambler (1929), War and Peace (1944)

Ballets The Prodigal Son (1929), Romeo and Juliet (1938), Cinderella (1945)

Orchestral music symphonies – no. 1, "Classical", D (1917), no. 2, d (1925), no. 3, c (1928), no. 4, C (1940), no. 5, B♭ (1944), no. 6, E♭ (1947), no. 7, c♯ (1952); Peter and the Wolf (1936); piano concertos – no. 1, D♭ (1912), no. 2, g (1913), no. 3, C (1921), no. 4, B♭ (1931), no. 5, G (1932); violin concertos – no. 1, D (1917), no. 2, g (1935); Cello Concerto, e (1938)

Choral music Alexander Nevsky (1939)

Chamber music string quartets – no. 1, b (1930), no. 2, F (1941); Flute Sonata (1943); Violin Sonata (1946); Cello Sonata (1949)

Piano music sonatas – no. 1, f (1909), no. 2, d (1912), no. 3, a (1917), no. 4, c (1917), no. 5, C (1923), no. 6, A (1940), no. 7, B♭ (1942), no. 8, B♭ (1944), no. 9, C (1947)

Songs   *Incidental music*   *Film scores*

111 Prokofiev's *The Love for Three Oranges*: scene from the Glyndebourne production, designed by Maurice Sendak, 1983.

nonsensical, served to stimulate Prokofiev to create a variety of musical and musical-dramatic situations suited to his sharp mockery and brilliant technique. Conventional operatic emotions of longing and love are exaggerated to a point of absurdity, and the orchestra takes on a toy-like quality of crisp definition and color. Then, Prokofiev launched into an opera of a very different kind, *The Fiery Angel* (1923), a tale of high passion and religious hysteria.

Prokofiev now returned to Europe and settled in Paris. His Second Symphony (1925) and a ballet follow the fashion for heavy-engineering music, with massive sonorities and chugging motor rhythms. Once he had returned to the Soviet Union, he gained a new stylistic balance, but continued to compose as prolifically as ever. Partly this can be put down to the natural development of an artist in his mid-40s. Partly, though, the more fulsomely Romantic style of his works from the mid-1930s onwards was a necessity in Russia.

The turning-point was marked by the ballet *Romeo and Juliet* (1938), written for the Bolshoy Theater in Moscow. At first rejected, it won eventual popularity for the vitality and variety of its rhythms, its skillfully etched orchestral sounds and its glamorous love music. Other major works of Prokofiev's early Soviet years include one of the very few masterpieces of music for children, *Peter and the Wolf* (1936), where his gifts for musical illustration are applied to a simple tale.

In the war most Soviet artists were evacuated to the provinces. There, in 1941, Prokofiev began an operatic setting of scenes from Tolstoy's epic novel *War and Peace*. Official encouragement spurred him to make it into a patriotic panorama. The opera occupied Prokofiev off and on for the rest of his life. His patriotism was genuine, and is expressed with genuine force in the choral scenes, while the "peace" scenes, focusing on the loves of the heroine, provide opportunities for the lyrical impulse that was also part of his creative personality.

Another wartime work, the Fifth Symphony, shows the grand, Romantic gestures of Prokofiev's Soviet style, with the triumphantly affirmative conclusion to suit a time of new hope. But a contrary feeling, of grim challenge, comes over in some of his piano sonatas of the time.

The war heightened the demand from government quarters for cheerful, inspiriting and direct music. After the war came the darkest hour, when, in 1948, Prokofiev and most of his outstanding colleagues were condemned for their "formalism" – a term applied to anything the government disliked but particularly to tendencies associated with the newest music of the West. Prokofiev was driven to works of bland character, but even a heroic opera about a World War II pilot was unacceptable and withdrawn until after Stalin's death. Prokofiev, ironically, died on the same day as Stalin, in 1953.

Shostakovich

The effect of Russian cultural dictates was even stronger in the case of Dmitry Shostakovich (1906–75). He lived all his life in Russia, and he grew up with the Soviet state. Moreover, he lived not only under Stalin's dictatorship but under Khrushchev's and Brezhnev's, and so had to deal with subtler forms of intervention than the blanket censorship of the 1930s and 40s. The constraints became a part of his musical personality, as did the irony and cynicism with which he coped with them.

The irony, as with Prokofiev, is there from his earliest works. It had been a quality of Russian music at least since Mussorgsky. Another characteristic was his prolific inventiveness. Indeed, after Prokofiev's departure in 1918 Shostakovich took over as the bold young innovator of Russian music. When in 1925 he finished at the Leningrad Conservatory, still only 18, he had composed a variety of instrumental works, including his First Symphony. This brought him international renown, but it was a curious start for a symphonic cycle that was to unfold as the most important since Mahler's. The First Symphony begins with an ambling, casual tune and then picks up the clear-cut outlines of Prokofiev's *Classical Symphony*. It at once established the vein of self-mockery in Shostakovich's music.

Meanwhile, Shostakovich had associated himself with the movement in Russia that saw

Dmitry Shostakovich   Works
born St Petersburg, 1906; *died* Moscow, 1975

Orchestral music symphonies – no. 1, f (1925), no. 2, "To October", B (1927), no. 3, "The first of May", E♭ (1929), no. 4, c (1936), no. 5, d (1937), no. 6, b (1939), no. 7, "Leningrad", C (1941), no. 8, c (1943), no. 9, E♭ (1945), no. 10, e (1953), no. 11, "The year 1905", g (1957), no. 12, "The year 1917", d (1961), no. 13, "Babi-Yar", b♭ (1962), no. 14 (1969), no. 15, A (1971); October (1967); piano concertos – no. 1, c (1933), no. 2, F (1957); violin concertos – no. 1, a (1948), no. 2, c♯ (1967); cello concertos – no. 1, E♭ (1959), no. 2 (1966)

Operas The Nose (1930), Katerina Izmaylova (1963) [revision of Lady Macbeth of Mtsensk, 1932]

Chamber music 15 string quartets; Piano Quintet (1940); 2 piano trios

Piano music sonatas – no. 1 (1926), no. 2 (1942); 24 Preludes (1933); 24 Preludes and Fugues (1951)

Songs   *Choral music*   *Incidental music*   *Film scores*

112   Shostakovich at work on his Symphony no. 7 in 1941.

artistic revolution as the necessary companion of political revolution. Its followers took a keen interest in what was being done by Stravinsky, Schoenberg, Bartók and other leaders of Western musical advance. This, however, was briskly quenched once the Stalinism of the arts got underway in the mid-1930s. Shostakovich's connection with it is strongest in his works of the early 1930s, including two symphonies with massive choral finales in praise of the revolution. There is also an opera, *The Nose*, whose overriding character is of grotesque parody: the libretto is based on a fantastic story by Gogol in which a man's nose takes on an independent existence. The story is clearer than Prokofiev's *Love for Three Oranges*, but the score is similarly a patchwork of brightly fashioned musical objects that satirize operatic convention or are just perverse.

Shostakovich's second opera, *Lady Macbeth of Mtsensk* (1932), also contains satire, but within a realistic tragedy. It is the bourgeois world in which "Lady Macbeth" is mocked; she herself is a strong, urgent character, driven to desperate acts by her stifling situation. After its first production, in 1934, the opera was praised as a major achievement in Soviet art. Then, in 1936, it was violently attacked in the official party newspaper and hurriedly taken from the stage. It was not seen again in Russia until 1963.

The enforcement of "socialist realism" affected Shostakovich's other works too. He withdrew his vast, Mahlerian Fourth Symphony, then offered his Fifth (1937) as what a Soviet commentator called "a Soviet artist's practical creative reply to just criticism", where the "finale resolves the tragically tense impulses of the earlier movements into optimism and joy of living". If this was a bow to state demands, one can also detect Shostakovich's irony infiltrating the underlying structure even of his splendid, optimistic last movement.

Shostakovich found another way of declaring the overriding importance of the self in his Sixth Symphony, where a long lament is succeeded by two short and flippant quick movements: optimism fails by being insufficient. After this, he decided to cultivate chamber music as a less public, less exposed platform. A string quartet appeared every two or three years until by the end of his life there were 15, equal in number to the symphonies.

Among the latter are two program symphonies concerned with critical events in the birth of the Russian Revolution. Similarly expansive is the "Leningrad" Symphony, no. 7 (1941), which interprets current events in order to edify and encourage its audience. Its subject is the German invasion, depicted in immense, obsessive repetition and overcome in a grand finale that truly conveys the optimism undercut in the Fifth Symphony. Shostakovich's Eighth Symphony (1943) is the private counterpart to this public affirmation, interpreted widely as speaking of appalled horror and gruff determination in the face of the war; it trails off into hopeless, resigned detachment. While the Seventh Symphony was positively welcomed by the authorities, the Eighth was denounced and not played again until the 1950s. The Ninth Symphony (1945), too, disappointed the Kremlin, since it was not the hoped-for celebration of victory but instead a brittle, brief work returning to the tradition of Prokofiev's *Classical Symphony*.

On Stalin's death Shostakovich might have taken advantage of the looser controls, but he came out into the open only cautiously. He brought forward his powerful First Violin Concerto (1948), but otherwise his works of the next few years avoided political dangerousness. So the Thirteenth Symphony (1962) came as all the more of a bombshell. In it Shostakovich set poems by Evgeny Yevtushenko, outspokenly critical of the government. The first movement is a lament at Russian complicity in the massacre of the Jews at Babi-Yar, the second a scherzo satire on the hypocrisy of rulers, the third an identification with Russian women bearing the burden of deprivation, the fourth a rebuke to those who fear the truth, and the last a cheer for those who speak it. Here at last was powerful optimism, but not of a kind to commend itself to the authorities. The symphony was withdrawn and Yevtushenko forced to change some of the text.

Shostakovich's creative thoughts were now turning towards death, the goal of most of the music of his last decade. His Fourteenth Symphony (1969) is a cycle of songs on the subject, his Fifteenth (1971) an orchestral work with enigmatic quotations from Rossini, Wagner and others. The mood of this late period, however, was one that favored chamber music, and the years 1968–74 saw the composition of his last four quartets, works with many original features and in increasingly elegiac tone.

Germany

Hindemith

In Germany, many composers – like Bartók in Hungary – viewed Schoenberg's atonality as a challenge to a new interpretation of tonality. While Bartók found his guidelines in folk music, Paul Hindemith (born 1895) as a German was closer to the central tradition. No other composer of this period was so classically neo-classical. After trying out various styles, he began in 1924 to write music that featured Bach-type counterpoint, Baroque form and that mechanical rhythm that often turns up when the twentieth century imitates the eighteenth. This "motor rhythm", propelling the music along without any clear harmonic progress, is a feature of Hindemith's quick movements.

Hindemith was exceedingly productive. However, his Bach-Stravinsky style of neo-classicism is summed up in the seven works called *Kammermusik* ("chamber music"), most of them concertos, written between 1922 and 1927. These have an unflagging contrapuntal energy and a sheer ebullience that point to a connection with the Brandenburg Concertos. Like Bach, too, Hindemith had a feeling for dance rhythms, including those of jazz.

Hindemith, a viola player of professional standing, wanted his music to be useful beyond international festivals or star performances. He suggested that composers ought to write with the non-specialist and the amateur in mind, and he formulated a concept of "music for use", with a decisive function (film scores, radio music) or aimed at performance by children or amateurs. He wrote much music of this kind, but his activities were cut short by the Nazis. In 1938 he left Berlin; from 1940 to 1953 he was a professor at Yale.

The problems faced by a creative artist in an immoral, strife-ridden state are explored in Hindemith's opera *Mathias the Painter* (1938). The central character is the sixteenth-century painter Mathias Grünewald, who forsakes his art to engage in political activity on behalf of the German peasants; but he discovers that his greatest need is the exercise of his creative talent, in which may also lie his greatest usefulness to society. The opera is evidently a personal document.

Hindemith's emigration to the USA brought little change in his style, which had become more mellow and less astringent. His most important American work was a *Requiem* for the dead of World War II, setting Walt Whitman's elegy on the death of President Lincoln, *When Lilacs Last in the Door-yard Bloom'd*.

Even though he had become an American citizen, Hindemith returned to Europe and made his home in Switzerland. He died in 1963. The main work of his last years was a second opera concerned with a visionary from the Renaissance: *The Harmony of the World* (1957), on the life and beliefs of Johannes Kepler. Here the "studies in tonal organization" have taken on a mystical fervor, and Hindemith seems to hope with his hero that an understanding of natural harmony will unlock the secrets of the universe.

Weill

Bartók and Hindemith were concerned with their music as the product of a society. For a more radical solution to the problem of artistic communication, however, we must turn to Kurt Weill (1900–50), whose musical background was similar to Hindemith's. Both were attracted by the expressionism of Schoenberg's pre-serial atonal works and by corresponding trends in German theater, and both were deeply influenced by neo-classical ideals.

Hindemith and Weill collaborated in 1929 on a setting of *The Lindbergh Flight* by the German dramatist Bertolt Brecht (1898–1956). But where Hindemith seems to have been happiest in pure music-making, Weill was very much a man of the theater, and recognized in Brecht one who shared not only his political ideals but also his esthetic. In their joint opera *Rise and Fall of the City of Mahagonny* (1929), they show in exaggerated image the monstrous exploitation of money, power, rank and sex in the real world. Set in a mythical America, the work aspires in part to the style of the American popular song. There is a delicate irony in the use of debased styles to criticize a society. At the same time, Weill's tonal harmony, spiked with dissonances, is a pervading symbol of decadence and corruption.

Weill's period of work with Brecht was brief. It began with *Mahagonny* and *The Threepenny Opera* (1928), whose popular success enabled Weill to live off his earnings as a composer; it ended five years later with *Seven Deadly Sins*, a song cycle-cum-ballet staged in Paris in 1933, three months after Weill had left Germany.

In 1935 Weill moved to the USA, and spent the rest of his life in New York as a composer for Broadway: a curious fate for the composer of the insidiously ironic *Mahagonny*. But Weill merely shows how the activity of an artist is conditioned by society. As a German Jew under the threat of Nazism, he addressed himself to the strains in that society. As an American in a time of prosperity and stability under Roosevelt's "New Deal", he was more relaxed, even entertaining. If Weill wanted to reach a large audience, the musical offered him the best chance: hence the shows for Broadway, including *Knickerbocker Holiday, Lady in the Dark* and *One Touch of Venus*. The style he had adopted in "Mack the Knife" from *The Threepenny Opera* now had to be the whole Weill, and the success of such a number as "September Song" is a mark not only of his musical skill but also of his artistic conscience.

America: the "ultra-moderns"

A remarkable number of great composers from Europe were driven by Nazism and war to seek a better life in the Americas – Schoenberg, Stravinsky, Bartók, Hindemith, Weill and the Spaniard Manuel de Falla among them. Their presence did much to stimulate the development of music in the New World: Schoenberg and Hindemith were both teachers, and apart from anything else, the presence of such names, like the earlier presence of Dvořák (see pp. 249–50), was a boost to the morale of American composers. However, American music was in fact strong enough to take care of itself: decades before, it had produced its first genius in Charles Ives (1874–1954).

Ives

A close contemporary of Schoenberg, Charles Ives also owed much to his upbringing. His father had been a bandmaster in the Civil War. Living in the small Connecticut town of Danbury, he was an enterprising musician: he encouraged his son to sing in a key different from that of the accompaniment and in other ways to take nothing for granted. This urge to experiment was pursued by the young Ives in psalm settings he composed around the age of 20, some in several keys at the same time or vaguely dissonant. Ives also had the benefit of a normal musical education at Yale, where he was a pupil of Horatio Parker (1863–1919), one of a group of gifted but unadventurous New England composers. The result was a creative splitting. At Yale, between 1894 and 1898, he continued his experiments, but he also composed works of a more conventional kind, such as his First Symphony. Academic training gave Ives the technique to improve and enlarge his experi-

---

Charles Ives   Works
born Danbury, Connecticut, 1874; *died* New York, 1954

Orchestral music symphonies – no. 1 (1898), no. 2 (1902), no. 3 (1904), no. 4 (1916); First Orchestral Set (Three Places in New England) (1914); Second Orchestral Set (1915); The Unanswered Question (1906); Central Park in the Dark (1906); Emerson Overture (1907); Washington's Birthday (1909); Robert Browning Overture (1912); Decoration Day (1912); The Fourth of July (1913)

Choral music Psalm 67 (?1894); The Celestial Country (1899)

Chamber music From the Steeples and the Mountains (1902); string quartets – no. 1 (1896), no. 2 (1913); violin sonatas – no. 1 (1908), no. 2 (1910), no. 3 (1914), no. 4 (1916)

Piano music sonatas – no. 1 (1909), no. 2, "Concord" (1915); Studies (1908)

Organ music Variations on "America" (?1891)

Songs The Circus Band (?1894); General William Booth Enters into Heaven (1914); *c*180 others

ments, and the orthodox background provides a frame against which his departures seem all the more extraordinary.

Ives went into the insurance business. Most American composers would have gone to Europe for further training, but he felt no such need. He would have found it limiting to take up either of the two professional courses open to a composer: teaching or serving as

---

Listening Note X.E   *Side 11, band 5*

Ives: *Three Places in New England* (1914, rev. 1929), no. 2 "Putnam's Camp"
Flute/piccolo, oboe/english horn, clarinet, bassoon
2 or more horns, 2 or more trumpets, 2 trombones, tuba
piano, timpani, drums, cymbals
1st violins, 2nd violins, violas, cellos, double bass

The original scoring, reconstructed by James B. Sinclair in his edition of 1976, was for a rather larger orchestra.

"Putnam's Camp" is a scherzo between two slow movements of *Three Places*. The first is "The 'St Gaudens' in Boston Common (Col. Shaw and his Colored Regiment)", which contemplates a memorial to heroes of the Revolution, and the finale is a more auto-biographical piece, "The Housatonic at Stockbridge", in which Ives recalled a walk by the river with his wife.

Time
0:00	orchestral flourish in quick time
0:10	dance tune, ex. i, first violins
0:51	five metrically independent lines played simultaneously
2:16	nine-note chord ("Goddess of Liberty")
2:28	"cause" theme, ex. ii
2:35	*The British Grenadiers*, ex. iii
3:25	arrival of Putnam, ex. iv
3:29	*The British Grenadiers*, flute
4:14	dance tune emerges out of collage of many marches
4:36	music returns to the complexity of 0:51
4:50	*The British Grenadiers*, added in trumpet
5:05	episode, for brass and drums
5:37	dense chords
5:51	(end)

ex. i

ex. ii

ex. iii

ex. iv

a church musician. Insurance gave him the livelihood which made it possible for him to compose in his spare time. He prospered, and his music silently prospered too. Most of his output dates from the two decades up to 1918, when he suffered a heart attack, but almost nothing of it was known outside a small circle of musician friends.

Ives's achievements, though, were immense. At the center stands a body of around 150 songs, from gentle hymn-like pieces (*At the River*) to robust philosophical meditations (*Paracelsus*), from student imitations of German *Lieder* (*Feldeinsamkeit*) to exuberant pictures of an America that had disappeared with Ives's boyhood (*The Circus Band*). In responding to a text, he was willing to use any materials that seemed suitable, and his enthusiastic identification with such a great range of poems was responsible for the vast range of his musical technique. The more nostalgic pieces may be filled with quotations from hymns, parlor songs, marches and dances, whereas the more strenuous mental exertions tend naturally to go with dissonant chords and complex rhythms that are awkward and difficult to grasp. These sometimes suggest the atonal Schoenberg, though Ives composed in ignorance of what was happening in Europe.

Because he was not building up a professional body of work, he had the freedom to make different versions of the same piece. This sprang in part from his conviction that what mattered was, in his own words, the "substance" and not the "manner". He could even be impatient of the physical practicalities of music-making: "Why can't music go out in the same way it comes into a man", he wrote, "without having to crawl over a fence of sounds, thoraxes, catguts, wire, wood and brass? . . . Is it the composer's fault that man has only ten fingers?" For him, therefore, there was an ideal beyond the notation: hence his continued revision of his scores.

A key work, typical in its marriage of personal vision and national destiny, is the set *Three Places in New England*. The second, "Putnam's Camp", is a graphic musical scene that presents a boy hearing jolly, brassy marches on a Fourth of July outing, then going off by himself and having a vision of ghostly soldiers from the Revolutionary War (see Listening Note X.E).

Many of Ives's other orchestral works, especially those for small ensembles, are similarly memories of place and time: *Central Park in the Dark*, with the darkness presented in the atonal strings which circle unperturbed while the other instruments enter in mounting clamor, or *All the way around and back*, a musical skit on a baseball maneuver. But there are also the symphonies, in which illustration plays only a secondary role. The first two, by Ives's standards, are mild and more than somewhat academic, but the third is more individual.

Symphony no. 4 is one of his greatest and most demanding works, and one of his most all-embracing. The third movement is a moderately well-behaved fugue, originally composed to open a string quartet and here a resting-place between more ambitious movements. The second movement is the most complex of those jumbles of quotations that represent Ives in vital spirits. In the Fourth Symphony the raucous enjoyment of these pieces is rather modified by the density of marches, hymns and dances woven together. Instead of depicting a particular moment, as "Putnam's Camp" and "The Fourth of July" (from the *Holidays* symphony) seem to, this second movement of the symphony is a vast panorama of mundane existence. The finale returns to the slower, quieter, more distanced manner of the brief first movement. But where that opening had appeared to ask the questions, with its hymn fragments (the symphony requires a chorus as well as a huge orchestra), the finale is a departure into higher realms of transcendent vision, with muted percussion and far-off voices. A similar sort of music is present in other works where contemplation comes at the end of strenuous questioning or in answer to abundantly physical music with quotations strewn throughout.

Another, more condensed product of the philosophical Ives is the orchestral piece *The Unanswered Question*. The "question" is posed several times by a solo trumpet, while offstage strings proceed through slow-motion diatonic chords, as if ignorant that any question needs an answer, and a quartet of flutes rushes about in vain panic. Composed in 1906, it antedates Schoenberg's properly atonal compositions. It provides an extraordinary instance of Ives's prefiguring of many of the techniques and interests that have guided the course of music in this century.

Ives's position as a precursor, as has already been suggested, is borne out by many other features. His use of recognizable musical quotations – found in most of his larger orchestral, chamber and piano pieces – looks forward as far as Stockhausen in the 1960s. He experimented too with tuning a piano in quarter-tones and with the close calculation of pitch, interval and rhythm structures. He seems to have felt that his musical "substance" should not be compromised by convention or technique. If a piano sonata demanded impossible spreads and the introduction of subsidiary instruments (like a flute in the finale), then so it must be: hence the colossal breadth and difficulty of his Second Sonata, sub-titled "Concord" and picturing the personalities of four writers associated with that Massachusetts town. First comes Ralph Waldo Emerson, the far-seeing thinker, then Nathaniel Hawthorne, in a stream of activity taken up again in the third movement of the Fourth Symphony. The Alcotts provide a slow movement of domestic tranquillity, and finally there is Henry Thoreau, the plain man's seer.

Not until the 1940s did Ives begin to be recognized as the first great American composer, the man who, in the great mix of styles and materials he cultivated, created musical images that could have come only from America. By then, he had long stopped composing: his health caused him to abandon composition in 1926 and insurance in 1930, even if he continued to dream of a *Universe Symphony* which would have been a still more comprehensive undertaking than any he achieved.

Cowell

Ives is the model of the truly American composer: unfettered by European norms, ready to go his own way, unashamed of the incongruous. The music of Henry Cowell (1897–1965) is similar. Cowell too was an experimenter from his boyhood. A Californian, he gave his first piano recital just before his 14th birthday, by which time he had already worked with "clusters" of adjacent notes in the bass to be played with the flat of the hand or the forearm. Later he introduced the idea of playing directly on the piano strings, wrote much for percussion in combinations with other instruments, and developed techniques for creating atonal melodies and providing rhythmic structures on the same mathematical basis.

Besides composing a great deal, Cowell was active as a teacher and promoter of other composers; he launched a publishing enterprise to issue challenging new works and bring to public attention the music of Ives and Edgard Varèse among American contemporaries.

Varèse

Varèse (1883–1965) should be considered an American because, although he was born in France and spent his first 32 years in Europe, almost all his surviving music dates from after his emigration to New York in 1915. He was in effect born as a composer with his first American work, significantly entitled *Amériques* (1921), for an enormous orchestra and "symbolic of new discoveries – new worlds on earth, in the sky, or in the minds of men." Having spent time in Berlin as well as Paris, Varèse was familiar with the atonal Schoenberg as much as with Debussy and Stravinsky. However, the importance of the percussion ensemble is something quite new, as is the rhythmic complexity of this many-stranded percussion music.

Amériques shows too Varèse's prodigious orchestral imagination. Ideas are not passed from one group of instruments to another: instead they are as if welded to a particular type of sound. If there is a change in the sonority, there has to be a change of idea. Those changes come with brusqueness and violence. In the most characteristic moments of *Amériques* this conveys the impression of the composer working directly with his raw material of sound.

The most compact of Varèse's works from the 1920s is *Hyperprism* (1923), for flute, clarinet, seven brass and seven percussion players – all the percussionists using untuned instruments except for the indefinitely pitched siren. The avoidance of strings is typical: Varèse distrusted expressiveness and liked the intensity that high woodwind and brass instruments could give him.

The fierce energy of *Hyperprism* went out of Varèse's music when he returned to Paris in 1928 for five years. His interest in percussion received expression in *Ionisation* (1931), one of the first Western works for percussion orchestra. Typically the music is concerned above all with intricate rhythmic polyphony. In Paris, Varèse met inventors who were developing electronic instruments, and he used two of these in his *Ecuatorial* (1934). But they were limited achievements by the standards of the technological breakthrough Varèse was looking for, and – after composing almost nothing for more than a decade – Varèse's creativity was reawakened by the arrival of the tape recorder. Earlier he had experimented with altering sounds recorded on disc, but the tape recorder made such techniques simple, for tape could be cut up and edited into compositions. Using this procedure, he composed *Déserts* (1954), where three "windows" of electronic music are let into a score for wind, piano and percussion. He went on to create one of the few masterpieces of music on tape, his *Poème électronique* (1958), before finally returning to live media for various projects on the subject of night, none of them completed.

Ives, Cowell and Varèse represent what was called "ultra-modern" music in the USA between the wars. But there was much else. This was, for instance, a golden age for popular song and musical comedy in New York. This repertory is discussed in the next chapter – including the music of its greatest exponent, George Gershwin. There was also a more traditional "mainstream".

1922 · NEW YORK · EXPERIENCES · FIRST PERFORMANCE OF VARÈSE'S "HYPERPRISM" —

113 Cartoon recording impressions of Varèse's *Hyperprism* after the first performance at the Klaw Theater, New York, on 4 March 1923.

Copland

A leading representative of the mainstream was Aaron Copland, born in Brooklyn in 1900. From a prosperous family, Copland had the benefit of formal musical training; at the age of 20 he went to Paris, where he was a pupil of Nadia Boulanger for four years – one of the first disciples of a famous French teacher who was to instill her precepts of clarity and technical command into many American composers. In 1924 he returned, to become a specifically American composer. From jazz he borrowed syncopated rhythms and certain harmonic features in his Piano Concerto (1926); he also set the words of various American poets in choral pieces and songs.

Like Cowell and Varèse, Copland was active in support of his fellow composers. He helped organize concerts of new music in New York between 1928 and 1931, and took an interest in the development of music within the southern neighbors of the USA. A visit to a nightclub in Mexico City gave him the stimulus for his first essay in light music, *El salón México* (1936), catching the exuberance of the dance music he heard there.

The opportunity soon came for a similar hybrid of popular material and serious setting on an American theme in the ballet *Billy the Kid*. This was followed by another rowdy cowboy ballet, *Rodeo*, and then by a treatment of the theme of Stravinsky's *Wedding* in pioneer New England: *Appalachian Spring* (1944). Like Ives, Copland uses folksong,

Aaron Copland   Works
born Brooklyn, 1900

Ballets Billy the Kid (1938); Rodeo (1942); Appalachian Spring (1944)

Operas The Tender Land (1955)

Orchestral music symphonies – no. 1 (1928), no. 2 (1933), no. 3 (1946); El salón México (1936); Lincoln Portrait (1942); Fanfare for the Common Man (1942); Orchestral Variations (1957); Music for a Great City (1964); Inscape (1967); 3 Latin American Sketches (1972); Piano Concerto (1926); Clarinet Concerto (1948)

Chamber music Vitebsk, Study on a Jewish Theme (1928); Violin Sonata (1943); Piano Quartet (1950); Nonet for strings (1960); Threnody I: Igor Stravinsky, in memoriam (1971)

Piano music Variations (1930); Sonata (1941); Fantasy (1957); Night Thoughts (1972)

Songs 12 Poems of Emily Dickinson (1950)

Choral music   *Film scores*

traditional dance and hymn, joined by modern notions of rhythm, harmony and orchestration. The difference is that Copland, welding these together, created a style in which he could move freely between quotation and original music. In *Appalachian Spring*, for example, the Shaker hymn "The Gift to be Simple" provides the music with something like an underlying mode from which much of its substance derives.

Its success also led him to contemplate more ambitious works in the same style, notably his Third Symphony (1946). No doubt this was encouraged too by the recent example of Stravinsky's Symphony in C, for the neo-classical Stravinsky had been a central influence on Copland since his time with Boulanger. Copland's energy is similarly owed to interruptions and displacements of a marked meter: both composers had learned from jazz. In his orchestral sonorities, too, Copland is closer to Stravinsky than to any other contemporary. Simple chords – most effectively in *Appalachian Spring* – can be refashioned by unusual wide spacing and luminous orchestration; even a major triad becomes something new, belonging only to the sound-world of this work.

Copland went beyond Stravinsky in the range of levels at which he composed, especially in the late 1930s and 1940s. The *Lincoln Portrait* for speaker and orchestra and the *Fanfare for the Common Man* (both 1942) represent the public composer, addressing the nation at a time of crisis and using a language that presents no difficulties, though it is definitely his own. At the other extreme are the more searching and rarefied chamber and instrumental pieces. Right at the end of this period came two sets of simple arrangements of Old American Songs (1952) and a Piano Quartet (1950) in which Copland, like Stravinsky at this time, began to test the waters of serialism. With the greater importance of serialism came a decline in his use of the popular style of the ballets and film scores. Copland also became much less prolific and after *Inscape* for orchestra (1967) he composed little.

Carter
An outstanding characteristic of American music is its diversity. But there are rare composers who draw from that diversity to build up their own style; the most notable is Elliott Carter (b. 1908). Like Ives, with whom he was in contact from his schooldays onwards, he developed an independence and a willingness to use highly complex ideas. Like Copland, he was greatly impressed by the neo-classical Stravinsky. Like Copland too, he was greatly concerned in his youth with creating a specifically American music.

As it happened, Copland-like folklorism was to be replaced in Carter's music by a much more individual style, though one no less American in its essential difference from the European tradition: its openness, its freedom from preconceptions.

Carter studied at Harvard and followed the trail blazed by Copland to Paris and Nadia Boulanger, whose pupil he was from 1932 to 1935. He returned to the USA as musical director for a dance company. In 1950 he set off for Arizona to compose in relative isolation, determined to strike his own path and not be troubled by the needs and tastes of potential audiences. The result was a 40-minute string quartet (1951) of powerful newness. This was music that spoke broadly, if in a difficult style, and the quartet was soon recognized as a major achievement.

An original feature is Carter's conception that a "movement" need not be the same thing as a chunk of music separated in time. His quartet is divided into three sections – I Fantasia, II (untitled) and III Variations – but the division into movements is different. The Fantasia consists of the cadenza introduction, a combative Allegro and the beginnings of the scherzo. This is then continued in the second marked section, which also includes a slow movement and the start of the final Variation – these creating change in so fantastic a way that they have begun before their nominal beginning.

Carter pursued this quicksilver variation technique in his next major work, the Variations for orchestra. The idea of bringing together different movement types is carried much further in, for instance, the Symphony of Three Orchestras (1977), where the separate ensembles converge and diverge in a kaleidoscope of 12 movements arranged within a single span. The rhythmic and textural intricacies – also the variety of the ideas and their sheer energy – are present in all Carter's later works. Stravinsky singled out his Double Concerto for harpsichord and piano, each with its own group of instruments (1961), as perhaps the finest musical achievement to date by any American.

Bernstein

If Carter belongs to the intellectual wing of American composition, one who embraces a multiplicity of traditions is Leonard Bernstein (b. 1918). His music looks to the twentieth-century symphonic tradition of Mahler and Shostakovich, to American jazz, to Jewish sacred music, to the rhythmic verve and clear scoring of Copland and Stravinsky, to the snappy melody of the Broadway musical. Usually these strands are moderated according to the nature of the work, and Bernstein has shown a rare ability to compose in different genres almost at the same time. Moreover, he has combined his career as a composer with that of one of the outstanding conductors of his generation, though most of his works

---

Leonard Bernstein   Works
born Lawrence, Massachusetts, 1918

Stage music On the Town (1944), Candide (1956), West Side Story (1957), Mass (1971)

Ballet Fancy Free (1944)

Orchestral music The Age of Anxiety [Symphony no. 2] (1949); On the Waterfront (1955)

Choral music Jeremiah Symphony [no. 1] (1943); Symphony no. 3, "Kaddish" (1963); Chichester Psalms (1965)

Piano music Seven Anniversaries (1943); Four Anniversaries (1948)

Chamber music Clarinet Sonata (1942)

Songs

date from before or after the period of his musical directorship of the New York Philharmonic (1958–68), and he has also been uniquely distinguished as a popularizer of music through his brilliant television programs.

The earlier group includes two symphonies, sub-titled *Jeremiah* (1943) and *The Age of Anxiety* (1949). The latter has a solo piano and a program derived from Auden's long poem: it was the first evidence of Bernstein's willingness, like Copland, to address the great issues of the day, in this case the conflicts and tensions of the cold war. Both these symphonies are in the Mahler–Berg–Shostakovich line of Bernstein's music; his Broadway style is more in evidence in the ballet *Fancy Free*, in the musical *On the Town*, and most successfully of all in the musical *West Side Story* (1957), an updating of the story of Romeo and Juliet where the warring families become rival gangs in New York. With its strong plot, its hit tunes and its big dance numbers, *West Side Story* has all the ingredients needed for the genre. It has taken its place among the classics of the American musical, while the brilliant overture to another stage work of this period, the operetta *Candide*, immediately gained a place in the repertory.

Bernstein's more serious works of the 1950s and 60s are broadly of two kinds, reflective and declamatory. The *Chichester Psalms* are melodious settings in Hebrew for choir and orchestra. Another Hebrew work, the *Kaddish* Symphony, his third (1963), belongs however stylistically and expressively with its two predecessors, though benefiting from the heightened grasp of different idioms that Bernstein had now achieved.

His *Mass* (1971) is a more startling mix. Using the words of the Roman Catholic Mass, and having the ritual enacted on stage, Bernstein attempts to explore the meaning of the ceremony for a contemporary audience: this brings the world of the *Chichester Psalms* into contact with that of *West Side Story*. In later works, however, Bernstein has been more selective in his style and has chosen to compose only to mark special occasions: his *Songfest*, for example, is an anthology of American poetry set to celebrate the Bicentennial.

Menotti

Perhaps the most successful opera composer working in America is Gian Carlo Menotti (b. 1911), an Italian who arrived in the country as a teenager and found his new environment a source of color and spice to reinvigorate the tradition of Puccini. His most successful works date from the immediate postwar years and include *The Consul* (1950) and the children's opera *Amahl and the Night Visitors* (1951); the former is representative of his bold melodrama, the latter of his tunefulness. Menotti has also been active as a festival administrator, opera producer and librettist for other composers: he wrote *Vanessa* (1957–8) for Samuel Barber (1910–81), a fellow conservative. Barber's roots are in the late Romantic symphonism of Strauss, Mahler and Elgar rather than the *verismo* of Puccini; correspondingly, his finest works are not his operas but his orchestral works and songs, and his best-known piece is his *Adagio* for strings.

Britain

If America's position to the far west of the European musical centers has tended to make her composers more adventurous, then Britain, on the fringe of Europe, has traditionally been musically rather conservative and mistrustful of home-grown originality. Hence, to some degree, the continuation in that country of genres widely considered obsolete around the middle of the twentieth century: opera (Britten, Tippett) and symphony (Vaughan Williams, Tippett).

Vaughan Williams

The rebirth of English music at the very end of the nineteenth century provided encouragement for such young composers as Ralph Vaughan Williams (1872–1958), Gustav Holst (1874–1934) and Frederick Delius (1862–1934), who together dominated English music between the wars and, in Vaughan Williams's case, long after. Vaughan Williams's influence was also the deeper because he put forward a general approach, whereas Holst and Delius were musical loners. That approach was the absorption of English folksong, which he began to collect at the beginning of the century and which gave his music a distinctive melodic and harmonic flavor.

Vaughan Williams's roots were all English; he looked not only to folksong but also to the art music of his country's Renaissance, and in particular to the sacred music of Byrd and Tallis. His Fantasia on a Theme by Thomas Tallis, for string orchestra (1910), utilizes the most harmonious chords in a quite original way, motivated by the modal relationships its composer discovered as much in English folksong as in Tallis. (Bartók at the same time was also struck by the potential usefulness of folk music modality.)

A further aspect of Vaughan Williams's Englishness is the feeling for landscape his music sometimes conveys. *The Lark Ascending* (1914) is a work of this kind, and one of Vaughan Williams's most perfect, with its solo violin etching the bird's flight against the warm, immobile orchestral accompaniment. There is also a cycle of nine symphonies, of which the angry no. 4, the pastoral no. 5 (linked with his opera *The Pilgrim's Progress*) and the desolate no. 6 are the finest.

Britten

When Vaughan Williams died, in 1958, there was no doubt as to his successor as the leading English composer. Benjamin Britten dominated the postwar scene in British music. As a young man, in the 1930s, he had looked to the European mainland more readily than most English had done: he was impressed by Berg and Bartók, and by Stravinsky. From

---

Benjamin Britten   Works
born Lowestoft, 1913; *died* Aldeburgh, 1976

Operas Peter Grimes (1945), The Rape of Lucretia (1946), Billy Budd (1951), Gloriana (1953), The Turn of the Screw (1954), A Midsummer Night's Dream (1960), Death in Venice (1973)

Church parables Curlew River (1964), The Burning Fiery Furnace (1966), The Prodigal Son (1968)

Orchestral music Variations on a Theme of Frank Bridge (1937); Sinfonia da Requiem (1940); Four Sea Interludes and Passacaglia from "Peter Grimes" (1945); The Young Person's Guide to the Orchestra (1946); Cello Symphony (1963); Piano Concerto (1938)

Choral music A Boy was Born (1933); Hymn to St Cecilia (1942); A Ceremony of Carols (1942); Spring Symphony (1949); Cantata academica (1959); War Requiem (1961)

Vocal music (with orchestra) Our Hunting Fathers (1936); Les illuminations (1939); Serenade (1943); Nocturne (1958)

Song cycles Seven Sonnets of Michelangelo; The Holy Sonnets of John Donne (1940); Canticles I–V (1947–74); Winter Words (1953); Songs and Proverbs of William Blake (1965); The Poet's Echo (1965)

Chamber music string quartets – no. 1 (1941), no. 2 (1945), no. 3 (1975); Six Metamorphoses after Ovid for oboe (1951); Cello Sonata (1961); 3 cello suites

Piano music   *Folksong arrangements*   *Incidental music*

them he drew his vital, elegant style, his brilliant technique and, at times, satirical wit –
exemplified in his *Variations on a Theme of Frank Bridge* for string orchestra (1937). Also
from this period is the song cycle *Les illuminations*, to words by the French symbolist poet
Arthur Rimbaud, for high voice and string orchestra (1939). Here Britten sets the original
French, as later he was to set Michelangelo in Italian, Hölderlin in German and Pushkin
in Russian.

The approach of war in 1939 led Britten to emigrate to the USA. However, he became
homesick, and the feeling was sharpened by his discovery of the subject for a more
ambitious work: he read an article on George Crabbe, like himself from the county of

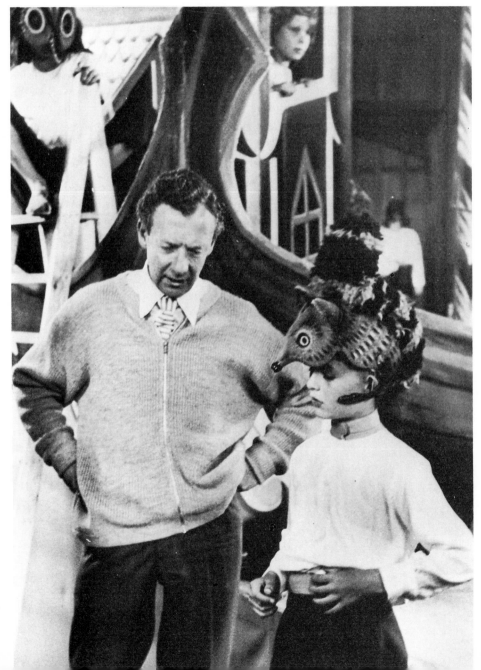

114   Benjamin Britten
and a Squirrel during a
rehearsal for *Noyes Fludde*,
Aldeburgh, 1958.

Suffolk, and author of the verse tale *Peter Grimes*. He returned to England in 1942 and in 1944 began the composition of his opera on the subject. *Peter Grimes* is the story of a man hounded by small-town society because he cannot contain his violence, and because he is an "outsider": it can readily be understood as a metaphor for Britten's own feeling of being an outcast because of his sexual orientation. Its first performance in London, soon after the victory in Europe in 1945, reawakened English opera after a long dormant period.

The role of Peter Grimes was the first of many that Britten wrote for his lifelong companion Peter Pears, for whom he had already composed his settings of Michelangelo and his *Serenade*, an anthology of English verse for tenor, horn and strings. Pears's distinctive voice – a razor-sharp lyric tenor of unusual expressive potential – colors almost the whole of Britten's output from this point onwards. The *Serenade* shows the depth of Britten's feeling for English verse – its sounds, its rhythms, above all its meaning, expressed in the rich imagery of the tenor line, fluid and wilful, and the pointed, poetic writing for the solo horn and the string orchestra. The poems range from a fifteenth-century dirge to Tennyson's Romantic vision in "The splendour falls on castle walls", with its mysterious echoing fanfares. Other songs treat the subject of evening and darkness more lightly, except for the setting of Blake's Elegy, a haunting miniature about the worm at the heart of the rose, the rottenness that is buried within beauty and can eat it away and destroy it (see Listening Note X.F).

Britten's only important orchestral score of the next 30 years was his Cello Symphony (1963), written for Mstislav Rostropovich, also the dedicatee of a sonata and three suites for cello. Other instrumental works were occasional or else written, like the Rostropovich pieces, for friends. Songs, too, Britten composed with particular performers in mind: chiefly Pears, with whom he regularly gave recitals. Pears was also one of the intended soloists for his biggest choral work, the *War Requiem* (1961), written for performance in the rebuilt Coventry Cathedral in memory of the dead of World War II, and adding a

---

Listening Note X.F   *Side 12, band 1*

Britten: *Serenade* op. 31 (1943), "Elegy"
solo tenor, solo horn
1st violins, 2nd violins, violas, cellos, double basses

This is the third movement of a song cycle setting English poems of the fifteenth to nineteenth centuries. Here the poem is by William Blake.

> O Rose, thou art sick;
> The invisible worm
> That flies in the night,
> In the howling storm,
> Has found out thy bed
> Of crimson joy;
> And his dark, secret love
> Does thy life destroy.

Time
0:00	first section of orchestral introduction
0:31	introduction continues ...
0:58	last part of introduction lingers ...
1:31	tenor takes over horn's role ...
2:12	horn re-enters for a repeat of section 0:05 to 1:30
3:40	the coda has the horn ...
3:58	(end)

personal melancholy by the insertion of war poems, often ironic in tone, by Wilfred Owen amid the traditional, impersonal ritual of the Latin Mass for the dead.

Otherwise the major works were all operatic. For the Royal Opera House in London Britten wrote *Billy Budd* (1951) on Herman Melville's story of an innocent seaman, the victim of envy and injustice, his starkest large-scale opera score, and since the action unfolds on an eighteenth-century man-o'-war, the cast is all male. But Britten came to prefer working with a small troupe of a few singers and a dozen instrumentalists, the English Opera Group, for whom he wrote a series of chamber operas, culminating in *The Turn of the Screw* (1954) on a story by Henry James – a chilling study of childish fantasy and one of his most theatrically effective works.

Britten's work in opera, and with chosen performers, centered on the festival he established in 1948 in the Suffolk coastal town of Aldeburgh. Many of his works had first performances there, including his adaptation of *A Midsummer Night's Dream* (1960), his three "church parables", which in somewhat Stravinskian fashion fall between opera and Japanese *nō* drama (1964–68), and his last opera, *Death in Venice* (1973), which provided Pears with one last star part as the German writer Thomas Mann's character, Aschenbach, infatuated with a boy.

Since 1945

Though the careers of many composers extend across World War II – Stravinsky, Shostakovich, Carter, Copland and Britten, among those already mentioned – 1945 is a useful boundary. Bartók and Webern died in that year, Schoenberg soon after, and the next years saw the first acknowledged works of the Frenchman Pierre Boulez, the German Karlheinz Stockhausen and others who were to play leading roles in the development of music. Even composers active before the war went through periods of stylistic change in the postwar years when serialism began to gain widespread attention.

Messiaen

In Europe the center for radical musical ideas of the late 1940s and early 1950s was the class at the Paris Conservatoire of Olivier Messiaen (b. 1908). At that time he was an organist-composer more concerned with the mysteries of the Catholic faith and the marvels of modality than with new techniques. His subsequent career has proved his readiness to bring into his music the fruits of his inquisitiveness. From stable foundations in the "church modes" he has gone on to incorporate serialism, rhythms calculated according to the patterns of ancient Indian music or Greek verse, dense harmonies chosen with his eye for the "color" of sounds, birdsongs collected in the field and transcribed, even sacred messages coded in musical notation. All these are applied, ultimately, to the celebration of the mysteries of the church, the central force behind Messiaen's music. They come into play in his hugely extended, hugely virtuoso meditation on the Christ child, *Twenty Glimpses of the Infant Jesus* (1944; see Listening Note X.G).

Such materials could not be accommodated in smooth, continuous forms. Messiaen's structures are made up of blocks, often in alternation or symmetrically arranged. His textures tend to be heterophonic rather than homophonic or contrapuntal, with several different levels of activity: this is particularly true of his orchestral works, such as the *Turangalîla-symphonie* (1948).

The title is made up of two Sanskrit words ("rhythm" and "play" or "love"). Messiaen

Olivier Messiaen
born Avignon, 1908

Works

Orchestral music L'ascension (1933); Turangalîla-symphonie (1948); Oiseaux exotiques (Exotic birds, 1956); Chronochromie (1960); Couleurs de la cité céleste (1963); Et exspecto resurrectionem mortuorum (1964); Des canyons aux étoiles (1974)

Choral music Trois petites liturgies de la Présence Divine (1944); La Transfiguration de Notre Seigneur Jésus-Christ (1969)

Vocal music Poèmes pour Mi (1936, later orchestrated); Harawi, chant d'amour et de mort (1945)

Piano music Vingt regards sur l'enfant Jésus (1944); Catalogue d'oiseaux (1956–8); two pianos – Visions de l'amen (1943)

Organ music Le banquet céleste (1928); L'ascension (1934, version of orch. work); Le nativité du Seigneur (1935); Le corps glorieux (1939); Livre d'orgue (1951); Méditations sur le mystère de la Sainte Trinité (1969)

Instrumental music Quatuor pour le fin du temps (Quartet for the end of time, 1940)

Opera St François d'Assise (1983)

Listening Note X.G   *Side 12, band 2*

Messiaen: *Vingt regards sur l'Enfant-Jésus* (1944), no. 18 ''Regard de l'onction terrible''
piano solo

The ''Regard de l'onction terrible'' (''Glimpse of the dreadful anointment'') is one of 20 pieces that make up a two-hour cycle of meditations on the Child Jesus.
The entire form can be represented as
X–A–A–B–A–C–A–B–A–A–C–X

Time
0:00	right hand climbs down chromatic scale
0:53	main subject a chorale, ex. i, based on symmetrical mode, ex. ii
	(the numbers indicate the size of the intervals in semitones)
1:24	repeat of preceding section, chorale in different mode
1:55	variations of *a* and *b* fragments of chorale
2:41	further repeat of 0:53–1:24
3:11	variations of *c*
3:59	repeat 0:53–1:24, transposed up a minor 6th
4:30	repeat of 1:55–2:41, transposed up a minor 6th
5:15	repeat of 0:53–1:24, transposed up an octave
5:44	varied repeat of preceding section
6:14	varied repeat of 3:11–3:59
7:30	reversal of the introductory section
	(end)

ex. i

ex. ii

115 Olivier Messiaen collecting birdsong, 1961.

has described this ten-movement work as a *Tristan* symphony, and in certain of the movements, notably the sixth, "Garden of the sleep of love", he is not afraid to wallow in lush string music. The co-existence of the mathematical (in the rhythmic structures) and the erotic is frequent in Messiaen: he praises God both as architect of the universe and as creator of the human body as his choicest work.

The *Turangalîla-symphonie* summarizes Messiaen's early manner. But the symphony also looks forward to the serialism in which Messiaen was soon to interest himself, following up the interest of Boulez and others of his pupils. Beginning here, he applies serialism to rhythm by making successions of durations chosen from an arithmetical series (e.g. from one to 12 thirty-second notes), and then performing serial operations of reversing and so on. The furthest he went in this direction was in his *Mode of durations and volume* for piano, a crystalline mixture of three lines passing through series of pitches, rhythmic values and dynamic levels.

This had an enormous influence on Boulez and Stockhausen. For Messiaen himself it was an isolated event and his least characteristic work. He soon turned to birdsong for his material, used almost exclusively in the *Catalogue d'oiseaux* (1956–8), a collection of impressions of different birds in their habitats around France, worked into substantial pieces each representing 24 hours' activity.

Messiaen sees himself as a musician-theologian who expounds the truths already revealed to the church. In his immense *La Transfiguration* (1969), for example, each of the 14 movements is an illustration of a text from the New Testament or St Thomas Aquinas. Though the range of reference is intensely personal – including birdsong along with the complex rhythmic apparatus, percussion ensemble, color chords, evocations of nature and modality – the usual building-block forms convey a sense of inevitability and objectivity.

Boulez

It is a measure of Messiaen's qualities as a teacher, as it is of Schoenberg's, that his pupils have not simply been imitators. Thus Pierre Boulez (b. 1925) has been able to learn much from Messiaen's calculated approach to rhythm, his vibrant piano writing and his scoring for percussion, but in harmony and form his style is wholly different.

At an early stage Boulez became a serialist, while drawing on a Schoenbergian turbulence; he soon moved on to "total serialism", applying serial principles to elements like rhythm, loudness and color, notably in *Structures* for two pianos (1952). Then he moved towards a different kind of elaboration, in which flexibility in time, ornamentation and sudden violence return. The climax of this came in *Le marteau sans maître* (1955), a setting of three short, surrealist poems by René Char, consisting of nine movements (the songs are interleaved with instrumental commentaries), for contralto voice, alto flute, viola, guitar, vibraphone, large xylophone and unpitched percussion. The tone colors recall Debussy and Schoenberg, but also Asian and African music. Yet the style is Boulez's own, with fast tempos, clear and brittle sounds, highly intricate structures (too fast-moving for the ear to grasp) and an expressive manner in which excitement is conveyed with complete coldness.

This taste is evident in his next completed major work, *Pli selon pli* (1962), a portrait of Mallarmé, the symbolist poet, for soprano and an ensemble strong in pitched percussion. The gestures are larger and some of the nervous energy is replaced by a flexibility deriving from Boulez's introduction of choice for his performers (for example in options over the order of sections). He has completed few compositions since *Pli selon pli*, though many have been begun: Boulez sees music as the proliferation of simple basic ideas in a variety of directions, so composition may be easier to begin than to finish. But in the 1960s and 70s he devoted much of his time to conducting and in the 1980s he has chiefly been occupied in running a computer-music studio in Paris. His first work from there, *Répons*, suggests a reawakening of creative vitality and a feeling – inherited from Varèse – that only the advent of sophisticated electronic equipment could allow music to move forwards.

Stockhausen

The involvement of Karlheinz Stockhausen (b. 1928) with electronic music has been more continuous than Boulez's, though both began at the Paris studio of Pierre Schaeffer (b. 1910). Schaeffer was the first to create effective electronic music from recordings in 1948, and his studio became a center of *musique concrète*, made out of recorded natural sounds (see p. 278). Boulez and Stockhausen both found the techniques too primitive.

Stockhausen found a more congenial studio in Cologne, where in 1953–4 he composed two studies which are among the first pieces of music realized entirely by electronic means (that is, the sounds are electronically synthesized, not recorded from nature). No less significant, though, was his *Kontra-Punkte* for ten players (1953), in which he reached beyond the single events of the earlier works to take charge again of note groupings. His pre-eminence was secured by three works of the mid-1950s: *Gesang der Jünglinge* ("Song of the Youths"), a brilliant tape piece merging a treble soloist into textures of synthetic sound (see Listening Note X.H); *Gruppen* ("Groups"), which divides an orchestra into

Listening Note X.H   *Side 12, band 3*

Stockhausen: *Gesang der Jünglinge* (1956), opening sequence

This is a piece of electronic music, composed on tape in the studios of West German Radio. There is no published score, but the source materials are usually clearly identifiable as a boy's voice and electronically generated sounds. The boy sings words from the canticle *Benedicite, omnia opera*, in German translation.

Preiset (*or* Jübelt) den (*or* dem) Herrn, ihr Werke alle des Herrn:	O all ye works of the Lord, bless ye the Lord:
lobt ihn und über alles erhebt ihn in Ewigkeit.	praise him and magnify him for ever.
Preiset den Herrn, ihr Engel des Herrn:	O ye angels of the Lord, bless ye the Lord:
preiset den Herrn ihr Himmel droben.	O ye heavens, bless ye the Lord.
Preiset den Herrn, ihr Wasser alle die über den Himmeln sind:	O ye waters that be above the firmament, bless ye the Lord:
preiset den Herrn, ihr Scharen des Herrn.	O all ye powers of the Lord, bless ye the Lord.
Preiset den Herrn, Sonne und Mond:	O ye sun and moon, bless ye the Lord:
preiset den Herrn, des Himmels Sterne.	O ye stars of heaven, bless ye the Lord.
Preiset den Herrn, aller Regen und Tau:	O ye showers, and dew, bless ye the Lord:
preiset den Herrn, alle Winde.	O ye winds of God, bless ye the Lord.

Time
0:00   purely electronic sounds
0:10   boy's voice heard in the distance, singing the word "jübelt".
0:29   boy soloist on the left, followed by an artificial "chorus" on the right.
1:01   a new chorus on the left, followed by soloist: "Preiset den Herrn".
1:29   choral entry on the left, then a pair of soloists, right, around the words "ihr Scharen des Herrn".
1:44   choruses across the sound picture.
1:57   a soloist in the middle: "Preiset den Herrn"; then short section recalling events already heard.
2:42   a solo n emerges, then recedes as electronic flourishes enter.
3:01 n returns in electronic facsimile, and the music becomes slower; solo voices contribute words.
4:19   (end: about a third of the composition.)

116   Karlheinz Stockhausen at his electronic control panel.

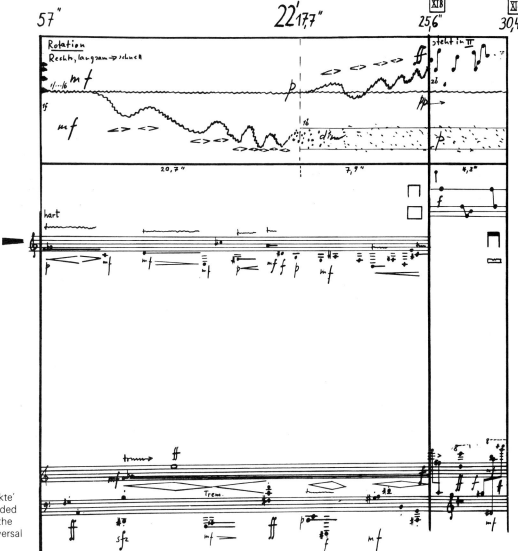

117 A page from Stockhausen's 'Kontakte' (the part for pre-recorded tape is symbolized at the top of the page). Universal Edition.

three ensembles situated around the audience, their music sometimes separate, sometimes joined; and *Piano Piece XI*, in which the soloist decides the order of the provided fragments. The culmination of this period of parallel electronic and instrumental exploration came in *Kontakte* ("Contacts") for piano, percussion and tape (1960), where "The known sounds ... function as traffic signs in the unbounded space of the newly discovered electronic sound-world". Stockhausen's score gives no more than an impression of the electronic part, and the work depends not only on sound but on space: on various levels of events seeming to take place behind the loudspeakers, on the rotation of sounds around the audience, and on the contrast between the placing of the piano-percussion sounds and the imaginary location of the electronic ones.

Kontakte is characteristic of Stockhausen's work in its emphasis on the collaboration of live and electronic components. Equally characteristic is the way the music achieves a form from a process, in this case one of sound transformation. Stockhausen's distrust of prescribed, outer form led him to develop the notion of "moment form", in which "moments" were to succeed each other without concern about their succession. But even in the work entitled *Momente*, the moments are arranged according to some pattern of resemblance and change.

During the later 1960s Stockhausen's methods became increasingly free, particularly in his works for his own ensemble including electronic appliances. This culminated in *Aus den sieben Tagen* ("From the Seven Days"), in which the players are provided only with short verbal texts as guides to their musical intuition. Stockhausen then drew back and wrote an hour-long, fully notated score for two pianos and electronics: *Mantra* (1970), his first work created around a melodic theme or formula. As in serialism, the whole composition is built out of a melodic idea by transposition, inversion and other transformations. Typical is *Inori* for orchestra (1974), where the formula is built up and used in various richly harmonized combinations, the whole process seemingly governed by two dancers who go through ritual gestures of prayer on platforms above the players.

Most of Stockhausen's later works offer the same mix of music and drama, ritualized and selfconsciously portentous. *Licht* ("Light"), the large-scale project on which he expects to be working until the end of the century, is a cycle of seven stage works devised to be presented operatically on consecutive evenings. It is concerned with a personal mythology centered on the figures of the Archangel Michael, Eve and Lucifer.

Berio

Luciano Berio (b. 1925) joined the Boulez–Stockhausen circle towards the end of the 1950s. Typically Italian, his music generally shuns angularities in favor of smooth, malleable musical forms, usually led by voices or instrumental soloists. Berio has been concerned with connections between vocal and non-vocal sounds. One of his finest pieces is *Circles* for soprano, harpist and two percussion players (1960), in which the sound and sense of poems by E. E. Cummings circle out of the voice and into the instruments. An important feature is the dramatization of the concert platform; the soprano is required to move nearer the ensemble as their music converges.

118 A page from Berio's 'Circles'. Universal Edition

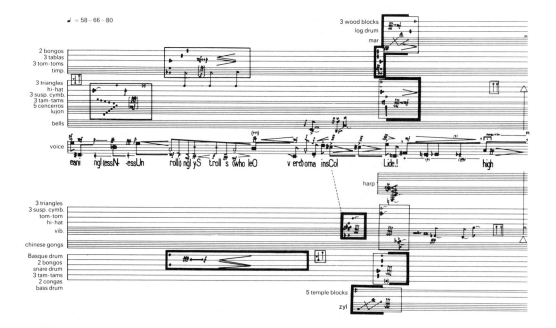

119   Cage's prepared
piano

Even without such imposed activity, Berio's work shows a response to the physical business of making music. His *Sequence* series for soloists are not merely essays in virtuosity but dramatic scenes deploying a soloist, whether comic, frantic or hopelessly trapped. Indeed, Berio's dramatic sense has been more often exercised in concert works than in music for the stage.

Cage

The aims of Boulez and Stockhausen in applying serialism to elements other than pitch in the late 1940s and early 50s were matched in America by Milton Babbitt (b. 1916). Sometimes regarded as Babbitt's precise opposite, John Cage (b. 1912) has spent most of his life trying to free music from mental control. However, besides studying with Cowell (see p. 308), Cage had lessons from Schoenberg in 1934 and wrote some serial compositions. Serialism even contributed, along with his awareness of Balinese and other exotic music, to the repetitious style he developed in works for percussion such as his *First Construction (in Metal)*. He discovered the possibilities of the piano as a one-man percussion ensemble, if miscellaneous objects are placed between the strings: he used the result, the "prepared piano", in various works of the 1940s.

By then Cage had settled in New York, where he was active as a teacher, ballet musician and composer. Partly through his association with other New York composers, partly through his contacts with painters, and partly through his studies of Eastern thought, he wanted to remove from music every trace of personal intention. This led him into a laborious process of coin-tossing to decide the nature and layout of events in his *Music of Changes* for piano (1951). He made *Imaginary Landscape no. 4* (also 1951) still more arbitrary by scoring it for 12 radio sets. Then, in *4' 33"* (1952), he realized a long-cherished ideal in creating a piece that has no sounds at all: the performer sits or stands as if to play, but

John Cage Works
born Los Angeles, 1912

Piano music Metamorphosis (1938); Sonatas and Interludes (1948); Music of Changes (1951); Music for Piano (1952); Seven Haiku (1952); Water Music (1952); Cheap Imitation (1969, later orchestrated)

Percussion music First Construction (in Metal) (1939); Second Construction (1940); Third Construction (1941); Imaginary Landscape nos. 1–5 (1939–52)

Electronic music Fontana Mix (1958); Cartridge Music (1960); Rozart Mix (1965); Bird Cage (1972)

Other music 4'33" (1952); Variations I–VI (1958–66); Music for Carillon nos. 1–5 (1952–67); Musicircus (1967); Atlas eclipticalis (1961); HPSCHD (1969); Quartets I–VIII (1976); Score (40 Drawings by Thoreau) and 23 Parts (1974)

120 An excerpt from Cage's *Atlas Eclipticalis* (Henmar Press/Peters Edition).

nothing is heard except the environmental sounds and any audience reaction. These, in Cage's view, have as much value as anything else: the artist's function becomes that of pointing people towards the potential art surrounding them.

Cage was a pioneer in the involvement of electronics in music-making. His earliest experiments go back to 1939. A mature successor is *Cartridge Music* (1960), for performers amplifying the "small sounds" they can make with objects to hand, using phonograph cartridges to pick them up. Later works use seashells and plant materials.

Another main thrust of Cage's activity has been in the direction of freeing music from the concert. In the 1960s he was responsible for stimulating jamborees bringing together musical performers, video and light shows, and so on. Cage produced few works in the later 1950s and 60s, but in the 1970s he became prolific again, partly in response to a reactivated conscience about the orchestra. As a body of skilled professionals, the orchestra might seem unsympathetic for Cage's music of non-intention and freedom: indeed, a performance by the New York Philharmonic of his *Atlas eclipticalis* (1961), where the parts consist of star maps from which the musicians play as the spirit moves them, had proved disastrous. In *Cheap Imitation* (1972), he tried to provide a model of what an orchestra might be in an age of musical democracy: not ruled by the composer, not swayed by the conductor, but working harmoniously at a common task. In later works for orchestra he has returned to looser forms of notation.

Texture music

The boom in serialism in the early 1950s was a west European and American phenomenon: there was no comparable movement in eastern Europe because of official policy. But in the later 1950s artistic constraints began to be loosened, and in Poland, in particular, the result was a sudden flowering of avant-garde activity, marked by boldly new textures. Witold Lutoslawski (b. 1913), as the most distinguished of Polish composers, played a leading part in this movement; Krzysztof Penderecki (b. 1933) produced some of the most striking effects in music of raw sound.

Lutoslawski's mature style became defined in *Venetian Games* for small orchestra (1961), the first work in which he used "aleatory counterpoint", asking instrumentalists to repeat phrases out of synchronization to generate textures in which details reappear in an atmosphere of constant, teeming change. Almost all Lutoslawski's later works combine sections in "aleatory counterpoint" with fully composed sections, using the latter to steer among the necessarily stationary harmonies of the fluid, dappled passages.

Ways to simplicity

One of the most conspicuous features of music in the 1970s was a seeking after simplicity and uniformity: it may be discerned too in the English composer Maxwell Davies's move from expressionist theater to symphony, or in the greater thematic content of Berio's later music. It is also found in the music of the Greek composer Iannis Xenakis (b. 1922), an originator of "texture music": his *Metastaseis* (1954) was the first work to treat each string player as a soloist in complex waves of glissandos. This sort of mass effect is his abiding concern.

A similar if more refined development can be detected in the music of the Hungarian György Ligeti (b. 1923): struck by the leveling-out when the elements of music are all in processes of rapid change (brilliant detail merges into gray generality), he removed in his *Atmosphères* (1961) all trace of harmony, melodic profile or rhythm, so that the work is compounded entirely of orchestral cluster-chords, constantly shifting in weight and color. Its awesome effect created a sensation and served well in Stanley Kubrick's film *2001* a few years later.

The Minimalists

The clearest indications of the new simplicity are to be found in the music of certain American composers sometimes classified as "minimalists": they include LaMonte Young (b. 1935), Terry Riley (b. 1935), Philip Glass (b. 1937) and Steve Reich (b. 1936). In Reich's music of the late 1960s, for example, the aim is the projection of a simple process of change involving repeating patterns in pure tonal harmony.

There are evident signs, however, that for Reich and his colleagues such simplicity is only a stepping-stone to complexity of another sort, for in later works, such as *Drumming* (1971), Reich has created much more ambitious and complicated processes while retaining the mesmeric intensity of his repetitive rhythm and glowing harmony. It is characteristic of our enigmatic times that this is one of the directions that music is now taking.

Chapter XI

The Traditions of Popular Music

Popular music, or "pop music", means "music of the populace". The term embraces all kinds of "folk" music which, originally made by illiterate people, were not written down. In most societies throughout European history different types of folk music have co-existed, usually in a rural environment, with "art" music, usually centered on courts, aristocratic houses or towns. For many centuries there was give and take between folk and art music, just as there was between a peasant society and an urban one.

The creation of a popular music that aims simply at entertaining large numbers is a product of industrialization, in which music may become a commodity. It is in the rapidly industrialized nations that we first encounter composers who have devoted themselves to fulfilling a demand for entertainment music.

A transition from the old world to the new is represented by the Vauxhall Gardens in London, for which such eighteenth-century composers as Handel supplied music for people seeking relaxation. Although the music was not radically different from that which they composed for more serious occasions, it was on the way to what we now call "easy listening". Early in the nineteenth century, in Britain and still more in America, some composers became professionally occupied with the production of popular pieces which may be defined according to their social purpose: music for the chapel, the bar and eating-house, the pleasure-garden and music hall, the parlor. We may further define them in terms of the needs they serve; they encourage hedonism (physical delight in the present) and nostalgia (sentimental regret for the past). These areas of experience, which continue to feature in popular music, are not necessarily discreditable. People need forms of escape. And even in an industrial community the borderline between "art" and "entertainment" is hazy.

That is particularly true of what might be described as religious music. A Mass by Byrd, in Shakespeare's England, or a cantata by Bach in Lutheran Germany, is an act of worship that embraces man's deepest needs and highest aspirations. One cannot say the same of most Victorian evangelical hymns, the purpose of which is to comfort with a repetitive, predictable tune and to lull with cozy harmonies, marshaled by a four-square beat. Such music reminded laboring people of their humble place while referring to their rewards in Heaven. The music is not insincere, and it may be moving, but emotional impact is usually disproportionate to musical merit. This is even more true of the "escapist" music of the Victorian parlor, which by the later nineteenth century was dedicated to sentimental ballads, or to superficial, brilliant piano pieces of no real technical difficulty or musical substance.

In America, where the production of parlor pianos increased prodigiously during the nineteenth century, the manufacture of music to match became an industry in itself. Charles Grobe, who emigrated from Weimar in 1839, turned out huge quantities of operatic transcriptions and pot pourris, piano arrangements of missionary hymns and military marches, along with dubiously original compositions that extend to opus 1995.

Of the numerous composers of nineteenth–century popular music, three figures stand out. All are "escapist": Foster by nostalgia, Sousa by hedonism, and Gottschalk by a mixture of the two.

Foster

Stephen Foster was born in 1826, near Pittsburgh, an urban industrial community on the edge of the wilderness; the Indians had left but their memory lingered. Foster worked as

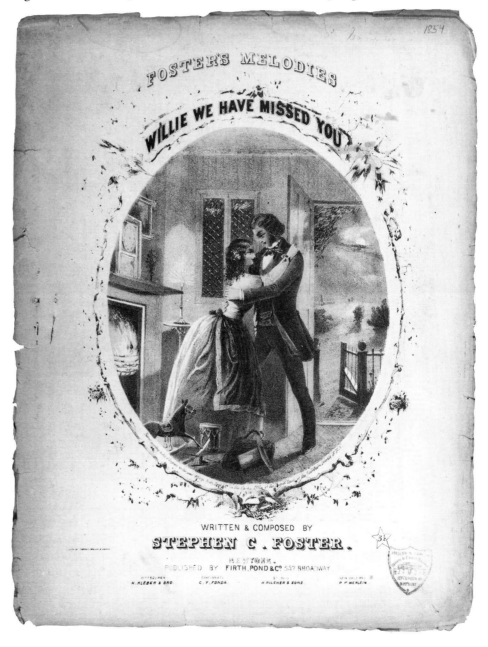

121 Title-page of Stephen Foster's song *Willie we have missed you* (1854).

a journalist, composing songs in his spare time. His aim was to amuse the middle-class public, and those conventions that were handiest and most familiar seemed best. The well-worn clichés were derived from early nineteenth-century British composers, from evangelical hymns and military marches, from Italian Romantic opera and from salon piano music (a reworking of European classical conventions). Foster's public was English, Irish, German and Italian by ancestry, with a heavy leaning towards Puritan heritage.

Foster's "Ethiopian" songs were based not on real black spirituals but on the songs of the Christy minstrel shows. These were an exploitation of the black man by white men with blackened faces, in an idiom closer to English ballad, march and hymn than to black music. The Christy show, with its comic presenter and two stooges armed with tambourine and bones, crystalized the white myth of the wide-grinning black man, lazy yet happy in his innocence. Foster's genius lay in revealing the other side of this myth: the black man, though happy, was also homeless, and therefore sad. His songs tell us that the black man's homesickness is related to the frustration and nostalgia in everyone, especially in a raw industrial city with an uncertain future. All Foster's songs yearn for the "good old days". But their yearning is not innocent, as real folk music is, since they express modern man's consciousness of loss. That is why, in no discreditable sense, they are sentimental and why their technique is at once simple and artificial. The ballad is an artistic contrivance combining elements from English music hall, French waltz and light Italian opera.

In the most celebrated of Foster's "Ethiopian" songs, Old folks at home (1851), the tune is restricted to five tones and the harmony does not depart from the rudimentary tonic, dominant and subdominant of evangelical hymn-books. Yet this song, epitomizing the instinct to return to one's roots, is known all over the world. It owes its obsessive quality to its simplicity: in the phrase repeated four times, a leaping octave is followed by a declining minor 3rd, representing an age-old yearning, while the closing phrase brings us safely to the security of home.

In spite of the appeal of his music, Foster's life was not successful. He was unable to establish relationships, especially with women; after the failure of his marriage he relapsed into alcoholic despair, and died in New York in 1864. The most deeply touching of his songs, Jeanie with the light brown hair (1854), is a dream-image of his lost wife. It is perhaps the only one in which the gracefully undulating melody has the haunting simplicity of a real Scots or Irish folktune, imbued with tender regret in the little cadenza that takes us back to the repeat of the first section, to end with the fleeting sigh of a closing chord of the 13th. The song may bring tears even to sophisticated eyes.

Sousa

At the opposite, "hedonistic" pole stands John Philip Sousa, born in Washington, DC, in 1854. He was the son of a Spanish trombonist in the US Marines band; he refuted the legend that his father's name was originally Antonio So, the "USA" being appended as a tribute to his adopted country, but it should be true, because Sousa had no doubt that although he was a professional composer, his most durable works were his marches for his military band. Inaugurated in 1892, it soon became internationally famous because it epitomized the youthful optimism of America, making the maximum appeal to body and nerves, the minimum to head and heart.

Sousa's marches (except for some late ones) generally follow the same pattern. After four or sometimes eight measures of introduction, the "verse" section falls into two groups of 16 measures. The first, like a classical sonata, modulates to the dominant. After the double bar the second 16 rarely depart from the tonic and are usually broader and more song-like, with richer harmony and a few chromatic passing notes. The "trio" section, derived from the classical minuet, is usually in the more "passive" subdominant and is

122 US Marine Band, c1880, with J. P. Sousa (*front right*).

more lyrical and quieter in rhythm. After its own brief middle section, often more strenuous, the chorus trio is restated, still in the subdominant but very loud.

The most famous of Sousa's marches, *The Stars and Stripes Forever* (1896), represents this type. The four-measure introduction, with its aggressive unison and cocky syncopation, makes us take notice; the verse section proceeds in a jerky triple meter over a swinging bass. When, in the second 16, the bass becomes the top line, transformed into a wide-intervaled tune, a sense of well-being is created. The trio begins in a narrower melodic range. In its final statement, however, animated by a prancing bass and by fierce descending chromatics, its majesty ("molto grandioso") carries all before it. The mixture of sentiment such a piece evokes – private and public, personal and communal, domestic and national – is finely judged, and unified by the design.

Gottschalk

Nostalgia and hedonism, represented by Foster and Sousa, meet in Louis Moreau Gottschalk, who of the three has the closest ties with Europe. Born in 1829 in New Orleans, of German-Jewish-French-Creole descent, Gottschalk was a child prodigy sent to study the piano and composition in Paris, where he was admired by Chopin, Berlioz and Liszt. Back in his native land, he became rather like an American Liszt, traveling the continent publicizing himself, his music and the rapidly expanding American piano industry. He spent his last years in South America, dying there in 1869.

Gottschalk was a man of commerce as much as of art. Drawing on his origins he incorporated into his music elements from black rag, French waltz and quadrille and Spanish habanera; often he used authentic Creole or black melodies for his elegantly pianistic pieces. Even his contributions to the sentimental parlor genre have substance. His greatest hit, *The Last Hope* (1854), treats a Presbyterian hymn-tune with seductive yet disciplined luxuriance. Gottschalk wrote it as a parody of the popular *The Maiden's Prayer*, but he played it, eyes closed, with total dedication. It sold 35,000 copies in a few years and is still in print: it pleases the player in being rewardingly pianistic but not as difficult as it sounds; it pleases listeners in entertaining them while also making them feel good morally.

All Gottschalk's pieces fulfill the prescription for entertainment music while never

123 Caricature of one of Gottschalk's "monster" concerts, performed by 56 pianists and two orchestras at the Teatro Lyrico Fluminse, Rio de Janeiro, 1869.

radically disturbing emotional equilibrium. *Souvenir de Porto Rico* (1857) is a set of variations in the popular convention of the arriving and departing procession. As the band approaches, the "chromatic grapeshot and deadly octaves", with which Gottschalk attracts our attention, fill us with the childish wonder of watching fireworks. But they are for fun. As the procession departs, we know our lives will go on.

That Gottschalk came from the Southern, European-affiliated city of New Orleans is significant; so too is the fact that his music incorporated elements from that of the city's black population. For it provides a transition to jazz.

Blues and ragtime

Though jazz is a twentieth-century phenomenon, mainly associated with cities, its origins were in Africa, in societies quite different from those of the West. Stravinsky's *Rite of Spring*, Bartók's *Cantata profana*, Orff's *Carmina Burana* and many elements in the visual art of such men as Pablo Picasso and Amedeo Modigliani might suggest that there had been a move away from the ego-conscious values of Western civilization from the beginning of the twentieth century. Yet that would not explain why the music of black Africans became a mouthpiece for white men too, throughout the Westernized world. Perhaps we are all, in some ways, if not black and enslaved, at least alienated and dispossessed. The black man's music, in the white man's world, asserted the violence of dispossession, that violence which was exploding in mechanized wars; at the same time it reaffirmed man's roots in the earth and Nature. That is why the techniques of "primitive" music could be transplanted to a strange land.

We have seen in earlier chapters how tonal progression has been used in Western music. The techniques of African music evolved differently. Forms tend to be circular rather than linear, repetitive rather than progressive. Melody is usually basically pentatonic, restricted to the five pitches (paralleled by the black notes on a piano; see p. 14) which for acoustical reasons are the most natural to sing. Almost always, African music avoids leading tones, so the harmonic finality of dominant-tonic cadences is impossible. Textures are not so much polyphonic as heterophonic – several different versions of the same melody are stated simultaneously. The resulting harmony therefore happens by chance.

African music expresses a communal way of life. People dance together. Unlike Western music, when solo voices sing or play they are seeking to lose, rather than to assert, personal identity. The singer is a mouthpiece for his people's culture and history. If he sings of himself or of topical and local events it is to affirm his oneness with the group to which he belongs, or to assuage his distress at having left it.

In his new, white American world the black man, enslaved, used the musical techniques he had been reared on. His wailing cries, on the cotton plantations, in labor camps or in prisons, were virtually unchanged from those he had uttered in his homeland, but his oppressed state lent a sharper edge to the distortions of pitch and flexibilities of rhythm typical of folk music conceived as a single line. He called on ancient vocal formulas of the pentatonic roulade and a tumbling descent from a high note, and on traditional techniques of vocal production – modified because he sang in the American language.

But the black man's African heritage was to suffer a change more radical than one of language. It came into contact, and then conflict, with the musical manifestations of the New World, especially the march and hymn. As we have seen, the hymn followed a pattern of tonic, dominant and subdominant harmony, while the march also provided a four-square beat. When the American black, responding to these types of music, took over the white man's guitar, the blues was born, and with it the heart of jazz.

Blues

There was no decisive break between folk holler and blues. Pete Williams, for instance, a black man in a Southern prison, uses the guitar in what he calls "Levee camp blues", but it is still a holler in which speech is heightened, with the guitar providing a repeated figure. A labor song (intended to be sung during strenuous work), it is metrically more regular and melodically more defined, but the guitar still plays mainly a tonic chord, with only fleeting touches of subdominant and dominant. The subject is the familiar one of the faithless woman. (The words of blues often concern the agony of desertion, betrayal and unrequited love and sexual references are frequent.) The guitar could sing-speak with the intimacy of a human voice, and provide a touch of white harmony to balance the plangent black vocal line. Blues "form" tends to fall into a pattern, as shown:

	a				a′				b′			
Bars	1	2	3	4	5	6	7	8	9	10	11	12
Chords	I————————				IV—		I—		V——		I——	

But the form is not static. It provided a harmonic framework against which the black singer could interpret his words or the instrumentalist could improvise. Thus black melody and white harmony interact.

This interaction may be heard in Robert Johnson's blues *At the crossroads* (1936). Johnson was a neurotic black murdered in 1937 at the age of 21. The rasping timbre of his voice and the contours of the improvised melody are profoundly African. Launching the phrase on a high, pinched note, he "tumbles" wildly from it, while his chittering guitar brokenly attempts to affirm a march-like beat and to establish the tonic, dominant and subdominant fundamentals of white tonality. This is a real 12-bar blues, effecting a compromise between black melody and rhythm and white harmony and meter. But the compromise is agonizing, vocal and instrumental elements cannot fit. Yet the desperate repetitions are still therapeutic. Strength springs from clashes of minor and major 3rd which happen by chance because black pentatonic and modal melody favors the vocally "natural" flat 7th while white guitar harmony prefers the sharpened leading tones appropriate to the closing cadences of the march and hymn. These "false relations" became an important feature of jazz idioms, where they are known as "blue notes".

Ragtime

The basic country blues form came from the Mississippi Delta. The pieces we have discussed are folk rather than popular music; but as black men moved into cities, white elements grew more obtrusive and barriers between folk and pop were scarcely discernible. It is not surprising that American blacks in the early years of the century should have evolved their own version of the white march: ragtime, basically piano music though often played by bands, was the black's attempt to make a "civilized", notated music that could compete with that of his white masters. Significantly, the most celebrated rag composer, Scott Joplin (1868–1917), known as the "King of Ragtime", moved from the South to the urban North. He took his musical convention from the white military two-step, more or less identical with Sousa's march form. But Joplin's music, both in the *Maple Leaf Rag* (1899) that made him famous and in more harmonically sophisticated pieces like *Euphonic Sounds* (1909), has an improvised feel mostly because the rhythms are "ragged" in being syncopated. The manner is dandified but in the music of the best rag composers a wistful vulnerability hides beneath mirth. The music has pathos but not sentimentality.

Piano jazz

Blues and rag meet in the evolution of piano jazz. When blacks came across broken-down pianos in bars they treated them as mechanized guitars, sometimes using them mainly as drone-like backgrounds to song or speech. "Barrelhouse" pianists came to make basic, usually very fast use of 12-bar blues harmony and to seek substitutes for the guitar's expressiveness by way of "crunched' tones, slides and displaced accents. The pianist exploited the power of a percussive keyboard, creating momentum with a pounding left hand, usually in patterns of repeated tones or unequal rhythms that came to be known as boogie basses. Gradually, the piano's capacity for polyphony, harmony and rhythm encouraged barrelhouse pianists to explore complexities of texture as well as to exploit rhythmic force.

Physical exuberance could hardly be carried further than in Mead Lux Lewis's famous *Honky tonk train blues*. Though Jimmy Yancey, a less virtuoso but more expressive Chicago pianist, also played frenetic train pieces, he was one of the few barrelhouse men to specialize in slow blues, achieving music of tough sinew yet of airy grace. His *At the window*, with its fragmented texture and electrically hesitant rhythm, is marvelously moving.

Most early bluesmen were itinerants who made their music at street corners or in bars and brothels. An exception is James P. Johnson, trained in both barrelhouse and ragtime traditions and distinguished for his command of an irresistibly "striding" bass and for the delicate precision of his right-hand figurations. Significantly, he moved to New York to work in white cabaret, even trying his hand at composing symphonies and musicals.

Blues singing

The fusion of blues and rag exemplified in Johnson's playing is crucial to the evolution of jazz, especially during the 1920s. The blues were now centered on traveling shows, and the most revered singers were women. A matriarchal image is fundamental to black American music, since African matriarchy (society ruled by women) offered an alternative to the white patriarchy on which Western culture had been founded. The earliest of the great women blues singers, Gertrude Rainey, received her nickname "Ma" at the age of 18, and she soon began to fulfill a role as Earth Mother and Priestess. Her searing vocal timbre often has a liturgical flavor; despite her secular material, in the early 1920s she worked with guitarists or pianists with church affiliations. Performing the traditional *Boeval blues* or *See, see rider*, she found no barriers between country blues, gospel and minstrel-show music.

Bessie Smith

Bessie Smith (1894–1937), the most famous blues singer of the 1920s, was known as the "Empress of the Blues". With a gargantuan appetite for sex and alcohol, she demonstrated what happened to the blues when it entered the city. Though her musical roots are black, she was a sophisticated performer within her convention and became a committed urban American. As with the finest jazz, her music sprang from tension: between country and town, black and white, art and entertainment.

Like other women blues singers, Smith usually performed not only with a piano and perhaps drums but also in dialogue with a melody instrument which both intensified and depersonalized the vocal line. She gave superb versions of folk blues like *Careless love* and *Reckless love* with Louis Armstrong playing a cornet obbligato, and of her own *Young woman blues* and *Poor man blues* with the cornet of Joe Smith, her favorite collaborator.

Jazz

New Orleans

Since women blues singers worked with jazz players and used conventions from jazz and minstrel show, their work had many features in common with the early jazz band. This began in New Orleans where a lively black population mingled with a cosmopolitan society of white Americans, Frenchmen, Spaniards, Italians and Germans. Blacks played waltzes, quadrilles, polkas and "mazookas" at white junketings, and also played in parade bands. From these cross-fertilizations the New Orleans (or Dixieland) jazz band became established, with instruments from the white military band. Typically, it was a group of five to eight players. The cornet (later trumpet), clarinet and trombone were the main melody instruments. A tuba (later string bass) provided the bottom line, reinforced by percussion. The banjo substituted for the guitar as harmonic fill-in, perhaps because it was easier to play and less "expressive", for jollity rather than pathos was the aim. Later, when bands no longer marched, the piano became the main harmony instrument.

New Orleans band music compromises between the 12-bar blues and a 32-bar form. Sometimes the band played traditional material with folk origins, at others it started from composed numbers, re-creating them in folk style. The musical substance lies in the tension between the military beat and the symmetries of white harmony on one hand, and on the other the black solo lines which, with their African flexibility of pitch and rhythm, try to override the basic form. Each tune is repeated several times, the cornet, clarinet and trombone usually improvising a solo in turn and combining noisily for the last statement.

Louis Armstrong

The supreme New Orleans soloists – Louis Armstrong (cornet and trumpet), Johnny Dodds (clarinet) and Sidney Bechet (soprano saxophone) – attain ecstasy with their soaring improvised melodies. They also imbue their instruments with the expressivity of the voice. This becomes obvious if we compare Armstrong's trumpeting with his gravelly singing. The voice and instrument speak, the body moves: so the heart of the music is in the spoken and unspoken word and in physical movement.

What is remarkable about New Orleans jazz, especially after the players migrated, under economic pressure, north to grimmer cities like Chicago, is that this word–body relationship flourished within the context of Westernized commercial music. We can hear this in the supreme achievements of band jazz, the recordings made by Armstrong with his Hot Five and Hot Seven in 1926–8, for instance *Tight like this* or *West End blues*.

The combination of black folk melody and the harmony of white art music in New Orleans–Chicago jazz is revealed in Armstrong's recording of "King" Oliver's *Weather bird*, which he presents simply as a duet with Earl Hines, the most eminent jazz pianist of the time. We might expect from only two players, rhapsodic improvisation, but we get a sequence of choruses planned to lead to a climax of disrupted repeated notes. The piano part is sometimes melodic and agile, sometimes merely a background to, and inspiration for, the wildly spurting trumpet. The stuttering repeated tones and the rising scale of the coda fuse exaltation and frustration, at once comic and tragic. Since the music has this effect it must, in spite of its basis in undeveloping variation, have some sense of beginning, middle and end. Armstrong and Hines have proceeded from the folk heterophony of early jazz to a true improvised polyphony, which creates tension between melodic direction and harmonic progression.

Armstrong left Chicago for New York, later to embark on a career as a show-business entertainer as well as a jazzman. Such rapprochement was inevitable and has been essential to jazz's development. That becomes clear if we consider those men who, working within black folk traditions while being influenced by white entertainment music, appropriated

124 King Oliver's Creole Jazz Band, early 1920s; Oliver plays the cornet, Louis Armstrong the trombone (*center*), Lil Hardin the piano, Johnny Dodds the clarinet, and "Baby" Dodds the drums.

white elements to their own ends, composing numbers that could serve as bases for improvisation. Jelly Roll Morton, a light-skinned New Orleans black, composed most of the numbers in the convention of the Sousa march and trio and even wrote down 12-bar blues with precise indications of harmony and figuration, if he wanted to modify established patterns. He notated his arrangements but the music involved improvisation and Morton, as pianist-director of his still basically New Orleans ensemble, the Red Hot Peppers, controlled the performance. His music generates passion while managing to sound blithely carefree. Its improvised composition, as distinct from Armstrong's composed improvisation, is an irresistible affirmation of the human spirit.

Duke Ellington

A refinement of Morton's approach occurs in the music of Duke Ellington who, born in Washington, DC, of a modestly genteel black family, worked mostly in New York nightclubs, for a predominantly white audience. If Morton was the first, Ellington was the second jazz composer; he remains the finest. Playing in a politer environment than that of the Chicago bars in which Armstrong and Morton performed, he scored for a bigger band, using a choir of saxophones blending, or playing in contrast, with brass and reeds, supported by string bass and percussion; he directed from or beside the keyboard.

Ellington composed using a 32-bar format more than the 12-bar blues and creating enlivening permutations between them. The more artful quality of his music, compared with Morton's, lies first in the tunes, which are memorable and recognizably his. *Black Beauty* (1928), for instance, has a most touching melody that attains, through an unobtrusive

125 Duke Ellington at the Royal Albert Hall, London, 1967.

irregularity, a delicate balance between innocence and sophistication. Ellington's melodies are inseparable from harmony and scoring and he adds chromatic richness that can plumb our emotions. But the music remains folk improvisation, in tune with the spirit of the blues and profoundly African. Although the sequence of musical events is written down, each is conceived in terms of a member of Ellington's ensemble, singing or speaking in his own voice. In Ellington's band (as in commercial dance-bands), the oily saxophones began to rival the sharper clarinets, enhancing the sensuous colors that smoothe over the hard reality of the blues.

One of the finest examples of the ambiguity between dreamy romanticism and harsher elements is the *Black and Tan Fantasy* (1927). Through an atmospheric background of liquid "creole" clarinet, saxophone and muted brass, the trumpet's 12-bar blues tune, a transformation of the popular anthem *The Holy City*, speaks painfully of the heart's truth. The piece is an elegy of the lost world the black man allegedly cannot inherit, which is why the quotation of Chopin's well-known funeral march in the coda seems appropriate.

Ellington fuses the spirit of New Orleans jazz with the precise realization of art. Compromise between black jazz and white art entails the acceptance of white show business which, in an industrial society, is art's popular manifestation. There are two complementary strands in this process. One develops black jazz into a mechanized power-house; the other combines popular conventions with the escape art of musical comedy. The two streams converge, as did blues, minstrel show and rag in the earlier generation.

American musical

The jazz musicians we have discussed have all been black, indirectly of African descent. The musicians who worked in Broadway theater music were white, mostly of Jewish European ancestry. Musical comedy had its roots in operetta, Viennese, French and English.

One of the earliest and most talented Broadway composers, Jerome Kern, though born in New York in 1885, studied in Europe. When he returned to the USA and to Tin Pan Alley, he did not forget his musical education. He produced his first show in 1912 and during the next 30 years composed such musicals as *Sunny* (1925), *Showboat* (1927) and *The Cat and the Fiddle* (1931).

Even the format of musical comedy steers it towards escapism, since a spoken play with musical interludes has two separate elements: the play, which is naturalistic, and the song-and-dance, which may be thought of as dream. In this, Broadway musical comedy emulates the operettas of such composers as the Strausses and Offenbach. Like those of minstrel show and vaudeville, the themes are either hedonistic or nostalgic. The forms follow a predictable pattern, the tunes constructed within rigidly diatonic, symmetrical eight-plus-eight-measure periods, though the harmony and modulations, especially in the middle eight, may be more adventurous than those of the old minstrel music. Verse and refrain have a relationship similar to that of the main section and the contrasting one in a Sousa march. A faintly jazzy element comes from the syncopated pianism of the black rag. The escapism of musical comedy is not necessarily negative. Men like Kern and Irving Berlin may demonstrate, as had Foster, how dreams may represent our real feelings. We shall understand this better if we consider two composers who represent opposite but complementary poles.

Irving Berlin

Irving Berlin, born in Russia as Israel Baline in 1888, grew up the hard way in the Bowery and lower East Side of New York City. He had no musical training so when he discovered that he had a gift for writing words and tunes he was content to pick out the melody with one finger on the piano, leaving harmonization and notation to a professional.

Berlin's songs have only two themes: an adolescent pleasure in the present and an equally adolescent nostalgia, sometimes tinged with self-pity. In songs like *Top Hat* and *Cheek to Cheek* (from the Ginger Rogers and Fred Astaire musical *Top Hat* of 1935), we can recognize or remember the experience. The tunes, with their narrow range and stepwise movement, more or less sing themselves. Yet this cannot be all there is to them or they could not have retained their appeal over half a century. Berlin acquired some expertise as a composer. He was able to achieve such subtleties as the gradual extension of the repeated phrase in *Cheek to Cheek* until it reaches its highest point on the words "hardly speak". Such songs do not deny that love may hurt; they seek pleasure from the hurt itself and create an illusion that we can live on the surface of our emotions.

Cole Porter

Musical comedy is most convincing when making an ironic point of its illusory nature. Cole Porter (1891–1964), unlike Berlin, the poor boy who made good, was a rich boy who made bad but richer. The cynical title of Porter's musical *Anything Goes* (1934) is typical; so too is the fact that it conveys the mood of the 1930s with carefree irresponsibility, with no trace of the bitterness of current social-political art. There is no positive element in it except the rudimentary boy–girl relationship, as expressed in the song "All through the night". Its tune is merely a descending chromatic scale that, prompting dreamy modulations, induces trance, making the love seem almost too innocent to be true. Porter's chromatics cast an ironic reflection on the diatonic love-songs of Berlin.

The satirical elements in Porter's songs are not sharp. Yet his irony sometimes carries an uneasy honesty that we do not find in later musicals such as Richard Rodgers's *Oklahoma* (1943), though that ostensibly deals with ordinary folk in a commonplace world, or in Rodgers and Hammerstein's *South Pacific* which, affected by World War II, attempts to embrace serious themes.

George Gershwin

Only one composer of Broadway and Tin Pan Alley overrode the illusory nature of the conventions to produce works of genius: George Gershwin (see p. 309). Many songs he contributed to ephemeral musicals have survived in their own right, for example "The man I love", one of many written with his brother Ira as lyricist; it is a song of remarkable melodic, harmonic and tonal subtlety which treats the stock theme of the adolescent dream with irony and compassion, though making no overt departures from Tin Pan Alley. Gershwin's *Porgy and Bess*, dealing with life among New Orleans blacks, started as an ambitious musical, but ended up as a fully-fledged opera exploiting an interplay of speech, recitative, arioso and pop "aria" and exhibiting a musical-theatrical craft to rival Puccini. Within the sophisticated harmonic and orchestral textures Gershwin finds scope for the tunes, which serve their dramatic function while having separate identity as numbers performable in dance-hall or cabaret. Art and entertainment are one, in a tale about corruption, oppression, alienation and the inviolability of a radical innocence of spirit. Gershwin was a poor boy who (neurotically) made good, a Jew who knew about spiritual isolation and had opportunity to learn about corruption. Perhaps he wrote such fresh music because even in the face of temptation he preserved, like Porgy, a modicum of innocence. This is manifest in the radiant lullaby, "Summertime", that opens the opera.

Swing era

That Gershwin's understanding of the black blues was profound is indicated by the fact that his tunes have been favored material for jazz improvisation. *Porgy and Bess* has been given superb jazz treatments by such distinguished musicians as Louis Armstrong and Ella Fitzgerald, Miles Davis and Gil Evans. This provides a link to the evolution of jazz, now both black and white, in the 1930s and 40s: the era of swing, during which the relationship of band to soloists changed. The big white bands were more a part of show business than of jazz. The earliest was Paul Whiteman's, for which Gershwin composed *Rhapsody in Blue*, and to which some of the most talented white jazz wind players contributed; notable among them was Bix Beiderbecke, who produced a sound on his cornet that was characteristically "white" in being pure, clean and vulnerable. Dominating the era of World War II was the big band of Glenn Miller. More interesting musically and sociologically is Benny Goodman, a white clarinetist who directed big and small bands and who looked, from the world of commerce, towards both jazz and art. In his small groups he played with many talented black jazzmen. He also flirted with serious music, as a concerto soloist and as commissioner of jazz works from "straight" composers. It is significant that Goodman, himself a fine musician, was the first white impresario to promote black jazzmen on equal terms.

Count Basie

However, the supreme achievements of jazz during the swing era remain black, notably the Kansas City bands of Count Basie. The Basie band is a successor to the barrelhouse music of the shanty-town piano thumpers; the obliviousness of the city takes over from the deprivation of earlier days. The machine-made energy of the massed brass is now set against the wiry agility of Basie's piano playing. His line and rhythm, though nervously fragmented, are strong as steel. Thus, in *Tickle toe* (1940), his sinewy, boogie-rhythmed piano solo is interrupted by the explosive shouts of brass chords. In the Chicago music of Armstrong and Bechet the soloists' ecstasy soared over the ensembles, leading to the recognition that the individual ought to triumph. In Basie's music, more blues-influenced than Ellington's, the outcome is more dubious. Rhythmic momentum liberates the soloist but at the same time threatens his individuality.

Cabaret singers

The big band era was also the age of the great jazz cabaret singers. Basie worked with male blues "shouters" such as the great Jimmy Rushing, creating a fiercely urban complement to the primitive country blues. He also worked with Billie Holiday, the finest female jazz singer since Bessie Smith, who, restricting herself mostly to pop standards, nonetheless revealed, especially in dialogue with Lester Young, emotional depths beneath the corniest material. In *If dreams come true* (1938), her simple enunciation of the words suggests that she wants to believe, but the lingering phrasing shows that she cannot. Her continually shifting verbal stresses are echoed by Young's saxophone, and she in turn answers his echoes almost instrumentally. Holiday died young, of heroin, but other great cabaret singers of the 1940s and 50s, notably Ella Fitzgerald, Sarah Vaughan and Betty Carter, have carried on performing into the 1980s.

Instrumentalists

The story of jazz has veered between the private and the public. The big band seemed to sell out to a commercial world, yet sometimes discovered in it new identities for the individual. During the 1950s and 60s what came to be called Modern Jazz reverted to private values. A pianist-composer like Thelonius Monk turned his back on his audience as he created a nervously tight, harmonically and tonally contorted revamping of old barrelhouse styles, whether in dialogue with a few brilliantly driving wind and percussion players, or as soloist, in the fragmented austerity of a blues with the pertinent title of *Functional* (1957). Miles Davis, in his "cool" jazz of the 1950s, tempered jazz heat with the muted sonority of his trumpet and with the grave modality of his melodic lines, akin to Spanish flamenco dance. Often he was abetted by the swinging lilt, the lucid chromaticism and the controlled filigree of Bill Evans's piano-playing. Evans was a white man. So is the composer-arranger Gil Evans, with whom Davis collaborated in some of the most beautiful jazz "tone poems" since Ellington, notably the suite derived from *Porgy and Bess* (1958).

Among modern jazz saxophonists Charlie Parker stands supreme, the most inventive and influential jazz soloist since Armstrong. Although he used blues and pop conventions, his rapid chord changes and flexible meter steered jazz improvisation once more towards a linear approach. This is evident too in the playing of Stan Getz, a white man who experiments in Latin-American as well as Afro-American idioms; and in that of John Coltrane and Ornette Coleman, who revealed relationships between country blues and the melodic arabesques of Indian and other Asiatic music. Players of the percussive and harmonic piano did not avoid Parker's influence either.

White country music

Black jazz began as the music of an alien people in a vast industrial land. Originally a minority activity, in its true forms it has remained one. In the eighteenth and nineteenth centuries white settlers on the American continent brought their folk music with them, and it too has been transformed into an industry: the pop music known as country and western. The music originated in the Eastern states, where emigrants from Britain had sung their old songs, rendered more rasping by the tough conditions of pioneer life. Even in the mid-twentieth century this is evident in the singing of men and women living in remote areas of the Carolinas, Kentucky and Virginia. The instrumentalists, who made music not so much to alleviate loneliness as to stimulate communal activity, transformed their models more radically. Georgian, Arkansas and Virginian fiddlers such as Fiddlin' John Carson played Scots and Irish reels with wild abandon, making a music of almost manic cheerfulness. To keep their spirits up, the old music had to be defused of pain and passion – and therefore, to a degree, of truth.

This provided a recipe for pop or entertainment music. Whereas such singing is folk music, the fiddling of the 1920s string bands abandons everything to hedonism. This euphoria is no less evident in the banjo and guitar pickers who often support the fiddlers or play European-based dance music, or accompaniments to songs, some derived from British sources, others newly invented. Fiddle and plucked string music tends to be fast, regular in meter and diatonic. The modal inflections of folk music are banished, though they occasionally creep back through the influence of the singing and playing of itinerant blacks. The musical interest of this functional music for dancing increases with such influence.

Bluegrass

Some fiddlers and string players formed bands such as the Skillet Lickers or the North Carolina Ramblers. The music they made in the 1920s and 30s was still a medley of British songs and dances drained of hurtful elements and seasoned with American hymnody, march and ballad, with exotic intrusions from new and old Mexico and from French Louisiana. At first it was still folk music in that, played by amateurs, it served the community's needs. During the 1940s it became more streamlined, exploitable on radio and recording. It was named "bluegrass" in homage to its Eastern mountain origins.

Bluegrass music was performed by a lead singer who also played the guitar, banjo or mandolin, vigorously supported by other players of guitar, banjo and harp, with an interlacing of fiddles. Tunes were fast and diatonic; in the work of the legendary Flatts and Scruggs, breathtaking virtuosity may bring a whiff of danger, and therefore of nervous reality, to the cozy themes of hearth and home, mother, love and duty. There may be a hint of desperation in the way in which the most melancholy local events – railway accidents, hangings etc – are recounted with glee. One finds something similar in the more jazz-influenced string bands that, in the 1940s, came to be known as "western swing".

Carter Family

Some of these musicians were not merely itinerant entertainers but stars on the radio networks. So were the Carter Family, a Virginian mountain family centered on A. P. Carter, who collected and arranged hymns and ballads and sang quavery bass in the vocal trio. This was led by the low, rasping voice of his wife Sarah; Maybelle, musically the most gifted, played banjo, fiddle, lute, autoharp and guitar. All the Carters' songs, whatever their origin or theme, are in moderate-to-fast tempo, regular meter and unsullied diatonicism. Enunciation is flat, tone pinched, whether the numbers are based on British ballads, gospel hymns or parlor songs in barbershop harmony. The Carters' importance is attributable to their incorruptible integrity: though commercialized, they were little changed between the 1920s and the 1950s.

Country music became an industry in which those opposite poles of pop music, hedonism and nostalgia, were identified. Mountain girls like Dolly Parton and Lacy J. Dalton have become pop stars, without destroying the folklike creativity from which they started.

Rock

The rock explosion that occurred in the wake of World War II was an attempt to re-create music as orgiastic magic. White country music, having become an industry, tried to absorb the life-giving primitivism of black jazz. Black–white integration worked both ways. Black culture was now eager to take advantage of white technology to boost its self-confidence. From this emerged what came, appropriately, to be called soul music: the passion and pain of black gospel music and of the blues are given greater punch by electric rather than acoustic guitars and keyboards, in powerful amplification.

The most distinguished soul singers – Otis Redding and James Brown, Nina Simone and Aretha Franklin – maintain contact with black folk traditions both in their vocal production and jazz-oriented rhythm and phrasing, and also in their use of gospel-style antiphony between lead voice and backing group. Also, in the 1960s blacks established their own record-producing industry, based in Detroit, manufacturing their own style, called Motown. This fast, regular-metered, cheerily diatonic music, reflecting the black's self-assurance, is best represented by Diana Ross and her Supremes. It is a mechanized version of the appeal typical, half a century earlier, of ragtime, a black music that had sprung from competition with whites. The sound of Motown has been widely imitated.

But the emergence of rock and roll was a white phenomenon, in that young whites listened to black rhythm and blues out of frustration with their society. It is possible to see Elvis Presley as a successor to the country singer Hank Williams. Both were Southern, with an evangelical background; both were nervously distraught. Williams composed most of his own material in an idiom related to that of the Carter Family, though with a touch of the black blues that gave a darker shade to the hymn-like and ballad style. He found a pleasurable zest in the sincerity of his corniness, reflected in his transitions between country waltz and blues, folk fiddle and electric guitar. His songs of disappointed love spring from the same emotion that informs his devotional songs.

Occasionally the black elements in Williams's songs, reinforced by the electric beat, guide him towards early Presley-style rock and roll, as in *Move it on over*.

Born a decade later than Williams, Presley responded to a small-town background far more rebelliously. Whereas Williams created his own songs, Presley at first used other people's manners to evoke a narcissistic image. Dressed extravagantly, he brought it off because he had ability.

Heartbreak Hotel, the number that brought him instant fame in 1956, was in origin a Southern country song. He sings it lyrically, inviting us to take the love experience straight. At the same time he undermines it by rhythmic displacements derived from the triple drag-style of piano boogie and by conscious pitch distortions suggested by gospel singing. But his ecstasy became sexual rather than godly. The two poles of his nature – white dream-maker and black rebel – were both attempted escapes. Slowly he succumbed to drink and drugs.

As rock music developed it took from gospel music the concept of the group. The rock group reached its climax not in the USA but in traditionally conservative Britain. The Rolling Stones, whose heyday was in the 1960s, represent the closest approach pop has made to an orgiastic music comparable with that created in tribal societies. This is seen in the group's singer Mick Jagger's Africanized yelling and bodily gyrations, as well as in the fact that he adapted much material from black bluesmen. The Rolling Stones' electric guitars and keyboards are vastly amplified versions of blues guitar, country harmonica, bagpipes and autoharp. Amplification intensifies primitivism, since electronics may create a nightmarish inflation of the pitch distortions typical of folk music. Percussion is more violent than real tribal drumming because it is metrically cruder and in amplification rendering one deaf as well as stunned. Breaking the sound barrier may become not a permissive euphoria but a destructive force. Primitive pentatonic melody relies mainly on the driving beat for its momentum; harmony, as in tribal music, is minimal or non-

Hank Williams

Elvis Presley

Rolling Stones

126 Elvis Presley in the film *Jailhouse Rock*, 1957.

existent. This may be observed too in "hard" American rock groups such as Grateful Dead and the drug-oriented Velvet Underground. Although language plays a part, it is mostly inaudible or, if audible, negative.

The celebrants at a concert by the black Jimi Hendrix, who identified his musical with his sexual instrument, regarded his violent magnificence as prelude to an affirmative act. The same might be said of the music of The Who, even as they concluded their performance by burning their instruments. Later more unorthodox groups like the Mothers of Invention offered a purgative experience in which song, dance, acrobatics, mime and clowning combine with narcotics and with what is usually called obscenity.

Sometimes attitudes are more benign. Groups such as the Moody Blues, Pentangle and Steeleye Span were triggered off by European folk-cults and the comic play of the Italian *commedia dell'arte*. Medieval and Renaissance techniques meet those inherited from folk styles of many cultures. From such fusions of techniques, both straight and electronic, springs a world of fairy-tale. The gentle modal tunes and sonorities imply a return to the child within us. Militantly hard rock and dreamily soft folk both opt out of a society considered hostile because materialistic. Yet both depend on that society.

Music-theater, rock musicals

In the 1960s there was a return, if in simple form, to the Greek concept of music-theater ritual. This is also demonstrated in the "tribal musicals" of which Galt McDermott's *Hair* (1969) was the first to achieve artistic as well as material success, offering a hippy's purification from the enemies, war and society, by way of freedom, sex and drugs. The same theme and structure appear in The Who's *Tommy* and in Andrew Lloyd Webber's *Jesus Christ Superstar*. The use of multiple media – word, sound, movement, lighting – and of improvisation and audience participation means involvement rather than passive reception. Most pop concerts have become theater ritual in this sense. Audiences no longer tolerate a pop concert without visual as well as audible appeal.

The Beatles

The most successful group in pop history, the Beatles, was the best. Their quality depended on the fact that, although they represented their culture, they made songs of pronounced individuality. The return to origins in the basic beat, the often modal tunes, the side-stepping harmonies, were given a location and a name. American blues and country music interlaced with British hymn and music hall in the memorable melodies. The innocence of the early, wide-eyed *I saw her standing there* (1963), the unsentimental nostalgia of *Yesterday* (1965), the witty pathos of *Eleanor Rigby* (1966), the magical mystery of *Strawberry Fields Forever* (1967), are all beyond the range of time and tarnish. With *Sergeant Pepper's Lonely Hearts Club Band* (1967) the Beatles made the first self-contained cycle prompted by the long-playing disc; they explored with instinctive verbal articulateness and in fresh, original music the problems of adolescence: loneliness, fear, friendship, sex, the generation gap, alienation, nightmare. They could do this because, although a group, they were four individuals, two of whom, John Lennon and Paul McCartney, had immense creative gifts. The cycle is about "A Day in the Life" of any young person, and the contrast between the tender pentatonic tune with which the song opens and the inhumane hubbub that simulates the atomic bomb remains potent and poignant.

127 The Beatles recording *Day Tripper*, 1965.

Bob Dylan

Alongside tribal pop has flourished the music of solo performers, who affirm the validity of the individual spirit. With the Beatles, Bob Dylan is probably the most remarkable pop musician. He has consistently written his own words and music. Opting out from college and the Establishment, he became a spokesman for American youth, starting from the minimal conventions of white country music and black blues. He at first castigated a sick society in "protest" songs in part inspired by those of his master, Woody Guthrie. Variations of pitch and inflection were part of the composition.

The social validity of Dylan's songs is deepened when he moves from protest to self-confrontation. This is initiated in *Mr Tambourine Man* (1965) which, related to white hillbilly music rather than to blues, looks like an escape from life to dream, and in a sense it is, in that a tambourine man is a dope pedlar. In the next phase Dylan uses rich poetry that prompts comparably rich permutations of country music and blues, calling on electric technology in the process. In *John Wesley Harding* (1968) he abandons this gadgetry, returning to his country roots and acoustic guitar; but the verses now have a fundamentalist Christian background. Dylan's gospel songs contain some of his blackest music, close to pentatonic yell and tumbling strain, abrasive in vocal production.

Joni Mitchell

It is not surprising that some of the finest singing poet-composers should be women. Joni Mitchell matriarchally complements Dylan's white-Jewish-black patriarchy. The pathos of her verses in early songs like *To a seagull* and *Margie* (1968) flows into modal tunes and empirical, guitar-derived harmonies that sound at once hopeful and vulnerable. In *Mingus* (1979), named after the neurotically brilliant composer-performer Charles Mingus who made the record with her, the fusion of her white lyricism with black jazz's vivacity brings rich dividends. Latterly, Mitchell's songs embrace white folk, black jazz and South American music with a ghost of the aboriginal Amerindians.

Dylan and Mitchell are not alone in these travelings through space and time. Among others are Randy Newman, whose musical spontaneity complements the rigor of his verbal wit; Tom Waits, the gravel-voiced bard of late-night New York bars; Bruce Springsteen, rockstar of "the darkness at the edge of town"; and the West Indian Bob Marley, who gave international status to his people's pop music, reggae (a Caribbean derivative of soul and Motown), and so became a national political hero. Among the women is another West Indian, the British Joan Armatrading, whose creative intensity is in part attributable to her ethnically varied roots; and Tania Maria, another hybrid, dazzling alike as jazz pianist and as a singing composer in an idiom somewhere between a New York jazz club and the Rio bars she came from.

128 Bob Dylan at Slane, July 1984.

Further Listening

The Listening Notes throughout the book (listed in the contents pages) treat in detail certain representative works or movements which should be listened to above all. The first priority for further listening should be the remaining movements of works of which only one or two are discussed in the Listening Notes. The lists below, which correspond with the arrangement of the historical chapters in the book, offer suggestions of works that may appropriately be used for following up. Most of them are mentioned, and some are discussed, in the text; all are relevant to points made in the text, nearly all are readily available in good recordings. And all should give pleasure to the listener.

Chapter IV
Any examples of plainsong
VITRY *Impudenter/Virtutibus* (motet)
MACHAUT *Douce dame jolie* (virelai)
DUNSTABLE *Veni sancte Spiritus* (motet)

Chapter V
DUFAY *Ave regina coelorum* (motet); Mass *Se la face ay pale*
BINCHOIS *Filles à marier* (chanson)
OCKEGHEM *Ma bouche rit* (chanson)
JOSQUIN *Ave Maria . . . virgo serena* (motet); *Mille regrets* (chanson)
JANEQUIN *Le chant des oiseaux* (chanson)
LASSUS *Salve regina, mater misericordiae* (motet); Lamentations
PALESTRINA *Tu es Petrus* (motet); *Missa Papae Marcelli*
VICTORIA Mass *Laetatus sum*
GIOVANNI GABRIELI *In ecclesiis* (motet)
GESUALDO Responsories; *Deh, coprite il bel seno* (madrigal)
BYRD Mass in Four Voices; *Sing joyfully* (anthem); *This sweet and merry month of May* (madrigal); *The Carman's Whistle* for virginals
MORLEY *Now is the month of maying* (madrigal)
WILBYE *Draw on, sweet night* (madrigal)
GIBBONS *O clap your hands* (anthem); *The silver swan* (madrigal)
DOWLAND *Lachrimae* (fantasia for strings)

Chapter VI
MONTEVERDI Vespers (1610); *Lamento d'Arianna*; *Chiome d'oro* and *Zefiro torna* (madrigals)
CARISSIMI *Jephte* (oratorio) (*excerpts*)
SCHÜTZ *Veni, sancte Spiritus* (motet); *St Matthew Passion*
PURCELL *Come, ye sons of art* (ode); *My heart is inditing* (anthem)
LULLY *Te Deum*; *Armide* (*excerpts*)
COUPERIN Harpsichord music, e.g. *Les barricades misterieuses*, *Soeur Monique*
CORELLI Concerto grosso in g op. 6 no. 8, "Christmas"
VIVALDI *Gloria* in D; Violin Concertos, *The Four Seasons*, op. 8 nos. 1–4
DOMENICO SCARLATTI Harpsichord sonatas
TELEMANN *Musique de table* (*excerpts*)
BACH Toccata and Fugue in d for organ; Brandenburg Concerto no. 5 in D; Partita no. 1 in B♭; Cantata no. 80, *Ein feste Burg*; *St Matthew Passion* (*excerpts*)
HANDEL *Water Music*; Organ Concerto (e.g. op. 4 no. 4 in F); *Giulio Cesare* ("Julius Caesar") (*excerpts*); *Jephtha* (*excerpts*)

Chapter VII
GLUCK *Orfeo ed Euridice* (*excerpts*)
HAYDN String Quartet in f op. 20 no. 5; Symphony no. 44 in e; *The Creation* (*excerpts*)
MOZART String Quartet in G K387; String Quintet in C K515; Symphony no. 40 in g K550; *Die Zauberflöte* ("The Magic Flute") (*excerpts*)

BEETHOVEN Piano Sonata in c op. 13, "Pathétique", String Quartet in F op. 59 no. 1; Symphony no. 5 in c; Symphony no. 9 in d, "Choral" (finale); String Quartet in a op. 132; *Fidelio* (*excerpts*)

Chapter VIII

SCHUBERT Songs, e.g. *An die Musik* ("To Music"), *Der Erlkönig* ("The Erlking"), *Die Forelle* ("The Trout"), *Heidenröslein* ("The Little Rose in the Heather"), *Tod und das Mädchen* ("Death and the Maiden"); *Wanderer* Fantasia for piano; Symphony no. 9 in C, "Great C major"

MENDELSSOHN Overture *A Midsummer Night's Dream*; Symphony no. 4 in A, "Italian"

SCHUMANN Piano Concerto in a; *Carnaval* for piano

CHOPIN Nocturne in E♭ op. 9 no. 2; Ballade no. 1 in g op. 23; Waltz in D♭ op. 64 no. 1

LISZT Piano Sonata in b

BERLIOZ *Fantastic Symphony*

ROSSINI *Il barbiere di Siviglia* ("The Barber of Seville") (*excerpts*)

VERDI *Rigoletto* and *La traviata* (*excerpts*)

WAGNER *Die Meistersinger* ("The Mastersingers") (*excerpts*)

BRAHMS Violin Concerto; Clarinet Quintet

Chapter IX

TCHAIKOVSKY *Romeo and Juliet* (overture)

MUSSORGSKY *St John's Night on the Bare Mountain*

RIMSKY-KORSAKOV *Sheherazade*

RACHMANINOV Piano Concerto no. 2 in c

SMETANA *Vltava*

DVOŘÁK Symphony no. 9 in e, "From the New World"; String Quartet in F op. 96, "American"

JANÁČEK *Katya Kabanova* (*excerpts*)

BRUCKNER Symphony no. 7 in E

MAHLER Symphony no. 4 in G

STRAUSS *Der Rosenkavalier* (*excerpts*)

SIBELIUS Symphony no. 5 in E♭

ELGAR Variations on an Original Theme "Enigma"

FAURÉ *Requiem*

DEBUSSY *La cathédrale engloutie* (Préludes, i)

RAVEL *La valse*

PUCCINI *Tosca* (*excerpts*)

Chapter X

SCHOENBERG *Verklärte Nacht* ("Transfigured Night")

BERG Violin Concerto

WEBERN Symphony op. 21

STRAVINSKY *The Rite of Spring*

BARTÓK Music for Strings, Percussion and Celesta; String Quartet no. 4

HINDEMITH *Mathis der Maler (suite)*

WEILL *The Threepenny Opera* (*excerpts*)

IVES *The Unanswered Question*

COWELL String Quartet no. 4, "United"

VARÈSE *Hyperprism*

COPLAND *Appalachian Spring*

CARTER String Quartet no. 1

VAUGHAN WILLIAMS Fantasia on a Theme by Thomas Tallis

PROKOFIEV *Romeo and Juliet*

SHOSTAKOVICH Symphony no. 5

BRITTEN *Peter Grimes* (*excerpts*)

MESSIAEN *Turangalîla-symphonie*

STOCKHAUSEN *Kontakte*

CAGE *4′ 33″*

BERNSTEIN *West Side Story* (*excerpts*)

LUTOSLAWSKI *Venetian Games*

Further Reading

Below is listed a selection of books which should help the reader who wants to look more deeply into any particular topic. The reference books contain fuller bibliographies which may usefully be followed up. Publication dates are normally those of the most recent edition.

There exist numerous biographies and other studies of individual composers. Here we confine ourselves mainly to the rather factual biographies in the *New Grove* series (largely reprinted from *The New Grove Dictionary*), which have comprehensive lists of works and full bibliographies. Other composer studies are cited only when they have something rather different to offer on a major figure; similarly, a number of non-biographical books (including the subject's own writings) are listed where they afford particular insights.

In the "Composers" section below, studies treating groups of composers are listed first, then books on individual composers in chronological order by composer.

Reference

The New Grove Dictionary of Music and Musicians, ed. Stanley Sadie (Washington, DC: Grove's
  Dictionaries; London: Macmillan, 1980)
Harvard Dictionary of Music, ed. Willi Apel (Cambridge, Mass. and London: Harvard UP, 1973)
Baker's Biographical Dictionary of Musicians, ed. Nicolas Slonimsky (New York: Schirmer; Oxford:
  Oxford UP, 1985)
The New Oxford Companion to Music, ed. Denis Arnold (New York and London: Oxford UP, 1983)

Special topics

INSTRUMENTS
Anthony Baines, ed.: *Musical Instruments through the Ages* (Baltimore and Harmondsworth: Penguin,
  1966)
Robert Donington: *Music and its Instruments* (New York and London: Methuen, 1982)
Sybil Marcuse: *A Survey of Musical Instruments* (New York: Harper & Row; Newton Abbot: David
  & Charles, 1975)
Mary Remnant: *Musical Instruments of the West* (New York: St Martin's; London: Batsford, 1978)

ELEMENTS, FORM
See individual subject articles in *The New Grove Dictionary of Music and Musicians* and the *Harvard
  Dictionary of Music* (cited above)

AMERICAN MUSIC
Charles Hamm: *Music in the New World* (New York and London: Norton, 1983)
H. Wiley Hitchcock: *Music in the United States: a Historical Introduction* (Englewood Cliffs, NJ, and
  London: Prentice-Hall, 1974)

JAZZ
James Lincoln Collier: *The Making of Jazz* (New York: Houghton, Mifflin; London: Granada, 1978)
Donald D. Megill and Richard S. Demory: *Introduction to Jazz History* (Englewood Cliffs, NJ, and
  London: Prentice-Hall, 1984)
Paul Oliver, Max Harrison and William D. Bolcom: *Ragtime, Blues and Jazz* [The New Grove]
  (New York: Norton; London: Macmillan, 1986)

OPERA
Donald Jay Grout: *A Short History of Opera* (New York: Columbia UP, 1965)
Earl of Harewood, ed.: *Kobbé's Complete Opera Book* (New York and London: Putnam, 1972)
Joseph Kerman: *Opera as Drama* (New York: Vintage, 1956)
Stanley Sadie, ed.: *Opera* [The New Grove] (New York: Norton; London, Macmillan, 1986)

NON-WESTERN MUSIC

William P, Malm: *Music Cultures of the Pacific, the Near East, and Asia* (Englewood Cliffs, NJ, and London: Prentice-Hall, 1977)

Bruno Nettl: *Folk and Traditional Music of the Western Continents* (Englewood Cliffs, NJ, and London: Prentice-Hall, 1973)

Elizabeth May, ed.: *Music of Many Cultures: an Introduction* (Berkeley, Los Angeles and London: U. of California Press, 1980)

History

GENERAL

Gerald Abraham: *The Concise Oxford History of Music* (New York and London: Oxford UP, 1980)

Edith Borroff: *Music in Europe and the United States: a History* (Englewood Cliffs, NJ, and London: Prentice-Hall, 1971)

Donald Jay Grout: *A History of Western Music* (New York: Norton; London: Dent, 1974)

Paul Henry Lang: *Music in Western Civilization* (New York: Norton; London: Dent, 1941)

PERIODS

Richard H. Hoppin: *Medieval Music* (New York and London: Norton, 1978)

Howard Mayer Brown: *Music in the Renaissance* (Englewood Cliffs, NJ, and London: Prentice-Hall, 1976)

Claude V. Palisca: *Baroque Music* (Englewood Cliffs, NJ, and London: Prentice-Hall, 1981)

Charles Rosen: *The Classical Style: Haydn, Mozart, Beethoven* (New York: Norton; London: Faber, 1972)

Leon Plantinga: *Romantic Music* (New York and London: Norton, 1985)

Gerald Abraham: *A Hundred Years of Music* (Chicago: Aldine; London: Duckworth, 1974)

William W. Austin: *Music in the Twentieth Century* (New York: Norton; London: Dent, 1966)

Nicolas Slonimsky: *Music since 1900* (New York: Scribner, 1971)

Eric Salzman: *Twentieth-Century Music: an Introduction* (Englewood Cliffs, NJ, and London: Prentice-Hall, 1974)

Paul Griffiths: *A Concise History of Modern Music from Debussy to Boulez* (New York and London: Thames & Hudson, 1978)

Paul Griffiths: *A Guide to Electronic Music* (New York and London: Thames & Hudson, 1979)

John Vinton, ed.: *Dictionary of Contemporary Music* (New York: Dutton; London: Thames & Hudson, 1974)

Composers

MIDDLE AGES, RENAISSANCE, BAROQUE

David Fallows: *Dufay* [Master Musicians] (London: Dent, 1983)

Joseph Kerman and others: *High Renaissance Masters* [Byrd, Josquin, Lassus, Palestrina, Victoria; The New Grove] (New York: Norton; London, Macmillan, 1984)

Denis Arnold and others: *Italian Baroque Masters* [Monteverdi, Cavalli, Frescobaldi, A. and D. Scarlatti, Corelli, Vivaldi; The New Grove] (New York: Norton; London: Macmillan, 1984)

Joshua Rifkin and others: *North European Baroque Masters* [Schütz, Froberger, Buxtehude, Purcell, Telemann; The New Grove] (New York: Norton; London: Macmillan, 1985)

Malcolm Boyd: *Bach* [Master Musicians] (London: Dent, 1984)

Christoph Wolff and others: *The Bach Family* [The New Grove] (New York: Norton; London: Macmillan, 1983)

Winton Dean: *Handel* [The New Grove] (New York: Norton; London: Macmillan, 1982)

CLASSICAL

Jens Peter Larsen: *Haydn* [The New Grove] (New York: Norton; London: Macmillan, 1982)

Wolfgang Hildesheimer: *Mozart* (New York: Farrar, Straus & Giroux, 1982; London: Dent, 1983)

Stanley Sadie: *Mozart* [The New Grove] (New York: Norton; London: Macmillan, 1982)

Emily Anderson, ed.: *The Letters of Mozart and his Family*, 3rd edn. (New York: Norton; London: Macmillan, 1985)

Maynard Solomon: *Beethoven* (New York: Schirmer; London: Cassell, 1977)
Alan Tyson and Joseph Kerman: *Beethoven* [The New Grove] (New York: Norton; London: Macmillan, 1983)
Joseph Kerman: *The Beethoven Quartets* (New York: Knopf; London: Oxford UP, 1967)

ROMANTIC
Nicholas Temperley and others: *Early Romantic Masters I* [Chopin, Schumann, Liszt; The New Grove] (New York: Norton; London: Macmillan, 1985)
John Warrack and others: *Early Romantic Masters II* [Weber, Berlioz, Mendelssohn; The New Grove] (New York: Norton; London: Macmillan, 1985)
Philip Gossett, Andrew Porter and others: *Masters of Italian Opera* [Rossini, Bellini, Donizetti, Verdi, Puccini; The New Grove] (New York: Norton; London: Macmillan, 1983)
Deryck Cooke and others: *Late Romantic Masters* [Bruckner, Brahms, Wolf, Dvořák; The New Grove] (New York: Norton; London: Macmillan, 1985)
Michael Kennedy and others: *Turn of the Century Masters* [Strauss, Sibelius, Mahler, Janáček; The New Grove] (New York: Norton; London: Macmillan, 1984)
Maurice J. E. Brown: *Schubert* [The New Grove] (New York: Norton; London: Macmillan, 1982)
Hector Berlioz: *Memoirs*, ed. David Cairns (New York: Knopf; London: Gollancz, 1969)
Leon Plantinga: *Schumann as Critic* (New York: Da Capo, 1976)
John Deathridge and Carl Dahlhaus: *Wagner* [The New Grove] (New York: Norton; London: Macmillan, 1983)
Barry Millington: *Wagner* [Master Musicians] (London: Dent, 1984)
Julian Budden: *Verdi* [Master Musicians] (London: Dent, 1985)
John Warrack: *Tchaikovsky* (New York: Scribner; London, Hamish Hamilton, 1973)

TWENTIETH CENTURY
Oliver Neighbour and others: *Second Viennese School* [Schoenberg, Berg, Webern; The New Grove] (New York: Norton; London: Macmillan, 1983)
László Somfai and others: *Modern Masters* [Bartók, Stravinsky, Hindemith; The New Grove] (New York: Norton; London: Macmillan, 1984)
Edward Lockspeiser: *Debussy: his Life and Mind* (London: Cassell, 1962)
Charles Rosen: *Arnold Schoenberg* (New York: Viking; London: Boyars, 1975)
Arnold Schoenberg: *Style and Idea*, ed. Leonard Stein (New York: St Martin's; London: Faber, 1984)
John Kirkpatrick, ed.: *Charles E. Ives Memos* (New York: Norton; London: Calder & Boyars, 1972)
Robert Craft: *Stravinsky: Chronicle of a Friendship* (New York: Vintage; London: Gollancz, 1972)
John Cage: *Silence: Lectures and Writings* (Middletown, CT: Wesleyan UP; London: Calder & Boyars, 1961)

Glossary of Musical Terms

Works given in capitals refer to other glossary entries. Page references are given for terms discussed more fully in the main text of the book.

absolute music Music with no extra-musical association or PROGRAM.

a cappella A Latin term, applied to choral music without accompaniment.

accent The emphasizing of a note in performance.

acciaccatura A "crushed" note, sounded just before the main one, used as a musical ornament.

accidental A sharp, flat or natural sign occurring during a piece, temporarily altering the pitch of a note.

adagio Slow; a slow movement.

aerophone A generic term for a wind instrument.

air A simple tune for voice or instrument; also AYRE.

aleatory music Music in which chance or randomness is an element (pp. 278, 325).

allegretto Less quick than allegro; a movement in moderately quick tempo.

allegro Quick; a movement in lively tempo.

allemande A moderately slow Baroque dance in quadruple meter, often the opening movement of a SUITE; also *almain, almand* etc.

alto 1 A female voice with a range lower than a soprano, or a high male voice (p. 25). **2** A term used for an instrument whose range is analogous to the alto voice, e.g. alto saxophone; hence *alto clef,* used by the viola.

andante At a moderately slow pace; a movement in moderately slow tempo.

andantino A little faster than andante.

answer A musical phrase that responds to one previously heard, particularly in a fugue.

anthem A choral work in English for performance in church services; a *national anthem* is a patriotic hymn.

antiphony Music in which two or more groups of performers are separated to create special effects of echo, contrast etc; hence *antiphonal.*

appoggiatura A "leaning" note, usually a step above (or below) the main note, creating a DISSONANCE with the harmony, used as a musical ornament.

arco A direction to bow rather than pluck the strings of a string instrument.

aria An air or song for solo voice with orchestra, usually part of an opera, cantata or oratorio (p. 56).

arioso A style of singing between RECITATIVE and ARIA.

arpeggio The notes of a chord sounded in succession rather than simultaneously.

Ars Nova A Latin term, meaning "new art", used for the new style of fourteenth-century French and Italian music (p. 67).

art song A composed, written-down song (as opposed to a folksong).

atonality Without TONALITY, not in any KEY; hence *atonal.*

augmentation The lengthening of time values of the notes of a melody (usually by doubling them), particularly of a medieval *cantus firmus* or a fugue subject.

augmented interval An interval that has been increased by a semitone (p. 15).

avant-garde A French term used to describe composers (also artists and writers) whose work is radical and advanced.

ayre An English song (or air) for solo voice with lute or viols (p. 56).

bagatelle A short, light piece, usually for piano.

ballad A traditional song, often with a narrative; hence *ballad opera,* which has spoken dialogue and uses popular tunes.

ballade 1 An instrumental piece in narrative style, usually for piano. **2** A medieval polyphonic song form.

ballata A late thirteenth- and fourteenth-century Italian poetic and musical form.

ballett A Renaissance part song with a dance-like rhythm and a "fa-la" refrain; also *balletto.*

bar MEASURE.

baritone A male voice with a range between a tenor and a bass (p. 25).

barline The vertical line marking off one MEASURE from the next.

bass 1 A male voice with the lowest range (p. 25). **2** An instrument of bass range, or the lowest of a group of instruments, e.g. bass clarinet; hence *bass clef,* used by bass instruments and a pianist's left hand. **3** The lowest-pitched part of a piece of music, the basis of the harmony.

basse danse A medieval and Renaissance court dance, usually in slow triple meter.

basso continuo The term for which the more commonly used CONTINUO is an abbreviation.

beat The basic pulse underlying most music (p. 16).

bel canto A style of singing, particularly in Italian opera, that allows the voice to display its agile and sensuous qualities; hence *bel canto opera.*

binary form The form of a piece of music with two sections, *AB* (p. 46).

blues A type of black American folk or popular music (p. 332).

bourrée A fast Baroque dance in duple meter with a quarter-note upbeat.

break In jazz, a short solo passage (usually an IMPROVISATION) between passages for ensemble.

bridge 1 A linking passage in a piece of music. **2** The part of a string instrument over which the strings pass.

cadence A progression of notes or chords that gives the effect of closing a passage of music (p. 18).

cadenza A virtuoso passage (sometimes an IMPROVISATION) towards the end of a concerto movement or aria.

canon A type of polyphony in which a melody is repeated by each voice or part as it enters (p. 23).

cantata A work for one or more voices with instrumental accompaniment (p. 57); hence *church cantata,* with a sacred text (p. 55).

cantus firmus A Latin term, meaning "fixed song", used for a borrowed melody on which composers from the late Middle Ages onwards based polyphonic compositions (p. 45).

canzona A short sixteenth- and seventeenth-century instrumental piece.

capriccio A short instrumental piece; also *caprice*.

chaconne A moderate or slow dance in triple meter, usually with a GROUND BASS.

chamber music Music for a chamber (or small room) rather than a hall; hence music played by small groups – duos, trios, quartets etc (p. 51).

chance music ALEATORY MUSIC.

chanson The French word for "song", used specifically for French medieval and Renaissance polyphonic songs (p. 56).

chant PLAINSONG.

characteristic piece A short piece, usually for piano, representing a mood or other extra-musical idea; also *character piece*.

chorale A traditional German (Lutheran) hymn-tune.

chorale prelude An organ piece based on a chorale.

chord The simultaneous sounding of two or more tones (p. 20).

chordophone A generic term for a string instrument.

chorus 1 A choir. **2** The music a choir sings. **3** The REFRAIN of a song.

chromatic Based on an octave of 12 semitones rather than a DIATONIC scale; hence *chromaticism*, *chromatic scale*, *chromatic progression* (p. 14).

clef The sign at the beginning of the staff that indicates the pitch of one of its lines and therefore determines all of them; hence *treble clef*, *alto clef*, *tenor clef*, *bass clef* (p. 13).

coda An Italian term, meaning "tail", used for a movement's closing section added as a rounding-off rather than an integral part of the form.

coloratura A rapid, decorated style of singing, often high-pitched.

common time 4/4 time, i.e. four quarter-notes in a measure (p. 17).

compound meter A meter in which the unit beats are divisible by three (e.g. 6/8), unlike SIMPLE METER (p. 17).

con brio With spirit.

concertino 1 The small group of soloists in a CONCERTO GROSSO. **2** A small-scale concerto.

concerto Originally, a work (vocal or instrumental) with effects of contrast, but now a work in which a solo instrument is contrasted with a large ensemble or orchestra; hence *solo concerto* (p. 50).

concert overture An overture written as a self-contained concert piece, not as the opening of a larger work.

consonance An interval or chord that sounds smooth and harmonious, as opposed to a dissonance; also *concord* (p. 21).

continuo 1 A term (abbreviated from *basso continuo*) for a type of accompaniment played, usually on a keyboard or a plucked instrument with or without a sustaining instrument, from a notated bass line to which figures may have been added to indicate the required harmony. **2** The group of instrumentalists playing a continuo part.

contralto A female voice with a range lower than a soprano (p. 25).

counterpoint The simultaneous combination of two or more melodies, or POLYPHONY; hence *contrapuntal* (p. 22).

countersubject A subsidiary theme played simultaneous with the subject of a fugue (p. 129).

countertenor A male voice with the highest range, similar to that of an alto (p. 25).

courante A moderately fast Baroque dance in triple meter, often the second movement of a SUITE; also *corrente*.

crescendo Getting louder.

cyclic form A form in which themes recur in more than one movement of the same work.

da capo An Italian term, meaning "from the head", placed at the end of a piece as an instruction to the performer to repeat the first part of the music up to a given point; hence *da capo aria* (p. 56).

development The process of developing (expanding, modifying, transforming etc) themes and motifs; the section of a movement in which development takes place (p. 47).

diatonic Based on a major or minor scale rather than a CHROMATIC one; hence *diatonic scale* (p. 14).

diminished interval An interval that has been reduced by a semitone (p. 15).

diminuendo Getting quieter.

diminution The shortening of time values of the notes of a melody (usually by halving them).

dissonance An interval or chord that sounds rough, not harmonious like a consonance; also *discord* (p. 21).

dominant The fifth step or degree of the scale (p. 19).

dotted note In notation, a note after which a dot has been placed to increase its time value by half (p. 17).

double 1 Lower in pitch by an octave; hence *double bass*. **2** A VARIATION.

double bar A pair of vertical lines to mark the end of a piece or a substantial section of it.

downbeat The accented beat at the beginning of a measure, indicated by a downward stroke of a conductor's stick, and sometimes anticipated by an UPBEAT.

duo A work for two performers (or a group who play such a work); also *duet*.

duple meter A meter in which there are two beats in each measure (p. 16).

duplet A pair of notes occupying the time normally taken by three of the same note value.

dynamics The gradations of loudness in music (p. 23).

electronic music Music in which electronic equipment plays a part.

electrophone A generic term for instruments that produce their sound by electric or electronic means.

ensemble 1 A small group of performers. **2** A number in an opera or large choral work for two or more solo singers (p. 56). **3** The quality of coordination in a performance by a group.

episode An intermediate passage, e.g. a section of a fugue or a rondo between entries of the subject.

étude The French term for a STUDY.

exposition The first section of a work, particularly of a movement in sonata form, in which the main themes are stated (p. 47).

expressionism A term borrowed from painting and literature for music designed to express a state of mind.

fanfare A ceremonial flourish for trumpets or other brass instruments.

fantasia In the Renaissance, a contrapuntal instrumental piece; later, a piece in free, improvisatory style; also *fantasy*, *phantasia*, *fancy*.

fermata The sign (𝄐) indicating that a note or rest should be prolonged; also *pause*.

figured bass A system of notating the harmonies in a CONTINUO part.

finale The last movement of a work or the closing ensemble of an act of an opera.

flat In notation, the sign (♭) indicating that the pitch of a note should be lowered by a semitone; also *double flat* (♭♭) (p. 14).

florid A term used to describe a melody that is highly ornamented; also *fioritura*.

form The organization or structure of a piece of music (p. 44).

forte, fortissimo (f, ff) Loud, very loud.

French overture A piece in two sections (a pompous, jerky introduction followed by a fugue) that originated in the late seventeenth century as an introduction to an opera or ballet.

fugato A passage in fugal style.

fugue A type of composition (or a technique) in which imitative polyphony is used systematically (p. 48).

galant A term for light, elegant, tuneful eighteenth-century music of no great emotional weight (p. 146).

galliard A lively sixteenth- and early seventeenth-century court dance in triple meter, often paired with a PAVAN.

gavotte A fast Baroque dance in quadruple meter, beginning on the third beat of the measure, often a movement of a SUITE.

Gebrauchsmusik A German term, meaning "functional music", used in the 1920s for music with a social or educational purpose.

Gesamtkunstwerk A German term, meaning "total art work", which Wagner used for his later music-dramas in which music, poetry, drama and the visual arts were unified in his concept.

gigue A fast Baroque dance usually in compound meter, often the last movement of a SUITE; also *jig*.

glissando A rapid instrumental slide up or down the scale.

Gregorian chant A repertory of PLAINSONG associated with Pope Gregory I, during whose reign chants were categorized for use in the Roman Catholic church (pp. 45, 62–3).

ground bass A bass melody repeated several times while upper parts have varying music (p. 48).

group A group of themes in a sonata form exposition; hence *first group, second group* (p. 47).

harmony The combination of tones to produce chords, and the relationship of successive chords; hence *harmonic, harmonize* (p. 20).

harmonics The sounds heard together when a tone is produced by a vibrating string or air column, through its vibration in parts (two halves, then thirds etc); hence *harmonic series*.

heterophony A texture in which several different versions of the same melody are stated simultaneously; hence *heterophonic*.

hocket A medieval technique of staggering rests and short phrases between two or more voices to give a "hiccup" effect.

homophony A texture in which the parts generally move together, a melody with accompanying chords; hence *homophonic* (p. 22).

hymn A song of praise, usually in several stanzas, sung congregationally.

idée fixe A term used by Berlioz for a recurring theme in his symphonic works (p. 212).

idiophone a generic term for instruments that, when they are struck, produce the sound themselves.

imitation A polyphonic technique in which the melodic shape of one voice is repeated by another, usually at a different pitch; hence *imitative counterpoint* (p. 22).

impressionism A term borrowed from painting to describe music that is intended to convey an impression (often of natural phenomena) rather than a dramatic or narrative idea.

impromptu A short piece, usually for piano, that suggests improvisation.

improvisation Spontaneous performance without notated music, but often with reference to a tune or chord progression.

incidental music Music composed as a background to, or interlude in, a stage production (see p. 198).

indeterminacy The compositional principle of leaving elements to chance (ALEATORY MUSIC) or at the discretion of the performer.

interval The distance between two notes (p. 15).

inversion 1 The rearrangement of the notes of a chord so that the lowest note is no longer the fundamental one. **2** The performance of a melody "upside-down", with the intervals from the starting note applied in the opposite direction.

isorhythm A fourteenth-century technique whereby a scheme of time-values is repeated, usually to a plainsong melody; hence *isorhythmic motet* (p. 67).

Italian overture A piece in three sections (fast – slow – fast/dance) that originated in the early eighteenth century as an introduction to an opera or other vocal work.

jig GIGUE.

Kapellmeister The German term for the musical director of a prince's private chapel or other musical establishment.

key 1 The TONALITY and major or minor scale of a passage of music according to the note to which it is gravitating; hence *key note* (pp. 18, 45). **2** The lever depressed by the player on a keyboard instrument.

key signature The group of sharp or flat signs at the beginning of each staff indicating the KEY (p. 19).

largo, larghetto Slow and grandly, slightly less slow; a slow movement.

lai A medieval song form.

leading tone The seventh degree of the scale, a semitone below the tonic, to which it therefore gives a feeling of leading.

legato Smoothly, not STACCATO, indicated by a SLUR.

leger lines Small extra lines above or below the staff for notes too high or low to be accommodated on the staff itself; also *ledger line* (p. 13).

leitmotif A German term, meaning "leading motif", used (chiefly by Wagner) for a recognizable theme or musical idea that symbolizes a person or a concept in a dramatic work (p. 227).

lento Very slow.

libretto The text of an opera (or oratorio), or the book in which the text is printed.

lied The German word for "song", used specifically for nineteenth-century German songs for voice and piano; plural *lieder* (pp. 58, 187).

madrigal A Renaissance secular contrapuntal work for several voices that originated in Italy and later also flourished in England (p. 56).

maestro di cappella The Italian term for the musical director of a prince's private chapel or other musical establishment.

Magnificat The hymn to the Virgin Mary, often set to music for liturgical use.

major The name given to a SCALE in which the distance from the first note to the third is four semitones, applied to keys, chords, intervals (pp. 15, 19).

manual A keyboard played with the hands, as opposed to a pedalboard, chiefly used with reference to the organ and harpsichord.

Mass The main service of the Roman Catholic church, frequently set to music for liturgical use (pp. 54, 61–3).

mazurka A Polish dance in triple meter.

measure A metrical division of music marked off by vertical lines (barlines); also *bar* (p. 16).

Meistersinger A member of a guild of German merchant musicians which flourished from the fourteenth century to the seventeenth.

melisma A group of notes sung to the same syllable; hence *melismatic*.

mélodie A French word for "song", used specifically for nineteenth- and twentieth-century French songs for voice and piano.

melody A succession of notes of varying pitch with a recognizable shape or tune; hence *melodic* (p. 17).

membranophone A generic term for instruments that produce their sound from stretched skins or membranes.

meter The grouping of beats into a regular pulse; hence *metrical* (p. 16).

metronome A device (mechanical or electrical) that sounds an adjustable number of beats per minute; hence *metronome mark*.

mezzo- Half, medium; hence *mezzo-forte* (*mf*), *mezzo-piano* (*mp*).

mezzo-soprano A female voice with a range halfway between a soprano and a contralto or alto (p. 25).

Minnesinger The German equivalent of a TROUBADOUR.

minor The name given to a SCALE in which the distance from the first to the third notes is three semitones, applied to keys, chords, intervals (pp. 15, 19).

minuet A moderate dance in triple meter, often a movement of a Baroque SUITE and later the third (occasionally second) movement of Classical forms like the symphony, string quartet and sonata.

mode A term used to describe the pattern of tones and semitones within an octave, applied particularly to the eight church modes used in the Middle Ages; hence *modal, modality* (p. 19).

moderato At a moderate pace.

modulation The process of changing from one KEY to another in the course of a piece (p. 19).

monody A term for music consisting of a single line, applied to the type of accompanied song that flourished in Italy around 1600 (p. 99).

monophony A single line of melody without accompaniment, as opposed to polyphony; hence *monophonic* (p. 65).

motet A polyphonic choral work, usually with a Latin text, for use in the Roman Catholic church, that was one of the most important forms from the thirteenth century to the eighteenth (pp. 55, 67).

motif A short, recognizable musical idea; also *motive*.

motto A brief motif or phrase that recurs during a work.

movement A self-contained section of a larger composition.

music-drama Wagner's term for his later type of opera.

musique concrète Music in which real (or "concrete") sounds are electronically recorded.

mute A device used on instruments to muffle the tone (Italian *sordino*).

natural In notation, the sign (♮) indicating that a note is not to be sharp or flat (p. 14).

neo-classical A term describing the music of some twentieth-century composers whose techniques draw on those of the Baroque and Classical periods (p. 277).

neume A sign used in medieval notation showing the groups of notes to which a syllable should be sung.

nocturne A piece that evokes night, usually a short, lyrical piano piece (pp. 54, 206).

nonet A work for nine performers.

note The written symbol for a tone of definite pitch; also the tone itself.

obbligato A term for an instrumental part that is essential to a composition, second in importance only to the principal melody.

octave The interval between two notes of the same name, 12 semitones (an octave) apart (p. 14).

octet A work for eight performers.

ode In ancient Greece a sung celebratory poem; in the seventeenth and eighteenth centuries, a cantata-like work celebrating events, birthdays etc.

Office The eight daily services (apart from Mass) of the Roman Catholic church.

opera A drama set to music (p. 58).

opera buffa Italian eighteenth-century comic opera.

opéra comique French opera, normally with spoken dialogue (not just "comic opera" and not necessarily comic at all).

opera seria Italian eighteenth-century opera on a heroic or tragic subject.

operetta Light opera with spoken dialogue, songs and dances.

opus The Latin word for "work", used with a number to identify a work in a composer's output.

oratorio An extended setting of a text on a religious topic for soloists, chorus and orchestra (p. 56).

orchestration The art and technique of writing effectively for an orchestra or large group of instruments.

Ordinary The parts of the Mass with fixed texts that remain the same each day, as opposed to the Proper (table, p. 63).

organum A type of medieval polyphony in which one voice or more is added to a plainsong (p. 65).

ornament One or more notes used to embellish a melody.

ostinato A musical figure that is persistently repeated while the other elements are changing; hence *basso ostinato*, a GROUND BASS.

overture A piece of orchestral music introducing a larger work; also CONCERT OVERTURE, FRENCH OVERTURE, ITALIAN OVERTURE.

part 1 The written music for a performer or performing section in an ensemble, e.g. the violin part. **2** In polyphonic music a "strand", line or voice, e.g. two-part harmony, four-part counterpoint; hence *part-writing, partsong,* a song for several parts.

passacaglia A GROUND BASS movement, in slow or moderate triple meter, in the Baroque period.

passing tone A tone, foreign to the harmony with which it sounds, linking by step two tones that are (normally) part of the harmony.

Passion An extended oratorio-like setting of the story of the crucifixion (p. 55).

pavan A slow, stately sixteenth- and early seventeenth-century court dance in duple meter, often paired with a GALLIARD; also *pavane*.

pedalboard A keyboard (e.g. on an organ) played by the feet.

pedal point A sustained tone, usually in the bass, round or above which the other parts proceed.

pentatonic A term used for a mode or scale consisting of only five tones (p. 15).

phrase A group of tones, often a unit of a melody, longer than a motif.

piano, pianissimo (p, pp) Quiet, very quiet.

pitch The highness or lowness of a sound (p. 13).

pitch class A term for all notes of the same name, such as C or A♭.

pizzicato A direction to pluck rather than bow the strings of a string instrument.

plainsong Liturgical chant to Latin texts used since the Middle Ages, also known as GREGORIAN CHANT.

polonaise A stately Polish dance in triple meter.

polyphony A texture in which two or more independent melodic lines are combined, as opposed to heterophony, homophony, monophony; hence *polyphonic* (pp. 22, 65).

prelude A short instrumental work originally intended to precede another, but from the nineteenth century a short, self-contained piece usually for piano.

presto, prestissimo Very fast, very fast indeed.

program music Instrumental music that is narrative or descriptive of some non-musical idea, often literary or pictorial (pp. 185–6).

progression A musically logical succession of chords; hence *harmonic progression, chord progression.*

Proper The parts of the Mass text that vary from day to day according to the church calendar, as opposed to the Ordinary (table, p. 63).

quadruple meter A meter in which there are four beats in each measure (p. 17).

quarter-tone An interval half the size of a semitone.

quartet A work for four performers (or a group that plays such a work).

quintet A work for five performers.

ragtime A type of early twentieth-century American popular music characterized by syncopated melody, usually for piano (p. 332).

rallentando Slowing down.

recapitulation The third main section in a movement in sonata form in which the thematic material stated in the exposition is repeated in the home key (p. 47).

recitative A type of writing for the voice with the rhythm and inflections of speech, used in opera, oratorio and cantatas by the soloists (p. 57).

refrain A verse of a song or vocal work that recurs after each new verse or stanza.

Requiem The Roman Catholic Mass for the dead, frequently set to music (p. 54).

resolution The progression from dissonant, unstable harmony to consonant harmony.

rest In notation, one of several symbols corresponding to a given number of beats or bars, indicating a period of silence (p. 16).

rhythm The distribution of sounds into groups with a perceptible meter or pulse (p. 15).

rhythm and blues A type of black American pop music of the 1950s.

ricercare A Renaissance instrumental work that usually displays skillful application of counterpoint; also *ricercar.*

ripieno The large group of instrumentalists in a CONCERTO GROSSO.

ritardando Becoming slower.

ritenuto Held back.

ritornello A passage that recurs, particularly the instrumental section of an aria or a passage for orchestra in a Baroque or Classical concerto; hence *ritornello form* (p. 48).

Rococo A term borrowed from art history to describe the decorative, elegant style of music between the Baroque and Classical periods (p. 146).

rondeau 1 A medieval polyphonic song form. **2** A seventeenth-century instrumental form, forerunner of the RONDO.

rondo A form in which a main section recurs between subsidiary sections (p. 46).

round A sung CANON in which the voices all sing the same melody at the same pitch.

row SERIES.

rubato The Italian word for "robbed", used as an indication that the meter may be treated with some freedom by a performer for expressive effect.

sarabande A slow Baroque dance in triple meter often with a stress on the second beat of the measure, normally a movement of a SUITE.

scale A sequence of notes going upwards or downwards by step; hence *major scale, minor scale, chromatic scale* (p. 14).

scherzo 1 A lively movement in triple meter that came to replace the minuet as a symphony movement. **2** In the nineteenth century, a self-contained instrumental piece, usually for piano.

score The music-copy of a piece for several performers; hence *full score*, containing complete details of every participating voice and instrument, *short score*, a compressed version of a full score; *conducting score, miniature score, piano score, vocal score.*

semitone Half a tone, the smallest interval commonly used in Western music.

septet A work for seven performers.

sequence 1 The repetition of a phrase at a higher or lower pitch than the original. **2** A medieval and Renaissance polyphonic setting of a religious text.

serialism A method of composing using a series of tones (usually all 12 of the chromatic scale), or other musical elements, which are heard only in a particular order; hence *serial* (pp. 46, 283).

series A fixed set of tones used as the basis of a serial composition (p. 46).

sextet A work for six performers.

sforzato, sforzando (sf, sfz) Strongly accented.

sharp In notation, the sign (♯) indicating that the pitch of a note should be raised by a semitone; also *double sharp*, × (p. 14).

simple meter A meter in which the unit beats are divisible by two (e.g. 2/4), unlike COMPOUND METER (p. 17).

sinfonia The Italian word for "symphony", used to designate a wide range of instrumental pieces; hence *sinfonia concertante*, a sinfonia with a concerto element; *sinfonietta.*

Singspiel A German eighteenth-century opera with spoken dialogue.

slur In notation, a curved line over a group of notes indicating that they should be smoothly joined in performance.

sonata A piece in several movements for small ensemble, soloist with accompaniment or solo keyboard; hence *sonata da camera* ("chamber sonata") and *sonata da chiesa* ("church sonata"), seventeenth- and eighteenth-century instrumental works in three or four movements; *sonatina* (pp. 51, 53).

sonata form A form used from the Classical period onwards, chiefly for the first movements of large instrumental works (e.g. symphonies, string quartets, sonatas) (p. 47).

sonata-rondo form A form that combines elements of sonata form and rondo (p. 47).

song cycle A group of songs unified by their texts, a general idea, a narrative or musical features.

soprano 1 The highest female voice (p. 25). **2** A term used for an instrument of high range, e.g. soprano saxophone.

Sprechgesang A German term used to describe a vocal style between speech and song, used extensively by Schoenberg (p. 282); also *Sprechstimme*.

staccato Detached, not legato, indicated by a dot or a dash over a note.

staff The set of lines on and between which music is written; also *stave* (p. 13).

stretto 1 The overlapping of entries in the subject of a fugue. **2** A direction to the performer to increase the tempo, or a passage containing such an increase; also *stretta*.

strophic A term applied to songs in which each stanza (verse) of the text is sung to the same music.

study A piece, usually for solo instrument, intended to demonstrate or improve an aspect of performing technique; also *étude*.

Sturm und Drang A German expression, meaning "storm and stress", used for an eighteenth-century literary and artistic movement the ideals of which were to convey emotion and urgency (p. 152).

subdominant The fourth step or degree of the scale.

subject A theme or a group of themes on which a work is based; hence *subject group*.

suite An instrumental work in several movements, usually a set of dances, which in the seventeenth and eighteenth centuries often took the form ALLEMANDE–COURANTE–SARABANDE–optional dance movements–GIGUE (p. 53).

suspension A harmonic device whereby a tone or tones of one chord are held while the next, with which the prolonged tones are dissonant, is sounded; there is a RESOLUTION when the suspended tones fall to those of the new chord.

symphonic poem An orchestral piece based on a non-musical (literary, narrative etc) idea, or program (p. 50).

symphony An extended orchestral work usually in several (most often three or four) movements (p. 49).

syncopation The stressing of beats of a meter that are normally unstressed.

synthesizer A machine that produces and alters sounds electronically.

tablature A system of notation by symbols that represent the position of a performer's fingers (e.g. on a guitar) rather than the tone to be played (p. 13).

tempo The speed of a piece of music (p. 15).

tenor 1 The highest normal male voice (p. 25). **2** A term used for an instrument whose range is analogous to the tenor voice, e.g. tenor saxophone; hence *tenor clef*, used by the cello.

tenuto A term telling the performer to hold a tone to its full length.

ternary form A form with three sections, the third a repetition of the first, *ABA* (p. 46).

texture The way in which the individual strands of a work are blended.

thematic transformation A nineteenth-century process whereby themes are modified during a movement (p. 210).

theme A musical idea on which a work is based, usually with a recognizable melody; hence *thematic, theme and variations* (p. 44).

thoroughbass CONTINUO.

through-composed A term applied to songs in which each stanza (or verse) is set to different music, as opposed to STROPHIC songs.

tie In notation, a curved line linking two notes of the same pitch, indicating that they should be one continuous sound.

timbre TONE-COLOR.

time signature The figures on the staff at the beginning of a piece indicating the meter and unit (p. 16).

toccata An instrumental piece in free form, usually for keyboard, intended to display the performer's technique.

tonality The feeling of gravitational pull towards a particular tone, determined by the KEY of the music.

tone 1 A sound of definite pitch and duration. **2** The interval equal to two semitones. **3** The timbre or quality of a musical sound.

tone-color The quality of the sound of a particular instrument or voice, or a combination of them.

tone-poem SYMPHONIC POEM.

tonic The main note of a major or minor key (p. 18).

transition A subsidiary passage that leads from one more important section to another, e.g. a BRIDGE passage in sonata form.

transpose To write down or play music at a pitch other than the original one; hence *transposing instrument*, which plays a tone at a fixed interval from the written one, e.g. a clarinet in B♭ (p. 18).

treble 1 A high voice, usually a child's (p. 25). **2** A term used for an instrument of range similar to the treble voice, e.g. treble recorder; hence *treble clef*, used by high instruments and a pianist's right hand.

tremolo A rapid reiteration usually of a single tone, e.g. by the trembling action of a bow of a string instrument; also *tremolando*.

triad A three-note "common" chord consisting of a fundamental tone with tones at the intervals of a 3rd and 5th above (p. 20).

trill The rapid alternation of two adjacent tones, used as a musical ornament; also *shake*.

trio 1 A work for three performers, or a group that plays such a work. **2** The middle section of a minuet, scherzo, march etc.

trio sonata A Baroque sonata for two melody instruments and continuo (p. 51).

triple meter A meter in which there are three beats in each measure (p. 16).

triplet A group of three notes occupying the time normally taken by two of the same note value.

tritone The interval of three whole tones.

trope A passage, with or without a text, introducing or inserted into Gregorian chant.

troubadours, trouvères French poet-musicians who performed songs of courtly love at the feudal courts of Europe during the Middle Ages (p. 64).

tune A simple, singable melody.

tutti An Italian term, meaning "all the performers", used (e.g. in a concerto) to designate a passage for orchestra rather than the soloist.

twelve-tone A term used to describe a technique of composition (SERIALISM) in which all 12 notes of the chromatic scale are treated equally (pp. 45, 283).

unison A united sounding of the same tone or melody; hence *unison singing*.

upbeat A weak or unaccented beat preceding the main beat (the DOWNBEAT), particularly the beat before a barline, indicated by an upward stroke of a conductor's stick.

variation A varied (elaborated, embellished etc) version of a given theme or tune; hence *theme and variations* (p. 48).

verismo An Italian term, meaning "realism", applied to some late nineteenth-century operas that feature violent emotions, local color etc (p. 239).

verse 1 A stanza of a song. **2** In Anglican church music, a term used for the passages for solo voice rather than choir; hence *verse anthem*.

vibrato A rapid fluctuation in pitch and/or volume, used for expressiveness and richness of sound, e.g. the "wobble" of a string player's left hand on the strings.

virelai A medieval polyphonic song form.

vivace Vivacious.

vocalise A wordless solo vocal piece.

voice-leading The rules governing the progression of the voices in contrapuntal music; also *part-writing*.

waltz A nineteenth-century dance in triple meter.

whole tone The interval of two semitones; hence *whole-tone scale*, a scale progressing in six equal tones (p. 270).

word-painting The musical illustration of the meaning of a work, or its connotation, in a vocal work.

Acknowledgements

John Calmann & King Ltd wish to thank the institutions and individuals who have kindly provided photographic material for use in this book. Museums, galleries and some libraries are given in the captions; other sources are listed below.

Alinari, Florence: 41
Artothek, Munich: pl. 9
Clive Barda, London: 27
Imogen Barford, London: 7
Bartók Archive, Budapest: 110
BBC Hulton Picture Library, London: 90
Biblioteca Nacional, Rio de Janeiro: 123
Bibliothèque Nationale, Paris: 50; 58; 86; 87; 89; 100
Trustees of the British Library, London: pl. 2; pl. 15; 3; 13; 31; 32; 37; 48; 51; 59; 65; 68; 76
Bulloz, Paris: 54
Bureau Soviétique d'Information, Paris: 93
Giancarlo Costa, Milan: pl. 14; 104
Brian Dear, Lavenham: 4; 5; 19 (Oxford University Press); 23; 24 (Macmillan Publishers Ltd, London)
Department of the Environment, London: pl. 8 (reproduced by gracious permission of Her Majesty The Queen)
Dover Publications Inc., New York: 78
Edison Institute, Henry Ford Museum and Greenfield Village, Dearborn (Mich.): 121
Editions Alphonse Leduc, Paris: 115
EMI Ltd, London: 102
Fotomas, London: 72
Freie und Hansestadt Hamburg: 56
Furstlich Oettingen-Wallerstein'sche Bibliothek und Kunstsammlung, Schloss Harburg: 29
Mrs Aivi Gallen-Kallela, Helsinki/Akseli Gallen-Kallelan Musesäätiö, Espoo: 101
Gemeentemuseum, The Hague: 18
Giraudon, Paris: pl. 4; 84
Glyndebourne Festival Opera/Guy Gravett: 111
Henmar Press Inc., New York © 1962 (reproduced by kind permission of Peters Edition Ltd, London): 120
Heritage of Music: pl. 2; pl. 13; 52; 81; 86; 87; 96; 119
Hungarian Academy of Sciences, Budapest: 85
Peter Hutten, Wollongong/Kurt Hutton: 114

Master and Fellows of St John's College, Cambridge: 35
Kerkelijk Bureau de Hervormde Gemeente, Haarlem: 21
Collection H. C. Robbins Landon, Cardiff: pl. 10; 81
Mander and Mitchenson, London: 64
Bildarchiv Foto Marburg: 38
Federico Arborio Mella, Milan: 61
Museen der Stadt Wien: 66; 70; 80
Ampliaciones y Reproducciones MAS, Barcelona: 52
National Library of Ireland, Dublin: 95
New York Public Library, Lincoln Center: 119
Novosti, London: 112
Öffentliche Kunstsammlung, Basel/SPADEM: 108
Österreichische Nationalbibliothek Bildarchiv, Vienna: 77; 97
Photo Service, Albuquerque: 22
The Photo Source, London: 127; 128 (Seán Hennessy)
Reiss Museum, Mannheim: 67
Réunion des Musées Nationaux, Paris: 109 (SPADEM)
Roger-Viollet, Paris: 103
Harold Rosenthal/Opera Magazine: 94
Royal Collection (reproduced by gracious permission of Her Majesty The Queen): 69
Scala, Florence: pl. 6; pl. 7; pl. 12; 43
Robert-Schumann-Haus, Zwickau: 83
Sotheby's, London: 8; 33
Mrs Sivvy Streli, Innsbruck: 107
Stuart-Liff Collection, Isle of Man: 92
University of Texas at Austin (Theater Arts Library, Harry Ransom Humanities Research Center): 121; 126 (from the MGM release *Jailhouse Rock* © 1957, Loew's Incorporated and Avon Productions Inc.)
Mrs Louise Varèse/W. W. Norton & Co., New York (from L. Varèse, *Varèse: a Looking-glass Diary*, 1972): 113
VEB Deutsche Verlag für Musik, Leipzig: 26
Courtesy of the Board of Trustees of the Victoria and Albert Museum, London: 34; 63
Universal Edition (London) Ltd: 117
Universal Edition AG Vienna (Alfred A. Kalmus Ltd): 118
Richard-Wagner-Museum, Bayreuth: 91
Allan Dean Walker, Santa Monica (Cal.): 105
© Galerie Welz, Salzburg: 98
Val Wilmer, London: 125
Joseph P. Ziolo, Paris: 106

Index

1750–1875 Music	1750	Art and literature	History and philosophy
			Diderot and others begin the *Encyclopédie*
C. P. E. Bach: *Essay on the True Art of Playing Keyboard Instruments*			Rousseau: *Discourse on Inequality* Johnson: *Dictionary*
D. Scarlatti dies (71); J. Stamitz dies (39) Handel dies (74)		Voltaire: *Candide*	
Gluck: *Orfeo*; J. C. Bach moves Milan–London			
Haydn becomes *Kapellmeister* to Esterházys		Fragonard: *The Swing*	
Boccherini settles as chamber composer in Madrid			
	1775		
Mozart visit to Mannheim and on to Paris			America becomes independent
Haydn: String quartets op. 33; Mozart settles in Vienna			Kant: *The Critique of Pure Reason*
Mozart begins great series of piano concertos Mozart: *Marriage of Figaro*		Beaumarchais: *Le mariage de Figaro*	
Mozart: last three symphonies		Reynolds: *Master Hare* Blake: *Songs of Innocence*	French Revolution
Haydn's first London visit; Mozart: *The Magic Flute*, dies (35)			
Haydn returns from second London visit (Symphonies 99–104); rejoins Esterházys (late Masses, 1796–1802) Paris Conservatory founded Haydn: *The Creation*			
	1800		
Beethoven: Symphony no. 3 Beethoven: *Fidelio*		Schiller: *William Tell*	Louisiana Purchase
Beethoven: Symphony no. 5 Haydn dies (77)		Goethe: *Faust*, part 1; Friedrich: *Winter*	
Vienna Philharmonic Society founded (Royal) Philharmonic Society, London, founded Schubert: *Erlking* (and about 150 other songs) Rossini: *The Barber of Seville*		Byron: *Childe Harold* Austen: *Pride and Prejudice* Goya: *The Third of May 1808*	Napoleon invades Russia Battle of Waterloo; Congress of Vienna
Weber: *Der Freischütz* Beethoven: Choral Symphony Schubert: Great C major Symphony Beethoven: late string quartets; Weber dies (39); Mendelssohn: Overture *Midsummer Night's Dream* Beethoven dies (56) Schubert: String Quintet in C, *Winterreise*, dies (31) Berlioz: *Fantastic Symphony*; Bellini: *Norma* Chopin: Nocturne in E♭ Mendelssohn: *Italian Symphony* Schumann: *Carnaval*; Donizetti: *Lucia di Lammermoor*; Bellini dies (34)	1825	Constable: *The Haywain* Delacroix: *Liberty leading the people* Pushkin: *Eugene Onegin*	Schopenhauer: *The World as Will and Idea* Hegel: *The Philosophy of Right* Bolivar liberates South America Faraday discovers electrical induction
Schumann: *Dichterliebe* New York Philharmonic Symphony Society founded Leipzig Conservatory founded			
Berlioz: *The Damnation of Faust* Mendelssohn dies (38) Chopin dies (39)			Marx: *The Communist Manifesto*; Revolutions sweep Europe; California Gold Rush
Verdi: *La traviata*; Liszt: Piano Sonata in b	1850	Dickens: *David Copperfield* Beecher: *Uncle Tom's Cabin*	
Schumann dies (46) Liszt: *Faust Symphony* Offenbach: *Orpheus in the Underworld* Wagner: *Tristan und Isolde*; Gounod: *Faust* Brahms: Piano Concerto no. 1		Thoreau: *Walden* Whitman: *Leaves of Grass* Baudelaire: *Fleurs du mal*; Flaubert, *Madame Bovary* Hugo: *Les misérables*	Darwin: *Origin of Species* American Civil War begins; Unification of Italy Emancipation of slaves in USA
Smetana: *The Bartered Bride*		Moreau: *Revelation* Dostoevsky: *Crime and Punishment* Ibsen: *Peer Gynt*; Zola: *Thérèse Raquin* Tolstoy: *War and Peace*	Marx: *Das Kapital*
Brahms: *German Requiem*; Grieg: Piano Concerto; Wagner: *Mastersingers*			Franco-Prussian War Unification of Germany
Mussorgsky: *Boris Godunov*; Smetana: *Vltava*; J. Strauss: *Fledermaus*; Verdi: *Requiem* Bizet: *Carmen*, dies (36); Tchaikovsky: Piano Concerto no. 1	1875	Degas: *Ballet Rehearsal* Twain: *Tom Sawyer*	

1875–present Music	Art and literature	History and philosophy

1875

Wagner: *The Ring* performed at new Bayreuth theater; Brahms: Symphony no. 1

Tchaikovsky: Symphony no. 4, *Eugene Onegin*

Bell invents the telephone
Edison invents the phonograph

Renoir: *Boating Party*; James: *Portrait of a Lady*
Manet: *Bar at the Folies-Bergère*

Bruckner: Symphony no. 7; Wagner dies (69)

Sullivan: *The Mikado*

Nietzsche: *Beyond Good and Evil*

Verdi: *Otello*; Borodin dies (53), working on *Prince Igor*
Franck: Symphony; Wolf, great creative spell (songs) begins; Rimsky-Korsakov: *Sheherazade*
Fauré: *Requiem*

Van Gogh: *Sunflowers*

Gauguin: *Two Women on the Beach*
Winslow Homer: *Coast in Winter*; Maeterlinck: *Pelléas et Mélisande*
Munch: *The Scream*
Chekhov: *The Seagull*

Dvořák: *New World Symphony*, String Quartet op. 96; Tchaikovsky dies (53)

Marconi invents wireless telegraphy

Strauss: *Till Eulenspiegel*
Debussy: *L'après-midi d'un faune*

Elgar: *Enigma Variations*; Joplin: *Maple Leaf Rag*
Puccini: *Tosca*
Mahler: Symphony no. 4; Rachmaninov: Piano Concerto no. 2
Debussy: *Pelléas et Mélisande*

1900

Cézanne: *The Bathers*
D'Annunzio: *Francesca da Rimini*

Wright brothers make first powered flight
Freud: *Psychopathology of Everyday Life*
Einstein's first theory of relativity

Ives: *The Unanswered Question*; Mahler: Symphony no. 8

Mahler: *Lied von der Erde*; Strauss: *Elektra*

Matisse: *Red Room*

Sibelius: Symphony no. 4; Strauss: *Rosenkavalier*
Ravel: *Daphnis et Chloé*; Schoenberg: *Pierrot lunaire*
Stravinsky: *Rite of Spring*; Webern: *Bagatelles*
Ives: *First Orchestral Set*

Shaw: *Pygmalion*

Russell: *Our Knowledge of the External World*

Braque: *Musical Forms*; Proust: *Swann's Way*;
    Lawrence: *Sons and Lovers*

World War I begins

Ives: Symphony no. 4

Russian Revolution

Janàček: *Katya Kabanova*; Prokofiev: *Love for Three Oranges*; Varèse: *Amériques*

Monet: *Water Lilies*; Joyce: *Ulysses*; Mann: *The Magic Mountain*
Picasso: *Three Musicians*
Frost: *New Hampshire*; Pound: *Testament of François Villon*
Kandinsky: *Little Dream in Red*; Kafka: *The Trial*

Schoenberg's first 12-tone works; Varèse: *Hyperprism*
Sibelius: Symphony no. 7; Fauré dies (79)
Berg: *Wozzeck*

1925

Lindbergh makes first transatlantic flight

Bartók: String Quartet no. 4; Webern: Symphony; Weill: *Threepenny Opera*;
    Louis Armstrong: *West End Blues*

Hemingway: *Farewell to Arms*

Wall Street crash, Depression begins

Schoenberg leaves Germany for the USA
Berg: Violin Concerto; Gershwin: *Porgy and Bess*
Bartók: Music for Strings, Percussion and Celesta; Cowell: *United Quartet*;
Orff: *Carmina Burana*
Shostakovich: Symphony no. 5

Faulkner: *Light in August*

Hitler comes to power

Eliot: *Murder in the Cathedral*
Lloyd Wright: *Falling Water*, Bear Run, Pa.
Sartre: *La nausée*

Spanish Civil War begins

World War II begins

Stravinsky: Symphony in C; Ellington: *Concerto for Cootie*
Copland: *Lincoln Portrait, Fanfare for the Common Man*
Bartók: Concerto for Orchestra; Britten: Serenade
Messiaen: *Vingt regards*; Prokofiev: *War and Peace*; Villa-Lobos: *Bachianas brasileiras*

Camus: *The Outsider*

First atom bombs used

Hesse: *The Glass Bead Game*

Messiaen extends serialism in *Mode de valeurs et d'intensités*; Miles Davis: *Birth of the Cool*
Weill dies (50)
Electronic music studios, New York and Cologne
Cage: *4'33"*; Tippett: *Midsummer Marriage*

Mailer: *The Naked and the Dead*
Mies van der Rohe: Seagram Building, New York;
    Wyeth: *Christina's World*; Orwell: *1984*
Pollock: *Blue Poles*

1950

Boulez: *Le marteau sans maître*
Stockhausen: *Gesang der Jünglinge*; Presley: *Heartbreak Hotel*
Bernstein: *West Side Story*

Le Corbusier: Chapel at Ronchamp; Beckett: *Waiting for Godot*

Russians put first Sputnik into space

Johns: *False Start*

Britten: *War Requiem*; Cage: *Atlas eclipticalis*; Lutoslawski: *Venetian Games*
The Beatles: *Love me do*; Dylan: *Blowin' in the Wind*

Warhol: *Marilyn Monroe*; Singer: *The Slave*

Berlin Wall built
President Kennedy assassinated

Henze: *The Bassarids*; Penderecki: *St Luke Passion*; Stravinsky: *Requiem Canticles*

Moore: *Reclining Figure* (Lincoln Center, New York)

Solzhenitsyn: *The First Circle*

America puts first men on moon

Stravinsky dies (81); Reich: *Drumming*

Stockhausen: *Inori*

IRCAM (Paris) opens

Utzon and others: Sydney Opera House; Bellow: *Humboldt's Gift*
Rogers and Piano: Pompidou Center, Paris

1975